DURHAM

by

SIR TIMOTHY EDEN

VOLUME TWO

London

Robert Hale Limited

63 Old Brompton Road S.W.7

First published 1952

Printed in Great Britain by
Billing and Sons Ltd., Guildford and Esher
G1584

CONTENTS OF VOL. II

APPENDICES

Frontispiece   BISHOP WESTCOTT

Reproduced by kind permission of Mr. G. F. Westcott and Messrs. Macmillan and Co. Ltd.

vi

LIST OF ABBREVIATIONS

A.A.D.N.	*Transactions of the Architectural and Archæological Society of Durham and Northumberland.*
Arch. Ael.	*Archæologia Aeliana.*
B.P.	*Bishoprick Papers,* by H. Hensley Henson (O.U.P., 1946).
Collingwood	*Roman Britain,* by R. G. Collingwood (Clarendon Press, 1934).
C. and M.	*Roman Britain and the English Settlements,* by R. G. Collingwood and J. N. L. Myres (Oxford, 1936).
D.N.B.	*Dictionary of National Biography.*
D.U.J.	*Durham University Journal.*
Durham Company ...	*Durham Company,* by Una Pope-Hennessy (Chatto and Windus, 1941).
Fordyce	*History of Durham,* by William Fordyce.
Hare	*The Story of my Life,* by Augustus Hare (G. Allen, 1900).
Headlam	*The Three Northern Counties of England,* edited by Sir Cuthbert Headlam, Bt. (1939).
Hutchinson	*History of the County Palatine of Durham,* by William Hutchinson (Newcastle, 1785).
Latimer	*Local Records,* by John Latimer (*Newcastle Chronicle* Office, 1857).
M.C.	*Monthly Chronicle of North Country Lore and Legend* (Newcastle, 1887-1891).
Mackenzie and Ross ...	*View of the County Palatine of Durham,* by Mackenzie and Ross (Newcastle, 1834).
Proceedings	*Proceedings of the Society of Antiquaries of Newcastle-upon-Tyne.*
Retrospect	*Retrospect of an Unimportant Life,* by H. Hensley Henson (O.U.P., 1946).

S.S. ...	...	...	...	Surtees Society.
Stenton	...	...	...	*Anglo-Saxon England*, by F. M. Stenton (Oxford, 1943) in "Oxford History of England."
Surtees	...	...	...	*History of the County Palatine*, by Robert Surtees (London, Vol. I, 1816; Vol. II, 1820; Vol. III, 1840).
Sykes	...	...	...	*Local Records*, by John Sykes (Newcastle, 1853).
Symeon	...	...	...	*The Historical Works of Symeon of Durham* (Surtees Society).
Trevelyan, England		...		*History of England*, by G. M. Trevelyan (Longmans, 1926).
Trevelyan, Social History	...			*English Social History*, by G. M. Trevelyan (Longmans, 1945).
V.C.H.	...	...	...	*Victoria County History*.

BOOK IV
MANHOOD
(1688-1832)

CHAPTER XVII

BEFORE THE DELUGE

"Qui n'a pas vécu avant 1789, ne connaît pas la douceur de vivre."
                                                        TALLEYRAND.

VAST were the changes which took place during the period which we have now approached. At the beginning of it the Dean of Durham was romantically dying in exile for love of a Jacobite king; at the end of it the first locomotive in the world was puffing its hideous commercial way between Stockton and Darlington. During these one hundred and fifty years the old ideals of chivalry and honour finally withered and died, and those portentous triplets, Science, Industry and Democracy, first saw the light of a refined and cultivated world which it would henceforth be their province to destroy. If we will put our finger on a spot somewhere between these two extremes, we shall hit upon the most civilised chapter in our story and, perhaps, in the whole long switchback history of the risings and fallings of mankind. Horne Tooke, the friend of Wilkes and teacher of Hazlitt and John Stuart Mill, and therefore no pig-headed reactionary, described the middle of the eighteenth century as our happiest time; Talleyrand corroborated its enchantment; Wheler, who lived through its morning beauty, praised the Lord that the lot had fallen unto him on so fair a ground; and our Durham historian, Robert Surtees, though he came when the light was beginning to fade, exclaimed that God had placed him in Paradise. It is a delusion, deliberately encouraged by democrats to obscure their own enormities, to presume that men have always compared the present disadvantageously with the past. No one was more certain than the Englishman of the eighteenth century that the age in which he lived had reached the high-water mark of civilisation, and no one was more right. If we grumble today about the sordid ugliness of life, it is for the very good reason that life today is ugly and sordid. If we have any eye for beauty, or any taste for quiet; if we can enjoy the stimulating contrasts of individuality, or take pleasure in the elegance of speech and the dignity of manners; if we can

admire a classical culture, or delight in the native poetry of
country tales and language, of local customs and beliefs; then
we can never cease to execrate a present marked with none of
these distinctive graces and to deplore a vanished past which
had them all.

Nevertheless, there are, as Doctor Johnson has reminded
us, "no Chinese perfectly polite." If this period was a paradise
to some, and a time of solid cheer and hard-won but certain
peace to the majority, it was a hell to others. The extremes of
wealth and misery were not to be reached until the century
had passed, but already there were men making fortunes out
of coal-mines, and women and children toiling in the bowels
of the earth, scarcely ever seeing the light of day. In 1765
was the first recorded coal strike. As the century advanced
the contrast became more pronounced. "The Poor, in many of
the townships," wrote an economist on the county of Durham
in 1795, "are in a miserable condition. . . . I hope I may
add, without being considered paradoxical, that the influx of
wealth within the last forty years has produced a more than
proportionable addition of Poor."[1]

Thus, when considering the details of this period, we have
constantly to remind ourselves not only that there are two
angles from which to look at every picture, but that those two
points of view, which towards the middle of the century
approximated as nearly, perhaps, as it is possible for them to
do in an imperfect but civilised world, were to become increasingly divergent as, with the development of Industry
and Commerce, Wealth leapt ahead of Poverty and Poverty
multiplied itself in the mire. In the first half of the century
particularly, though the coal-pits were slowly increasing, our
county was agricultural, sylvan and pastoral. By the time that
the Reform Bill came to strike the first decisive blow for
Democracy more than half the trees were down, where the
lone farmhouse or the rustic hamlet had stood towns were
sprouting like fungi, and not only the coal-mining but the
shipbuilding and the iron industries were being rapidly developed. The number of inhabitants of our county rose from
135,000 in the year 1750 to 250,000 in 1832. But more
noteworthy than this general rise in population is its concen-

[1] *The State of the Poor,* by Sir Frederick Eden (J. Davis, 1797),
Vol. II, p. 162.

tration in towns. In 1681 the population of Sunderland was estimated at 2,500; in 1781 at 21,000.

But in the middle of the century the village was still "the normal unit of society,"[1] and Durham was a county, not of industrial towns and furnaces, but of village greens and duck-ponds, of village churches and thatched roofs. In this atmosphere the points of view of the squire who worked with his men in his own fields and woods, the parson who kept his cow and his pig, the farmer who jogged to market, and the peasant who tilled the land, were not so widely divergent. They all spoke more or less the same language, they all loved more or less the same things, they were all born and bred, were married, lived and died, in the same little corner of England. The differences of that period were differences less between classes than between localities. Joe Brown and his squire knew every little detail of each other's lives and were, as often as not, foster-brothers. No question of "class-consciousness" entered their heads. But there was a great feeling of local patriotism. There was much "country-consciousness." Between the North and the South there was still a vast gulf. "There," said a Member for the county[2] on some project of equalising the land-tax, as he placed a brown loaf and a pair of wooden clogs on the table of the House, "there—when the *South* eats and wears what we do in the *North*, then mak' us like and like."[3] (Now we do, and now we are!)

The surest key to an understanding of this period is a constant alertness to its extraordinary individuality, variety, contrast and independence. It will not be very difficult for a future historian to describe the age in which we are now living. We all look alike, dress alike, speak alike, eat alike, live alike, and, to judge from the effects of our popular system of education, we almost all think alike. The characteristics of this age are obvious, and a generalisation based upon them would be as true as any generalisation can be. But it is far otherwise with the eighteenth century. We can with justice both belaud its gracious refinement and reprove the coarseness of its manners, wonder at its conscientious charity and be aghast at its callous cruelty, delight in the beauties which it

[1] Trevelyan, *England,* p. 524.   [2] Sir John Eden.
[3] Mackenzie and Ross, Vol. II, p. 286.

created and deplore its lamentable lapses of taste, envy its quiet leisure and marvel at its skill and capacity for work, condemn the godlessness of its clergy and be charmed by the holy sweetness of their lives. It was an age of individuals, an age of contrasts, an age when every man, from highwayman to bishop, could live his own life, restricted by little more than his conscience, and when every man had within him enough of youth, of zest, of blood, to make him wish to live that life to the utmost. The nervous complaisance and the anæmic self-depreciation of the present time would have seemed effeminate and ridiculous to the robust manhood of the eighteenth century. It was an age when an empire was conquered or lost, not an age when it was given away.

These contradictions and peculiarities, so far as they were manifested in the county of Durham, will become apparent as our story unfolds, but we may at once consider some little anecdotes, some traits of character and expressions of opinion, which will illustrate the idiosyncrasies of this period and serve to fix its lively contrasts in our memory.

Doctor Bathurst, a Prebendary of the Cathedral, entreated the Chaplain of Durham Gaol not to remain uncovered while talking with him in the close. "I am in your territory, Doctor Bathurst," was the reply. Soon afterwards they met each other by the prison gates. "Now, Mr. Chaplain, I am in *your* territory," said the canon, taking off his hat, "and I must follow your example until you put your hat on in the close."[1] Gracious manners and pretty customs were more than mere ribbons of adornment. They reflected the minds of that period, and not only the cultivated minds. The fishermen of the little port of Hartlepool, who were rough, independent and peculiar, without even the rudiments of education, were remarkable for their courtesy, particularly to strangers. It was the custom of the clerk of Coniscliffe, "all smiles and crimson," to yell out, on his own initiative, as soon as the banns of a couple had been read in church: "God speed them weel!"[2] It was the custom for a nanny, when dosing her charges with some nauseating mixture, to exclaim: "God bless it to you, my dear!"[3] And it was the custom for pretty

---

[1] *Sylvestra,* by Anne Raine Ellis. (George Bell, London, 1881.) Vol. II, p. 14.   [2] Longstaffe, *History of Darlington,* p. 218.
[3] *Sylvestra,* Vol. I, p. 7.

girls, on their engagement, to sit in the wishing chairs at
Finchale and at Jarrow and pray for bonny children. All this
is charming. But it was also the custom to butcher beasts in
the streets of Durham, which is not so attractive. It was also
the custom to bait bulls and to regard a cockpit as "a perfect
paradise"[1] and to play rough practical jokes and to be far
from mealy-mouthed and to indulge in the oddest behaviour
in the most unsuitable places. "I have but one whore in my
congregation, and I'll fell her," said the Rev. Daniel Burgess,
picking up his Bible in his pulpit. Everybody in church
ducked, whereupon he said: "I think I have nothing else but
whores."[2] No doubt this was only the parson's little joke, but
to us it is a somewhat surprising jest for a clergyman to make
from his pulpit. Curious, too, is the trick which was played on
the unfortunate wife of Bishop Crewe, who was renowned
for her piety and care of the poor. A ball of hair full of
lice was hidden in the seat of her coach, which "forced
her to strip," and the suspected joker was an alderman
of the city![3] Practical jokes and fantastical wagers were
as typical of this period as wit and repartee. The most
respectable could not contain the exuberance of their spirits.
Who, in these dull times, would think of riding down St.
James's Street, on a day when the King was holding a Court
in the palace, mounted upon a cow?[4] Or who would back his
own wife for twenty-five guineas against a neighbour's for
the first delivery of an infant?[5] It was a light-hearted,
dancing, singing, waggish age, an age when pitmen sported
flowered waistcoats, an age which produced the "Keel Row"
and "Elsie Marley," and twisted ribbons round maypoles,
and ate enormously, and told bawdy stories over bumpers of
port and kissed its hand to the ladies, and finished off bravely
in apoplectic fits. "You have worn out the coat of your stomach
by too high living," said his grave doctor to an ecclesiastical

---

[1] Longstaffe, *History of Darlington*, p. 298.
[2] *North Country Diaries*. Diary of the Rev. John Thomlinson, p.
147. (S.S., 1910.)
[3] *North Country Diaries*, p. 138.
[4] The feat of a certain Brooke Richmond, a friend of R. S. Surtees,
creator of "Jorrocks." (See *Robert Smith Surtees by Himself and E.
D. Cumin* [Blackwood, 1924], p. 37.)
[5] Wager between Mr. Liddle and Sir John Eden. (*North Country
Diaries*, p. 227.)

dignitary. "No matter for that!" replied his patient gaily, "I'll live in my waistcoat."[1]

Even with death itself they could not help being flippant, not out of malice or irreverence, but because they enjoyed life so much:

> "Here lies John Lively, Vicar of Kelloe,
> Who had 7 daughters and never a fellow,"

runs an epitaph in a parish church; and in the Cathedral Registry Book there is an entry for "Mrs. Dougwith, old virgin, Elvet, bur: 17th June 1779."

The Vicar of Darlington and the Vicar of Gainford were two good, jolly parsons who loved their God and who loved their dinners. Mr. Heyrick, of Gainford, had prevented Mr. Wood, of Darlington (whose appetite he dreaded), from being invited to an excellent meal, whereupon his friend, resolving to be avenged, waited until Heyrick came to town to buy himself a fine pair of soles, of which he was exceedingly fond. Then the Reverend Wood pressed his brother to dinner. "No, no!" cried the Vicar of Gainford, longing to get home and devour his favourite fish. "But," said the other, "I have a fine pair of soles for dinner." This argument was irresistible. To share his friend's soles now and to look forward to his own on his return was more than a civilised parson could resist. So Mr. Heyrick, of Gainford, remained to dinner and innocently consumed a portion of his own soles, while his host, who had abstracted them from his overcoat pocket, thoroughly enjoyed the rest.

Scratched on the window-pane of a small room at Crook Hall, in the outskirts of Durham, may be read the following inscription:

> "This is the sleeping room of Peter Wag, also of
> Mustapha and Paddy."

These were, presumably, three dogs. But the real sleeping room of "Peter Wag" is the whole of the eighteenth century.

The treatment of the poor at this period, but particularly of prisoners and of children, is shocking to us. For the first there was no machinery of beneficence, no centralisation, no bureaucracy, no committee meetings or bazaars to raise funds, no

[1] *Sylvestra,* Vol. I, p. 163.

newspapers to draw attention to distress; but nevertheless private charity was active and benevolent, and practically the only rates that Englishmen would pay at this time were the poor rates. The upkeep of roads, bridges and buildings was a very secondary matter. "The humanitarian spirit of the eighteenth century, with the care it bestowed on the bodies and minds of the poor and the unfortunate, made a real advance towards better things."[1] Of this humanitarian spirit the wealthier inhabitants of our county possessed a goodly share. It can be said, practically without exaggeration, that whether by will or by gifts during the life of the donor, from Sir George Wheler's bequests, amounting to over £1,100, down to Bishop Barrington's present of nearly £3,000 for the benefit of schools in Weardale, the poor were never forgotten by any person of consideration and standing. These charities generally took the form of schools or almshouses or both. Those at Cornsay, built and endowed by William Russell, of Brancepeth, will serve as an illustration for the rest. This endowment was for a home for six men and six women over fifty-five years of age, and for a school for the education of twenty poor children, boys and girls, who were all to be taught reading, writing and arithmetic by the master, and the girls sewing and knitting by the mistress. Each man and woman, in addition to provisions, was given £12 a year (the purchasing power of which today would be about ten times as much) and three loads of coal; and the schoolmaster was to read prayers for the old people every Wednesday morning at eleven o'clock, and the Morning Service every Sunday to those who were unable to go to church.

But admirable though these private charities were and probably sufficient to relieve distress in country districts, there is another side to this picture. This was the age when people were alive to their responsibilities to the deserving poor, but it was also the age of the negro slave trade, of women and children toiling in the mines, and of innumerable instances of cruelty to apprentices and other helpless infants left unprotected by society to the mercies of their employers or schoolmasters or brutish parents. Even the Workhouses devised by the nation for the relief of the poor seem to have served as often as excuses for tyranny as for opportunities for work. No

[1] Trevelyan, *Social History*, p. 363.

doubt "the evil that men do lives after them"; the numerous
instances of happy childhood are taken for granted and passed
over unmentioned, and in Crabbe's picture of the Workhouse
boy, "sad, silent, supple, bending to the blow," we may be
seeing an exception rather than the rule. We have had cases
in our days, with all our elaborate machinery for protection,
which would throw no pretty light upon our treatment of
orphan children, were they to be regarded, at some future
date, as typical of our system of administration. We must
therefore, when reading of a child at Chester-le-Street
"played for at cards, at the sign of the salmon, one game, four
shillings against the child,"[1] be careful not to jump to the
conclusion that this was a common occurrence; or, when we
hear of drunken Ann Potts burning herself and her infant to
death "in a hole in Pilgrim-street Gate, Newcastle,"[2] not to
presume therefrom that all the poor were drunken and lived
in holes. But nevertheless, the general roughness of the age,
the still practically complete ignorance of the principles of
health and hygiene, the absence of that supreme boon of
modern science, the anæsthetic, and, above all, the unlimited
free play given to the brutalities as well as to the benevolence
of individuals, force us to the conclusion that, with all the
politeness above, there was much suffering beneath the surface
of these civilised times. Though delightful to the educated,
grown man, it was a terrible age for the poor who were
crowded in cities (but these formed but a small percentage of
the mainly rural population), and it was by no means an ideal
age for children. Certainly later, and probably earlier, they
were treated with more understanding. The very names
"Cuthbert Godsend" and "Thomas Amongus," bestowed in
the Middle Ages on foundlings, seem to speak of love in the
hearts of those who adopted them, while the eighteenth-
century "Richard Mondays" and "Obadiah Sundays" sound
harsh and impersonal in our ears. The Workhouse brat had
taken the place of a gift from the saints.

The children of the well-to-do, though in obvious respects
better off than those of the poor, were, in some ways, less
fortunate. More sheltered from the rough but wholesome
nursing of nature, their bodies overheated, their brains often

---

[1] *Local Records*, by John Sykes, Vol. I (Newcastle, 1865), p. 151.
[2] *Ibid.*, p. 169.

overworked, their stomachs stuffed with food, and suffering, with all other children, from the medical ignorance of the times, they were prone in infancy to spread infectious diseases throughout all their numerous kith and kin, to die off like flies, and often to take their exhausted mothers with them. "Underneath this stone," runs an inscription in the churchyard of Great Stainton, "lie the remains of Robert Rickerby, who died May 23, 1745, aged 70, Jane his wife, died April 9, 1728, aged 49, and their numerous issue—

Robert,	bur. 29 Aug.	1703, aged	1 year.
Jane,	— 31 Jan.	1706, —	2 years.
Robert,	— 26 Nov.	1707, —	1 year.
Margaret,	— 30 May	1715, —	2 months.
Robert,	— 7 July	1717, —	1 year.
Elizabeth,	— 5 April	1718, —	18 years.
Jane,	— 3 May	1718, —	9 years.
Thomas,	— 12 May	1722, —	26 years.
Sarah,	— 21 Mar.	1726, —	15 years.
John,	— 26 April	1754, —	46 years.
Watson,	— 14 Octo.	1759, —	61 years."

Large families were, of course, no innovation. In the preceding centuries multitudes of children came and went with the same clockwork regularity. Sir William Bellasis, of Morton House, Houghton-le-Spring, had seven sons and four daughters between the years 1612 and 1623. What became of them we do not know, though we may guess, but his wife survived for another fifty-eight years.

As for the prisoners and other outcasts from society, there was little mercy for them. A lunatic woman at Houghton-le-Spring was kept in a stable (perhaps only for a short time), where her head was shaved for her, she was dosed with medicine, bled and handcuffed. And Howard writes a terrible report on Durham Gaol in 1774. "The debtors have . . . two damp, unhealthy roofs, 10 ft. 4 inches square. . . . No sewers. At more than one of my visits I learned that the dirt, ashes etc. had lain there many months. The felons . . . are put at night into dungeons; one 7 feet square for three prisoners; another, the great hole, 16½ ft. by 12, has only a little window. In this I saw six prisoners chained to the floor. In that situation they had been for many weeks, and were

very sick. The straw on the stone floor was almost worn to
dust. (This was a punishment for an attempted escape.)
Commonside debtors, in the low jail, whom I saw eating
boiled bread and water, told me this was the only nourish-
ment some had lived on for nearly twelve months. At several
of my visits there were boys, thirteen and fifteen years of age,
confined with the most profligate and abandoned."[1]

If we now turn our attention to the æsthetic qualities of
this age, we can at first find nothing but praise. The Queen
Anne silver; the Georgian houses; the beautiful clothes; the
quaint little towns, with not an ugly building to blotch them;
the smiling landscape, with its great woods, its cornfields, its
pasturage, its air of peace and prosperity, almost purring with
contentment in the evening sun; the country songs and dances,
the smocks and muslin caps and ribbons; the horses and the
coaches and the sound of the horn; the good food, the love
and knowledge of wine; the stately prose; the learned, witty
conversation; the drowsy libraries and the roaring fires—
when we consider all these, harmoniously combined and based
upon a solid sense of religion and duty, we may well believe
that here was to be found all the dignity and grace of civilisation and that the people of this century had learnt, what we
have now forgotten, the secret of the Art of Life. And no
doubt we should be right. If Beauty be indeed Truth or, at
least, a right method of seeking Truth, then the civilisation of
the eighteenth century, without approaching the magnificence
of the Middle Ages, with nothing to compare with a Norman
Cathedral or the glorious ceremonies within it, nevertheless,
by its combination of taste and learning, of reserve with colour,
and of humanity with dignity, in the high level of its conduct
of life and of its artistic creations, in its *savoir faire* and *savoir
vivre*, has approached more nearly to the ideal standard of
excellence than that of any other period of our history, before
or since. Yet even here we find strange paradoxes, though
chiefly as the century advances. These people who themselves
created so charmingly seemed unable to appreciate the grander
and more rugged works of their predecessors. They represented (and so they believed) the acme of taste and the peak
of civilisation, and therefore any building belonging to a past
period of barbarism must inevitably be "inelegant" or "mean."

[1] *Correspondence of John Cosin* (Appendix), p. 337.

The impression of Durham Cathedral left upon the mind of a young Cambridge graduate is that of "a large but inelegant pile of Saxon architecture," and even the greatest intellect of his age dismisses the same unpolished edifice with a few well-chosen words. "The Cathedral has a massyness and solidity such as I have seen in no other place," writes Dr. Johnson to Mrs. Thrale. "It rather awes than pleases, as it strikes with a kind of gigantick dignity, and aspires to no other praise than that of rocky solidity and indeterminate duration." It could not, at any rate, aspire to the praise of "elegance," and therefore could evoke little enthusiasm from a cultivated mind. This typical eighteenth-century word is sprinkled so thickly over the otherwise admirable writing and fine enthusiasms of our historian, Hutchinson, that we are tempted at times to wish him and his elegance to the devil. "This entrance," writes Mr. Hutchinson of a shocking innovation which ruined the proportions of the great Barons' Hall at Raby, "is the most judicious and elegant improvement the castle has received in any age."[1] Similarly, the "Gothic order" receives a modicum of praise because it is "elegant"; a boiling cauldron of sea-spume off the iron Northumbrian coast is described, à la Watteau, as a "fine *jet d'eau*"; old Norman buildings are contemptuously labelled "inferior structures" (though, maybe, "showing some marks of antiquity"); and the little Saxon chapel at Escomb, perhaps the most interesting parish church in the county, is dismissed without a single comment on its appearance. We know where all this elegance led to. Before the century was fairly over Mr. Wyatt was setting to work on his elegant improvements to Durham Cathedral.

It cannot, unfortunately, be denied that the educated people of this age, with all their virtues, perhaps because of them, were somewhat inclined to be smug. In Sedgefield Parish Church are two inscriptions, the one composed in the eighteenth century, the other towards the end of the thirteenth. Nearly five hundred years separate these two "points of view" about the dead, and each inscription may be regarded as typical of the age in which it was written. Highly though we may esteem the balanced and unhurried progression of eighteenth-century phraseology, not lacking in a charm of its own, there can be no hesitation as to which of these two

[1] Hutchinson, Vol. III, p. 270.

epitaphs speaks more beautifully and appeals more directly
to the heart. Here is the later and more civilised one:

"To the memory
of MARY ANNE SPEARMAN,
daughter of Robert Spearman,
late of Old Acres, Esquire,
and ANN his wife.
If elegance and amiableness of form,
united with simplicity of manners,
innocence of life,
and a truly benevolent disposition,
could have prolonged her existence upon earth,
many had been her days,
and her example continually instructive:
but He, who seeth not as man seeth,
ordained otherwise;
and to the inexpressible grief of her nearest relations
and sincere concern of all who knew her value,
called her unexpectedly from hence,
May the 9th, 1777, in the 21st year of her age."

And here is the uncivilised one:

" Sir : Andrew : de : Stanelai :
Metir[1] : de : Gretham : git : icy : pur :
deu : priez : pur : li :"

[For the love of God, pray for him.]

The "godlessness" of the eighteenth-century parson has
been heavily laboured in the past, particularly by those who,
at first or second hand, have been influenced by the opinions
of John Wesley and his disciples. The more "nonconformist"
and Puritan elements our consciences may contain, through
heredity or force of circumstances or conviction, the less shall
we appreciate the card-playing, wine-bibbing and fox-hunting
propensities of the eighteenth-century clergyman of the
Church of England. The more catholic and latitudinarian
our views, the less shall we be shocked by these little idiosyncrasies, the more shall we be delighted by the courteous

[1] "Maître"—*i.e.,* Master of Greatham Hospital. He was the first.

manners, the ease, the dignity and learning of the clergy, the more ready to recognise the fundamental religious convictions which often underlay their polished civility. There is a natural tendency in this democratic age to assume that virtue is synonymous with boorishness and to take for granted that, because a man had the manners of a gentleman, he could not, *ipso facto*, have had the morals of a Christian. But in the eighteenth century a glass of port and a good horse were the natural concomitants of a clerical life, no more scandalous or remarkable than the present-day curate's motor-bicycle and glass of water or bad beer; and a game of cards or chess after a comfortable dinner, in a snug parlour, was as much a part of the ordered ecclesiastical round as a modern vicar's rough-and-tumble on the football field with his illiterate parishioners. Bishop Henson laments that during the whole of this period all the Bishops of Durham, from Crewe to Shute Barrington (with the single and remarkable exception of Butler, who was of humble origin), owed their position to their birth and had but their birth to recommend them to their position. They were courtiers first and prelates for their courtliness. Of Bishop Crewe this criticism can hardly be denied, though even in his case there is surely more to be said. A charitable heart underlay his super-courtly conduct. For the others, without the presumption to contradict so eminent an authority, we may perhaps be able to find a softening word or two when we come to consider their individual lives. Meanwhile, in reply to the general condemnation of eighteenth-century clergy, the judgment of a great modern historian will serve our turn. "It is a common error to regard the eighteenth century in England as irreligious,"[1] writes Professor Trevelyan; and again, after quoting the numbers of candidates for Confirmation in various parts of the country: "It is impossible, in face of such figures, to say that the Bishops were entirely neglectful of their ecclesiastical duties, or that the religious zeal of the population ran wholly into the Wesleyan mission. There is much evidence that Church life, in many districts at least, was strong and vigorous. Nevertheless, there was elsewhere much laxity and neglect. At any rate the aristocratic clergy we have described were more often examples of Latitudinarian merits than of the Methodist virtues."[2]

[1] Trevelyan, *Social History*, p. 353.   [2] *Ibid.*, p. 361.

Apart from the rights and wrongs of the accusation, is it not an approach to impertinence when we, of all people, describe another age as "godless"? With our churches less than half full, and that small half composed almost exclusively of old women, with our education deliberately secularised, our ritual conforming to everything but our Book of Common Prayer and our priests and bishops generally engaged in shortening and "brightening" services in order to popularise Christianity,[1] we might be pardoned if we refrained from criticism of an age which, if it were godless, was at least not both godless and vulgar. But let us now consider the examples of the strength and vigour of the Church in the Palatinate and mark its derelictions to "laxity and neglect."

We will take, this time, the bad side first. There exists a diary of a certain Rev. John Thomlinson, whose opinions and those of his relatives on the conduct of life are more amusing than edifying. He tells a few good stories, some of which I have quoted (but of which one is too vulgar to be repeated) and may be partly excused for his worldliness and flippancy on the score of his youth. But, nevertheless, the insight which the diary gives into the less gentlemanly clerical mind tends to confirm the accusation of indifference to their religion which has been levelled at the clergymen of this age. His chief preoccupation, and that of his clerical uncle for him, seems to have been the pursuit of money to marry, and meanwhile to enjoy himself to the best of his ability.

August 9th, 1717: "Uncle Robert would have me court Mr. Ord's daughter, well educated, religious and 2 or 3,000l. fortune." August 19th, 1717: "Uncle told Mrs. Bilton, etc., that either he or I must marry, for he wanted a housekeeper." January 1st, 1718: "Uncle says he will have us both marryed before another year—me first and then Jane—and then next winter he will go to Bath." March 9th, 1718: "Cousin Jackson's wife beats him, or at least scolds him abominably. . . .

[1] "As to the public worship and life of the Church of God, a serious tendency . . . seems to me to be . . . a discredit of extra-sacramental worship, such that the traditional treasures embodied in Morning Prayer, for example—the Lessons, the Psalms, the *Te Deum*—are becoming unfamiliar to many church people."—Handley Moule, Bishop of Durham. (See p. 362 of *Life* by Harford and Macdonald.)

Uncle Jos Dickman's wife was an arrant whore." June 28th, 1718: "Uncle told a story of Judge Hales marrying his maid, and inviting his children, asking them their opinion. He said it was the Lord's doing, to which they replied it was 'marvellous in our eyes.'" August 18th, 1718: "Passed a few minutes in Stanton garden very agreeably, in thinking what pleasant scenes had been acted of love and gallantry."

While it is possible to over-emphasise the importance of such jottings, even as revelations of an individual character, we cannot wholly ignore them as illustrations of one aspect of the times, particularly when the young parson goes on light-heartedly to inform us (August 28th, 1718) that the "clergy in Cumberland are near as vitious [as in the Bishoprick]. Mr. Gregory as bad as Mr. Nicholson here. Jefferson, lewd. Whittingdale, lewd and drunken." There was, perhaps, some reason for the behaviour of that poor lunatic, Jonathan Martin, who, a hundred years later (after a personal experience of "Thomlinsons," no doubt), stood up in the middle of the sermon at St. Andrew's, Auckland, and cried aloud: "Thou hast no business in that pulpit, thou whitened sepulchre, thou deceiver of the people! How canst thou escape the damnation of hell?"[1]

But here again there is another side to the medal. At the time when young Mr. Thomlinson was considering the prospects of a lucrative marriage and meditating agreeably on forgotten acts of gallantry, Sir George Wheler, within a distance of a few miles, was setting an example of almost saintly conduct in the famous parish of Houghton-le-Spring. In Wheler we have the beau ideal of the eighteenth-century parson, the proof that a man could combine the tastes of a gentleman with the devotion of a disciple, and could face the world with a tolerant and learned mind and yet be as bountiful in love and charity and as rigorous in self-discipline as any more popular and obvious evangelist.

George Wheler, son of a colonel of the Guards, was born in Holland during the exile of his parents for their loyalty to Charles I. In his youth he travelled abroad, and later published an account of his adventures in the Holy Land and in Greece, which revealed him as a classical scholar, a student of history, an antiquary and a numismatist. In 1683 he entered

[1] *M.C.* (1887-1891), Vol. I, p. 419.

the Church and in 1708 was made Rector of Houghton-le-Spring. He was, at heart, a Jacobite, but (unlike his uncle by marriage, Denis Granville) he believed that his loyalty to the Church of England must override all other considerations and that it was his duty to ensure its protection from the attacks of arbitrary power. He wrote a book called *The Protestant Monastery,* wherein the keeping of canonical hours, vigils and fasts was advocated, and the gathering together of the family three times a day for prayer. He regulated his own life and family according to these rules. But "his religion," says Surtees, "though austere in regard to himself, never rendered him harsh or severe in his judgment of others . . . and his zeal and charity embraced the whole Christian world."[1] It is interesting to note that Sir George (who had been knighted after his return from his travels) was far from condemning those dinners of Durham prebendaries at which we are inclined to look askance. "The noblest remains of this English, and I think I may say Christian hospitality," he writes, "is the Residential Entertainments of the Cathedral Church of Durham, where each prebendary in his turn entertains with great liberality the poor and rich neighbours and strangers with generous welcome, Christian freedom, modest deportment, good and plentiful cheer, moderate eating and sober drinking. They give God thanks, read a chapter in the midst between the courses, during which all men reverently uncover their heads; and after grace again there is seldom more drunk than the *Poculum Charitatis,* or the Love Cup, and the King's good health; and then every one to his own home, business and studies."[2] The contrast presented in these dreary days, even before the second world war, is remarkable. Now, writes Bishop Henson, "no suggestion of conviviality, hardly a suggestion of hospitality" is attached to any ecclesiastical entertainment. "There is no wine, and the company consists of diocesan officials, and holy women of one sort and another."[3]

Nor was Sir George an enemy of horse-flesh. "Most considerable men of quality have fine stables belonging to their

---

[1] Surtees, Vol. I, pp. 172-173.

[2] *The Protestant Monastery,* by Sir George Wheler, p. 175; *vide* Surtees, Vol. I, p. 172.

[3] *Retrospect of an Unimportant Life,* Vol. I, p. 307.

seats: I should be glad to see them as well furnished with
horses and more accomplished riders. Hunting, indeed,
savours more of the race of Esau than of Jacob, yet I doubt
not but it may be moderately used very innocently . . . and
I had much rather hear good musick and see fine dancing,
than the harsh ratling of dice and the shuffling of cards."[1]

Wheler never fought for his own rights. His was ever the
soft answer which turneth away wrath. "Sir,—I do assure you
that any trespass which I or mine have committed on your
ground has been through meer inadvertency, and not through
any design to offend: and next, as to the matter which you
say is in dispute betwixt you and my steward, so small a matter
shall never break the peace which has hitherto been betwixt
me and any of my Parishioners."[2] In another letter he pleads
for an old woman: "If you would give me leave to intercede
for your choyce of old Margery Watson, I shall think myself
obliged to you: her work is done and her sight failes, and is
a very honest good creature, and it would be very good charity
to relieve her in this her age, w^h is neer seventy."[3] He left,
amongst other charitable bequests, £600 for the establishment
of a school for twenty girls and for clothes for twelve of them.
The school no longer exists, but the charity still continues for
the clothing of poor girls.

The virtues and intellectual qualities of Sir George Wheler,
though exceptional in any age, were emulated by other incumbents of the same parish. His predecessor, Bagshaw, had
something of the quietness and sweetness of George Herbert,
with "the greatest inclination to gardening plants and flowers
which began from my infancy in coats."[4] Wheler's successor,
Thomas Secker, became Archbishop of Canterbury, and a
later Rector, John Rotheram, was remarkable for his charity
and hospitality, "the hearty kindness of his manner,"[5] his
learning and his exalted ideals. "I am happy to find that you
are pleased with the conclusion of my History," he writes to
a friend, "but that which gives me most pleasure is your
thinking it may be useful to the highest interests of mankind,
by inculcating a right sense of morality and religion, without

[1] Wheler, p. 156; Surtees, Vol. I, p. 172.
[2] Surtees, Vol. I, p. 175.
[3] *Ibid.*   [4] *Records of Houghton-le-Spring, ut cit.*
[5] Surtees, Vol. I, p. 178.

the hope of which I could not have gone through the drudgery
of it with any satisfaction."[1] I cannot refrain from quoting
from a fragment found amongst this good man's papers, both
for its own sake and for a further illustration of the mind of
a country parson living at the height of that period which has
been so recklessly condemned for its materialism and selfish-
ness. "Change gives room to the faculties to renew their
vigour, which would be impaired by too long an exertion.
Perpetual joy would be as fatal to the mind as perpetual
sunshine to the earth. As the finest musical compositions consist of various movements, and the hand of a master runs
through the whole compass of the instrument, one while
striking the sprightliest notes, and then again changing to
some soft and melting air: so is there in our minds a constant
change and succession of feelings and emotions. Indeed, we
may justly complain that the instrument is here often out of
tune, which occasions many ungrateful and jarring notes: but
the time will come when the Divine Master shall again attune
and retouch our frame, and then shall we bear a part in the
Heavenly Choir, and no more discord will remain but what
will be necessary to mix and fill up the harmony."[2]

It might be argued that in a parish of such importance as
Houghton-le-Spring particular care would be taken in the
appointment of the clergy. (This, incidentally, speaks well
for the Bishops.) But we need not confine ourselves to this
neighbourhood for examples of Christian conduct by both
priests and laymen. In Sunderland there was the famous Dr.
Paley, author of the *Evidences of Christianity*, who certainly
enjoyed the good things of life, but also proved that he could
bear excruciating pain without a murmur of complaint. He
was a shocking rider, rolled in his walk like Dr. Johnson,
always wore a court coat and a white wig, was most generous
to his tenants, and won all who knew him with the charm of
his smile. [Later on, in this neighbourhood, at Cleadon, there
lived kind, vague Mr. Abbes, round whom, like a second St.
Francis, the birds would cluster for protection if a hawk
appeared in the air.] In the early nineteenth century there was
Rector Gray, of Sunderland, who devoted himself to his
poorest parishioners and died of a fever caught while visiting
them. There was old Dr. Burgess, canon of the Cathedral,

[1] Surtees, Vol. I, p. 178.   [2] Surtees, Vol. I, p. 178.

who discovered his housekeeper, during a storm of thunder and lightning, sitting on the floor against his study door, believing that she would be safe there, in such close proximity to so holy a man. Thereafter they sat together whenever it thundered. There was Mr. Birkett, Vicar of Stranton (now submerged under West Hartlepool), who sat at his door distributing apples to his parishioners, George Carpendale, Rector of Middleton-in-Teesdale, whose name "deserves to be held in perpetual remembrance"; James Grahame, curate of Sedgefield and a distinguished poet, whom Walter Scott described as "an Israelite without guile"; and the "good old parson," Peter Fisher, who died in 1793 and had been for over fifty-six years Vicar of Staindrop. "Of the sick he was a diligent and conscientious visitor; to the poor and needy a liberal benefactor. Mildness and condescension, humility and gentleness beamed from his countenance. . . ."[2]

Of the laymen the most noteworthy example is that of Robert Surtees, who modelled his own life on Wheler's *Protestant Monastery*. But he was not the only pious squire. In the numerous bequests and gifts made by laymen for the benefit of poor children the greatest care was generally taken to ensure that the teaching of the Church of England should form the basis of their education.

The social customs of the eighteenth century have been condemned as subservient. No doubt this was "the age of well-defined social distinctions, and it used a language in accordance with its social structure."[3] The presumption that all men are equal, upon which we base all our political theories and all our social behaviour, would have seemed manifestly false to the vast majority of thinking persons before the days of the French Revolution. The people of the eighteenth century believed in an ordered society, advancing rank upon rank, like an army on the march, not in a homogeneous herd tearing with frantic haste to its destruction. Such a theory of society involved an elaborate code of manners, not only between persons of different social rank, but between equals,

[1] R. A. Waters in *D.U.J.* (April, 1919).
[2] *Gentleman's Magazine*, Surtees, Vol. IV, p. 133.
[3] *The Charity School Movement*, by Miss M. G. Jones, p. 4. Quoted by Professor Trevelyan in *English Social History*, p. 364.

even as officers in an army salute each other and are saluted
by the private soldiers. But there is nothing in manners to
imply subservience unless the individual is already obsequious
by nature. Nor is there anything in a difference in rank, in
intellect, in property or in birth, to involve the loss of an
independent spirit. The English yeoman and peasant of the
mid-eighteenth century would have resented as a lying insult
any implication that he was a servile, cringing person, while
the pitmen and the keelmen, Crowley's Crew and Hawks's
Blacks, give any impression rather than that of subservience.
They would at least not have tolerated our modern queues.
There is a verse of the period, referring to the custom of
shaving by women barbers on the quayside at Newcastle,
which illustrates this and gives us a vivid glimpse of those
bold and picturesque times:

> "There pitmen with baskets
> And fine posey waistcoats,
> Discourse about nought but who puts and hews best;
> There keelmen just landed,
> Swear 'May they be stranded,'
> If they're not shaved first, while their keel's at the fest;
>
> With face full of coal-dust,
> Would frighten one almost,
> Throw off hat and wig while they usurp the chair;
> While others stand looking,
> And think it provoking,
> But, for the insult, to oppose them none dare."[1]

These swaggering keelmen, moreover, sported their own
fine and individual feathers. No dreary utility clothes could
reflect the force of their personality, but a blue jacket, yellow
waistcoat, slate-coloured trousers and five or six inches of
ribbon streaming from a flat-brimmed hat. Indeed, it is difficult to believe that an age which produced so much marked
individuality, in every walk of life, was remarkable for a lack
of free and manly spirit or suffering from an "excessive
emphasis on the difference of classes."[2] Of course, the difference was there, but whether the emphasis upon it be judged
excessive or rational and healthy must depend upon the

[1] From "The Retrospect," by William Stephenson of Gateshead
(b. 1763), M.C., Vol. III, p. 175.
[2] Trevelyan, Social History, p. 364.

greater or less degree of faith which we are inclined to put in our modern theory of democracy and its works. It is, perhaps, significant that "Rule, Britannia," with its too confident but superb refrain, "Britons never shall be slaves," was written and composed in that period, and is with reason rarely sung in ours.

The career of Brass Crosby provides an example of an independence of spirit combined with a love of freedom and justice for which it would be difficult to find a parallel in modern times. Born at Stockton on May 8th, 1725, the son of a "respectable burgess," Crosby worked his way upwards to wealth and honour, until he became Lord Mayor of London. On his election, which occurred at a time—for thus does history repeat itself—when the freedom of the press was being threatened by Parliament, he promised the citizens of London "that at the risk of his life he would protect them in their just privileges and liberties." And manfully did he keep his promise. On a charge (which again smells strangely of our own days) of misrepresenting the speeches of Members of the House, the printers of two newspapers were summoned before the Bar and, on their refusal to attend, were arrested by order of the House. The Aldermen of the City before whom they were brought on their arrest discharged them, whereupon the Sergeant-at-Arms applied to the Lord Mayor for their surrender. But meanwhile another printer had been arrested by a Messenger from the House, and the Mayor, asserting "that no power on earth shall seize a citizen of London without authority from me or some other Magistrate of the Franchise," declared all the printers to be at liberty and made out a warrant to arrest the Messenger of the House of Commons for assault and false imprisonment. Thereupon he was himself committed to the Tower by a large majority of the House. While on his way there in his coach, with the Deputy Sergeant-at-Arms beside him, the crowd took the horses from the carriage and drew him in triumph to the Mansion House. Only by pretending that the deputy was an intimate friend of his, on his way to stay with him, was Crosby able to save the life of the man who was arresting him and of whose presence the people were suspicious (April 28th, 1771). Then next morning he slipped off quietly to prison. Ten days later (May 8th, 1771), when the Session came to an end, the Lord

Mayor was automatically released, was received by the
citizens in triumphant procession and given a vote of
thanks and a silver cup "for having nobly supported the
privileges and franchises of this city, and the rights of the
subjects."[1]

There was what must seem to us an extraordinary sense of
stability in this period. Like the Romans, the people of the
eighteenth century had no mean opinion of themselves and
seemed to believe that the world as they knew it would continue until the end of time. There could be no other form of
civilisation, no possible convulsion of society to mock and
dislocate the careful provision they always made for the
future. "I give and bequeath," wrote Mrs. Baxter, of
Edmundbyers, "for the use of the poor of the parish, the sum
of fifteen pounds of good and lawful money of Great Brittain
for ever; and the use thereof to be distributed, upon my tombstone, yearly upon Christmas Day *for ever*, by my cousins
. . . and their heirs and successors *for ever*."[2] There is a
satisfying, self-confident ring about such a will which speaks,
as surely as any direct evidence, of quiet and ordered lives,
long-settled habits and the smooth, unbroken procession of
days. But the many-wheeled engine was at the door, Stephenson's and others'. Soon portents of prodigious events would
be witnessed in the Durham skies, the French Revolution
would fall like a knife on the white neck of Beauty, and all
this order and symmetry and quiet and stability would be
shovelled and consumed in an industrial furnace.

But meanwhile the age proceeds upon its leisurely way, not
perfect by any means, guilty of many injustices, blind to
many wrongs, but virile and various and displaying many
human virtues, rising to many human heights, which we have
not been able to show nor had the power to scale since those
distant, care-free days. Meanwhile the fairies dance their
moonlit circles in their Cradle near Hetton-le-Hole, the
Durham ploughman "sosses as much milk as the Lambton
worm,"[3] the canon quaffs his loving cup, the girls sit in the

[1] Surtees, Vol. III, p. 195-196.
[2] Surtees, Vol. II, p. 364.
[3] *Bishoprick Rhymes*. Old Proverb. For Lambton worm see Chapter
XIX.

sunshine weaving their willow crosses for Palm Sunday, and a squirrel swings light-heartedly from branch to branch (where now the chimneys smoke and the sad miners' houses succeed each other in endless rows) all the way from Axwell Park to Shotley Bridge.

CHAPTER XVIII

A CIVILISED CITY

"The City of Durham is famous for seven things—Wood, Water
and Pleasant Walks, Law and Gospel, Old Maids and Mustard."
                                                    OLD SAYING.

THE most learned, the most polished and the most lively
elements of Durham society in the eighteenth century were
concentrated in its capital.

Today the city presents a curious contrast of magnificence
and dreariness. It is a cathedral city, a county town, a university, and, though not itself industrial, with no pithead
visible from its hills, it lies in the heart of the oldest coalfield
in England and is a holiday centre for the surrounding
miners. It has a population, amounting to 18,500, of clergymen, professors, undergraduates, local government officials,
shopmen and pitmen. It possesses, in the Bailey, one of the
most beautiful Georgian streets in England, looking in the
half-light of evening, with its rare lamps lit, like an
eighteenth-century Utrillo. But the North Road is a shopping
centre which has been described as "worthy of a mining
village." There is a market-place which must once have been
charming, but is now not so; there are a few hotels of the
English provincial variety; beautiful bridges and steep,
narrow little streets, which threaten the most alert with instant
death and present a major traffic problem. In its "Abbey"
Durham has the finest cathedral in England and a building
in the very first rank of all the greatest in Europe; and in its
Shire Hall, erected at the beginning of the twentieth century,
it has another building, in the very last rank. In its rocky,
tree-girt peninsula looped by the River Wear and superbly
crowned by Castle and Cathedral it possesses a site unique in
Europe, described by Ruskin as one of the seven wonders of
the world; but the river itself is now black with the pollu-
tions of industry. In the "banks" on the slope of the peninsula,
which belong to the Dean and Chapter but are open to the
public, one wanders, shaded by bosky trees, through idyllic
surroundings; and a few yards further off, in the direction of

Kepier, the riverside is a slatternly stretch of waste land; while from the ruins of the old "Hospital" itself, so quiet and sprinkled with apple blossom and singing birds, an uninterrupted view is obtained of a revolting iron gas balloon and depressing rows of ugly slate roofs. Over all the town, from the great central tower of the Abbey down to the ridiculous little kiosk in the market-place, where the policeman sits twiddling the traffic, there hangs a sort of blight, difficult to describe but impossible not to feel, and due, perhaps, to a combination of circumstances—to the grey, northern climate; to the abstraction of the old Cathedral, enveloped, as in cerements, in its pontifical past; to the quiet sadness of the beautiful Bailey, with no bright faces, no periwigs, no bustle of fine clothes or scraping of fiddles, no champing of horses to relieve it, no Prince of Charming Manners ever henceforth to appear to rouse it from its deathlike slumber; to the uncomfortable consciousness that we are here in the middle of a vast mining area, long torn with social animosities and political hatreds, long distressed, ugly and dispiriting in itself, far removed alike from the humility of Cuthbert and the splendour of Pudsey, which has cast up material and visible signs of its propinquity all round the feet of the Cathedral, but has thereby only succeeded in isolating it, not, for all the occasional gala services, transfusing it with its own life, not transforming it into the great spiritual centre of a new industrial community; and finally to the appalling depression and ever-increasing instability of the times in which we live, to the sense of hopelessness inseparable from disruption and decay, to the miserable apprehension, intensified in a place bearing upon it so many marks of antique glory, of a Christianity that is fast waning and a civilisation that is almost dead. Thus, like a majestic old woman who has seen better days, tired, bent and chilled with age, with many a false tooth and with her skirts bedraggling the mire, but still gamely striving to keep up appearances, still talking hopefully of how well she will look and feel tomorrow, the city of Durham waits . . . for what? There are splendid schemes afoot for new houses, new roads, new hotels and factories and workshops, for new law courts and technical colleges, for concert halls and public gardens and open spaces. This is very fine (or may be), and all honour is due to those who seek to save this

ancient city from drifting into worse ugliness and confusion
by a systematic plan of development which recognises the
dominating factor of the Cathedral—architecturally. But it is
not new roads nor open spaces nor community centres that
give life to any unit of civilisation. These are but its garments,
more or less attractive and more or less necessary, but an
outward expression of civilisation, which must find its essence
and its impulse in tradition, culture and religion. Without
these it must inevitably perish, were the new roads as broad
as the road to Hell and the community centres multiplied a
thousandfold.

But in the eighteenth century Durham must have presented
a very different appearance and inspired a very different feeling. Then the permanent population, of about a third of its
present number, consisted almost exclusively of ecclesiastics
and tradesmen—old freemen of the city—with their various
apprentices and appendages. But to these were added, in the
season, and in some cases all the year round, families "of the
first fortune" in the county, who, with merry widows and the
proverbial old maids, lived for the most part in the borough
of Elvet or in the Bailey, and danced and played their evenings away in the Assembly Rooms or at private parties. The
Bailey, lining the old ramparts of the city and once echoing to
the tread of men-at-arms, now became the centre of elegant
hospitality, and fat horses (called by their devoted coachmen
their "hinnies") waited in the moonlight in their glistening
harness for the end of the revels, where before a Hilton or a
Conyers had gone the rounds of his sentinels upon the walls.
The days of Scottish terror had passed, the days of democratic
depression had not yet arrived; there was mustard, the
famous biting Durham mustard, first made by Mrs. Clements
in 1720—but no gas works, and all was merry as a marriage
bell. Walter Scott saw something of the tail end of these happy
days. After the banquet given by Bishop van Mildert to the
Duke of Wellington, in 1827, he went on to the Assembly
Rooms, "where I saw some very pretty girls dancing merrily
that old-fashioned thing called a country dance, which Old
England has now thrown aside, as she would do her creed if
there were some foreign frippery offered instead."[1]

[1] *M.C.*, Vol. V, p. 390.

Dancing, however, was not the only nor the most usual form of entertainment. Cards and backgammon were more suitable amusements for the relaxation of a learned and sedate society, "the last so clerical a pastime that young ladies about to marry country parsons were advised to learn it."[1] There was, indeed, "a decorous coffee-house in the town, where the clergy met to read the newspapers and to play their games."[2] The elder ladies did not lag behind in this passion for cards. The parties, for this purpose, of old Madame Poisson, a Huguenot refugee, were a feature of life in the Bailey, where sometimes three or four similar entertainments would be given in the same evening. Apart from these, invitations to a mild gossip, *entre dames,* were issued and accepted for an hour when our unfortunate wives are struggling in the kitchen or our unfortunate daughters beating an uninspiring typewriter. "Miss ——'s compliments to Mrs. ——, and shall be glad of her company to drink tea with them this afternoon, Tuesday, 12 o'clock." Incidentally, this actual invitation throws some light on the regular habits of those civilised citizens. Now, in order to catch our friend, we should have to ring her up half a dozen times, find her out on most of them, and eventually agree on some day weeks ahead which she would be obliged to cancel at the last moment. Such are the pressure, rush and uncertainty of our days.

But it must not be supposed that dancing and cards and gossip occupied the whole time of Durham society. No doubt, as there were no communal activities, no W.V.S. and G.F.S. for the women, no offices for the men and girls, there was infinitely more leisure than in the present day. No doubt, also, there were idle people and those who overrated their amusements, such as are not unknown in our time, but leisure could also be, and often was, both studious and industrious, an opportunity to improve the mind or to see to the ordering of the house or to teach one's own children, an occasion to make the most of the duties and graces of a cultured life—to pray more regularly, to read more deeply, to walk more quietly, to dress more becomingly, to converse more carefully, and to indite more elaborately worded, more beautifully written epistles to distant relatives in the South. Life in "Golden Durham" was as free from care and worry

[1] *Sylvestra,* Vol. I, p. 61.   [2] *Ibid.*

as, perhaps, it is possible for human life to be, but it was not, therefore, a useless existence. Certainly the prebendaries were among the richest in England. The Dean's income in the early nineteenth century was £7,200 a year; the occupant of the eleventh or "golden" stall received £3,367 annually, and of the ninth, which was the poorest, £2,279. "York has the highest rack," it used to be said, "but Durham has the deepest manger." Nevertheless, money was not the criterion of society. It was possible for a Master of Arts, in 1771, to keep good company and be lodged and boarded for £6 10s. a quarter. Certainly there were ecclesiastics who were better gentlemen than they were parsons, but "side by side with these sat men whose piety might have saved cities."[1] They were all, guilty and innocent, involved in the abuse of the Wesleyans, and this harsh judgment of their religious and political opponents is now generally accepted as a statement of fact. There are few, in these democratic days, who would stand up for the Golden Canons of Durham. Yet it may be a congenial and a not dishonest task to whisper a word or two in their favour.

We cannot whisper much about Prebendary William Warburton, afterwards Bishop of Gloucester. Though his was certainly a formidable, it was not a particularly agreeable personality. This "tall, robust, large-boned"[2] man, the friend and editor of Pope, a furious champion of the Church, and the bitter enemy of many whom he offended by his rude personalities and contemptuous gibes, became a Prebendary of Durham Cathedral in 1755, and, although consecrated Bishop of Gloucester in 1760, continued to hold his stall until his death. His delight in paradox induced him, in his most famous work, *The Divine Legation of Moses Demonstrated*, to advance the ingenious but unconvincing argument that, because no reference to a life hereafter was contained in the law of Moses, it therefore followed that this law must have been divinely inspired, since, without such supernatural support, any system of society based on the negation of a future state must have inevitably collapsed. His clerical brothers did not thank him for this argument. But in an earlier work,

---

[1] *Sylvestra*, Vol. I, p. 166.
[2] Bishop Newton. (See *D.N.B.* Article on Warburton by Leslie Stephen.)

Alliance between Church and State, he had set down vigorously and clearly the doctrine of the orthodox clergy, and in his attack on Wesley, launched under the characteristic title of *The Doctrine of Grace, or the Office and Operation of the Holy Spirit vindicated from the Insults of Infidelity and the Abuses of Fanaticism*, he evinced that contempt of hysterical enthusiasm which was typical of eighteenth-century divines and which was turned by their adversaries into a counter-charge of coldness and indifference to religion. In spite of his violence and brutality, Warburton "was never a small man."[1] He fought *pro aris et focis*, for the altar and the hearth, "nor did his paradoxical or incorrect arguments, or his lack of languages, take from him the respect due to ingenious and original thought."[2] He lacked neither courage nor warm feeling. At a time when the slave trade was supported by so many influential persons, both laymen and ecclesiastics, that even Bishop Butler hesitated to criticise it with more than gently deprecatory phrases, he denounced it unequivocally in a sermon before the S.P.C.K. But impatience and intolerance seem to have been his most prominent characteristics. It is said that it was thanks to him that the beautiful mediæval copes formerly worn in the Cathedral (and now resuscitated) were discarded, because their high collars deranged and ruffled both his temper and his wig.

But Warburton is not the only nor the best specimen we can produce of the Cathedral clergy of the eighteenth century. Of the Deans, there were Bland and Cowper and Dampier; Bland, perhaps, not a noble figure, but not to be overlooked, for he was Headmaster and Provost of Eton as well as Dean of Durham. He owed his advancement to his steady adherence to Walpole and the Whigs, and must have felt somewhat forlorn amongst his Tory colleagues.

For Spencer Cowper we have the tribute of his cousin and namesake the poet:

> *"Humility may clothe an English Dean;*
> *That grace was Cowper's—his, confess'd by all—*
> *Though placed in golden Durham's second stall."*[3]

Dean Dampier, who had himself been Lower Master at Eton,

---

[1] Kitchin, *Seven Sages of Durham*, p. 247.   [2] *Ibid.*
[3] *Truth*, by William Cowper.

was the father of a Durham prebendary, who became Bishop of Ely and was celebrated for his love of literature and for his splendid library.

William Markham, who was prebendary of the second stall from 1759 to 1771, became Archbishop of York. "Pompous and warm-tempered, with a magnificent presence and almost martial bearing," he represents more faithfully than most that ecclesiastical type which was so obnoxious to the Wesleyans. But his powers of mind and his scholarship were "of the very first order,"[1] and by his staunch friendship for Warren Hastings he showed that he was no time-server.

Thomas Sharp, the studious vegetarian, who wrote an 'Enquiry about the Lawfullness of Eating Blood[1]; Thomas Secker, Archbishop of Canterbury and at one time Rector of Houghton-le-Spring, who "on almost all public questions was on the side of enlightenment and large-hearted charity"[1]; Joseph Spence, the anecdotist and friend of Pope, urbane and gentle and fond of gardening; Edmund Law, "of the mildest and most tranquil of dispositions,"[1] disciple of Locke and author of the *Theory of Religion*; and John Moore, another Archbishop of Canterbury, an "amiable and worthy prelate"[1] and a promoter of Sunday-schools—all these were members of the Durham Chapter during this century, and they sound singularly unlike our preconceived notions of that body.

Robert Lowth, Bishop of London, a man of refined and courtly manners and an accomplished and elegant scholar, Wesley himself described as one "whose whole behaviour was worthy of a Christian Bishop"[1]; while to the modest and learned John Ross again it is Wesley who pays a tribute, for his "genuine and unaffected courtesy."[1] Ross became Bishop of Exeter, and both these men were prebendaries of our Cathedral.

Henry Phillpotts, another Bishop of Exeter, who was in Durham from 1806 till 1828, though not strictly belonging to this century, may here fairly be set in balance against these mild and tranquil clergymen. For it is he, at one end of the line, with Warburton at the other, who seems most nearly to justify our somewhat jaundiced views of all these ecclesiastical dignitaries. Yet there is something to be said for Phillpotts. He was, no doubt, more hated by most people than any man of

[1] *D.N.B.*

his time, and for two excellent reasons: the first, that he was
an irreconcilable enemy to reform; the second, that his enmity
was formidable, for he was a born controversialist and a
magnificent debater. These were the times when Lord Londonderry was attacked by a London mob and even the good
Bishop van Mildert was burnt in effigy before the doors of his
palace. It was not safe to oppose reform, and those who did
so were subjected to the sort of language with which we have
become familiar in recent times: "Let the Lords refuse this
Bill *if they dare*. And if they do, dearly will they rue their
obstinacy hereafter," and so on. It was bad enough to be
opposed by a Wellington and a Londonderry, but that a
Phillpotts, the son of an innkeeper,[1] should dare to cross the
path of a Lambton in his own county was more than these
aristocratic Radicals could stomach. So this prebendary was
singled out for abuse and challenged to come forward and
proclaim his views at a public meeting. His stinging replies
did not lead to an increase of amity. "The hon. gentleman
shall have his own way, as far as I am concerned, when he has
a mob on his side. But I have not the same difficulty in
meeting him in print; we are then on terms of equality . . .
and I cannot affect, what assuredly I do not feel, that there is
anything, either in the authority or in the talents of that
gentleman, to make an ordinary man backward to cope with
him."[2]

The treatment of Queen Caroline complicated and further
embittered the bitter feelings between the Durham clergy and
the reformers. When she died no bell was tolled for her in
Durham, whereupon the *Durham Chronicle*, champion of the
Radicals, cried "Out!" upon the prebendaries for hypocrites
and proclaimed that "it is such conduct that renders the very
name of our established clergy odious *till it stinks in the
nostrils*."[3] Mr. Phillpotts, of course, was one of the stinkers.

Such were the extreme feelings on both sides, which make

[1] Although his father kept an inn, Phillpotts came of an ancient
family of yeoman-squires, who had owned a property in Herefordshire
for two hundred years. This Bishop's father had evidently lost money,
for he sold the property.
[2] *Life of Dr. Henry Phillpotts*, by R. N. Shutte (Saunders, 1865),
p. 48.
[3] "The Libels on the Durham Clergy," by W. L. Burn. (*D.U.J.*,
December, 1945.)

4

it difficult to appraise the character of one who, even today, is looked upon with disfavour from the outset as an uncompromising opponent of "liberal" measures. Apart from his politics, the main accusation against him is that, on elevation to the See of Exeter, he continued to hold the rectorate of Stanhope and to draw a huge salary for which he was doing no work. The accusation is hardly fair. Phillpotts was not a rich man, he had a large family, and he had only accepted the See, whose emoluments amounted to less than £3,000 a year, on the distinct understanding that he would be allowed to retain Stanhope, where he had recently spent £12,000 on a new rectory and a house for the curates.[1] Though today it seems shocking to us that any parson should hold a living *in commendam*, in those days it was a normal procedure, particularly for such a parish as Stanhope, whose chief revenues were derived, not from local tithes, but from the See itself. Moreover, three recent predecessors of Phillpotts—Thurlow, Keene and even the noble Butler[2]—had all continued as Rectors of Stanhope while acting as bishops elsewhere. Nothing had been said against them. But when the hated Phillpotts followed suit it was the pleasing duty of Cuthbert Rippon, the rich reforming M.P. for Gateshead, who had just built himself a castle at Stanhope, to whip up his fellow-parishioners against the avarice of their old rector. "Those were the days when it was easy enough to excite clamour against a clergyman,"[3] and its echoes still reverberate in our ears. Yet the fact remains that, of the last twelve Golden Canons and their Dean (Phillpotts was one, but the rest have not been mentioned here), nine of them have found their place in the *Dictionary of National Biography*. And these thirteen were the virtual founders of Durham University.

But we must not become further involved in the agreeable task of laundering muddied surplices. Enough has been said to show that not all, at any rate, of the golden prebendaries of Durham were nothing but "stall-fed dignitaries," but within their ranks were to be found men of learning and character, gentlemen of courteous and graceful manners, and priests remarkable for their charity and humility. The real grievance

---

[1] Eventually he exchanged it for the sixth stall, but did not keep residence at Durham.

[2] Though he only for one year.   [3] Shutte, *op. cit.*, p. 283.

against them was not their existence, but their frequent absence from Durham. Plurality was the custom of the time, and a bad custom; but close residence during a brief period of the year was incumbent (save for extraordinary reasons) upon every canon, and it is impossible to say, without knowing the details of each individual's life, how often the prebendaries were away during the rest of the time and how much, or how little, was affected by their absence. On major promotion, such as to a See, it was the normal custom to surrender the prebend. A sweeping condemnation is probably not justified. There may have been those who were negligent, but there were those who were not.

One of the most charming old Durham customs lingered long into the nineteenth century and has been faithfully described by an eye-witness[1] of almost our own day. This was the regular prebendal hospitality, those "Residential Entertainments of the Cathedral Church of Durham," which Sir George Wheler commended so highly. The Dean and the twelve prebendaries each kept three weeks of "close residence" in turn. During this time they attended every service in the Abbey and gave their famous dinners. There were five or six of these given by each member of the Chapter, on a basis of two a week. The first was to the nobility and gentry, fellow-prebendaries and the more important of the county clergy; the second was to the headmaster of the Grammar School, to lesser clergy and to lawyers and doctors; the third to the Mayor and Corporation and leading citizens; the fourth to the singing men of the Cathedral and the tradesmen of the town; and the fifth to the King's Scholars of Durham School. The sixth was probably to personal friends, while, once during each residence, old widows were entertained at twelve o'clock in the Servants' Hall. Each of these dinners was succeeded by a little ceremony, the "Poculum Charitatis" of Wheler, or "the ceremony of grace," as it was later called. A chorister, appointed to come to the Canon's house for the purpose, entered the room, attended by the butler and attired in a brown gown faced with white.[2] He

---

[1] "Residence Dinners in Durham." Recollections by Canon J. T. Fowler in *Notes and Queries*, Tenth Series, Vol. III, p. 1.

[2] His morning habit was brown faced with scarlet.

took up his position behind the host, with the butler beside him holding a wax candle in one hand and a shilling on a silver tray in the other. So standing, the boy read out, in Latin, a portion of Psalm cxix. "Tu autem," replied the Canon, when he had finished; "Domine miserere nostri," concluded the child in his sweet monotone. "Amen." The Prebendary thereupon handed the boy the shilling over his left shoulder ("I remember well," says Canon Fowler, "the sweet smile with which Canon Jenkyns used to do it"), and the chorister bowed and retired to the kitchen, where he was given a posset of hot milk and wine, a jelly to eat on the spot, and a tart and cheesecake to take home with him. Meanwhile the grace-cup went the round of the assembled guests. If a King's Scholar were present, he stood up when the cup reached him and proposed the following toast, which it was the custom to rattle off as fast as possible: "Church, Queen, Bishop, Dean, Residentiary." A French chef was specially kept for these dinners and spent his time going from house to house preparing them. The last took place in 1870.

Canon Fowler's father and grandfather, happening to pass through Durham, were accosted by the Cathedral Verger, after afternoon service, with the following message: "Archdeacon Bouyer's compliments. Would you favour him with your company at dinner?" The invitation was accepted, and here the visitors met, perched on a high chair, with his own little knife and fork before him, the Polish dwarf, Count Joseph Boruwlaski. They were highly entertained by his graceful and witty conversation.

This remarkable man, 3 feet 3 inches high, beautifully proportioned and very intelligent, was a well-known figure in Durham society in the early years of the nineteenth century. In his youth he had lived a short time in Vienna, where he had been presented to the Empress Maria Theresa, who received him kindly and perched him upon her knee. In this exalted situation he distinguished himself by his ready tact and charming manners, and was the little hero of a little incident which, in the light of after events, is tinged with a little pathos. "The Empress," he writes in his memoirs, "had on her finger a ring, upon which her cypher was set in brilliants with the most excellent workmanship. My hand being by chance locked in hers, I happened to look upon the ring attentively, which she perceived, and asked whether the cypher was pretty. 'I beg your Majesty's pardon,' replied I, 'it is not the ring I admire, but the hand which I beseech you to give me leave to kiss'; and with these words I took it to my lips. The Empress seemed charmed at this little gallantry, and would have presented me with the ring which had caused it; but the circle proving too wide, she called to a young Princess about six years old, took from her finger a very fine brilliant she wore, and put it on mine. This young Princess was the unfortunate Queen of France, wife of Louis XVI."[1]

After various adventures the Count came to England in 1782 and eventually, delighted with the society which he found there, settled in Durham. A very poor man himself, often hard put to it to find the means of livelihood, he saw nothing to envy or to contemn in the possessions or the behaviour of the prebendaries, whom he describes as "a body distinguished for their munificence, employing their revenue chiefly in the practice of good actions, and in repairing the Cathedral, or their splendid houses."[2] They were kind to him, for it was impossible not to like the little man, so good and amiable, with his experience of many countries and his fund of anecdotes; and he repaid their kindness by enlivening their parties with his flashes of humour, his gifts of mimicry and his charming talent for musical composition and for playing on the violin and guitar. In his old age he would walk along the "banks" with his friend Ebdon, the Cathedral organist, or with Stephen Kemble, the actor, and perhaps Kemble's sister, Mrs. Siddons. The pitmen would follow him about, not a little to his annoyance, with open-mouthed amazement, occasionally breaking into hearty oaths of admiration. Whereupon he, who hated swearing, would stop and gravely reprove them, and they would look down on him with tolerant good-nature, fascinated by the "canny aad man."[3] Towards the end of his life he lived in a little house near Prebends' Bridge, which has since been pulled down. He died in the ninety-eighth year of his age and was buried in the Cathedral, a

[1] *Memoirs of Count Boruwlaski*, written by Himself (Durham, 1820), p. 28.
[2] *Op. cit.*, p. 353.   [3] *M.C.*, Vol. I, p. 175.

strange little companion for Anthony Bek and Hatfield. A tiny suit of clothes belonging to him may be seen today at the entrance to the Town Hall.

Stephen Kemble, Boruwlaski's friend, was a member of the great acting family, which comprised, besides himself, his brothers, Charles and the far more famous John Philip, and his sister, Mrs. Siddons. Stephen's wife was also an actress, who had played as Polly at Covent Garden, and Charles's daughter was the lovely Fanny Kemble. Stephen also had a daughter called Fanny, who seems to have been an equally, or an even more fascinating creature. She and her mother and father—hailed by Sheridan as the best declaimer he had ever heard on or off the stage—with his brother's sister-in-law and daughter, lived for many years at Durham, where Stephen managed the local theatre[1] and where his sister, Mrs. Siddons, sometimes played. A niece describes the happy life led by Fanny and her cousin. "They learned and acted their parts; devised and executed, with small means and great industry, their dresses; made pies and puddings, and patched and darned in the morning; and by dint of paste and rouge became heroines in the evening. . . . A merrier life than that of these lasses, in the midst of their quaint theatrical tasks and homely household duties, was seldom led by two girls in any sphere of life. They were full of fun, but well conducted, good young things."[2] Her famous cousin and namesake thus describes our Fanny: "She had inherited the beauty of her father's family, which in her most lovely countenance had a character of childlike simplicity and serene sweetness that made it almost angelic."[3] She seems to have been one of the first and most successful *diseuses*, an English Yvette Guilbert, for she composed, wrote and sang the most charming little songs, which made a sensation in London. "It was in vain," says her generous cousin, "that far better musicians, with far finer voices, attempted to copy her inimitable musical recitations; nobody ever sang like her, and still less did anybody ever look like her while she sang."[4] She married Arkwright, the son of the inventor of the spinning-wheel, and so became exceedingly rich, found a lifelong and devoted (but platonic) friend in the Duke of Devonshire, and, after the loss of her

[1] It has been pulled down. There is no theatre now.
[2] *M.C.,* Vol. V, p. 411.   [3] *Ibid.*   [4] *Ibid.*

children, grew sad and quiet in her old age, while still retaining all her tenderness.

Her father Stephen lies in the Cathedral near his friend Boruwlaski.

A personality scarcely less remarkable than the Polish Count's was that of John Gully, who, though he did not settle in Durham until fairly late in life, is so essentially a Regency figure, who might have walked straight out of the pages of *Rodney Stone*, that he must not be omitted from our chapter. As a boy Gully was apprenticed to his father, a Somerset butcher, and, happening to catch the eye, as a likely lad, of some patrons of "the fancy," was trained and set up against the famous "Game Chicken," Henry Pearce. He was beaten after a tremendous battle of sixty-four rounds, but, as Pearce soon afterwards retired, Gully became the acknowledged champion of England, beating "the Lancashire Giant" in two contests in two successive years, the second fought in white breeches, silk stockings and without shoes before about a hundred noblemen and Corinthians in Sir John Sebright's park in Hertfordshire. The same year Gully retired from the ring and took up racing. In the course of his subsequent adventures he lost on horses, on two separate occasions, £40,000 and £85,000, recovered somehow, and eventually won the Derby twice, the Oaks and the Two Thousand. He horse-whipped a man with whom he was once part owner of a racehorse, sat as Member for Pontefract in the Reformed Parliament, invested his winnings in Hetton, Thornley and Trimdon collieries, came to live at Cocken Hall, was married twice, had twenty-four children and a house in the Bailey in Durham, and died there in his eightieth year.

"The Pleasant Walks" round Durham mentioned in the proverb at the head of this chapter were once enjoyed by a poet—Thomas Gray. "I have one of the most beautiful vales here in England to walk in," he writes to his friend Mason,[1] "with prospects that change every ten steps, and open something new. Wherever I turn me, all rude and romantick, in short, the sweetest spot to break your neck or drown yourself in that ever was beheld." Let us see how our Hutchinson deals with this wonderful landscape, a panorama even more

[1] December 26th, 1753.

remarkable than that which enthralled him at Binchester. We cannot doubt that he will do justice to its superlative charms, for he saw the surroundings of Durham about the same time as Gray, at the very height of their beauty, and must have known them far better than he. Let us therefore allow ourselves to be transported for a moment to his magic land, to see a little corner of it with his eyes, having steeled ourselves beforehand to swallow some inevitable "elegance" in the process. Can we not afford to grant him this? Would not even he be hard put to it today to find a single object which he could with truth and propriety—and he was a friend of both —invest with the qualities implied by his favourite epithet? Then let us welcome his "elegance," and even enjoy it while we may. It will not last long.

He knows where to go to suck the full sweets of this paradise: down from the city, across Elvet Bridge, through the borough of Elvet, then up the steep hill on the other side to the crowning church of St. Giles, built in 1112 by our friend Ralph Flambard and bearing upon it, as the reader may not be surprised to hear, some "marks of distant antiquity." Here, in the churchyard, Mr. Hutchinson halts and takes his "noble prospect," lamenting at once that it is "too extensive for a picture, and too rich for description." "The inadequate ideas which language can convey," he continues, "are to be lamented by the reader who has a taste for rural beauties and the elegance of landscape." Nevertheless, after this preliminary canter he is off. We have not space to reproduce the whole of his excellent word-picture, but the following extract will suffice to carry us far from all modern problems of Industry, Social Welfare and Traffic, and all modern schemes of Improvement.

"The church of St. Giles stands upon very elevated ground, open to the south where the view is unobstructed. In front the meadow grounds form a steep descent to the river. At the foot of the hill the Wear forms a beautiful canal, terminated by Elvet bridge to the right, and by the wooded inclosures of Old Durham on the left. On the opposite shore is the race ground, from whence, by a gradual ascent, rise the two Elvets, bordered with gardens, and terminated by Elvet church. On the brink of the ascent stand the Bailies, object rising gradually above object, guarded with the remains of the town wall, and crowned with the cathedral church, which in this view presents the north and east fronts, like the mitre which binds the temples of its prelate; giving the noblest supreme ornament to the capital of the principality. To the right, Elvet bridge, with seven arches, receives the stream: over it, tier above tier, rise the buildings of Sadler-street, the gloomy and solemn towers of the gaol, and the battlement and octagonal tower of the castle; the trophies of civil jurisdiction wearing the aspect of old secular authority, and the frowns of feudal power. Thus far description has proceeded without much faultering, but in the other divisions of the scene it is faint and totally inadequate. Over the meadows, in the center, a precipice rises near one hundred perpendicular feet in height, called MAIDEN CASTLE, scar, or cliff; the steep sides of the hill to the right and left are covered with a forest of old oaks, and the foot of the cliff is washed by the river. To the left of Maiden castle you look upon a rich valley, highly cultivated, through which the river winds its silver stream: Hanging woods shut in each side of the nearer vale, where are finely disposed, the pleasant village of Shincliff, the bridge of three arches, the villa of William Rudd, esq; and Hough-hall house: The extreme part of the valley is closed by the woods of Shincliff, Butterby, and Croxdale, forming an elegant amphitheatre; over these rise distant hills, lined out with inclosures, giving the yellow and brown teint to the landscape over the richer coloured woods. To the left, again, you look down upon Old Durham house, its terraces and hanging gardens, with a fine bend of cultivated country stretching away through another opening of the hills towards the east; more rustic than the other views, and being in a simpler nature, affords a pleasing variety to the eye of the man of taste, who stands (if we may be allowed the extravagant expression) *on this enchanted ground.*"[1]

A word about the fate of some of the details of this landscape. Old Durham House, the home of the Tempests, was taken down in the early nineteenth century. There are still some remains of its "terraces and hanging gardens" surrounding the farmhouse which is now known as Old Durham. The races were abolished in 1881, and the racecourse is now the University playing-fields. The old gaol, the original North

---

[1] Hutchinson, Vol. II, p. 304.

Gate of the city and one of the most impressive of its kind in
England, was quite unnecessarily pulled down in 1820. The
last remains of the town wall have practically disappeared.
Maiden Castle, once a British camp, is still covered with
trees; and the village of Shincliffe is still pleasant, but its
thirteenth-century bridge was destroyed in 1824. "The villa
of William Rudd esq." continues to be a villa, and was lately
occupied by land-girls; Houghall became eventually a farmhouse. In its grounds much of the mustard was grown which
Mrs. Clements made famous. Some surrounding woods still
remain, but those at Butterby and Croxdale have been mostly
felled during the last war. Apart from these details and the
inevitable accumulation of public buildings, Victorian houses
and post-Victorian bungalows, with the multiplication of hard,
high roads, the whole prospect which delighted the heart of
Hutchinson has disappeared from view, and for the strangest
of reasons, in these days: not, as one would expect, because
the monstrous works of man have destroyed it, but because
trees have grown up round the churchyard and hidden the
country from sight. Some portion of it, however, can be seen
from lower down the street, and there are other, if not
"noble," at least fine, popular prospects which may still, in
spite of blemishes, afford pleasure to the eye of the modern
"man of taste." The most famous of these is from Observatory
Hill.

Having climbed so high to view the landscape o'er, it is a
disappointment to be bereft of the opportunity of comparing
the past beauties of Hutchinson with what may remain of
them at the present day. No doubt the old church is still here,
though "mucked about" as usual. The north wall remains,
and one or two Norman windows, and a pleasant wooden
ceiling, and old Heath of Kepier lying under his Tudor tomb.
But it was not to see the Normans and the Tudors that we
have climbed St. Giles's hill. It seems that the days of the
Georges, though so much nearer, are more difficult to grasp
than those remoter periods. These still frown down and over-
awe even the bumptious vulgarities of modern architecture,
but, save in some backwater, like the Bailey, the gentlemanly
grace of the eighteenth century has abandoned with shudder-
ings our inelegant and ignoble scene; or, like some down-and-
out aristocrat, lies perdu in a slum, with a cracked fanlight

and a pretty doorway disguised by dirt and cheap paint, and
an unsuspected mouldering staircase, once bright under the
brisk rubbing of a saucy girl in a mob-cap. Yet stay! Here, at
our very feet, lies a sad relic of those happier days. It is a
tombstone, on which the following epitaph is inscribed:

"Sacred to the Memory
of
ANN HILTON
who for many years conducted
the principal boarding school for young ladies
in this City.
d. 22nd Feb: 1832
aged 86.
Deeply lamented by her surviving pupils
and an extensive circle of relatives and friends,
to whom she had endeared herself by the kindness of her
disposition
and the genuine goodness of her heart."

Was this the last of the hoary Hiltons? those antique and
bloodstained barons, with their grey, haunted castle, their
murders and their jesters, ending here, under this elegant
inscription, with this gentle and scholastic dame?

The mists from the river rise above Prebends' Bridge and
overwhelm the spot where once stood the dwarf's little house.
Is it imagination, or do we hear the threading of a violin in
the stillness? wisps of uncertain sound floating upwards with
the wisps of uncertain mist? But these grow thicker and
stronger and bolder. They creep up the banks, creep up the
gardens of the old houses on the other side, up Rotten Row,
up Bow Lane, steal across Palace Green, shroud the great base
of the Cathedral, and gather for the night attack all the way
down the long, deserted Bailey. Not a footfall is heard. And
the music now, if there ever was any, has completely ceased.
But in the darkening twilight, behind those veils of vapour,
surely that is a little group of people, vaguely forming and
then dissolving and re-forming in the street? Surely there
gleams for a moment in the dusk what alone could gleam so
white, the well-kept periwig of Dr. Burgess as he takes off
his hat to salute a passing lady—*three* passing ladies. Can

these be those terrible old maids we have heard of, whom some saucy tongue had christened "Plague, Pestilence and Famine"? Who called them that, I wonder? Possibly Miss Peart; possibly that "charming Miss Peart" (charming but otherwise unknown) whom her lover has commemorated on a window-pane in South Street. . . .[1] What is this little procession coming up the hill? Children, evidently, for they are chattering quite merrily, untouched by the eeriness of the hour. Are these Miss Hilton's young ladies, perhaps? . . . Ah, no. They are the boys of the Blue-Coat School. We recognise the outline of their gowns as they pass. . . . With a sudden rattle a window of the house opposite is thrown open, that house at the corner of Bow Lane, and a little head is poked out to watch the boys go by. Another child, it seems. The world is full of children. She is wearing a white rose at her breast, the sentimental little Jacobite! Then that must be Jane Porter,[2] of course—such a clever child!—and that other one, trying to peep under her arm, she must be her baby sister, Anna Maria. But now there is a burst of laughter from a little higher up. There is a party going on in that house, and is not this the sound of wheels and horses, clattering on the cobbles? Somebody's carriage come to fetch them, no doubt. . . . Where is it? . . . We cannot see it. . . . *Boom!* . . . Suddenly the curfew[3] rings out above us from the Cathedral tower. Its reverberations startle our dreams and drive a long funnel through the mysterious mist. We can see far down the length of the long Bailey now. There is not a soul in sight, and we wend our way slowly to the railway station.

[1] No. 56.   [2] Vol. II, p. 419.
[3] This is still rung on every night except Saturday. For that was the night of the week in which a ringer once climbed the belfry to ring the curfew as usual and was never seen again! *The County of Durham,* by G. E. Mitton (A. and C. Black and Co., 1924), Chapter V.

Chapter XIX

GENTLEMEN OF LEISURE

"He lived in that past Georgian day
When men were less inclined to say
That Time is Gold, and overlay
With Toil their Pleasure;
He owned some land and dwelt thereon,
Where I forget—the place is gone—
His Christian name, I think, was John,
His surname, Leisure."   Austin Dobson.

And his daughters were called Lydia and Philadelphia,
Petronell and Troth, Maryanne, Thomasine and Margerie.
His sons were sturdy Roberts and Johns, Richards and
Williams, with an Ambrose to give a flavour of the cloisters,
and a Tobias to spice them. His home was E-shaped, medium
sized and "gavel-ended,"[1] tucked away in "a grove of old
gentlemanly sycamores" growing on "a gentle declivity
sloping from the west."[2] Its mossy stone slates were secured
by sheep bone, and the plaster ceiling of its hall was decorated
with roses and lilies and the intertwining initials of the young
couple who had fashioned it. Here he passed his quiet days,
busy with his trees and his farm; dozing in his garden amongst
his herbs and his bees, or over a Virgil or the campaigns of
Cæsar before a roaring fire, with a glass of port at his elbow;
or in his large square pew, where he could not conveniently
be seen by the parson, and where a fine copper stove, in the
middle of it, pleasantly warmed his toes; occasionally taking
his boys to school or his girls to dance in York or Durham,
occasionally even to London where, perhaps, he had to go to
represent his county in Parliament; occasionally fluttering
forth, rather old and rather agitated, to welcome his son home
from sea or from the wars, or to escort a distinguished son-in-
law, some statesman or bishop perhaps, to admire the tremendous pillars in his Cathedral or to attend service with him
in his local church and thereafter to "take a prospect of the
adjacent country"; occasionally, alas! to bury his children or,
with his heart still full of their curls tossing from the garden
swing, to visit their graves; occasionally to wait on a new

[1] Surtees, Vol. II, p. 335.   [2] Surtees, Vol. II, p. 208.

Bishop on his arrival at the River Tees, or in Durham, or in his palace at Auckland, and to compare him critically with his predecessor; but for the most part steadily enjoying his quiet and unnoticed days, riding and walking and eating a good deal, discussing the weather and the crops and their families with the villagers, entertaining his neighbours, arranging marriages between their children, making absurd bets, cracking rather vulgar jokes, and, above all, pursuing his long-determined objective, to acquire land and more land and yet more land, steadily to build up the fortunes of his family, to provide amply for all his girls and younger sons, but to leave to his first-born the jewel of his heart, more richly, more firmly, more beautifully set and settled than ever—his own and only English home. His name was Lambton and Tempest, and Bowes and Shafto and Eden, and Surtees and Greenwell, and Salvin and Liddel, and Williamson and Chaytor. . . . "Greencroft, where I was born," wrote old Baker, that stout Jacobite of whom we have read, "where I was born and could be willing to dye."[1] "Sed aliter visum est deo," he added—and so they can all add now.

It would be wearisome and insipid to plough through all the families who, at various times, have held lands in the parishes of this county. We will consider the fortunes of one or two of the better known amongst them, but for the most part it will be sufficient to remember that, while in most corners a single family would remain settled for generations, in others a whole number would succeed each other with startling rapidity, generally through the failure of the heir male and a marriage with the heiress. But the names of these successive owners are, more often than not, familiar from having been encountered in other parts of the Bishoprick or from a prominence in its story. Thus, of two important properties in the county, one, that of Wynyard, had been successively in the hands of Langton, Conyers, Claxton, Blakiston, Davison, Rudd, Tempest and Vane-Tempest before it came to its present owner, Vane-Tempest-Stewart, Marquis of Londonderry; while Brancepeth, the old Bulmer stronghold which passed by marriage to the Nevilles, has, since their attainder, been the property of the Crown, Cole, Bellasis, Bellasis (Lord Fauconberg), Tempest, Russell,

---

[1] Surtees, Vol. II, p. 353.

Hamilton-Russell (Viscount Boyne) before it returned once more to the Crown as headquarters of the Durham Light Infantry. Of the families associated with these two properties, Conyers, Claxton, Blakiston, Davison, Tempest, Vane and Bellasis are all well-known Durham names and all have held lands elsewhere in the county. Conyers we remember at Bishopton, protecting his bishop, and at Sockburn, killing his worm. Claxton was once lord of Horden and, later, forfeited his estate at Old Park, near Bishop Auckland, after the rebellion of the Northern Earls. Blakiston owned Coxhoe and Cocken and built Gibside. Davison, a Newcastle merchant, bought Beamish in the seventeenth century. From Tempest, who lost Holmside for his part in the rising of '69, sprang shoots at Old Durham, the Isle and Stella. Vane was at Raby and Longnewton, and Bellasis exchanged Bellasis, as we remember, for Henknoll. Bellasis, the place, links us up with two other families, Lambton and Eden, both of whom were, in turn, its owners; while Lambton also held lands, at various times, at Bishop Wearmouth, Hardwick (Sedgefield) and Great Stainton, besides Lambton itself; and Eden at Auckland, Beamish and Preston-on-Tees, besides Windlestone. Lumley, as well as being lord of Lumley, owned Hartlepool at one time, and Cocken, Buttersby, Tunstall, Bradbury in the Palatinate, with other property in Yorkshire and the South; while Surtees of Dinsdale crops up again at Mainsforth, Redworth and Hamsterley. Thus a few families, some twenty well-known names, dance, as it were, a pleasant country dance throughout the ages, shifting and changing and bobbing and curtsying to each other, now encountering in the north, now in the south, now crossing each other in the centre; buying up acres and messuages and farms and manors here and there, selling them again, or settling them on their younger children, or passing them with a daughter in marriage. They have their fingers in every pie, they pick out plums all over the county, only to scatter them again perhaps, or perhaps to gather them all together and suddenly proclaim their importance in the world by building a great mansion such as Lambton or Streatlam or Wynyard. . . . But now the plums can be gathered no more, the mansions are down or derelict or turned into some ghastly institution, the pavane is over. Even the old "gavel-ended" houses, from which these land-adventurers set forth, no longer shelter their descendants. Where the old squire drowsed over his Virgil the overworked farmer receives an unexpected visitor in a cold, cheerless parlour under a ceiling of roses. Where the squire's lady and her daughters and her maid Betsy dried their herbs and baked their lovely white bread and mixed their syllabubs and possets, the harassed farmer's wife tries to cope with her innumerable duties without the slightest assistance, while two dirty children cling, staring, to her skirts.

It may not be amiss, in view of the fact that we must now believe that the country is well rid of them, to see if they ever did anything, these gentlemen of leisure, besides begetting innumerable children and buying innumerable acres of land. For one thing, and it is not a little thing, they beautified and adorned the landscape, precisely there where their successors, the industrialist and the Government official, have desecrated and destroyed it. They built pleasant, and sometimes more than pleasant, houses, employing even great architects for the purpose—Ravensworth was refashioned by Sir Thomas Liddell after a design by Nash, and Vanbrugh left his mark on Lumley Castle. They set these houses gracefully in the picture and planted them about with trees, grew gardens beside them full of herbs and flowers, let peacocks strut about their lawns, and drove pretty avenues up to their doors. Gray, the poet, delighted in the loveliness of Old Park, that former home of the Claxtons, but then of Gray's friend, Dr. Wharton. "Whatever my pen may do," he wrote, "I am sure my thoughts expatiate nowhere oftener, or with more pleasure, than to Old Park"[1]; and again: "Happy they that can create a rose-tree or erect a honeysuckle; that can watch the brood of a hen, or see a fleet of their own ducklings launch into the water."[2] Let Surtees's description of this idyllic retreat stand for that of any other eighteenth-century home. All are more or less appreciative and alluring. "The house of Old Park stands retired about half a mile from the Wear, shaded by large elms, and fenced on the south by a moat, beyond which is the *Old Park*,[3] a piece of weeping ground,

---

[1] August 26th, 1766. Letter to Wharton. *The Works of Thomas Gray.* (London, 1825.)   [2] *Op. cit.,* 1761.
[3] So called because it once formed part of the Bishop's Auckland Park.

sloping towards the house. The shell of the old mansion of the Claxtons was repaired (with some additions) in the monastic style by the late Dr. Wharton. The sequestered situation suits well with the style; the modest, quiet front, with its panes of stained glass, and the cross rising in the centre, is seen dimly glimmering through the huge elms. The neglected grounds, once trim as Abbot's garden, are still sprinkled over with evergreens and matted with peri-winkle. The whole neglected spot affords an interesting specimen of the taste of Dr. Wharton and of his friend the poet Gray, whose genius may, I think, be plainly traced in the style of the building, and in the sequestered character of the grounds."[1] . . . Thus these amiable gentlemen assisted the uncultivated beauties of nature and intensified its repose.

But they did more than this. They studied and practised the latest methods in agriculture and forestry. By the end of the seventeenth century the native oak had become extremely scarce, having been wasted, in early days, for smelting pur-poses, or, like the great wood at Aycliffe, felled during the Commonwealth for the repair of long-neglected bridges and fences, or picked out for His Majesty's wooden ships. Now landowners began to plant trees in their parks and round their houses, until, early in the nineteenth century, regular planta-tions were being formed all over the countryside. Sir John Eden, of Windlestone, who had his own nurseries, was one of the first of these regular foresters in the kingdom. But they turned their attention much more to agriculture. They are reputed to have enclosed innumerable acres of common land, for the eventual good of the community, no doubt, but with a ruthless disregard of the poor commoner and his wandering beasts. Whatever the truth may be about the rest of England, this is a very broad exaggeration so far as our county is concerned. "Common fields were probably never very numerous or extensive in Durham," and "such as there were generally had been enclosed before the eighteenth century."[2] The enclosures of the seventeenth century, by Chancery Decree, were at least twelve times as extensive as those for private benefit in the eighteenth and nineteenth

[1] Surtees, Vol. III, p. 298.
[2] "A Hand List of English Enclosure Acts and Awards," by W. E. Tate, *Proceedings,* Fourth Series, Vol. X (1947).

5

centuries combined.[1] Such enclosures as took place at this time were mostly of moorlands in the unpopulated west. The eighteenth-century landowner concentrated far more on increasing the value of his property by the purchase of additional acres already enclosed or by the development and improvement of the land. Arthur Young, in 1768, found in Lord Darlington's Home Farm, at Raby, one of the finest in England. It consisted of 1,075 acres, of which 430 were under the plough and 288 were meadow, the remaining 357 acres pasturing 104 head of cattle, 442 sheep and 27 horses. This farm found occupation for 33 labourers, 20 horses and 18 oxen. Nor was the breeding of horses neglected. Both for popular local races, such as those at Woodham and Auckland and Durham, and for fox-hunting, which Mr. Bowes initiated with a pack of hounds at Streatlam in 1735, the neighbouring squires entered their own racers or rode their own hunters, which had been reared in their own homes. The dam of Eclipse, the most famous racehorse in the world, was bred at Windlestone.

The activities of these leisurely gentlemen were not, however, entirely confined to the pursuits and pleasures of a country life. Between 1675 and 1832, when the Reform Bill doubled the number of seats, the county of Durham (as distinct from the city) sent two representatives to Parliament. From the first of these—Tempest of the Isle and Vane of Raby—down to the last—Russell of Brancepeth and Williamson of Whitburn—the county was represented by its country gentlemen. We find a Tempest five times elected during that period, a Bowes ten, a Lambton twelve, an Eden thirteen, and a Vane sixteen times. Such, with their charities to the poor (which, as we have seen, were not neglected) and their duties as justices of the peace, including such county business as is now the affair of local councils, were the principal occupations of the heads of families.

But the head of a family, though the chief, was only a single member of a unit of society of which every individual— the girls by marriage and the formation of another unit, the boys by their own endeavours—had to play their part in the world. If there were no other justification for the existence of a landed aristocracy, the influence on our national affairs exerted by these younger children would amply suffice. The

[1] *Ibid.*

greatness of England was founded upon them. In the Church, in the Services and in Politics, and, to a less degree, in Literature, the younger sons of country gentlemen not only blazed a splendid trail by occasional examples of genius, but—which was even more valuable—formed a solid and dependable body of individuals upon whom the country could rely for normal leadership. Well educated in classical culture and therefore capable both of rational and original thought, inheritors of proud names and traditions and therefore not easily subject to the temptations of office, accustomed from childhood to country life and therefore unvitiated by exotic tastes and familiar with the daily problems of those who formed the bulk of the population, fortified often by sincere religious opinion and practice, and, if not so fortified, protected from outrageous conduct and unbalanced enthusiasms by an innate sense of seemliness, their naturally courageous and self-confident characters toughened in schools which, though harsh, erratic and even cruel in discipline, were never inimical to independence of thought, they combined in their persons the spirit of adventure with what amounts almost to a genius for common sense, and thus provided precisely that type which is necessary for the direction of public affairs and for the foundation of a great empire. Such were the characteristics of the average English gentleman which, when fully developed and allied with kindness of heart and courtesy of manner, were, at one time, proudly proclaimed by the nation to be the highest product of individual excellence that any society had hitherto evolved. It was a product whose roots were in the English countryside, and therefore bound to wither, with the trees and hedgerows, in the blast and fury of indiscriminate industrial manufacture. Drooping an eversicklier head, it yet managed to survive the nineteenth century, to be consumed at last on the battlefields of the first world war in a sudden and final conflagration of glory.

Let us now seek for particular instances of public service in the records of one or two families of our own county.

Richard Lumley, first Earl of Scarbrough, commanded a regiment of horse against Monmouth at the battle of Sedgemoor, and himself discovered that miserable fugitive hiding in a ditch. But later he signed an invitation to William of Orange to come to England, and upheld his cause in the

North. He served at the battle of the Boyne and in Flanders and was made a General. His younger brother was also a General, Governor of Jersey and M.P. for Sussex. Of the next generation of brothers, four were Members of Parliament, one was an ambassador, and one was killed in action. A little later we find, in the same generation, a Prebendary of York, a Captain of the Navy killed at sea, and a very distinguished General, Sir William Lumley. He commanded the 22nd Dragoons at Antrim during the Irish Rebellion, where "his judgment prevented the sack of the town by the rebels,"[1] and he was severely wounded. He later commanded the attack at Montevideo, and a brigade in an expedition to Italy, and in 1810 joined Wellington in the Peninsula, where he was in joint command with Beresford of the cavalry at Albuera. He was eventually made Commander-in-Chief and Governor of Bermuda. Of another contemporary Lumley, a Captain in the Navy who lost his arm in action, Lord Nelson not unnaturally wrote that such a loss "does not in my opinion at all interfere with his being imployed"[2] and that he would do his best to find work for him. In the first world war (1914–1918) the heir to the earldom was killed in action, and his brother, the present Lord Scarbrough, has been Governor of Bombay.

The legend of the Lambton Worm bears witness to the antiquity of the family of that ilk, but the family, in this instance, is older than the supposed origin of the story. This is ascribed to the fourteenth century, but there are traces of Lambtons as far back as the twelfth. The legend is the best known of those connected with the county of Durham. Its hero, a certain John de Lambton, Knight of Rhodes, was profanely fishing in the River Wear on a Sunday, when he caught a small worm which he unhooked and tossed into a well. Soon afterwards he reformed his life and became a Crusader. During his absence in the wars the worm grew. It grew to such vast dimensions that the well was no longer able to hold it and it betook itself to the river, where it lay sleeping on a rock in the middle of the stream. Here, and at a green hill in the neighbourhood, about which it wound itself nine times, the worm would pass its somewhat vacant hours, unmolested and molesting no one, so long as it was daily

[1] *D.N.B.*   ·   [2] *Records of the Lumleys*, p. 284.

supplied with the milk of nine cows. But when this supply failed, through forgetfulness or through inability to provide it, then havoc was let loose and man and beast were crushed and slain by the infuriated reptile. Such was the state of affairs when Lambton returned from the Crusades and boldly resolved to rid the neighbourhood of a pest for which he was directly responsible. Unfortunately, he was unable at first to achieve his object. Though he repeatedly cut the animal to pieces, the creature, after the habit of worms, repeatedly joined itself together again, and then proceeded, with increased fury, to its terrible depredations. The baffled hero consulted a wise woman. She gave him the shrewdest possible advice, but at the same time warned him that, his triumph once achieved and the worm slain, it would be his duty to immolate the first living creature which he thereafter encountered. Lambton faithfully promised so to do and then joyfully began his preparations, which consisted in studding his coat-of-mail with razor-blades, according to the woman's instructions. Next, in order to avoid any possible disaster, he warned his father that, were he this time successful in his adventure, he would wind his horn, and he directed the old man, at the sound of the third blast, to release his favourite greyhound, which would naturally come bounding to greet its master and so be slain in fulfilment of the vow. It was cruel, but he obviously could not take the risk of killing the first-comer. So, satisfied with these careful preparations, the gallant soldier, covered with razor-blades, took up his position on the serpent's rock in the middle of the stream and there awaited the onslaught of his adversary. It was not slow in coming. At the sight of his old enemy the worm promptly swam his way towards him and, meeting with no resistance, wound himself triumphantly about the man's body. The razors thereupon cut the creature to bits, and the pieces of worm, falling into the river and being carried off by the current to the sea, were unable to join themselves together again. The terror of the neighbourhood had been at last destroyed. All was so far well, but now the absent-minded and excitable old father, on hearing the joyful notes of the horn, instead of releasing the dog, as he had been told to do, himself ran forward to greet his son, and thus became the first living creature to cross the path of the conqueror. In despair the hero visited the wise woman again and begged for absolution from his vow, in view of the peculiar circumstances. This was granted, but only on the understanding that for nine generations no chief of the house of Lambton would be permitted to die in his bed.

The Worm Well has disappeared, though it existed more than a hundred years ago, at the time when Surtees wrote. The Worm Hill can still be seen and is thus named on the ordnance map. The creature, when represented in art, was always shown to have feet, and if we consider this circumstance with its partiality for milk and its habit of resting in the middle of the river, is it not permissible to surmise that we have here the distorted recollection of an extinct animal of the genus crocodile, which actually infested this region in the remotest past and the stories about which, handed down from generation to generation, were at last crystallised into a single tale in honour of the principal family in the district? "I have been lately often near the supposed haunts of the Lambton Worm,"[1] wrote Surtees to Walter Scott, "and I really feel much inclined to adopt your idea, that animals of this description may have been formerly nourished to a much larger size in our woods and waters. . . . The country around Lambton seems particularly favourable for the production of such a creature. The banks of the river have been, time immemorial, a thick, tangled forest; and part of the adjoining flats are low and marshy, and full of willows and brushwood." But Mr. Binnall is, perhaps, on safer, if duller, ground in ascribing the origin of such tales to "a reminiscence of belief in the guardian serpent-spirit."[2]

It would have been impossible to mention the Lambtons without telling the story of the famous legend with which their name is associated, but the worm, whether real or imaginary, has lured us away from our main purpose, which is to mark the more authenticated services rendered by the members of Durham families. To this purpose we shall now return.

The Lambtons, as we have already seen, were amongst the stoutest of the many stout Cavaliers of the Palatinate. Both Sir William, knighted by Charles I, and his eldest son and

[1] May 13th, 1810. (See Fordyce, Vol. II, p. 632.)
[2] *Proceedings,* Fourth Series, Vol. X (1947), "Holy Wells in Northumberland and Durham," by Rev. P. E. B. Binnall.

namesake were killed in the King's service, the first at Marston Moor and the second at Wakefield. Another member of the same family, John, lost his life in a skirmish at Bradford. Succeeding generations of Lambtons then represented Durham City (as well as the county) in Parliament, until their political genius culminated in John George, first Earl of Durham and Governor-General of Canada. This irritable, overbearing, vain, high-spirited and brilliant man was so remarkable, in those days, for his democratic opinions that he was popularly known as "Radical Jack." A Whig Member for the county between 1813 and 1828 (when he was created a peer), he was made Lord Privy Seal in Lord Grey's Cabinet and, with Lord John Russell, was entrusted by the Prime Minister with the preparation of the first Reform Bill. When it seemed probable that the House of Lords would throw out the Bill, Lord Durham wished to ensure its passing by the creation of an unlimited number of peers—a threat which we have heard more than once since. In 1833, on his resignation from the Government after a quarrel with Palmerston, he was created Earl of Durham, and five years later, in consequence of the rebellion of the French Canadians, he was sent out to Canada as Governor-General to put matters right. The steps which he took upon arrival were disavowed by the Government in England, whereupon he sailed for home and issued his "Report on the Affairs of British North America." This famous "Durham Report" laid the foundation-stone of the present Dominion of Canada. "The logical and complete application of the principle of responsible parliamentary government for the Dominions," writes Professor Trevelyan, "owes its timely triumph to the wisdom and energy of Lord Durham. He had the peculiar merit of regarding freedom as the means of preserving the Imperial connection, and not as a step towards separation. . . . He was both an Imperialist and a democrat at a time when hardly any other person of Cabinet rank was either the one or the other."[1]

Lord Durham inherited his zeal for reform from his father, William Henry Lambton, who was Member for Durham City, and whose talents promised a brilliant career which was cut short by his early death from consumption. William's brother, Ralph, also Member for Durham City, is better

[1] Trevelyan, *England,* pp. 660-661.

known to us as the Master of "Mr. Lambton's Hounds" and
the paragon of North-country sportsmen. Their father, John,
and their uncle, Hedworth, both younger sons of the preceding generation, were both generals in the Army. John was
also Colonel of the 68th foot, afterwards the 1st Durham
Light Infantry. Of a later generation, Sir Hedworth Meux,[1]
younger brother of the third and fourth earls, commanded the
Naval Brigade at the siege of Ladysmith, was M.P. for Ports-
mouth from 1916 to 1918, and Admiral of the Fleet.

The Vanes are said to owe their coat-of-arms—azure, three
sinister gauntlets or—to the capture by a member of their
family of King John of France at the battle of Poitiers. After
their purchase of Raby from the Crown they played a prominent part, as we have seen, in the Civil War, and not long
after the Restoration we find them representing the county in
Parliament, which they continued to do, off and on, with unflagging zeal for several generations. The second of these
M.P.s was created Lord Barnard, and the third Lord Barnard,
whom the Duke of Norfolk described as "Harry Vane, who
never said a false thing or did a bad one," was made Earl of
Darlington. His son was the keen agriculturist whose Home
Farm was praised by Arthur Young, and the third earl was
created Duke of Cleveland in return for his support of the
Reform Bill. The dukedom expired in 1891, when the father
of the present Lord Barnard succeeded to the barony and the
estates. His eldest son died as a result of active service in the
Great War.

Meanwhile a younger son of old Sir Harry Vane (who
bought Raby) had settled at Longnewton, where his descendant eventually married the sister and sole heiress of the last
of the Tempests of Old Durham and of Wynyard. Their
grand-daughter, Frances Anne, heiress both to the Tempests
and to the Vanes of Longnewton, married the third Marquis
of Londonderry, half-brother to the famous Castlereagh and
himself the *beau sabreur* of Wellington's army. His descendant was Secretary of State for Air between 1931 and 1935.
It is to him, the late Marquis, that we owe a share of our
gratitude for the eight-gun fighter, for it was during his
tenure of office that the specification for this machine was
passed. The idea of concentrating all the armament in the

[1] He changed his surname.

wings of an aeroplane was an entirely new one and aroused considerable technical opposition, but from this specification emerged both the Hurricane and the Spitfire, which, with the courage and skill of their pilots, saved England in her darkest hour.

We cannot omit to mention a few more Durham families, but we must dismiss them more briefly. Sir Thomas Liddell (the ancestor of Lord Ravensworth) won his baronetcy for his gallant defence of Newcastle against the Scots. His earlier descendants, as merchants of this enterprising town, were amongst the first—with the Carrs and the Ellisons, the Vanes, the Tempests and others—to appreciate the importance of coal and to busy themselves with its development. In the course of generations they represented various constituencies in Parliament. The sixth baronet, another Thomas, was created Lord Ravensworth and was a leading partner of the eighteenth-century colliery company known as the "Grand Allies," as well as a patron of George Stephenson, the builder of the first railway. Lord Ravensworth's nephew was that Dean of Christ Church whose share in "Liddell and Scott" has earned him the respect, if not the affection, of every schoolboy struggling with the classical Greek tongue. He was born at Binchester and was the father of "Alice," for whom Lewis Carroll wrote his famous book.

The Roman Catholic Salvins of Croxdale, with their proud motto, "Je ne change qu'en mourant," and their noble quarterings of de Ros, Bruce, Lancaster, Umfraville . . . are one of the oldest families in the county. Jocelyn came over with the Conqueror and settled in Nottinghamshire. His grandson, Thomas, founded Welbeck Abbey. This founder's brother went to live in Sherwood Forest and so acquired the name of Ralph le Silvan, later unfortunately corrupted to Salvin. In 1402 the Salvins, through marriage with an heiress, became the owners of Croxdale, where they settled in 1402, and where they remained until 1943. Their faith precluded them for many years from serving the State in any public office, but did not prevent them from taking arms for Charles I. One Salvin was killed at Northallerton and another at Marston Moor.

The first and second baronets of the Chaytor family were M.P.s for Sunderland and Durham City respectively.

Williamson of Monkwearmouth and Whitburn, Shafto of
Whitworth, Clavering of Axwell Park, and Burdon of Castle
Eden, have all represented their county in Parliament; a
recent Baker of Elemore, descendant of another gallant
defender of Newcastle, was an Admiral in the Royal Navy[1];
the very ancient stock of Surtees suddenly brought forth new
fruit when, in 1816, their descendant, Robert of Mainsforth,
produced the first of his magnificent volumes on the history
of the Palatinate, and again when, a few years later, his
cousin of Hamsterley created "Jorrocks."[2] Within the last
two hundred years there have sprung from the Eden family
of West Auckland and Windlestone quite a posse of admirals
and generals, of bishops and ambassadors and Governors and
Cabinet ministers.

Having scampered through a few records, let us now take
a glance at the houses which sheltered these families, as they
appeared in the eighteenth century and as they are today.
Proceeding in the order which we have selected, we come first
to the home of the Lumleys. "Lumley Castle," says Surtees
in a happy opening sentence, "stands glittering with a bright
open aspect, on a fine gradual elevation above the Wear."[3]
He goes on to inform us that it was built "of bright yellow
freestone."[4] The sight of this golden splendour, embosomed
in blue-green trees above the bubbling river, must have
seemed to the traveller on the great north road like a glimpse
of the towers of the New Jerusalem. But all glitter and
brightness has now left it. Now, no longer yellow in un-
tainted air, it stands blackened and smoke-grimed in close
proximity to coal-pits and to the mining town of Chester-le-
Street, and its aspect is rather grim than jocund. Nevertheless,
it remains the most satisfying and unspoilt secular building in
the county. Built in the fourteenth century, not so large
as Raby, nor nearly so remarkable in outline, it has a com-
pact and solemn beauty of its own which has not suffered,

[1] William Henry Baker, O.B.E., 1862-1932.
[2] Robert Smith Surtees. (See Chapter XXV.)
[3] Surtees, Vol. II, p. 153.
[4] *Ibid.* The builder was possibly John Lewyn, master mason to the
Bishop of Durham (Hatfield). (*The National Trust,* edited by James
Lees-Milne, Batsford, p. 54.)

as Raby has done, from the vandalisms of the eighteenth and nineteenth centuries. In the inner court, with its beautiful tower covered with Lumley coats-of-arms in various stages of evolution and its sixteenth-century clock chiming a sweet, ancient and plaintive note, one feels far removed from the ugly world without, brought slowly and peacefully backwards to an almost cloistered time. The castle within is impeccable. Only Vanbrugh has been at work on its walls, and he has done his work well, not imposing his pompous Castle Howard personality on this tough little fortress, but letting in light and air discreetly, making one or two noble reception-rooms and crowning them with a grand fireplace in the Barons' Hall. The whole house is in good condition, not too large for comfort, charming, light and civilised in spite of its exterior grimness, full until recently, at any rate—of fine pictures and good furniture. In fact, there is little to be done to it, save the one thing that cannot be done in this enlightened age—to live in it and enjoy it. It is now leased to Durham University, which thus has the distinction of being doubly castel-lated.[1] No better destiny could be found for it under the present conditions of society. But it is, nevertheless, both from the national and civilised points of view, sad and wrong that a home, built and intended for private purposes and occupied by a particular family for generations, should have to be surrendered to an institution devised for the benefit of the public generally, however admirable in itself. Durham University has its own excellent purpose in the world to fulfil, but this has nothing to do with the life and meaning of a private house which has been for centuries the citadel of a private family. The fact that the house is architecturally beautiful and historically interesting but serves to emphasise the value of these private associations. The beauty was created by the Lumleys and the historical interest is due to them. To hand over a home to "the nation," to make of it a monument or museum or institution, in whatever shape or form, is to destroy its personality, to kill it and stuff it, to rip the soul out of its body and to present the public with the corpse. The whole of England is littered with these corpses.

Old Lambton Hall was pulled down in 1797, and all that is left of it now is a charming little cottage. The new "castle"

---

[1] Durham Castle and Lumley Castle.

was built on the site of Harraton Hall, which belonged at
one time to the Hedworth family, whose two co-heiresses
married a Lambton and a Williamson. Lambton bought
Williamson's share and out of the old Hedworth and the old
Lambton grounds made the present most beautiful park,
which for size and variety of scenery, with its steep banks and
valleys and the River Wear running through its centre, is the
most romantic in the county. But it is an oasis in an industrial
desert. The great room of the new house, which measured
ninety-four feet by thirty-six, has recently been pulled down
in an endeavour to make the place habitable according to
modern standards.

Raby Castle still remains the most magnificent private
house in the county, but it can only be with the greatest
difficulty and at the cost of much care and anxiety that its
owner and his family continue to occupy even a corner of it.
Nine great towers built by one of the proudest nobles in the
North for military defence, an enormous entrance hall with a
fireplace about twelve feet wide, a Baron's Hall of prodigious
length,[1] a suite of reception rooms, a fourteenth-century
kitchen occupying the whole of one of the towers, muniment
rooms, a chapel, bedrooms up and down the narrow twisting
stairs, bathrooms tucked away in the thickness of the walls,
and a Servants' Hall nearly sixty feet long, however admirably adapted to the needs of Neville and his seven hundred
retainers or to the sumptuous hospitality of the Early Victorians, are not likely to be acclaimed with shouts of rapture
by the unfortunate châtelaine of today. The outside of this
magnificent building can hardly be rivalled in the North and
will bear comparison with any castle in Europe. It is set,
rather surprisingly, in no commanding position, but almost
too humbly, and yet sweetly, in a long, rolling English field.
The different heights and shapes of all the nine towers (of
which the highest is eighty feet) and the perfect placing of
them in the irregular building, the colour of the old stone,
the green of the surrounding park (just out of sight of the
pits), the deer seen browsing over the low park wall, the
woods and plantations crowning the slopes beyond—all these,
illumined by the rays of a slanting sun, are charged with that
curious mixture of romantic peace and rustic solidity which was

---

[1] 132 feet.

so typically and wonderfully English. Here is no elegantly
bedraggled French château, no exotically pinnacled mid-
European *Schloss*, as alien in this modern world as a marquise
or a fairy prince, but a home which still fits into the surrounding landscape, which is still as natural and right and proper
to England as an elm-tree and a hedge of flowering may.
How long will it remain so? How long *can* it remain so?
The machine-made bungalows of the newly deified "Common
Man" are bound to win in the end.

"I never weary of watching the red deer," wrote the
Duchess of Cleveland in her charming account of her home,[1]
"for they are always beautiful: beautiful, in their indolent
moods, when they will scarcely deign to turn their graceful
heads to look at you from their green couch under the trees;
beautiful when bending down to drink, and reflected in the
water below as in a setting of silver; most beautiful of all,
when roused and excited, tossing their antlers in disdain, or
levelling them at each other in their fencing-matches." The
red deer still survive. Their couch under the trees is green as
ever. But, with the castle which they grace with their tossing
antlers, with the minstrel gallery and the chapel, with the
two little boys[2] in the Barons' Hall and the fascinating little
minx in the dining-room,[3] they survive from an age which is
gone.

Brancepeth Castle, the old home of the Bulmers, which in
the past must almost have rivalled Raby, was ruined at the
beginning of the nineteenth century, when it was completely
rebuilt by Matthew Russell. It is strange that the vandals
of that period seemed to admire what they destroyed
and to imagine that by imitating it they could go one better.
Thus the genuine Norman church of Merrington was pulled
down and built anew according to the Victorian ideas of what
Norman should be, and Brancepeth still remains a castle, very
much a castle, with a mock antique archway to the main staircase which looks as if it had been made of Norman cheese.
Only the South Tower remains of the original building.

[1] *Handbook for Raby Castle* (1870).
[2] Henry Vane, afterwards First Lord Darlington, and Morgan
Vane, his brother, both by Allan Ramsay.
[3] Lady Catherine Margaret Powlett, afterwards Countess of
Darlington, by Sir Joshua Reynolds.

Of the various homes of the Tempests, Surtees says of Old Holmside: "Part of the old court-yard is remaining; the Chapel forms the North side, and its West window is still perfect. . . . Above it a mutilated figure is fixed in the wall, with a full moony face, and a kind of round helmet or *pot en tête*."[1] The "moony face" is still there, and is known locally as "Moll." The chapel is part of the outbuildings of what is now a whitewashed farm heavily strutted to prevent collapse from the extraction of the coal beneath. There are the remains of a moat visible and a general air of antiquity from the arrangement of the buildings, but nothing of particular interest. The Isle, near Bradbury, is another farmhouse; Old Durham likewise; Stella and Wynyard still remain.

Stella Hall, a Jacobean manor-house with late eighteenth-century alterations, stands hard by the scene of the rout of the English by the Scots in 1640, and is now surrounded by the industrial activities of the Tyne. Originally built by a branch of the Tempests, it came through an heiress to Lord Widdrington, who was attainted in 1715, and it was eventually bought by Sir Joseph Cowen, a Radical M.P. knighted by Gladstone, whose son was a friend of Mazzini and entertained within these very Catholic walls such popular anti-clerical heroes as Garibaldi and Kossuth. But today the house speaks neither of the devout Tempest—his chapel is here, but it is no longer a chapel—nor of the unhappy Jacobite Widdrington—though here is the hall where he and his tenants assembled and drank the health of their legitimate sovereign—nor of the romantic Garibaldi. The Cross of St. Cuthbert and the White Rose and the Red Shirt, so different and even hostile in intention, yet so sympathetic in a common heart-felt belief and a common reckless adventure, have all been crushed by the surrounding materialism. The smoking chimney has superseded all. Even the old Jacobean walls, even the charming pillared hall and the Italian plaster-work in the drawing-room, though they live on indeed, and pretty well to the material eye, live on with that apathetic parody of life which draws its sustenance only from the past, because it knows that it can have no future.

Wynyard was bought by the Tempests of Old Durham in the eighteenth century and is still the property of their

[1] Surtees, Vol. II, p. 324.

descendant, the Marquis of Londonderry. The present Palladian palace, built about a hundred years ago, has been the scene of more splendid entertainment and more generous hospitality than any other house in the county. Kings and queens, statesmen and writers, soldiers, sportsmen and artists, all who were noblest with all who were loveliest in the land, over a period of sixty years and more, have been the guests of the Londonderries at Wynyard. The bagpipes have skirled round the dinner-table, the gold plate has blazed under innumerable candles, the loving cup has gone the round. Again and again the great "saloons"—as Disraeli must have called them—have been filled from end to end with light, warmth and beauty, the hum of voices, the glitter of wonderful jewels and the scent of flowers; again and again the tenants and employees and their families have gathered here together for the private theatricals and other Christmas festivities, mingling their happiness and laughter with the laughter and happiness of many grateful children. Now the house is a training establishment for county council school-teachers.

The Ravensworth of Nash has been pulled down, its walls having been split by the extraction of coal. Only two uninhabited towers, belonging to the original castle, still remain above ground. The Salvin house at Croxdale, remarkable for its walled garden[1] of nine acres in extent and situated on a picturesque wooded ridge above the Wear, after having been occupied by that family for over five hundred years, is now a public Maternity Home—practically empty owing to the lack of nurses. Within the grounds of this property is the old manor-house of Butterby, or Beautrove, "a name probably bestowed by the earliest Normans, who discovered or appropriated this beautiful sequestered spot, hid in the bosom of woods and waters. . . . The house, offices and gardens are defended by a moat, walled, and though now dry, capable of being flooded to a depth of fifteen feet. The entrance is by a bridge and an arched gatehouse, which glimmers through an avenue of limes, like the entrance to a small monastic house."[2] So wrote Surtees over a hundred years ago. There is still an

[1] See *Country Life* for September 2nd and September 16th, 1939.
[2] Surtees, Vol. IV, p. 109. The manor belonged to an old Norman family called d'Audre, then to Lumley, Chaytor and others and was finally bought by Salvin.

avenue of limes, but the Gatehouse, no longer glimmering, looks forlorn and derelict at the end of them, standing in a farmyard mire with a bull rampaging about it. The outer walls and moat are in good condition, and even now this place is sequestered and lovely, though a farm has been made out of the ruins and the once-wooded hills around have been ravaged for timber during the last war. The farmer longs for a villa.

Another quondam home of a branch of the Salvin family, Burn Hall, a conspicuous and attractive early nineteenth-century house on the opposite side of the river, is now a Roman Catholic seminary.

The Chaytors still live at Witton Castle, which was built in the fifteenth century and much altered in the nineteenth; the Williamson home at Whitburn has been split into three; and the Shaftos at Whitworth are almost engulfed by the mining town of Spennymoor, which, in 1820, was a single farmhouse and, a hundred years later, had a population of 23,000. Axwell Park, where the gay squirrel once started on his green career, was a late eighteenth-century house of some importance, and is now an industrial school with a belch of monster chimneys at its front door. Two sad stone lions here pitifully lift their broken paws in a wasted, derelict park. Castle Eden has seen the last of the Burdons, the Bakers have just left Elemore, and Mainsforth, where Surtees rejoiced in his "Paradise," lies deserted of its owners and its peacocks at the edge of a mining village. Bellasis is in ruins, Hamsterley is an uncertain oasis, Windlestone is empty, surrounded with rusting wire and fallen trees, and the Tudor manor-house at West Auckland is a brewery. The fate of the two homes of the Bowes family, Gibside and Streatlam, is described elsewhere. As for the Old Park, where Gray watched the ducklings and smelt the sweet honeysuckle of his friend Dr. Wharton—"the place is gone."

The list is far from complete, but one grows weary of this mournful catalogue. I will mention but two more houses, which were sought out with eagerness because of the description of them in a book quite recently published. They are Cocken Hall, near Durham, which Mr. Mitton eulogises as "one of the prettiest gentlemen's seats in the county,"[1] and

---

[1] *The County of Durham,* by G. E. Mitton (1924), Chapters V and VI.

Newton Hall, not far from it, which he describes as "a grand Queen Anne mansion." This second house, of red brick with stone facings and graced with an old bowling green, belonged to Anthony Lax Maynard, the Master of the North Durham Hounds. Here, on November 3rd, 1873, and on many a day thereafter, the grandson[1] of "Nimrod" "partook of Mr. Maynard's good breakfast, which he had provided for all comers," horsemen and footmen alike, or danced the night away on New Year's Eves with the servants and the hunt servants.[2] But before Mr. Maynard's day (and before Queen Anne had taken it in hand) Newton Hall belonged to the Blakistons. So that it must have been along these wooded banks of the Wear that young John Cosin directed his steps when he came to court his future wife, Frances.

Both Newton and Cocken have now disappeared, pulled down by "builders"—a curious name to give to destroyers—and every brick and stone has been removed.

Standing in the brambly wilderness of what was once the garden of Cocken Hall, I wished that I had the gift of vision of those good ladies who saw the vanished beauties of Versailles. Yet what could be seen of interest here? No tragic queen, for certain, no mud-spattered messenger arriving with disastrous news. Only a placid Durham dame, sitting at her window with her embroidery; or a young girl with a high waist and a long flowered skirt, swinging her straw bonnet by its ribbons as she skips through the orchard. . . . But I saw nothing but weeds.

[1] N. W. Apperley.
[2] *North Country Hunting Half a Century Ago*, by N. W. Apperley. (W. Dresser and Sons, Darlington, 1924), pp. 60, 123, 282, etc.

Chapter XX

IT WAS A DREAM

"O! then, I see, Queen Mab hath been with you."
"Romeo and Juliet."

As so often happens in this contrary world, that which I vainly sought in the waste grounds of Cocken Hall came upon me several days later, with no conscious desire of it on my part, and, incidentally, at a most inconvenient moment. It happened in this way.

I had arranged to go to Billingham to see the great works of the Imperial Chemical Industries and, at the same time, to ascertain whether there was anything left of the old manor-house at Bellasis. But, as the car was to pick me up at midday, I decided that I had plenty of time meanwhile to walk across the fields to Middridge and look at the house of Anthony Byerley, the Cavalier who had garrisoned it with his "Bull-dogs." But it was a lovely summer's day, so that by the time I had reached the village green and cast an eye upon the building in question I felt too lazy to bother about its interior. It was now a farmhouse, doubtless resembling many others I had seen; a good staircase, an eighteenth-century niche for china with a pretty shell top, perhaps some remains of old plaster-work on a ceiling—was it worth while, on this beautiful day, to disturb the owners (and incidentally myself) for the sake of these few relics of a bygone age? And even these might not be there. To hell with the possible staircase and its possible cobwebs! The blue sky was better than any plaster ceiling, the buttercups in the meadows were worth a hundred Tudor roses, and the little wind running along the tops of the trees was more exciting than a china cupboard. So I turned to retrace my steps across the meadows, deciding that I would arrive back just in time to fortify myself with liquor before I had to face industrial Billingham. It had taken me longer than I had expected to come down here. I must not, therefore, dawdle on the way back. Nevertheless, I did. It was one of those days on which it would be an insult to nature to attempt a greater speed than a saunter. Her charms were about one

350

everywhere: in the gently waving beeches, in the tiny fleecy clouds, in the invisible lark, in the field flowers and the grass. It was as if one were caressed by the wanton creature and to resist her was impossible. Moreover, the sight of a cottage which I knew very well, not far from the gates of old Byerley's house, had started within me a train of thought far more in keeping with this idle summer's day than the Imperial Chemical Industries at Billingham.

When we were children we did not look forward with any great enthusiasm to our Sunday mornings. There was, first of all, church, which was rather a lengthy business from "When the wicked man . . ." down to the Blessing, particularly as one dared not turn round more than once or twice to catch the eye of Barbara Teasdale, the dairymaid. She was a sport. She did not mind if you slipped into her dairy and helped yourself to cream (when you were supposed to be taking ten minutes of fresh air between your French lesson and your music lesson), and on Sundays she always looked so pretty and pink and cheerful in her little black bonnet. It was really a pleasure to sit opposite her in the wagonette on the way to church. But the service, though long, was not too bad. That was only the beginning of the torture. It was after church that the trouble started (unless, by shamming a headache, you could manage to go straight home with the servants), for then began the weary round of visits to endless cottages and mournful old women. They were all worthy, perhaps, and it was excellent training for the young; but we did not appreciate that at the time. Only one of these calls was regarded by us as anything better than a boredom which had to be endured: that was the visit to the cottage the sight of which had started this train of memories. Its inmate, in those days, was a poor old widow with the surprising name of Mrs. Richelieu. Not only was her name a surprise, but so was her personality. She was generally the last in our round, and the contrast between her quiet, gracious and almost stately demeanour, with the profuse blessings and plaintive whinings of the other old women, was remarkable even to a small boy. Who was she? I have no idea; but the combination of that princely name and those princely manners can surely have been no accident. The obvious explanation is that she was the widow of the descendant of a French Protestant refugee. But who ever heard of a Huguenot called Richelieu! There is, by the way, another minor mystery, of a similar kind, in this neighbourhood. In the church of St. Andrew's, Auckland, there is a plaque bearing the following inscription :

"Ernest Maximilien Charles,
Marquis de Lerven de Limoelan, B.A.
Headmaster of King James's Grammar School."

That "B.A." seems rather absurd! And why should a Breton(?) Marquis (long after the French Revolution) become the headmaster of a grammar school in a small mining town in the north of England? No doubt this could be satisfactorily explained, but I fear that the origins of Mrs. Richelieu will remain wrapped in mystery.

Whoever she was, we liked her, and not because she invariably regaled us with cake and home-made wine at a time of day when we were beginning to feel decidedly peckish. Indeed, though her cake was delicious, we could not abide her wine and would practise our skill in surreptitiously watering her pot of geraniums with it while our mother engaged her attention. But we liked her because she did not embarrass us, because she did not call on the good Lord to bless our bonny cheeks nor expect us to drop a sympathetic tear over her ailments. Indeed, she alone, of all the numbers we visited, appeared to have no ailments. At least, she never mentioned them. She just seemed always to be pleased to see us, and the sun seemed always to be shining through her little window, lighting up the pretty pink geranium; and the cat was always purring on the hearthrug.

One day I was left alone with her. My mother had gone off to pay another visit, deciding to pick me up on the way back, for she did not wish me to accompany her. My brothers, for some reason, were not with us that day. I was therefore left in charge of Mrs. Richelieu and was beginning to fear that even she might seize this opportunity to embarrass me with some personal observations when she engaged my closest attention by asking me if I believed in fairies. I assured her that I did, though I had never seen one. I had read about them, I explained rather grandly, in the Red Fairy Book. "But you need not go to books for fairies," she said, "when you have them here." Here! I looked round me in amazement. "Not in the cottage," she continued, to my slight disappointment, "but in the village. Didn't you know that Middridge was famous for fairies?" A delicious shudder ran through me, for she had lowered her voice when talking about the little people, as if she were fearful of being overheard. "No," I whispered back eagerly, "I didn't know." So she told me the following story.

Middridge has always been famous for fairies, but once upon a time, a canny bit sin,[1] there was a daffley[2] young man who did not believe in them. He kept his silliness to himself, however, until one night after a champion harvest, which was followed, as was the custom in those days, by a grand mell supper at the farm opposite, he took too much cowslip wine . . . and he began to talk and talk, so fondly that all the girls fell to giggling and whispering at him. At last he said right out, before all the company, that he did not believe in fairies, and in particular that there were none at Middridge. Then the master's son got up and said to him, winking at the rest: "Thou must prove the truth of thy words now, Wull Jordan (for that was the daft lad's name), thou must prove the truth of thy words or aa'l nevell[3] thee for a tume-bellied[4] braggart." "Aall reet," says Willy, "aa'll prove 'un." "Then tyek ma fayther's best horse," says the master's son, "an' ride up to the green hill yonder an' shoot[5] these magic words in the night:

> *"Rise little lads,*
> *Wi' your iron gads[6]*
> *An' set the Lad o' Middridge hame."*

So up rose Will and saddled the horse and away he went, under the harvest moon, while all the company waited round the table. But they were no longer as merry as they were. And one young lass was there whose name was Patience Hall, and very particular for looks she was, and her eyes were as blue as the gentians at Langdon Beck. And she began to greet a little, quietly to herself, for she loved the lad. She rocked herself gently to and fro on the bench, murmuring, "Doan't ye do it, hinny,[7] doan't ye noo," which was a daft thing to say, for the fond loon had already gone.

---

[1] A long time ago.   [2] Silly, feckless.   [3] "Beat" from "nief"—fist.
[4] Empty-bellied, *cf.*, Old Proverb "A tume belly makes a lazy back."
[5] Shout.   [6] Lances.   [7] Honey, darling.

So Willy came to the hill and he called his magic words aloud; he shouted them fairly to the moon, for he was full of wine. And lo! hundreds and hundreds of fairies, with Oberon, their king, at the head of them, suddenly surrounded the foolish mortal and kept him stone cold with fear, with all the wine gone out of him and his mouth open. Then Oberon came up to him and shook his great iron gad in the lad's face and piped out in his lug:

> *"Silly Willy, mount thy filly;*
> *And if it is'na weel corn'd and fed,*
> *I'll ha' thee afore thou gets hame to thy bed."*

Willy did not stay to be bidden twice, but flung himself on the mare and rode home through the moonlight as if old Belgey Bub[1] were after him. Well was it for him that he had been lent his master's best horse, for the little folk pressed him so close that he had no time to halt even when he reached the yard, but came riding helter-skelter right into the hall where all the company was assembled, and they slammed to the great doors behind him . . . and he never laughed at fairies any more. But what do you suppose they found the next morning when they came to open the doors? Oberon's great javelin sticking in the midst of them, so fast that it took two smiths, with all their tweezers and instruments, to remove it. And they kept it in the Hall yonder, where it has been ever since. And that's not quite true, for it has gone now. But Mrs. Richelieu, when she was a girl, knew an old woman who, when she was a girl, had seen it and touched it and been never the worse.

This was the story which was in my mind as I strolled back across the field to keep my appointment with Imperial Chemicals. But stronger than the story was the vivid memory of the teller, of her white cap wagging as she told it, with the plum ribbon in it, and the old-fashioned brooch at her throat and the sparkle of her eyes in a network of wrinkles. And I sat down under a hedge, feeling suddenly tired, and plucked idly at the grass, while my thoughts delved deeply into the past that was gone. . . .

I must have been lying there some little time when I

[1] Beelzebub.

heard, from far away, the sound of a girl singing. I did not recognise the song, but there was such a singular sweetness in the notes that the absurd thought flashed through my mind that I was dead and that this was the voice of an angel. Then the singer, though still invisible to me, evidently drew nearer, for I began to make out the words, though they seemed quite fantastic; something about "two turtle doves and a partridge on a pear tree." After this there was a pause, and then, quite close, though I did not look up for fear of disturbing the singer, I heard the following verse, sung through with the clearness and the sweet impersonality of a silver bell:

> *"The twelfth day of Christmas, my true love sent to me*
> *Twelve lords a-leaping, eleven ladies dancing,*
> *Ten pipers playing, nine drummers drumming,*
> *Eight maids a-milking, seven swans a-swimming,*
> *Six geese a-laying, five gold rings,*
> *Four colly birds, three French hens,*
> *Two turtle doves, and a partridge on a pear tree."*

The notes of the "pear tree" dropped, lingering, through the air until they melted into silence; and I looked up. I saw the most beautiful girl that it has ever been my good fortune to see, with the skin of a dusky rose and eyes like chips of a summer sky. She was dressed in an odd sort of white skirt, somewhat full behind, but lifted well up to show her pretty ankles. Above the skirt was a pale blue bodice, laced rather tight and cut rather low, with a brooch fixed in it made of some curious rough stone. Her billowy white sleeves stopped short above the elbow, a string of coral was fastened round her brown wrist, and her chestnut hair, glistening with gold, was loosely gathered up and tied behind with a blue ribbon. She looked about seventeen, and she carried a milking stool, which she rested against her hip as she looked down on me with a half-shy, half-mischievous smile. I struggled to my feet.

"Ye've dovered off,[1] I'm thinking," she said, "so ye will not ha' seen ma coo?"

"I am afraid not," I replied. "Have you lost her?"

She nodded her head as she looked round the field.

"What sort of a cow?" I asked rather stupidly (but anyone would have been stupid at the sudden sight of her).

[1] Fallen asleep.

She laughed. "It's no matter," she said. "Aa don't believe it was ma Blossom at all. Blossom'd ne'er carry on like that. 'Twas the Hedley Koo." I continued to look stupid. "Ha' ye ne'er hard tell o' the Hedley Koo?"

"No, never."

"Then sit ye doon and aa'll tell thee aboot 'un, and a deal more things that ye're wanting to knaa."

"Am I?" At the moment I was only conscious of an all-absorbing admiration of the beautiful creature who was talking to me. But I was willing enough to sit down on the grass.

"Ye're an outman,[1] aa reckon?" she continued, "a Jarmin maybe?"[2]

"I am nothing of the sort," I replied indignantly; "I was born and bred here."

"Ay, an' Headlam hens lays twice a day,"[3] said she dryly.

"I presume you mean, by that, that I am a liar. But I am not. I was born here."

"Then wey do 'ee crack[4] so strange like?"

"That's not my fault," I answered sadly. "That's the fault of the B.B.C."

She looked puzzled at this for a moment, but then continued. "Ef ye wor born an' bred heor, ye'll knaa Blue Bell Farm, for sure?"

"Of course I do. Mrs. Robertson's."

"I ken ne Mistress Robertson," she said, "but Blue Bell Farm is whor aa leeve." I was too dumbfounded to say anything, for I knew well enough that she did not, and yet I did not like to give this radiant creature the lie, as she had done to me. Besides, there was a feeling of unreality about the whole conversation, about the whole scene, about herself even —for all the duskiness of her skin—in which I seemed to be caught and floundering like a fish at the bottom of a net. But, unlike the fish, I did not want to get out. There was something here which I could not understand, but I did not want to understand it. I only hoped that I might sit here for ever,

---

[1] Foreigner.

[2] Some north-country gentlemen in a coffee-house in London were once taken for Germans.

[3] A phrase to express incredulity. (See Hodgkins, *op. cit.,* p. 158.)

[4] Talk.

looking at her face and listening to her voice. "But aa must tell 'ee aboot the Hedley Koo," she said.

She then told me how she had come out that morning to milk her favourite Apple Blossom. But first the creature— most unaccountably, for she was as sweet as her name—had declined to let herself be caught, and then, when at last she had been secured and milked with difficulty, had suddenly kicked over the pail and galloped off out of sight. The girl had been looking for her, as I had seen, when it had suddenly occurred to her that of course this was not her Blossom at all, but that mischievous spirit or goblin, the Hedley Kow. "'Tis a favourite trick of his'n," she said seriously, "and aa ought to ha' knaan, for he's ketched me oot many a time, but ne'er wi' that one."

"What else does he do?" I asked lazily. . . . "By the way, I know your name. It's Patience Hall."

"That's reet," she said. "Ye seem to knaa me. Hoo is it that aa doesn't knaa thee?"

"Because I was born too late, unfortunately. But never mind that. Go on with the Hedley Kow."

So she told me that her lover—oh, what a pang, in spite of all my grey winters!—she told me that her lover . . . "Will Jordan," I interrupted rudely. "Wully Jordan it is," she said curtly. "An' what hast thou to say to that, aad man?" The old man, abashed, had nothing to say, and she continued her story. It appeared that Will Jordan, her lover, had called her one summer's night from the garden of Blue Bell, but when she had risen eagerly from her bed and put her head out of the window she saw nothing but the stars and heard only a faint snigger in the distance. It was the Hedley Kow. "Or the village lout," I suggested drowsily.

"There's ne lad in this village would dare to play such a trick on me," she replied composedly.

"And why not?" I asked. "You don't look very fierce to me, somehow."

"Because of this," she said, pointing at the curious grey stone at her breast.

"What is it? May I see?" She handed it to me. It looked to me like an old flint arrow-head.

"'Tis an elf-stone," she said. "Ye can find them sometimes on the moors, but there's few dare wear them. They are the brooches given to the elves by the old fairies, who had got them from the mermaids. They're not for mortals."

"Then how do you dare to wear one?" I asked, handing the brooch back to her. She hesitated a moment and then, lowering her eyes, she answered, with a little shudder: "Because aa'm different." I was silent, feeling that she was going to add more, and presently she said in a low voice: "Because aa hev seen the fairies."

"And where have you seen them?" I enquired in that silly, chatty, condescending tone with which one humours a small child.

"Everywhor," she replied. "Aa hev seen them heor an' at Pensher[1] Hill an' at Worm Hill, an' at Castleton, an' on the Tower Hill at Middleton, an' at their Cradle 'twixt Hetton an' Eppleton; an' at Clint's Craggs in Weardale, whor aa saw the Queen herself an' she gev me this [touching the brooch]; an' at Byers Green aa hev watched 'em dancing the grass off in a night; and at Bishopton aa have set ma lug te the groond an' hard 'em whistlin' their roundelays to the wind."

In spite of myself, I shivered a little, as I had shivered long ago when I was listening to Mrs. Richelieu.

"An' aa've seen more then that," she continued almost fiercely. "Aa've seen the great Tudhoe Mouse itself,[2] an' the Glassensikes at Darnton,[3] the dorg that's as big as a calf and stares at ye wi' eyen like moons; an' Peg Powler wi' her green hair, she that rises oot of the Tees so beautiful and draas the bonny bairns unto her for love of 'em; an' the Cauld Lad of Hilton, an' the ghost of the nun at Hall Garth,[4] an' old Lady Barnard[5]—her that they caa 'Aad Hell-cat'—knitting on the battlements at Raby wi' her red-hot needles.

---

[1] Penshaw.

[2] A gigantic ghostly mouse at Tudhoe, near Spennymoor, *M.C.,* Vol. II, p. 140.

[3] Darlington.

[4] At Hall Garth, near Coatham Mundeville, is the ghost of a nun supposed to have been buried alive.

[5] Wife of Christopher, Lord Barnard; a wicked woman, who loathed her son and encouraged her husband to pull down the castle in order to spite his heir. He was stopped by an injunction (1714). Besides her appearance on the battlements, she used also to be seen at midnight, driving through the park in her black coach and six. (See *Handbook for Raby Castle.*)

. . . Boggles[1] and goblins and fairies and a', good an' wicked, fair and foul, aa've seen 'em a', aa've seen 'em a'." And she fell to moaning a little to herself.

"What does it mean?" I asked gently. "Why have you seen so much?"

"What can it mean but that aa must dee?" she said, looking at me with all the colour drained from her face. "What can it mean but that aa must dee young, that aa must dee a maid? Ay, aa ken fine that Wull is a seventh son and that, come Martinmas, I am to place ma hand in his at the altar. But can aa endure until then? For there is something whispering in ma heart that aa'll dee afore he takes me. An' the mirror'll be shrooded,[2] an' the clock'll be stopped, an' the bidders'll gan oot i' their long black cloaks an' sashes[3] to bid the neighbours to ma funeral, an' ma maiden's garling[4] of white flowers will be hung aloft in Andra's Kirk.[5, 6] Listen!" she exclaimed, suddenly gripping me by the wrist. "The other neet aa fancied aa hard the Hoonds themselves, the Hoonds o' Gabriel[7] howling i' the clouds above the hoose, and the sound of a heavy, heavy hearse comin' up the lonnin.[8] That may have been only fancy, or maybe the Koo again, or the Picktree Brag.[9] Aa canna tell, but aa fear, aa greatly fear, that one neet, suen, wi' the going oot o' the tide, ma time'll come to me an' aa shall dee." And with that she broke out into a plaintive little song:

> *"A garland fresh and fair*
> *Of lilies there was made,*
> *In token of virginity,*
> *And on her coffin laid."*

[1] Ghosts.   [2] Lest the ghost of the corpse should be seen in it.

[3] It was the custom for two "bidders," men friends of the family, dressed as described, to go round the houses of acquaintances in the neighbourhood inviting their occupants to attend the funeral.

[4] Garland.   [5] St. Andrew's, Auckland.

[6] This pretty custom was last observed in the church of Witton Gilbert. (Surtees, Vol. II, p. 392 and *Memorials of Old Durham.* Chapter on Folklore by Mrs. Apperley, p. 52.)

[7] Dogs of the air with human heads whose pause over a house foretold death.   [8] Lane.

[9] A goblin who haunted Picktree, near Chester-le-Street. His mischievous tricks were similar to those of the Hedley Kow, and an old woman told Sir C. Sharpe that, when her father died, she heard it "coming up the lonnin like a coach and six." (*M.C.,* Vol. V, p. 407.)

I tried to comfort her. "Don't be afraid. Will will save you," I said.

She looked up a little wanly. "Wull?" she echoed. "Ay, he's a dear lad."

"And he loves you," I said, and she nodded her head emphatically. "And he's a seventh son," I continued, not having the least idea what I meant.

But she visibly brightened at this. "Ay, it's true enough," she said, "he hes the magic touch. Many a time hev aa seen him, wi' butterflies aal roond him, settlin' upon his fingers as ef they were flowers. 'Le, la, let,' he'd sing, 'ma bonnie pet; le, la, let.'[1] But no," she continued, shaking her lovely head, "he offended the King of the Fairies, an' they'll never forgive 'un."

"But you are the friend of the Queen," I urged.

"An' that's true, too," she said thoughtfully, "but it's a bad thing te hev seen the little folk, not a good one."

"But to have received a present from them," I persisted, pointing at her brooch, "surely that means that they will befriend you? They cannot want you to die."

She looked at me for a moment and then broke into a little laugh and laid her hand on mine. (I can feel the warm softness of it now.) "Eh, but ye're a canny man," she said. "Ye're putting new heart into me. Maybe ye're reet, after aa. It's certain that ma mother took ivvory precaution when aa was born."

"What did she do?"

"Wey, she gev me this to wear roond ma neck"—touching the coral[2] at her wrist—"an' she's never sold ma cradle, an' she carried me oop before ivvor she carried me doon."

"What on earth do you mean?"

"Ef ye carry a bairn doonstairs fust, ye carry her luck doon wi' her. So oop she must gan afore ever she makes a move downwards."

"And how can she do that if the room is on the top floor?"

"Wey, her mother holds her in her arms and climbs on a chair or a cracket,[3] an' that's what ma mother did with me.

---

[1] See Mrs. Apperley, *op. cit.*, p. 49. The seventh son used also to cure the King's Evil.

[2] A protection against theft by fairies and the substitution of a changeling.   [3] Stool.

An' on the way to Baptism she gev the fust wee lad we met a bonny piece of silver in ma name an' a slice of ginger cyek. An' when aa was baptised she took me straight to three houses, one after the other, where the neighbours were waitin' for me, and in each one aa received ma 'almison'—that is, egg and bread and salt—an' a piece of money. Ay, she's done everything for me, has ma mum, an' she was so fearful lest aa might look into a mirror afore aa was one year aad that she put our only glass in the cupboard under lock and kay. It may be that she will have saved me after aa, she an' Wull atwixt 'em."

"Of course they will," I said briskly. "Besides, my dear, if you will forgive me for saying so, you think too much of all these little superstitions. They're very pretty and all that, but it's absurd in these days to set any store by them or to worry about them."

She turned and looked at me very gravely, her blue eyes wide with wonder and reproach. "An' what mayst thou be meanin' by that?" she answered. "Wey, mon, be careful what thou sayst. Mind ye doan't go past yourself. Aa'm not playin' the band,[1] but aa knaa what aa'm aboot. Aa've seen strange things an' aa've hard 'em, an' knaa the marvels that can be wrought. Hev ye no mind above your bit o' meat or your sup o' crowdy?[2] Do 'ee think nought has been, because the sound of it has deed away from your dull ears? or nought still is, because ye canna see ut wi' your eyen? Would ye pass the cross[3] where the battle has been and never lay your lug to the groond te heor it? or loiter under an aad yak-tree[4] and ne'er turn your cloak?[5] Oh, do not be like ma poor daft Wull that

[1] Making a fuss about nothing.

[2] A sort of porridge. Originally "corrodium," given by the monks of St. Cuthbert to guests and pilgrims.

[3] Neville's Cross. Walk nine times round it (if you can do so without being killed by a motorcar) and lay your head to the ground, and you will hear the clash of arms and the noise of battle. (*Memorials of Old Durham.* "Folklore," by Mrs. Apperley.)

[4] Oak-tree. Aycliffe, where grew the great oak forest, is known as Yakley in the local dialect.

[5] "Turn your cloaks,
For fairy folks
Are in old okes."

(*Legend and Lore of County Durham,* by Eleanor Dover.)

neet at the farm yonder—an' *he* is no runaway Dr. Bokanki[1] —nor like aad Harry Langthorne, lest worse things betide ye."

"Who is Harry Langthorne?"

"Wey, he is ma feyther's man that he hired at the fair at Aakland last back-end,[2] and a grand chap for theking[3] he is, and he told me the tale himself one neet in the kitchen at home, when aa was making Tom Trot[4] for the bairns and he dropped in te hev a bit crack."[5]

And thereupon she told me that Harry Langthorne, in his youth, was one day leading a cart with two horses up the steep slope of Pensher Hill, where you can hear the fairies patting their butter in the dark. But it was broad daylight at the time and there was no sound nor sight of the little folk, and he was far from thinking of them, jogging peacefully on his way and whistling "Bobby Shafto" when suddenly he heard a voice in his ear say, quite distinctly: "Mend that peel."[6] He looked round, and there was no one, but by the roadside lay a broken shovel. So he took it home and mended it, and the next time he passed that way he put it carefully where he had found it. When his work was done he was coming down the hill that same evening, and he looked out to see whether the peel was still there or not. And he saw that it had been removed and that in its place lay a thick slice of bread spread with the most delicious-looking butter. He was very hungry, but still he durst not eat it, for he was very frightened, because it was magic butter. So he went on his way without touching it, and before ever he got to the bottom of the lonnin both his horses fell down dead. "It was to larn him not to doot the fairies' honour," said Patience Hall, "and do not thou doot it, neethor."[7]

"I will not, I will not," I hastened to assure her. "I promise always to treat them with the greatest respect. But that story has nothing to do with this fear of death which seems to be obsessing you. You have never doubted the fairies. Why should

---

[1] A saying which owed its origin to the flight of Dr. Balcanquall, Dean of Durham, from the Scots, after the rout at Stella, 1640.

[2] Autumn.   [3] Thatching.

[4] A sort of toffee, generally made at the New Year.

[5] For a gossip.   [6] Shovel (*cf.* French "pelle").

[7] *M.C.,* Vol. III, p. 548.

they punish you? I think, on the contrary, that you are favoured by them and that they love you. (I know I would, if I were a fairy.) Do you never look in the mirror? Can you not see the bloom on your skin and the light in your eye? Would not your cheeks be wan and your glance lack lustre if the fairies had set their mark for evil on you? But I don't believe you have ever been ill in your life."

"Save once," she replied quite cheerfully, "save only once, when aa was a wee slip of a lass some ten years sin'. Aa hed a nasty cough one winter, but ma mother cured it at last. She shaved off ma hair one neet an' hung ut on a bush in the garden, and the next mornin' the cough was gone."[1]

"Good heavens!" I exclaimed, "what an extraordinary idea! But it doesn't seem to have done your hair any harm, to judge from what it looks like now."

"It's middlin'," said Patience, pulling forward the ends of her luxurious locks to have a look at them. "Wull says it'll do."

"Jolly gracious of him," I remarked, feeling, in spite of myself, a slight dislike of the fellow, "but tell me now about your Will. I want to hear all about him. What's he like? Is he good to you? Do you really love him? When are you going to be married?"

"Eh? What a power of questions!"

"But, first of all, you must promise not to think any more about death!"

"Aa will not, then. Aa believe ye've put new heart in me, for noo aa ca' to mind two signs that wor given me, an' aa think they may mean that aa'm goin' to live."

"What were they?" I asked.

"Wey, aa saw the fust lamb of this year with its face towards me, an' only last week aa fell upstairs."

"Nothing could be better. Then away with death! It's a shame to think about it on such a day as this. And now tell me about Will."

"Weel," said Patience, stretching herself out comfortably on the grass, "it's a longish tale, for the course of true love nivvor did run smooth, and Wull an' aa are true lovers."

"The longer the better," I replied. "I could listen to you for ever."

[1] A Sunderland prescription.

"Weel, then, as to his looks, fust . . . well, they're champion. He's dark, ye knaa, not a pink and blue creature like myself—which is well enough for lassies—but black and lish[1] and limber on the hills—oh, a proper dalesman!—an' jest the colour for a fust foot. Aa ken see him noo, last New Year's Eve. There was aa settin' sad-like and dowly[2] within doors listenin' to the bells and thinkin' to masel', 'Wull's left me, after aa, else for sure he'd hev been over heor to fust fut for us,' when aal of a sudden like, when the bells had scarce done ringin', there cooms a knock on the door and a voice cries oot—ah, a voice that aa knaad well—'A happy new year to yer, mistress; have yer had a fust fut?' And, 'No, aa hev not,' says ma mother. 'But what be ye? Be ye dark or fair?' (though she knaad weel enough who he was). An' 'Aa'm dark,' says Wully, 'dark as Belzey Bug,'[3] he says. 'Then howay in, hinny,' says mother, 'here thou is. Thou must be starved.'[4] And in he came, wi' a lump of coal in his hand, which he popped on our fire, and there was kyek an' Wensleydale[5] an' wine waitin' for him on the kitchen table and . . . an' summat else besides. 'Eh, lad! aa thought thou'd failed me,' aa whispers. 'Then thou's daft for sure,' says he, 'daft as soods[6]; have aa e'er failed thee yet?' And that was true enough, for at every merry-making, come two years, he's allus sought me oot—at Easter an' Yule an' Royal Oak Day an' Bounder Day,[7] an' at every mell supper sin' he wor a wee lad—save only once, when he happened an accident an' was bedfast for three weeks.

"He wor a champion guiser,[8] too, and might hev ganged anywhere for money, he and his pals. But wherivver they ganged, an' they wor to a' the grand hooses round aboot, they allus came to Blue Bell Farm—he saw to that, did Wull. He was the best of all the guisers. I reckon he must hev played ivvory part in his time, from King George to Johnny Funny. But it was as Dr. Brown I liked him best, when he didna black his face like the rest of the mummers, and came on, after they'd a' been fightin' to cure them a'.

---

[1] Strong.   [2] Lonely, melancholy.
[3] Another corruption of Beelzebub.   [4] Very cold.
[5] Wensleydale cheese.   [6] Soap-suds.
[7] During Rogation week, when the parish boundaries were perambulated.   [8] Christian mummer.

"'*Aa've got a little bottle in ma pocket,*
Tak' a drop an' rise!
Ma feyther''s coom te life again,
We'll nivvor fight ne mower,
But we'll be kind as ivvor we wor,
As ivvor we wor befower.'

"Eh, but aa wish ut wor true. But men will allus be fightin'. . . .

"Before he wor a guiser, when he wor quite a lad, he would carry the dolly aroond to his neighbours in Weardale. It was too far for him, then, te coom te us. But aa mind once, when we wor stayin' wi' Auntie Sue for Christmas, her that lives at Hangin' Wells,[1] how he came roond to her hoose one bright, frosty neet, he an' other bairns, wi' the dolly in its box an' a' the bonny-coloured papers to deck it, and sang their little song. This is how ut goes. Dost knaa ut?

"'*God bless the Master of this house,*
God bless the Mistress, too,
And a' the merry little bairns
Aroond the table too.
'Cos it's comin' on to Christmas Time,
An' we travel far and near,
An' we wish you a merry Christmas
An' a happy New Year.'[2]

Aa can see him singin' it noo, wi' his cheeks aglow wi' the frost withoot an' the fire within, an' his hair all tousled over his forehead an' his eyes shinin' in the candlelight. 'Twas then that aa fust loved un."

"How old was he then?" I asked.

"Sixteen, an' aa wor thirteen. Aa hed not fancied him before at a', although aa'd knaad un so long, for aa wor a great one for books when aa was a little lass, and he used to tease me for it. He was allus wantin' me te play some silly game—hitchy-bays, or tiggy or Bellasis, or some sich dratted foolishness, but aa——"

"Hold on a minute!" I interrupted. "What's 'hitchy-bays'?"

"Wey, it's a game the bairns play. Ye stand on one leg, ye knaa, and kick a stone ower a mark on the groond. . . ."

"Hop-scotch."

---

[1] A farm in Weardale.　　　　　[2] This custom still prevails.

"Ay, I've heard 'em ca' it that; and in 'tiggy' whoever is touched last chases the rest; an' as for 'Bellasis,' aa reckon ye must hev seen that game, ay, and played it yourself?"

"Do you mean 'Bell-horses'?" I asked tentatively.

"Ne, ne; Bellasis. 'Bellasis, Bellasis, what time o' day? One o'clock, two o'clock, horse and away!' That's what ye sing. It's playin' at horses, of course."

"Yes, of course, but it's not 'Bellasis.' It's 'Bell-horses,' as I supposed. 'Bell-horses, bell-horses, up and away!'—from the packman's leading horse, which always has a bell to give notice of the long train coming round the corner."

"That may be," said she obstinately, "but it's 'Bellasis' as we play ut heor."[1]

"Well, never mind. Please go on with your story."

"Weel, as aa wor sayin', aa wor a great one for books when aa wor a lass. Aa couldna rest until aa had learned to read at Heighington School,[2] an' then aa would set at ma bedroom window in the summer, or by the kitchen fire in the winter, readin' an' readin', till I was nigh daft with it, aal aboot the old monks an' St. Cuthbert, an' of the Lambton Worm an' the Pollard one an' Hodge of Ferry, an' St. Aidan pouring his oil on the troubled watters, and of hoo Conyers gev oop his son to the Holy Ghost afore he set oot te kill his worm, an' aal sorts. Aa ca' to mind that, one summer's day, aa was so settin' an' readin' when who should appear under ma window but Wull himself, settin' on his little cuddy,[3] as bold an' as bright as brass! 'What fettle?' pipes he in his impudent, laughin' way. 'Middlin',' aa says, stiffly-like; 'an' what mayst thou be doin' heor, a' the way frae Weardale? Hast thou ne school as this week answers?'[4] 'Not today, ye fond lass,' he replies. ''Tis Yak-Apple Day. Canst na see the sprig i' ma coat?' And then he bursts oot singin':

> 'Royal Oak Day,
> Twenty-Ninth o' May,

---

[1] And still is. It is played at Bishop Auckland. (*Darlington and Stockton Times,* Feb. 2nd, 1946. Article by Miss Peggy Hutchinson.)

[2] Founded by Mrs. Jenison in 1601. Now an elementary school. (*V.C.H.*, Vol. I, p. 399.)

[3] Donkeys are called "Cuddies" in the North, after St. Cuthbert, as they are called "Neddies" in the South, after St. Edward.

[4] This week.

If ye don't gev us holiday,
We'll a' run away.'

" 'So we've run away,' he continues, 'an' aa've locked the door masel' an' left the key in the inside an' climbed oot of window, an' taken the cuddy oot of feyther's field, and heor aa is!' 'Ye'll get wrong for this,'[1] I says, shakin' my head at him. 'No matter for that!' says he, 'but coom 'ee back with me noo,' he says; 'art as light as a fairy an' cuddy will carry us both, an' we'll gan on the moors an' seek elf-stones. Ne halvers,[2] ne quarters, ne pin point!'

"Aa don't knaa whether ut wor the blueness of the day, or whether it wor the sight of him or the cuddy, or jest the gran' sense of adventure, but aa felt sore tempted to gan. 'An' hoo can aa?' aa says. 'Mother will nivvor let me.' 'Whor is she?' he axes. 'Doon at Sim's Pastures.' 'Then coom doon quickly, lass, and awa' we'll gan.' So, to cut a lang story short, aa went, but with sore misgivin's, an' ma faith! didn't aa ketch it when aa kem hyem late in the evenin' an' sumper wet,[3] for ut had kem on to rain after noon an' we did na dare te gan te Wull's hoose, but we sat on the moors, under a boulder, wi' the rain drippin' doon the backs of oor necks, eatin' carlin's.[4] (It was aal he could find to steal, the wafflin' Johnnie![5]) An' we quarrelled most of the day an' he pulled my hair an' made me cry—but aa gev him a bat on the lug for that—an' aa wished mony a time that aa had stayed at hyem wi' ma books, aa was that clashed[6] and miserable afore he brought me back again. But the ride oot was champion, aal in the bright silver light, wi' the hills comin' ivvor nearor like the Promised Land, an' ma arms clutched roond Wull's waist an' the bonny little cuddy rattlin' awa' beneath us, so blithe and so gamesome. Maybe aa looved him already then, but I surely

---

[1] Be punished.
[2] "No halves!" etc.—*i.e.,* no sharing by the finder.
[3] Soaking wet.
[4] Dried peas. These are particularly eaten on "Carling Sunday," the Sunday preceding Palm Sunday, in memory, it is supposed, of a time of famine, when a ship-load of peas was wrecked off the coast and saved the people from starvation. Publicans used to supply the dish free on this day, and highly seasoned, so as to encourage thirst.
[5] Anyone who makes a muddle of an errand is "a wafflin' Johnnie," who comes back "with his fingers in his mouth."
[6] Tired.

hated him sometimes. Maybe the two things is not se far apart as parson says.

"But it was na until the followin' Christmas, that neet at Hangin' Wells, that aa knaad aa loved un. An' after they had sung their song an' the rest of 'em had gan awa, he stayed behind—for my Auntie Sue axed him kindly—an' we played snapdragon[1] together, an' the blue flames danced on his fyece, an' he felt for ma hand in the dark. Then we eat our frumity; it's a gran' dish, made of barley and milk, ye knaa, an' flavoured with cinnamon and sugar, an' we allus eat ut on Christmas Eve. But a little of ut gans a lang way, an' aa couldn't finish mine, an' Wull seized ma plate an' supped it all oop. Aa ca's him a greedy pig for ut, but he whispers it was because he wanted te eat wi' ma spoon. An' afore he left he kissed me, not under the mistletoe, whor aal the folks could see, but in the cree,[2] whor Auntie Sue had sent me oot te see te an aad sow that was poorly. Aa sometimes think she knaad he would come wi' me an' wished te give us a chance, like. Eh, he was a gradely lad! . . ."

"And then what happened?" I asked at last. "What was it that went wrong?"

"Wey, nowt happened," she replied, "an' aa couldna tell for a long while what had gan wrong. But the years passed, an' though at fust he wor as tender as a lass could wish, he suddenly seemed to grow cold and kept awa' from me, for no reason that aa could tell. An' of course aa was not one to ask him. For instance, he wor a great one at egg-jaaping when he wor a boy, and he kep' it oop when he wor well-nigh a grown man, he had sich a boyish heart. Ye knaa, at Easter we dye our eggs wi' onion peelin's an' flowers—whin flowers are the best, they mak' a bonny purple colour—an' then we gan an' bowl 'em on the village green, or the boys will jaap 'em, holdin' an egg 'twixt thumb and forefinger an' strikin' ut against another lad's until one of 'em breaks. Weel, at this bowlin' on the green, aal the lads and lasses turn oot, jest as they do for the maypole on May Day, an' Wull would ride over on his cuddy or a gal[3] aal the way frae Weardale, jest te be at the bowlin' at Middridge, 'cos aa would be there too.

---

[1] Raisins soaked in whisky and set alight in a dark room, when the children played at snatching them through the flames.

[2] Pig-sty.   [3] Galloway pony.

An' it's the custom, ye knaa, for the boys to chase the girls, an', if they catch 'em, to tyek off one of their shoon, an' not to give it back again until it's paid for with an egg or, maybe, a wee kiss. An' Wull would allus chase me so, an' aa'm thinkin' that's why he kem frae Weardale. Weel, last Easter, a year sin', aa went doon te the bowlin', feelin' heavy in ma heart, for Wull had been very strange of lyet, an' aa could make nowt of ut. So aa was resolved to oop and ax un and to knaa the worst. But he never came. He had happened an accident, but aa was not to knaa that. Aa thought he had na coom o'purpose. So when aa was jest desperate Nelly Jackson says te me (she, that's ma great friend), 'Wey dost not gan te see Dorothy Stranger?' she says. 'She'll help thee.' An' at that aa fairly shooddered, for aad Doll Stranger wor a witch, as we aal knaad weel, an' mother had told me hoo she hersel' had pricked the woman, unbeknownst, wi' a pin to let the devil oot of her, an' aad Doll had grunted like a swine. How-somever, aa was desperate, so aa gan'd alang, takin' Nell wi' me for company; an' Dorothy set the letters of the alphabet in a circle on the floor of her kitchen an' took a sieve an' a pair of shears an' spun the sieve on 'em till ut stopped an' pointed at a lettor.[1] An' it pointed at M. Then she took the sieve and spun ut again an' it pointed at T. An' aa cried oot: 'That's enough! That's enough! For aa knaas aal aa want te knaa. It's Molly Thrower, as I knaad weel aal alang.' An' aa rooshed oot of the hoose like a mad thing an' left poor Nelly to follow as she might an' ran hyem sobbin' aal the way. An' all that summer, that was last summer, aa didna fairly knaa what aa was aboot, for aa nivvor seed Wull the whole of that time—he nivvor came nigh me—save once at the mell supper, when aa couldna get a word with him alone, an' he looked aal queer and dowly; an' aa tried te banish the thought of un from ma mind, but aa slep' ivvory neet wi' a sprig of rose-mary under ma piller, that aa might dream of un.

"An' twice aa set in the Prior's seat at Finchale, an' once in Bede's chair at Jarrer, an' aa prayed for un. An' aa dropped ma pins in the well at Whitworth an' the Worm Well, an' aa wished for his love again. An' aa gan'd te Stob-Cross, near Cornforth, whor the poor maid had put hersel' doon for love An' aa seed the white dove that was her spirit an' the three

[1] *M.C.*, Vol. I, p. 212.

crimson spots on her breast.[1] An' aa greeted sore for her and for me.

"Then, one day, it was late in the back-end, when the devil had set his foot on the bumblekites,[2] ma feyther catched me gapin' oot of winder when aa should hev been scrubbin' the kitchen table with herbs. But the herbs lay in a heap in ma lap. 'Oh, whistle an' ride me, lass,'[3] he says gaily; 'what ails thy bonny white fyece?' 'Things ain't as they used to be,' I says, 'and nivvor was,' I says. 'Aa'm ridin' over te Auntie Sue's,' he says; 'wouldst care to coom a-pillion?' And aa said aa wuld not. 'Weel, gan thy own gait, then,' says feyther; 'but aa'm startin' in half an hour.' An' in half an hour aa was settin' behind him an' we wore trottin' oot of yard. An' when we got te Auntie Sue's, there in the kitchen—for they'd arranged it aal beforehand, she and ma feyther, as aa hard later—there wor Wull, lookin' uncommon daft, I must say. An' after a bit pause, whiles Auntie and feyther were crackin' together, he whispers to me: 'Shall us tak' Darnton Trod?'[4] So we went an' walked on the heather, which was dying under our feet.

"An' he said nowt aal the time an' looked as glum as midnight.

"So aa says to him at last: 'What ails thee, lad?' An' he answers: 'Nowt.' An' aa says: 'That's grand; then thou'rt happy, aa reckon? Thou surely dost sound as blithe as a laverock,[5] and aal.' But he answers: 'Aa'm not happy.' 'Then art poorly?' aa axes. But he says: 'Ne.' Then aa says, greatly daring, though ma heart wor flutterin' in ma bosom: 'Is ut summat thou'rt missin', maybe, summat thou dost want?' And 'Ay, it is se,' he answers, 'summat as aa wants like hell.' 'Then ax for ut, ye fond loon,' aa tells him. 'Dost not knaa that blayte bairns gits nowt?'[6] But still he wouldna say a word. An' with that aa lets flee. 'Aa sees hoo ut is,' aa says in a fine

---

[1] The man who deserted her drowned himself some time afterwards, and was buried as a suicide, at the four cross-roads, with a "stob," or stake, through his breast. (Surtees, Vol. III, 14.)

[2] When the blackberries had withered.

[3] Said to a girl who is not getting on with her work.

[4] Slip away unnoticed. "Darnton Trod" = Darlington road or path; and perhaps the reference is to the sanctuary granted to criminals, once Darlington (just within the Bishoprick) had been reached.

[5] Lark.   [6] "Silent children get nothing." An old proverb.

passion (though less in a passion than aa pretends), 'it's that Molly Thrower, that jumped-up Judy Calico,[1] that's bridlin' thy lollicker[2] an' keepin' thee from the side of the lass that loves thee an' that's loved thee with her heart aal her life,' aa says. 'Jest let me ketch the trollop, thet's aal,' aa says; 'an' aa'll gie her Washin'ton,[3] the donnat[4]!' 'Ne, thou munna,' he says. ''Twas ma fault.' An' then aa gets the story oot of un.

"'Twas the neet that Master Wesley visited Wolsingham that it aal happened. Wull had been to heor him, an' bein' curdled inside wi' the power of his words an' the spirit of love—but I couldna mak' oot whether 't wor the love of Gawd or the love of me, or a mixture of the two—he ganged for to quench his emotion with a gill. An' he tyook mower than wor good for un, bein' se excited, he said, an' at last, on way hyem, it bein' pitch-dark, he boompted inte Molly Thrower. An' she, bein' no better than she ought to be, put her arms roond his neck an' bussed him, an' he busses her back (troying te pretend it wor me, he says), an' she swears that he axed her te wed, an' he swears he didna, yet he canna be sarten sure, for that the drink was in him. An' se he felt bound te her, he said, for he might hev axed her te wed him, but he knaad (though he loved me) he had nivvor axed me. 'Ne, but thou'lt ax me the noo,' aa says to him, 'an' leave me te deal wi' Moll.' 'Aa begged her to let me off,' he says, 'an' aa told her aa loves thee, but she threatened, ef aa made for to wed thee, to come into the kirk an' forbid the banns. An' aa didna wish te bring shame on thee an' thine,' he says. 'An' ef she comes to the kirk to forbid the banns,' aa answers, quite happy noo, for aa wor na feared of Molly Thrower, 'then it's the fust time she'll hev set foot in a kirk in her life, savin' at Butterby.[5] Leave Moll te me, aa tell thee, an' dena be deceived ba that hussy. Dost not knaa her sort? Aa'm surprised at thee, Wull,' aa says, 'acting se fond.' But he wor allus high an' lofty in his thoughts an' like a cavalier wi' the lasses.

---

[1] Girl that gives herself airs. [2] Tongue.

[3] "A washing down" or, as we say now, "a dressing down." Obviously corrupted into the name of a Durham village—"Washington." cf. French "laver la tête."

[4] "do-naught," worthless creature.

[5] "To go to church at Butterby" = not to go at all, for there was never a church at Butterby.

'For helmet bright wi' brass an' gold,
An' plumes that flout the sky,
Aa'll wear a mind of harder mould
An' thoughts that sweep as high.'[1]

"Ay, that's ma Wull, sure enough."

She had repeated the lines dreamily, almost lazily, and now she fell silent, gazing over the landscape with a wistful smile on her lovely young face.

"So what happened?" I asked at length.

"Weel, what dost think?" She turned and looked at me, and, for the last time, I felt the magic of those blue eyes. "Do 'ee think aa'd be stopped ba Moll Thrower an' her threats? The third banns wos read oot last Sunday in St. Andra's, an' nivvor a word hev we hard from her. An' noo aa'm to be a bride," she said, stretching out her arms in the sunlight, "an' gan to kirk wi' a bonny bride-wain drawn by white oxen aal stuck wi' flowers.[2] An' ma feyther an' the Middridge lads an' the Weardale folk an' aal Wull's brothers'll ride afore me firin' their guns, an' the Nominy Sayer'll[3] sing ma praises, an' the lads'll run races te Blue Bell door for the sake of a bit ribbon.[4] . . . An' aa'll need ne more rosemary under ma piller," she added softly, "te mak' me dream of Wull."

Once more she fell silent, and I had no desire to speak, for, in spite of the beauty of the day and the joy of my companion, a quiet sadness was stealing over me like a mist and I felt a pricking at the back of my eyes. I suppose that's what women feel like when they cry at a wedding, I remember thinking to myself, when suddenly the most joyous song came sparkling through the air. What a tune! What a lilt! My feet began shuffling in the grass with the very first sound of it. And what a voice the man had! Every note of it, so gay, so careless, was like an imperious summons to the dance.

"As aa cam' thro' Sandgate,
Thro' Sandgate, thro' Sandgate,
As aa cam thro' Sandgate,
Aa heard a lassie sing:

---

[1] The second verse of a song that used to be sung in Weardale, called "Were I a Haughty Cavalier." (*Weardale Men and Manners,* by Jacob Ralph Featherston, 1840.)   [2] Surtees, Vol. II, p. 344.

[3] The speaker of complimentary verses, on a marriage.

[4] These bridal races were still run, until quite recently, at Croft and at St. Helen's, Auckland.

'Weel may the keel row,
The keel row, the keel row,
Weel may the keel row
That ma laddie's in!' "[1]

At the first sound of it Patience had sprung to her feet, and now, with outstretched arms, she was dancing across the field to her lover, who had just vaulted the gate at the further end. And her voice floated through the air towards him as she answered:

"An' weel may the keel row,
The keel row, the keel row,
An' weel may the keel row
That ma laddie's in."

I watched, fascinated, between tears and laughter, as they met in the middle of the pasture and joined hands, singing and dancing together:

"He wears a blue bonnet,
Blue bonnet, blue bonnet,
He wears a blue bonnet,
A dimple in his chin.
An' weel may the keel row,
The keel row . . ."

"Stop! Stop!" I shouted, and began ludicrously capering after them. But they paid no attention to me. They were dancing off into the sunlight, into a golden light that seemed to wrap them in a haze.

"An' weel may the keel row,
The keel row, the keel row,
Weel may the keel row
That ma laddie's in.
He wears a blue bonnet,
Blue bonnet, blue bonnet . . ."

Their voices were growing fainter and fainter. I could hardly see them now. Were they melting into the air? "Stop! Stop!" I shouted, still dancing like a lunatic. But they were gone.

And when the music ceased I was standing stock-still,

[1] The "keel" was the special boat designed to carry coal from the staith to the mouth of the river. Sandgate, in Newcastle, was the stronghold of the keelmen. The first known version of this famous song appeared in 1752. ("The History of the Keelmen and their Strike in 1822," by W. Stanley Mitcalfe, *Arch. Ael.,* Vol. XIV, Fourth Series, 1937.)

looking up at an enormous man who towered above me and gripped me violently by the shoulder. "Wake up!" he shouted. "I'm Mug. What's your name?" "Wake up!" shouted another voice, even louder and ruder. "I'm Con.[1] What's your name? . . . Wake up, there! Wake up!" And I opened my eyes, to find that I was still lying under the hedge, that the day was almost gone, and that a man in a blue uniform was bending over me and shaking me by the shoulder. "Come along, now!" he said. "You don't want to sleep there all night as well as all day. I heard you were here from Mr. Snowden. This is Government property, you know. What are you doing here? Show me your identity card." And with these words I realised, as I fumbled for my pocket-book, that I had returned to the blessed days of Civilisation.

[1] Mug, Ben and Con (Muggleswick, Benfieldside and Consett) were three giants who amused themselves by tossing to each other an enormous hammer, which, when dropped, made dints in the sides of the hills, which may still be seen.

CHAPTER XXI

SOME BISHOPS AND MR. WESLEY

"The Spirit of the Lord is upon me, because He hath anointed me to preach the gospel to the poor."
TEXT OF A SERMON BY JOHN WESLEY.

"The pretending to extraordinary revelations and gifts of the Holy Ghost is a horrid thing, a very horrid thing!"
BISHOP JOSEPH BUTLER.

"FROM Cosin to Shute Barrington," says Bishop Henson, in a sentence to which we have already alluded,[1] "with the single exception of Butler, all the bishops of Durham were men of family and influence, whose appointment was easier to explain than to justify."[2] Presumably, as Cosin is clearly not included, Shute Barrington, at the other end of the list, although a "man of family," is not intended to be ranked with the herd of well-bred ecclesiastics whose elevation is thus deplored. The appointments therefore denounced as unjustifiable are those of Bishops Crewe, Talbot, Chandler, Trevor, Egerton and Thurlow. Of these six we have already considered one, Lord Crewe. Let us now briefly glance at the remaining five, to whom, for the sake of completing the roll of eighteenth-century Bishops of Durham, we may add the name of Shute Barrington. We shall follow (out of chronological order) with a sketch of Joseph Butler, who is excepted, by general consent, from all animadversions on the ecclesiastical dignitaries of this period; and we shall conclude the chapter with some reference to the man who exercised a more lasting influence on the religious thought of the county than all these bishops combined—John Wesley.

The first name on our list of five goes far to warrant Bishop Henson's stricture, to such an extent that one is tempted to believe that the characters of Crewe and Talbot, standing in the first place, in point of time, in the long line of "courtier prelates," have played a regrettable part in colouring, to a disgusted eye, the conduct of their successors. We must, however, be careful to distinguish between individuals, and not

[1] Vol. II, p. 299.   [2] *Retrospect of an Unimportant Life,* Vol. II, p. 79.

condemn a bishop who happens to succeed a gentlemanly self-seeker merely because he succeeds him and is himself a gentleman.

William Talbot, who was enthroned as Bishop on the death of Lord Crewe, was a member of one of the most ancient families in England, and doubtless owed his elevation to the Bishoprics of Oxford, Salisbury and Durham more to the influence of his cousin, the Earl of Shrewsbury, than to his own peculiar talents or piety. Such nepotism was an accepted principle of public life in the eighteenth century; nor is our own purity so remarkable that we can afford to condemn it, though today it has adopted the less natural, more disagreeable form of political, rather than avuncular, favour. If it be wrong to assist a nephew for no other reason than his kinship, it cannot be right to promote a stranger for no better cause than that his political principles (or lack of them) are in correspondence with our own. Conversely, so long as due regard is paid to individual merit and suitability, it is no more reprehensible to help the ambitious relative than the aspiring partisan. But for their influential relations there would have been no Pitt in England and no Wellington in the Peninsula to counter-check the ambitions of Bonaparte.

But it must be admitted that, in the case of William Talbot, the personal favour extended was more natural than judicious. This rosy-cheeked, pop-eyed, Toby Jug of a man was probably well fitted, by taste and appearance, to ride (as he did) at a royal review dressed in a layman's suit of purple cloth, with jack boots, a cocked hat and a military wig. But apart from this attractive, if somewhat undignified, picture with which he has presented us, we can find but one weight which we can fairly set in the scales for him. This is a happy instance of the proper use of that system whose abuse only is rightly labelled as "nepotism." He made, and he kept, a promise to his dying son that he would extend his favour to the young man's friend Joseph Butler. It was thanks to this worldly jack-booted dignitary that the deepest thinker and one of the sweetest natures that ever graced the throne of Durham was brought to the notice of authority and launched, with every advantage, upon his ecclesiastical career. Let us not, therefore, forget this debt of gratitude which we owe to the memory of

Bishop Talbot; but, having paid it, we must turn our face from him. He was greedy and wildly extravagant and rendered himself obnoxious to the county by the zeal with which he pursued his own pecuniary interests, regardless of those of others. "As a prelate," says Fordyce curtly, "nothing can be said in his praise."[1]

Edward Chandler was not a "man of family," but an Irishman of obscure parentage who owed his elevation to his own learning, which was considerable, to the assistance of the Bishop of Winchester, whose chaplain he was, and perhaps to some money inherited from his father, who had settled as a merchant in Durham City. There is little to be said about his episcopate of twenty years. During this time Wesley first visited the county, but we know nothing of the opinions of the Bishop concerning the extraordinary ministrations to his own flock of this uninvited shepherd. "Of more learning than capacity,"[2] perhaps, Bishop Chandler was a good and upright man who gave generously of his wealth and wrote a masterly *Defence of Christianity*. For the last years of his life he suffered tortures from the inevitable "stone."

We next come to Joseph Butler, who reigned for only two years and whom we will pass over for the moment, in order to consider another of those whom Bishop Henson has included in the ruck of gentlemanly ecclesiastics.

Richard Trevor, a scion of an ancient Welsh family, is warmly praised by all three of the principal historians of the county. He left behind him, says Hutchinson, who was his junior contemporary, "an example of Christian piety, fortitude and resignation, which no human being ever exceeded, and few have equalled."[3] "Bishop Trevor's person and countenance were strikingly handsome," wrote Surtees, "his manners noble and dignified, and he justly merited the praise of a sincere friend, a generous patron, and a splendid and munificent Prelate."[4] And finally Fordyce, writing as an Early Victorian rather censorious of the vices than appreciative of the virtues of the eighteenth century, says of Richard Trevor that, besides the competence of his learning and his high character as a man, "as a bishop he seems also to have been ever attentive to his duties; of a mild, tolerant and

[1] Fordyce, Vol. I, p. 81.
[2] *D.N.B.*
[3] Hutchinson, Vol. I, p. 583.
[4] Surtees, Vol. I, p. 123.

liberal disposition, and of a modest piety."[1] Owing to his handsome face and sweet expression, he was known throughout the diocese as "The Beauty of Holiness."[2]

No doubt Richard Trevor cannot be included in the small category of the great Bishops of Durham. He was extraordinary neither as a thinker nor as a statesman. As a man of taste, however, he is not to be despised. He added a charming wing to Auckland Castle and he bought (from a Spanish pedlar for £124 5s.) eleven of those excellent and interesting Zurbarans which are now most happily hung in the great drawing-room.[3] But it is simply and principally as a Christian that we have learnt to value him. He was content to practise Christian humility and to cultivate Christian faith and to suffer with Christian fortitude. For his care for the first two of these virtues his own reported words, when added to the testimony of contemporaries, may suffice. "We may boast ourselves," he would say, "in the advancement we have made in the theory of our religion; but how must our pride be humbled when we compare our practice with our theory! Surely principles so great and glorious as those of the gospel cannot always remain without their effect. No. Revelation may be slow in working the full purpose of Heaven, but it must be sure. . . . Christian charity cannot always be to the world a light without heat, a pale cold fire. Its warmth at length must be universally felt. The time must come when our zeal shall appear to be kindled by this heavenly fire and not by human passion; when all our little earthly heats shall be extinguished, and that pure and divine flame alone shall burn. The time will come when animosity and violence and rage shall cease; and when union, love and harmony shall prevail."[4] Whatever we may think of their prophetic character, these words cannot be regarded as the typical utterances of a complacent and well-fed eighteenth-century divine.

For his fortitude we have the evidence of his last illness and of the manner in which he bore it. A great walker all his life, he died of blood poisoning after nearly six months of suffering, during which his leg was gradually mortified and

[1] Fordyce, Vol. I, p. 85.
[2] *Auckland Castle,* by Rev. James Raine (Durham, 1852), p. 96.
[3] His statue by Nollekens is in the ante-chapel.
[4] Hutchinson, Vol. I, p. 585.

the toes of it dropped off one by one. Yet he was never heard
to utter one peevish word or to heave one desponding sigh,
and, although he was well aware of the fatal nature of his
illness, he persisted in sitting up until the last possible
moment and leading, so far as he was able, the life of a
normally healthy man, transacting his business, seeing his
friends and constantly having visitors to dine with him and
forcing himself to partake of the food. When he felt that the
end was near, he resigned himself to die without a murmur,
thanked God for having given him strength to support his
illness, thanked the world for its tenderness and care, and
murmured to his nephew, after he had been shaken by convulsions into which he was frequently thrown towards the
close: "Jack, you see me clinging to life much more than it
deserves."[1]

Bishop Trevor was succeeded by John Egerton, who, having
been promoted at the early age of forty-nine to the See of
Durham, where he soon became deservedly popular, was
known there throughout his career as "the amiable young
bishop."[2] He was the grandson of the Earl of Bridgewater
and the nephew of the Duke of Portland, but does not appear
to have been otherwise vicious. On the contrary, finding the
county suffering from a plethora of politics and divided, as a
consequence, into Whigs and Tories who entertained towards
one another feelings of unusual animosity, he exerted himself
to reconcile these rival factions and to unite them in social
harmony round his own table. An unambitious man, who
seems to have had greatness thrust upon him and never to
have sought it for himself, he was well suited for his self-
appointed rôle of peacemaker, both by the natural sweetness
and calmness of his temper and by his knowledge of the
world, his charming manners and his presence of mind. It was
impossible to maintain a rancorous behaviour before him, and
in the warmth of his hospitality old hatreds were thawed and
old envies were dissipated. But though he entertained lavishly,
he himself, following the custom of the best amongst his
predecessors, was abstemious. His pleasures lay in scholarship
and occasional games of chess and bowls, which his chaplains
were pleased to allow him to win. But he never neglected
the public duties of his office. He made considerable altera-

[1] *Op. cit.*, p. 583.   [2] *Sylvestra,* Vol. I, p. 62.

tions to Auckland Castle, rebuilt that portion of the Tyne bridge (swept away in the great flood of 1780) for which he was responsible, reclaimed many acres of waste land, and granted a new charter to the citizens of Durham which was received by the Mayor on bended knee, while the market fountain ran with liquor for the populace. This charter remained valid until the Municipal Corporations Act of 1835. He was also most careful in his ecclesiastical appointments. "But the feature which in him was as prominent as it is lovely," says Hutchinson, "was a perfect union of dignity and humility."[1] He believed that true religion, in his own words, "consists in the love of God and the love of our neighbour . . . in such a love of our neighbour as must prove itself to be undissembled, disinterested and productive of all social virtues. But let us never be unmindful that the first and great duty is the love of God, for it is this which exalts our morality into Christianity, and it is Christianity alone which can entitle us to a lasting happiness."[2] Generous to all, but firm of disposition, quick in decision, and never courting that popularity which his merits alone had earned for him, he seemed to hold himself above the life of this world, while yet enjoying it, and when death came to take him at a comparatively early age he welcomed it calmly as the medium of his translation to a better country. "Of the many noble and generous Prelates who have held the See of Durham," says Surtees, "none ever exercised his Palatine privileges with more liberal discretion, or passed through his high office with less of blame or envy, than Bishop Egerton."[3] It would, indeed, appear that "nepotism" has seldom been more justified of her nephews.

The next, and the last, of those six bishops whom we have endeavoured to present as the owners of six separate individualities, rather than to confuse in one conglomerate mass of courtiers, was Thomas Thurlow. He, like the others, owed his promotion to the influence of a powerful relative, but, unlike most of them, he was not "a man of family." When some parasite attempted to flatter his brother, the Lord Chancellor, with the suggestion that he was of noble descent, that dignitary replied in his rough, rude way: "Tcha! tcha! All the world knows that old Thurlow, the carrier, was my

---

[1] Hutchinson, Vol. III, p. 12.   [2] Ibid.
[3] Surtees, Vol. I, p. 123.

grandfather."[1] But Thomas was far more punctilious and polite. "My Lord," he said to the Chancellor, when he himself was made Bishop of Lincoln, "I have called to thank your lordship . . ." "Bah!" interrupted his lordship roughly. "I think you might have said 'brother,' and be damned to you!"[2] But though he damned poor Thomas, he nevertheless secured his translation to Durham.

But little is known of this bishop, who only occupied our See for a period of four years, during which he seems to have behaved as an amiable nonentity, which perhaps he was. The kindly Hutchinson, however, who was his contemporary, says that he was very shy and that he shone in an intimate circle of friends. That is hardly a sufficient recommendation to one of the most important bishoprics in England, but nevertheless, if we cannot praise highly, neither can we blame severely a man who was judged by those who knew him best to be "an attentive diocesan, a generous patron, a judicious adviser, an agreeable companion, and a sincere friend."[3] He was succeeded, in 1791, by Shute Barrington, a gentleman of very different calibre.

The Honourable and Right Reverend Shute Barrington, LL.D., Bishop of Durham, was the youngest son of the first Lord Barrington and descended from the family of Shute which had played its part for Parliament during the Civil War. Unlike his more recent predecessors, who, for one reason or another, had lived somewhat withdrawn from the world, Bishop Barrington enjoyed the scope which his position afforded him for the exercise of his energies and talents. As Bishop of Llandaff he had vigorously maintained in the House of Lords the authority of the Church against those liberal latitudinarians who desired the abolition of the Thirty-Nine Articles; as Bishop of Salisbury he had busied himself with the repair of the cathedral, and after his translation to Durham he spent the remainder of his long life in acts of munificence hardly equalled even by the most princely of the mediæval prelates, and in the expression of a taste for architecture not as impeccable as his public spirit. No doubt, thanks to the steady development of coal throughout the eighteenth century, the Bishop of Durham was, by this time, a very

[1] *Fordyce,* Vol. I, p. 86.   [2] *Ibid.*
[3] Hutchinson, Vol. III, p. 16.

wealthy man. But the richest men are not always the most generous. Bishop Barrington promoted learning, improved agriculture, greatly encouraged the education of the poor, and is said to have given away, in one cause or another, as much as £100,000. "There has scarcely been any social reform," said Bishop Westcott, one of his greatest successors, "which has been accomplished during the century which Bishop Barrington did not start. He started the idea of co-operation and was really the first inventor of the familiar phrase of 'Three acres and a cow.' He was anxious that every one should possess some small holding. His object was that every one in the county should feel a real interest in the life of his parish, and have a stake in it."[1] For Reform, that sweet and sober maiden whom over-indulgence can so swiftly debase into a flame-slinging fury, was now making her debut in the political world, and Bishop Barrington was one of those who had the sense to go forward and to greet her and to lead her calmly by the hand. His common sense was indeed one of his most striking characteristics. He was ever careful to dissociate political and even religious differences from personal relationship, and the golden mean between extremes of opinion, between Romanism and Methodism and between absolutism and radicalism, as between personal extravagance and austerity, seems to have been the determination of his life. Only his generosity was boundless.

With all this he was an engaging companion. "A store of honey is to be found in his polite conversation,"[2] said one of his contemporaries, and he was not above cracking his little joke. "I am the only licensed poacher in England," he once observed, "since 'I, Shute, by the Grace of God . . .'"[3] When Walter Scott paid him a visit at Auckland Castle he insisted on speeding his parting guest and rode with him for ten miles on the way to Rokeby. The Bishop was then seventy-nine. "I like to feel my horse under me, Mr. Scott,"[4] said the gallant old man, for he had always delighted in the pleasures of the country. He died, at last, peacefully and painlessly, in

---

[1] *Life and Letters of Brooke Foss Westcott*, by Arthur Westcott (Macmillan, 1903), Vol. II, p. 275.

[2] Boruwlaski, *Memoirs*, p. 361.

[3] *The Story of My Life*, by Augustus Hare.

[4] Lockhart, *Life of Scott*, Vol. III, p. 14. (Cadell, 1837.)

his ninety-second year. Thanks to his own moderation, power of mind and amiability of disposition, his life had been a happy, golden link between the age that was dying and the new one that was coming to pass.

For all through the eighteenth century the voice of modern industry, faintly at first, but with increasing assurance, was heard through the lowing of primordial cattle and the bleating of patriarchal sheep. The time had not yet come when these immemorial and living witnesses to the presence and travail of man would yield pride of place, as our inseparable companions, to the cacophonous screaming of machinery. But the time was at hand. Already, at the beginning of the century, Sir Ambrose Crowley had established his iron works in the Derwent Valley at Winlaton and Swalwell, where he was soon forging everything "frev a needle tiv an anchor" and governing his growing community under a system compounded of the benevolence of a despot, the theorisation of a Socialist and the meticulousness of a university proctor. Fifty years later a rival firm was set up by William Hawks below Gateshead, and "Crowley's Crew" and "Hawks's Blacks" were later notorious throughout the county for their extremely advanced political views and for the lawless vigour with which they enforced them. For these works, and for the glass industries at Sunderland, South Shields and Gateshead, and for the building of ships, coal was required, while the rapid deforestation of England and the increasing population were calling for more and more of it as a domestic fuel.[1] At the beginning of the century the making of coke began. About 1718 the first steam-engine ever used for pumping a coalmine was erected at Oxclose, near Washington.[2] These two inventions opened out enormous possibilities in the coal trade, and a few years later the foundations were laid of a partnership known as "The Grand Allies"—an association afterwards joined by several rich landowners and

[1] Headlam, *op. cit.*, Chapter IX, "History of Coal Mining," by A. Wedgwood, M.Sc., M.I.M.E.

[2] *Ibid.*, and *Local Records of Washington, No. 3*, p. 31, by Frederick Hill. This steam-engine is claimed to be the first by both the above, but Sykes mentions one set up at Byker Colliery, Northumberland, in 1714. (*Local Records*, Vol. I, p. 133.)

business-men, who between them came to own the best coal-pits in the North. In 1753 cast-iron wheels were first made for haulage tubs; in 1765 took place the first recorded strike; in 1779 the making of coal-tar was begun at Cockfield; and in 1787 two million tons of coal were shipped from the Tyne and the Wear. Industry was now fairly launched on its way, the population of the county was more rapidly increasing, while, as the pits sunk deeper and the working became more complicated, explosions of fire-damp became more frequent. In 1743 some seventeen lives were lost at North Biddick. Many other disasters were to follow, including an accident at Lumley, which destroyed thirty-nine human beings, and the terrible explosion at Felling in 1812, which resulted in the deaths of ninety-one men and boys. Female labour was used for work in the mines. As early as 1705 some women were killed in a pit near Gateshead. They no longer worked underground after about 1780, but at the close of the century children as young as six and "drunk almost from infancy" were still going down the pit. Meanwhile colliery villages were springing up to house the increasing number of mine-workers, dreary places ill-disguised by their romantic names —Philadelphia, Bunker's Hill, Porto Bello, Gibraltar—bestowed upon them in honour of British arms. Here the men and women and children drank and quarrelled and amused themselves with handball and cockfighting, and were extravagant and dirty and "in every respect inferior to other labourers."[1]

Now, if we reconsider the lives of our eighteenth-century bishops, we are bound to confess that we can read in them little indication of all these industrial activities, which were exercising the minds, affecting the characters and transforming the lives of an increasing number of their diocesans. The sheep were beginning to congregate on strange pastures, whose herbage must have tasted bitter to them, and where was the shepherd to console and enfold them and refresh them with the waters of life? Now we are forced to perceive the true sense of Bishop Henson's criticism. We trust we have saved the memory of two, at least, of these men from confusion with a generality of "Talbots." Bishops Trevor and Egerton

[1] *V.C.H.*, Vol. II, p. 346 (quoting MS. of Mr. Thomas of Denton Hall, *c.* 1800).

were Christians of exalted ideals and noble virtues, while against Chandler and Thurlow there is nothing opprobious to say. But, worthy or unworthy, these eighteenth-century "courtier-prelates" were completely out of touch with the life of the common man, on whose welfare, spiritual and physical, from now onwards would increasingly depend the spiritual and physical welfare of their diocese. The best of these bishops did not neglect their duty, as they conceived their duty to be. They transacted their business, improved the land, looked after their clergy and soothed the rancorous animosities of gentlemen. They exerted their influence upon those who were still governing and representing the county, on whom it was their obvious duty to exert their influence and with whom, as gentlemen themselves, it was their natural habit to consort. But they do not seem to have had the wit, or to have been induced by any suspicion, to pull aside this gentlemanly mask and look at the face of Durham behind it. No doubt it was the business of the rank and file of the clergy to report to their lord on the holes at Gateshead and the squalor of South Shields, but the Bishop was responsible for his clergy. While it is easy for us, with a knowledge of what was to come, to criticise the neglect of an aspect of social life which was still in its infancy—very far from the gross and dark dimensions which it was to attain in Early Victorian times—we are bound to admit that, for all their Christian virtues and lofty ideals, the prelates of this period failed where a great man would have succeeded. The influence they could have exerted on the first phases of industrial development, not only as bishops, but as rich and powerful potentates, might well have been decisive for all future relationships between the modern master and the modern man. But they missed the opportunity. Some of them were good men, whose memory we must reverence and admire. But they were not good shepherds, for they did not know their sheep.

We have, however, still the life of one Bishop, the greatest of them all, to consider. Let us now see how Bishop Butler affected, or was affected by, the first troubled whispers of our approaching industrial revolution.

Joseph Butler, born at Wantage in 1692, was the youngest son of a tradesman of that town. He was brought up as a Nonconformist, but, while still being educated at a dissenting school, he began to entertain grave doubts concerning the doctrine of his teachers, as the result of which he converted himself, in spite of protests, to the Established Church. It was about this time, at the age of twenty-one, that he began an anonymous correspondence with a learned divine, Dr. Samuel Clarke, to whom his first letter opened, after a preliminary apology, "with this astonishing declaration"[1]: "I have made it, sir, my business, ever since I thought myself capable of such sort of reasoning, to prove to myself the being and attributes of God."[2] This business, which he had made for himself so young, he adhered to throughout his life; the embodiment of this search for truth is to be found in his sermons and particularly in his great work, *The Analogy of Religion to the Constitution and Course of Nature.*

Having taken orders in the Church, Butler was in 1718, thanks to Dr. Clarke and young Talbot, appointed preacher at the Rolls Chapel. In 1722 Bishop Talbot fulfilled his promise to his dying son by the gift to his friend of the living of Haughton-le-Skerne, and in 1725 he transferred him to the rectory of Stanhope. In 1736 Butler was made Clerk of the Closet to Queen Caroline and presented her with his *Analogy,* the fruits of his retirement among the heather and sheep of Weardale. In 1738 he was made Bishop of Bristol, and in 1750 was translated to Durham, only two years before his death.

Butler's life was entirely uneventful. During the short time in which he occupied the northern See he gave evidence of his generosity, his hospitality, his love of building and the sweet and sad reflectiveness of his disposition; but he had no opportunity, even had he had the desire or been gifted with the necessary practical enthusiasm, for any large schemes of statesmanship or far-reaching plans of social regeneration or religious revival. Moreover, at the time when he came to Durham, though the wheels of industry had indeed begun to turn, they could still easily escape notice in the general peace and hush of the countryside. This was one of the happiest periods in England. Hints of what was to come were being thrown out, here and there, in the small, restricted colliery and manufacturing districts, but the country as a whole was predominantly agricultural, still steeped in a profound, blue

[1] Bishop Henson in *Bishoprick Papers*, p. 151.   [2] *Ibid.*

calm. Only something too earthy, something too self-satisfied and material, in this prosperity troubled the sensitive conscience of the Bishop. The want of faith, the lack of an earnest spiritual religion was manifest to him. He deplored this in his primary charge at Durham, he had taken steps to remedy it at Bristol by providing a church for the miners there, and he was at all times zealous in exhortations to his clergy and in charitable benefactions.

Though Butler was studious of the rights of his Palatinate, as well as its duties, his personal simplicity was saint-like. He could never resist beggars, who, quickly discovering this weakness, would importune him at all hours. "How much money have I in the house?" he once asked his steward at Auckland. "Five hundred pounds," was the reply. "It is a shame for a bishop to have so much," said Butler, and he gave it all to his petitioner.

Joseph Butler was essentially a thinker, with all the power, the humility and the sweet reasonableness of a gentle mind and a mighty intellect, earnest in the pursuit of truth. Yet he was not, as might be supposed, a vague and incapable philosopher, but a man of ability conscientiously desirous to fulfil his episcopal duties. Nevertheless, the practical side of such a man's nature must inevitably be subordinated to the philosophical, apart from the fact that the very brief time allotted to him in the northern See gave him scant opportunity to exert his influence. "The Bishop of Durham has been wafted to that See in a cloud of metaphysics," said Horace Walpole, "and he has remained absorbed in it."[1] "Is Mr. Butler dead?" Queen Caroline had asked on an earlier occasion, when her protégé had disappeared into the remote seclusion of Stanhope. "No, Madam," was the reply of Archbishop Blackburne, "but he is buried."[2] If we look at the portrait of him as a young man, we are fascinated by the serene and thoughtful melancholy of a face that is almost feminine in its beauty and almost angelic in its expression, but little suited, we cannot forbear from noticing, for a rough *corps à corps* with the devil in the back lanes of Gateshead or amongst the swearing colliers of North Biddick. The description of his appearance towards the close of his life, both by Hutchinson (who had doubtless seen him) and by Surtees, reveals, indeed, his

[1] *Ibid.*, p. 145.   [2] Surtees, Vol. I, p. 122.

ethereal and spiritual development, but, *ipso facto*, no practical, mundane advance towards a more robust or coarser form
of Christianity. "He was of a most reverend aspect," says
Hutchinson. "His face thin and pale; but there was a divine
placidness in his countenance, which inspired veneration, and
expressed the most benevolent mind: His white hair hung
gracefully on his shoulders, and his whole figure was patriarchal."[1] To which Surtees adds that "during the ministerial
performance of the sacred office a divine animation seemed to
pervade his whole manner, and lighted up his pale wan
countenance, already marked with the progress of disease, like
a torch glimmering in its socket, yet bright and useful to the
last."[2]

The fame of Joseph Butler rests upon a single work, his
Analogy, which occupies only some 380 pages of a broadly
printed octavo volume[3]—a very considerably smaller space
than *Gone with the Wind*. "But size," says Bishop Henson,
"has no relation to value,"[4] and within the compass of these
few sheets of paper is packed the most careful and the deepest
thinking of a master. For that reason, because the thinking is
deep, not because the expression is obscure, the book is not an
easy one to read nor ever likely to be popular with the general
reader. It has been described as "the greatest theological work
of the time and one of the most original of any time"[5]; it has
been praised for its "solid structure of logical argument in
which it surpasses any other book in the English language"[6];
it exercised a profound influence on the thought of Cardinal
Newman,[7] and it has endured until the present day, when a
modern historian has acclaimed it as "one of the world's
greatest philosophic works."[8] It is this book which has raised
Joseph Butler to a place of the first lustre amongst the most
illustrious Bishops of Durham. Its purpose is to prove logic-
ally, by an analogy between the moral and natural world, the
probability of the existence of God and of the truth of revealed religion. By balancing likelihoods and examining

---

[1] Hutchinson, Vol. I, p. 578.   [2] Surtees, Vol. I, p. 122.
[3] Vol. I of the Gladstone edition of Butler's works. (Clarendon
Press, 1896.)
[4] *Bishoprick Papers*, p. 151.   [5] *D.N.B.*
[6] Mark Pattison, quoted in *Bishoprick Papers*, p. 145.
[7] *Apologia,* Part III.   [8] Trevelyan, *England*, p. 518.

parallels, quietly, sweetly, reasonably, we are led to the conclusion that, so far as the finite mind can apprehend the infinite, the evidence in favour of a future life, of the probationary nature of this one, of the truth of Christianity, and of the authority of a living Church, is compelling and, if not irresistible, extremely difficult to resist.

The dying words of this saintly philosopher reveal to us the cautious, probing nature of his humble but hopeful mind. He must test each step. He must be sure of the way. " 'Though I have endeavoured to avoid sin,' he said to his chaplain, 'and to please God to the utmost of my power, yet, from the consciousness of perpetual infirmities, I am still afraid to die.' And the chaplain replied: 'Surely you have forgotten that Christ is the Saviour?' 'True,' he said, 'but how shall I know that he is a Saviour *for me?*' And the reply was: 'It is written, Him that cometh unto Me, I will in no wise cast him out.' 'True,' said the Bishop finally, 'and I am surprised that though I have read that Scripture a thousand times, I never felt the virtue of it till this moment. Now I die happy.' "[1]

True, true, true; yes, a thousand times true; but such truth as was the lifelong quest of Bishop Butler's philosophic mind was not likely to appeal to "Crowley's Crew" or "Hawks's Blacks," to the lead-miners in Weardale, to the weavers and dyers of Darlington and Barnard Castle, to the shipbuilders and colliers on the banks of the Wear, or to the keelmen and glassmakers on the Tyne. Someone else was needed for these, and someone else came.

John Wesley paid his first visit to County Durham in 1745, when he preached at Whickham, and, soon afterwards, at Tanfield Lea. It was not a cheerful beginning. "So dead, senseless and unaffected a congregation," he said of his hearers at Tanfield, "I have scarce ever seen, except at Whickham." From that time until a few months before his death he constantly visited the county.[2] During these forty-five years he changed the hearts of the people and laid the foundations of a religious influence which deeply affected the spirit of society

---

[1] *Seven Sages of Durham,* by G. W. Kitchin, p. 277. (T. Fisher Unwin, 1911.)

[2] His last appearance in County Durham was at Stockton on June 15th, 1790. He died on March 2nd, 1791.

in the North during the troubled times of industrial development and has endured, though lately with failing strength,
until the present day. Professor Laski is said to have lamented
this influence because it diverted the passions of the people
from indignation against social injustice into the love of God,
and thereby postponed the advent of the Socialists' Utopia.[1]
Wesley was not, indeed, interested in political theories for the
problematical improvement of society. He was not even
interested in the formation of a new religion. He believed in
the Church of England and had no more desire to be separated from it than St. Francis from the Church of Rome. But
he was interested in individual men, and an individual man
to him was, not his wages, however small, nor his conditions,
however hard, nor his complaints, however justified, but his
soul. This was the kernel in the nut, the gold in the nugget,
the only possible key to every man's happiness, and, what was
far more important than his happiness, to every man's salva-
tion. And to get at that soul he would do anything, he would
endure anything. He would seek it in the worst, the roughest
places, because there the need for it was greatest. He would
plead for it and implore, and thunder for it and terrify. "I
preached at Gateshead," he writes in his journal, "and declared the loving-kindness of the Lord. In the evening,
observing abundance of strangers at the Room, I changed my
voice, and applied these terrible words: 'I have overthrown
some of you as I overthrew Sodom and Gomorrah, and the
rest of you were as brands plucked out of the burning; yet
have ye not turned unto me, said the Lord.'" It was the
individual at whom he was aiming and it was the individual
whom he struck—"You, some of you, the rest of you." The
effect he produced was astonishing. "His countenance," said
one of his hearers, "struck such an awful dread upon me
before I heard him speak, that it made my heart beat like the
pendulum of a clock; and when he did speak, I thought his
whole discourse was aimed at me."[2] Nothing could daunt him.
Obstacles delighted him. For they showed that the Devil
disapproved of his plans, and that was precisely what he
wanted the Devil to do. Nothing could hurt him, no one

---

[1] *Daily Telegraph,* November 28th, 1946.
[2] John Nelson, a Yorkshire mason. See *Life of John Wesley,* by
Southey, p. 200. (Hutchinson, 1903.)

could harm him, for he was under the special protection of God. Storm-clouds parted before his path and passed on either side of him, stones thrown at him failed to touch him, the sun shone and did not dazzle his eyes, and a high wind was stilled as soon as he began to speak. So he went, from Gateshead in the north to Darlington in the south, from Teesdale in the west to Sunderland in the east, in main streets, in market-places, in stable-yards, under oak-trees, everywhere preaching the word of God.

This was a different aspect of religion indeed, not only from its parody in a Talbot, but from its virtues as exercised by the best of these gentle bishops. Here was no placid, Christian gentleman, but a thunderbolt of God; no sweet reasonable-ness, no melancholy, meditative glance, but a voice that terri-fied like a lion's and an eye that pierced like an eagle's. This was a prophet, an enthusiast, a man possessed and posessing, who inspired and shook and captured and captivated, and drove his hearers into physical ecstasies and agonies at his feet. "The Lord was wonderfully present," he writes in his diary, "more than twenty persons feeling the arrows of con-viction. Several fell to the ground, some of whom seemed dead: others, in the agonies of death; the violence of their bodily convulsions exceeding all description. There was also great crying and agonising in prayer, mixed with deep and deadly groans on every side." Little children rivalled their elders in enthusiasm. "They could not refrain from crying aloud to God," exclaims Wesley delightedly, and, on another occasion: "Among the children who felt the arrows of the Almighty, I saw a sturdy boy, above eight years old, who roared above his fellows, and seemed in his agony to struggle with the strength of a grown man." And the miners were melted down as wax before the fire, and their tears made white gutters on their black cheeks.

It was not surprising that such scenes, such frantic exhibi-tions of "corybantic Christianity" should have shocked and scandalised the gently searching Joseph Butler. It would have been strange if all this hysteria had not seemed "a very horrid thing" to his refined and sensitive mind. But Wesley's mission was not to refined and sensitive minds, but to colliers and mechanics. Moreover, to do him justice, it was not his object to throw people into convulsions, but to win their souls. He knew that these outward expressions of inward bliss or agony were natural to rough and uncontrolled characters. They were better, at any rate, than a dumb indifference; and he played as often the part of a tender, soothing parent as of a spiritual agitator. But he was himself so sincere that he could not fail to welcome sincerity in others (or what he believed to be sincerity), however crudely it might be expressed.

We are not called upon to decide between the rival merits of these two great Christians. There is no decision possible. But it is a strange and perhaps a sad reflection that the most profound religious influence ever exerted upon the minds of the people of Durham since the days when they worshipped at the shrine of St. Cuthbert did not emanate from any of the saint's successors, but from the stranger priest, John Wesley.

DATES OF THE BISHOPS OF DURHAM MENTIONED IN THIS CHAPTER

William Talbot	...	...	...	... 1721-1730
Edward Chandler	...	...	...	... 1730-1750
Joseph Butler ...	...	...	...	... 1750-1752
Richard Trevor	...	...	...	... 1752-1771
John Egerton ...	...	...	...	... 1771-1787
Thomas Thurlow	...	...	...	... 1787-1791
Shute Barrington	...	...	...	... 1791-1826

[John Wesley (in Durham) 1745-1790]

CHAPTER XXII

AIRS AND GRACES

I. AIRS

"Brave lads in olden musical centuries
Sang, night by night, adorable choruses,
Sat late by alehouse doors in April
Chaunting in joy as the moon was rising."
R. L. STEVENSON.

THE gaiety of the workaday world in bygone times is surprising to us, who sombrely gather in our state-controlled, azoic crops and have no reason to associate merriment with mining or any other branch of Industry. We have no song for a sheaf, no dance for a lump of coal. But in those days there was gratitude for these mercies, the ringing of bells, thanksgiving in church, subterranean balls and singing in the fields. "In this part of the country," writes Hutchinson, "are retained some ancient customs evidently derived from the Romans, particularly that of dressing up a figure of Ceres during harvest, which is placed in the field whilst the reapers are labouring, and brought home on the last evening of reaping, with music and great acclamation. After this a feast is made, called the 'mell supper,'[1] from the ancient sacrifice of mingling the new meal."[2] This "figure of Ceres," called locally the "mell doll" or the "Kern babby,"[3] was a sheaf, fashioned and decorated as a puppet; and the singing with which it was escorted homewards was known as "shouting the mell." The song, begun by the farmer's head man, ran something as follows:

"Blest be the day that Christ was born!
We've getten mell o' Mr. Hodgson's corn:
Weel won and better shorn,
Hip, Hip, Hurrah!"[4]

[1] "Mell" (Norse) = corn. *Memorials of Old Durham*, chapter on "Folklore," by Mrs. Apperley, p. 58.
[2] Hutchinson, Vol. II, p. 583.
[3] Mr. William Alsop of Gainford still makes beautiful "Kern babbies," according to information kindly supplied by Miss Peggy Hutchinson.   [4] Mrs. Apperley, *op. cit.*, p. 58.

For the ensuing festivities we cannot do better than quote the account of a participant in one of the last mell suppers held in the county of Durham.

"I have a recollection of being invited to a Mell Supper, or Harvest Home Supper, in the first year that my father came to Windlestone to work. That would be in 1887. It was held at the Home Farm, in the granary there, and it was well attended, but not crowded. Joseph Burlinson was the musician for the dancers, and to accompany songs; his instrument being his banjo, which we all loved to hear. The place was decorated with corn and small branches and leaves, and the lighting was from the farm lanterns—quite a number of them, too.

"The supper was the first event and was laid on a long table, the length of the big barn. A large joint of roast beef and also one of pork, besides pies and cakes and blancmanges in profusion. *Home-made ginger beer*, as they used to make it in those far-off days—and good. Everyone enjoyed the feast. Then came the toasts. The lord and the lady of the manor and all the family. The farmer and all his family. Loud cheers for each toast. At the end of the cheering everyone took a hand in clearing away and preparing for the dancing and the songs. The floor was just a little rough, but I think we managed to dance and enjoy ourselves. I have a memory of one man who asked me to dance, and his clothes had been put away in *pepper*, as used to be the custom, when they were not being worn. I was kept sneezing and had to give up trying to go through that dance, and there was great laughing and jokes about the pepper.

"Between the dances came singing. I can only remember one song, and it had a jolly refrain that everyone could join in, *and they did.*

> 'Blow the winds, I, O!
> Make the good ship go!
> I'll sail no more
> From England's shore,
> Ten thousand miles away!'

B. Thrower sung it.

"A general sing-song, led by Joseph on the banjo, brought the evening to a close, and Mr. Martindale, the farm bailiff, came and spoke a few words about the good harvest of that year, and hoped everyone had had a jolly evening. A big

Yes. Then we had to get to our homes, in the dark and across fields. I believe that was the last Harvest Home at Windlestone."[1]

And now the sneezing and the laughter and the songs have died away, and the banjo has thrummed itself to silence.

It was not only in the fields and barns that the people made merry, but in the streets of towns and on the banks of smoky rivers, and even in the bowels of the earth. The winning of coal from a new colliery was celebrated with much the same joyful ceremony as the garnering of the last sheaf of corn. A procession with banners escorted the first waggons from the pit-head to the staiths, cannon were fired, bells were rung, uniformed bands played "Weel may the keel row," and all the people cheered. Sometimes a "grand subterranean ball" was held, when the pit was illuminated with lamps and candles and, after each visitor had hewed a piece of coal in memory of the occasion, the pitmen and their lasses enjoyed cold punch and biscuits and "the pleasures of the ball-room."[2]

Not only the end or the beginning of work was celebrated in song, but the holidays too. All England has heard of Blaydon, on the Durham outskirts of Newcastle, not for the industries, "all dirty and some odoriferous,"[3] which are responsible for its existence, but for the races which have given it its gay and melodious distinction.

"Aa went to Blaydon races, 'twas on the ninth of June
Eighteen hundred and sixty-two on a summer's afternoon.
Aa tyuk the bus fra Balmbra's[4] and she was heavy laden,
Away we went doon Collingwood Street that's on the road to Blaydon.

Chorus:

Oh! lads ye shud a' seen us gannin
Passin' the folks upon the road just as they were stannin.
Thor wis lots o lads and lasses there, aall wi smilin faces,
Gannin alang the Scotswood Road to see the Blaydon Races."

The origin of these horseraces is obscure. They probably first took place in the eighteenth century as one of those

[1] Personal recollections of Miss Lily Brown. The "jolly refrain" is from an old music-hall song.
[2] Sykes, Vol. II, p. 243.   [3] Hodgkin, *op. cit.*, p. 67.
[4] A public house.

innumerable "flapper meetings" held all over England at that time, which were eventually condemned by law. They received a fresh lease of life in 1861, and thereafter appear to have been held irregularly, sometimes at Blaydon and sometimes at Stella. There is a picture of these races which can be seen today in a hotel in Newcastle and which illustrates well the boisterous, care-free spirits of a hundred and thirty years ago. The names of many of the characters have come down to us. They smack of Smollett and Borrow, of Cruickshank and Hogarth, of the days when individuals, blackguards and otherwise, distinguished with sobriquets crude and vivid as their personalities, fought and swore and laughed and danced and swindled their ways through life. In the foreground is "George the Plunger" with his whippet, and "Cuddy Billy," complete with "cuddy," backchatting with "Big Ben" from Prudhoe. The "Strolling Mike" from Gateshead is seen with his Punch and Judy show. "Scrapper Anderson" is rolling up his sleeves for a fight, and the "Swalwell Cat" is fleecing pigeons in the three-card trick. And there, crowned with flowers like any May-morn maiden, is Ned White, one of Hawks's toughest "Blacks," dancing with Nanny the Mazer and Billy Lauder the Piper.

There is an amusing story about this Ned White. "Ye knaa Ned and other twenty-fower o' Hawks's cheps went oot te the Peninsular War, whor Wellin'ton was, ye knaa. Se, as we wor hevin' a gill[1] tegithor, aa says te him, 'Ned, d'ye mind when ye wor in the Peninsular War?' 'Aa should think aa de,' says he. 'Did ye ever faall in wi' Wellin'ton?' says aa. 'Wellin'-ton!' says he; 'wey, man, aa knaa'd him. Wey, just the day afore the battle o' Watterloo he sent for me. "Ned," he says, "tyek yor twenty-fower men," he says, "an' gan up and shift them Frenchmen off the top of yon hill." "Aall reet," says aa, "but it winnit tyek all the twenty-fower," aa says. "Ah! but it's Napoleon's crack regiment," he says; "ye'd better tyek planty." "Aall reet," aa says, "we'll suen shift 'em." Se doon aa cums te the lads, an' aa says: "Noo, ma lads, Wellin'ton wants us te shift yon Frenchmen off the top of yon hill." "Aall reet," they says. "Heor, Bob Scott," a says, "hoo many Frenchmen are thor up yondor?" "Aboot fower hundred," he says. "Hoo mony on us will it tyek te shift them?" aa axes.

[1] A drink.

"Oh! ten," says Bob. "Wey, we'll tyek fifteen," aa says, "just
te humour the aad man." "Aall reet," they says. Se off we set
at the double alang the lonnen;[1] but just as we torned the
corner at the foot of the hill whe should we meet but Bonni-
part himsell on a lily-white horse, wi' a cocked hat on. "Whor
are ye off te, Ned?" says he. "Wey, te shift yon Frenchmen
off yon hill!" "What!" he says; "wey, that's my crack regiment," he says. "Nivvor mind that," aa says; "Wellin'ton
says we hev te shift 'em, and shifted they'll be, noo!" "Ye're
coddin,'" says he. "Ne coddin' aboot it," aa says; "we'll suen
shift them off." Aa says, "Cum by!" "Had on!"[2] he says, and
he gallops reet up the hill te them and shoots oot, "Gan back,
ma lads, gan back! Heor's Ned White from Haaks's and his
twenty-fower lads comin' up te shift ye. Ye hevvent a
happorth of chance!" And back they went.'"[3]

Such were the devil-me-care, swaggering, chapleted rascals
who, with their strapping lasses, "aall wi' smilin' faces," once
took the bus from Balmbra's on a summer's afternoon.

And it is the song that has made them live, this gay song
that was written for us by poor George Ridley, a native of
Gateshead, who had started to work in the pits at the age of
eight and was permanently injured in an accident at the age
of eighteen. Thenceforward he supported himself as a singer,
and eventually a composer, of Tyneside songs. He died at the
early age of thirty.

The last of these meetings was held at Stella Haughs in
1916 and finished in a style almost worthy of Ned and George
the Plunger and Billy Lauder and all the rest, for, dissatisfied
with the result of one of the races, the crowd tore up the track
fittings and tossed them into the river.[4]

At Hamsterley and Byers Green, Winlaton and Swalwell,
and elsewhere, there were regular "hoppings," when the
smiths of the iron works or the local pitmen wrestled and ran
races against each other, and grinned for tobacco, and danced
for ribbons with the ruddy farm-girls of the neighbourhood.
These annual fairs were famous for their great hilarity. "No
one is so happy as we," sang the revellers:

---

[1] Lane.   [2] Hold on.   [3] *M.C.*, Vol. I, p. 141.
[4] I am indebted to Mr. Arthur Wilson, News Editor of the *Newcastle Chronicle,* for most of the details about these races.

> *"No courtier fine,*
> *Nor grave divine,*
> *That's got the whole he wishes, O,*
> *Will ever be*
> *So blithe as we,*
> *With all their loaves and fishes, O."*[1]

But all songs were not hilarious. Nostalgia and love, in this county as elsewhere, were the themes of many of them. "O it's home, boys, home," sang the sailors, "it's home I'd like to be."

> *"Home, boys, home, in the old countree,*
> *Where the ash and the oak and the bonny ivy tree*
> *Are all growing green in the North Countree.*
>
> *O, if it is a girl she shall wear a golden ring,*
> *And if it is a boy, he shall fight for his king;*
> *With his breeches all so white and his jacket all so blue,*
> *He shall toddle up the rigging as his daddy used to do.*
>
> *But its home, boys, home . . ."*[2]

Home, home, home! The eternal lament of the exile, of the sailor at sea and the "North-country lass, who to London did pass, although with her nature it did not agree," and of the lad who 'listed for a soldier. This last was the theme of an old song, very popular in the mining districts some sixty years ago.

> *"Oh! now my love has 'listed,*
> *And I for him will rove;*
> *I'll write his name on every tree*
> *That grows in yonder grove,*
> *Where the huntsman he does hollow,*
> *And the hounds do sweetly cry,*
> *To remind me of my ploughboy*
> *Until the day I die."*[3]

Huntsmen and hounds, if they cry not so sweetly, strike a merrier note from Weardale, where the chasing of hares was a favourite pastime a hundred years ago and was celebrated there in a song with a rough and jolly metre suitable to the district.

> *"There's no joys can compare*
> *To the hunting the hare,*
> *In the morning, in the morning,*
> *Being fine and pleasant weather.*

---

[1] *M.C.*, Vol. IV.   [2] *Notes and Queries*, Ninth Series, Vol. XII.
[3] *M.C.*, Vol. V, p. 439.

With the horses and the hounds
We will sport upon the grounds,
Sing tantara, hurra, and tantara;
Brave boys, we will follow!"[1]

But even parliamentary elections provided excuses for singing. The most famous Durham song (if we except the Tyneside "Keel Row" and "Blaydon Races") owes its revival, if not its origin, to the election of 1761, when Robert Shafto, Esq., of Whitworth, alias "Bonny Bobbie Shafto," was returned as first of the two Members for the county. Mary Bellasis, the heiress to Brancepeth Castle, died of love for this handsome Robert, who favoured another heiress, Anne Duncombe, and married her. His portrait, painted by Reynolds, is still at Whitworth in the possession of his descendant.

Although some of the words seem applicable to an election, and the verses may have been written for this occasion and to put into the mouth of Miss Bellasis, it is probable that the song itself is much older than the eighteenth century. The family, originally Northumbrian, was celebrated in Border warfare, and the name and the air may owe its origin to these remoter times. Here are some of the verses:

"Bobby Shafto's gone to sea,
Silver buckles at his knee,
He'll come back and marry me,
Bonny Bobbie Shafto.

Bobby Shafto's bright and fair,
Combing down his yellow hair;
He's my ain for evermair,
Bonny Bobbie Shafto.

Bobby Shafto went to Court,
All in gold and silver wrought,
Like a grandee, as he ought,
Bonny Bobbie Shafto.

Bobby Shafto rode a race,
Well I mind his bonny face,
Won it in a tearing pace,
Bonny Bobbie Shafto.

Bobby Shafto throws his gold
Right and left like knights of old,
Now we're left out in the cold,
Bonny Bobbie Shafto."

---

[1] *Weardale Men and Manners,* by J. R. Featherston.

Another verse, which was doubtless added on the occasion of
Bobbie's marriage, has a different consonance and a charm of
its own:

> Bobby Shafto's gettin' a bairn
> For to dangle in his airm,
> In his airm and on his knee,
> Bonny Bobbie Shafto.

With his racing and his gold-throwing Bobby seems to have
been a lively member of a lively family, not unworthy of his
relative, Mr. Jennison Shafto, who won a bet of a thousand
guineas by riding fifty miles in well under two hours, a feat
which he performed by using ten horses. "Five-Bottle Mark"
was another bonny Shafto, whose distinction is revealed by his
gallant sobriquet and is celebrated in a neat Latin epitaph in
Whitworth Parish Church.[1]

In 1818 there was a terrible affray in Stanhope between the
keepers of the Bishop of Durham—"the fat man of Oakland,"[2] as the song called him—and the Weardale lead-
miners. These had come to regard the shooting of the "bonny
moor hen" as their particular prerogative. Times were hard,
the grouse were useful both for the pot and for converting
into cash, and, when the Bishop attempted to interfere and
protect his birds, his action was bitterly resented. At length,
on the arrest of two of the poachers, a gang of their fellows
pursued them and their captors and overtook them at an inn.
The subsequent battle was conducted with brutal ferocity on
the part of the miners, who kicked the keepers as they lay on
the ground and battered them with the stocks of their guns.
One of the Bishop's men had his eye knocked out, three others
were severely injured, and the result was the rescue of the

[1] Vir erat in omni amabilis,
Et Exemplum
Pietatis erga Deum,
Liberalitatis in Egenos,
Hilaritatis inter Amicos,
Humanitatis erga omnes,
Facilius laudand. quam imitandum,
Posteris reliquit.
(Surtees, Vol. II, p. 292.)

[2] Auckland.

prisoners and the complete discomfiture of the episcopal officers.[1]

The story of this battle was related in a ballad still popular in the North, called "The Bonny Moor Hen."

"You brave lads of Weardale, I pray lend an ear,
The account of a battle you quickly shall hear,
That was fought by the miners, so well you may ken,
By claiming a right to their bonny moor hen.

Oh, this bonny moor hen, as it plainly appears,
She belonged to their fathers some hundreds of years;
But the miners of Weardale are all valiant men,
They will fight till they die for their bonny moor hen. . . .

There's the fat man of Oakland, and Durham the same,
Lay claim to the moors, likewise to the game;
They sent word to the miners they'd have them to ken
They would stop them from shooting the bonny moor hen.

Oh, these words they were carried to Weardale with speed,
Which made the poor miners to hang down their heads;
But sent them answer, they would have them to ken,
They would fight till they died for their bonny moor hen. . . ."

And so on.

But better known to the English public at large than the Moor Hen, or even perhaps than Bobby Shafto, is Elsie Marley.

"Elsie Marley's grown so fine,
She'll not get up to feed the swine."

We have, many of us, read this couplet in our childhood with the rest of our nursery rhymes, without caring or suspecting that they formed part of a song in honour of Mistress Alice Marley, the most popular wife of the innkeeper at Picktree, near Chester-le-Street. The song was called "Di' ye Ken Elsie Marley, honey?" and one of the verses ran:

"The pitmen and the keelmen trim,
They drink bumbo[2] made of gin,
And for the dance they do begin
To the tune of Elsie Marley, honey."[3]

Poor Elsie, being in a fever, escaped unnoticed from her

---

[1] *The Bonny Moor Hen*, by W. M. Egglestone. (Republished by T. H. Egglestone. Weardale, 1933.)

[2] Gin and water and sugar.   [3] *M.C.*, Vol. I, p. 399.

bed, and, wandering across a field in a delirious state, fell into an old coal-pit and was drowned.

The county of Durham can produce no Mozart, but it can lay claim to a link with Haydn. This was provided by William Shield, born at Whickham, near Gateshead, Master of the King's Music in 1817, and friend of the great Austrian composer, who made his acquaintance in London in 1791. Shield, who was at one time musical director at Covent Garden and was the author of operas and of numerous songs, is supposed to have written the tune of "Auld Lang Syne." But this claim is disputed by the Scots, who assert that he borrowed an old Lowland air. He was, at any rate, a considerable musician. The last movement of his "Trio for Strings," "a particularly charming work," is a very early instance of a composition in that rare 5/4 time which was much later immortalised by Tchaikowsky in his "Symphonie Pathétique."[1] Shield now shares the grave of Clementi in the musicians' corner of Westminster Abbey.

Not content with claiming from the haughty Scots their greatest national hero and their most popular national air, their old enemies of the Palatinate have also pretensions to another well-known song, generally regarded as pure and perfect Scots—"Ye Banks and Braes o' Bonnie Doon." It is their greatest national poet, Burns himself, who has betrayed them in this instance. He wrote his famous words to fit a tune called "The Caledonian Hunt's Delight," and, according to one of his letters, this tune was composed in the following manner. A certain Mr. Miller said one day to his musical friend, Mr. Clarke: "I wish I could compose a Scots air." And Clarke answered cheerfully: "Stick to the black notes, accentuate the rhythm, and you will, my boy." So, a few days later, Miller brought Clarke the rudiments of a melody which were fashioned by the expert into what is now the tune of "Ye Banks and Braes." Now, this Stephen Clarke, who was editor of the *Scots Musical Museum*, was a Durham man, born in the county.

Nicholas Kilburn, conductor of the Sunderland Philharmonic and of the Bishop Auckland Musical Societies, with his enthusiasm, his friendship with the great artists of his time,

[1] Lecture by Dr. Bridge. (*D.U.J.*, March 11th, 1914.)

and his gracious manners, did much to arouse the interest of his county in good music. One of his sons played the viola in the London Symphony Orchestra; the other was reputed to be the best amateur performer on the clarinet in England. Those who were lucky enough to hear them will long remember the trios played by father and sons—piano, violin and clarinet—Mozart and Haydn and Beethoven, played as one can seldom hear them played in private, in the drawing-room of a small mining town. It was to Nicholas Kilburn that Elgar dedicated his "Music Makers."

But most of the music composed in the Bishoprick was of a religious character and the work of the organists and precentors of the Cathedral. Of the precentors the best known is J. B. Dykes, the author of many hymn-tunes, including the famous "Eternal Father, strong to save" and "Jesu, lover of my soul."[1] He was a warm supporter of the Oxford Movement, on account of which he was hardly treated by his Low-Church Bishop, Baring. Philip Armes, a later precentor, and a typical composer of Victorian Church music, wrote the tune of another well-known hymn, "Jesus shall reign." He was Professor of Music in Durham University.

Dykes was not the only musician to have difficulties with the ecclesiastical authorities. Some of the organists also fell foul of their superiors. John Brimley, who was Master of the Choristers at the time of the Rising of the Northern Earls, was present at Mass in the Cathedral "and did divers times help to sing Salves and played on the organs, and went in procession, as others did, after the cross."[2] But he expressed his contrition and was allowed to retain his post as a Protestant organist until his death. Richard Hutchinson, though he wrote one or two anthems, was better known for the "frequent haunting of alehouses and divers other evil demeanours; and especially for the breaking of the head of Toby Brooking, one of the singing men of this church, with a candlestick."[3] He was sacked, reinstated, and sacked again, for he appears to have been constitutionally incapable of even a pretence of that

---

[1] The tune of this second hymn is still known as "Hollinside" after the name of Dykes's house. The house was originally, and more beautifully, called "Buck's Hill."

[2] From a letter from Brimley's successor, William Brown.

[3] Minute of a Chapter meeting.

"sober, quiet and religious deportment of himself" which the
Dean, not unnaturally, required of him. James Heseltine, not
so turbulent but probably more disagreeable, had a row with
one of the canons, refused to apologise and vented his rage on
his own music, most of which he destroyed. But these three
are exceptions in a long, respectable line of organists who
contributed their share of anthems, responses and services,
some of which are still sung at Durham and elsewhere. The
collection of music manuscripts in the Cathedral Library is
almost unique and includes "a very fine set of choir-books,
eight large folios, written with diamond-headed notes in a
noble seventeenth-century hand. They contain music by
Parsons, Shepperd, Byrd and others and are the only existing
authority for Byrd's 'Great Service.' "[1]

II. GRACES

"Laudemus . . . homines pulchritudinis studium habentes."
VULGATE (Inscribed on choirstalls in Durham Cathedral).

As a frontispiece to the fourth, and last, volume of Surtees's
History there is a line-engraving from a water-colour of Raby
by Turner. The Earl of Darlington and his hounds and
huntsmen are in the foreground, the deer gaze mildly from
the middle distance, and the castle rises beyond, magnificently
illuminated by a stormy sky. There is a gentler, more con-
ventional view of Gibside,[2] from a water-colour by the same
artist, in the second volume of the *History*; and there is a
grand panorama of Hilton Castle with sweeping foreground
and rolling sky, taken when the place was no ruin with a
dejected public tennis-court in front of it, as it now appears,[3]
but with all the sweet appurtenances of a civilised epoch—the
well-knit house, the winding drive, the flock of sheep, the
loaded waggon with its plodding horses, the countrymen with
their sickles at work in the cornfields, and a rustic pair in the

---

[1] Information kindly supplied by the Very Rev. P. H. Cecil, Dean
of British Honduras and formerly Precentor and Sacrist of Durham
Cathedral.

[2] Surtees, Vol. II, p. 254. This water-colour is in the collection of
the Earl of Strathmore.

[3] Since this was written, the castle has been taken over by the Office
of Works.

foreground binding sheaves. This engraving is also from a water-colour by Turner.[1]

Other illustrations in these great volumes, even after we have made allowances (if we think necessary) for the euphemistic pencils of the painters and engravers, speak to us too tenderly for our comfort of a beauty and a grace that is dead. The grounds of Lambton, where the pellucid river flows past umbrageous banks, bear as yet no stains from smoke and chemicals, no suggestion of anachronism and decay; while the dreamy, rather woolly scenes of Dinsdale and Sockburn speak of the evening calm and peace, not of a backwater, but of what was once a normal English countryside. The cattle are reflected in the still waters of the Tees or lie ruminating on the banks, the young herd-boy is stretched beside them in a quaint beaver hat, and elegant ladies with extended parasols lean gracefully against a five-barred gate. Hutchinson has, in his history, a view of Axwell Park which is so staggeringly unlike its present condition as effectively to remove the pain of comparison, while in the work of Mackenzie and Ross there is a reproduction of Darlington Market-Place of which only the spire of the church can be identified today. Yet this book was published little more than a hundred years ago.

While Turner and Cotman (notably in his water-colour of the Cathedral[2]) have perpetuated the beauties of our county, we are forced to confess that there are no great painters indigenous to Durham. Of the five whose names here follow, Francis Place, a member of the family which succeeded that of Surtees as the owners of Dinsdale, was, although an amateur, probably the most important. Charles II asked him to paint the ships of the Royal Navy, promising a pension of £500 a year, but Place declined the honour. He preferred to follow "the roving life which he loved," to paint and to etch and to experiment with the manufacture of porcelain, accord-

[1] Surtees, Vol. II, p. 20. This water-colour also belongs to Lord Strathmore. The original pencil drawings, from which these three water-colours were made, are in the *Raby Sketchbook* (Turner Bequest, No. 156) in the British Museum. I am indebted to the courtesy of Mr. E. C. Murray, Assistant Keeper at the British Museum, for information about these drawings and about the water-colour by Cotman mentioned on p. 208.

[2] Now in the British Museum Print Room.

ing to his fancy. He "paid a strict attention to nature," says
Surtees, "and his mind was illumined by many a ray of true
genius."[1] Walpole praises him[2] and Bryan[3] opines that he must
have been a good painter, but his works are now forgotten.

William Bewick, who was born at Darlington (and must
not be confused with the famous Thomas, of whom he was no
relation) was "inspired with a passion for the grandiose and
historic."[4] The little Quaker money-making town was ill-
provided for the satisfaction of such an enthusiastic aspiration,
but an aunt near Barnard Castle came to the young man's
rescue and, encouraged by her, he left for London and
became the pupil of the unhappy Haydon. Thus it was not
long before Jacob was meeting Rachel on a canvas ten feet by
seven, and the girl's sweet face of unripened innocence so
delighted Keats that he prophesied that Bewick "would do
some of the tenderest things in art."[5] Unfortunately, the days
for these great pictures were passing. People preferred to
admire their own physiognomies rather than enjoy the con-
templation of a gigantic biblical or historical scene. Bewick
was forced to prostitute his art "to the gratification of personal
vanity,"[6] and his next great work was, apparently, never completed. Constantly in pecuniary difficulties, like his master
Haydon, he seems to have been a man of rare sensibilities and
intelligence, and doubtless deserving the friendship of the
most famous characters of his day. It is for this that we must
envy him now, for the list of his friends and acquaintances is
a staggering one. What should we not give to have stood in
the shoes of this little Darlington upholsterer's son and shaken
hands and talked and breakfasted, as he did, with Wordsworth, Shelley, Keats, Hazlitt, Haydon, Lawrence, Wilkie,
Horace Smith, Miss Mitford and Sir Walter Scott!

One would not expect a gentleman who had been born in
the Bailey at Durham, that genteelly beautiful and unosten-
tatious provincial street, to marry a Russian princess, to paint
the portrait of Simon Bolivar, to fight at Corunna, to be
decorated by the Shah of Persia, to be knighted by three

---

[1] Surtees, Vol. III, p. 238.
[2] Walpole's *Catalogue of Engravers* (1786), p. 93.
[3] Bryan's *Dictionary of Painters*.
[4] *D.N.B.*   [5] Longstaffe, Vol. II, p. 348.
[6] His own words. (See Longstaffe, Vol. II, p. 346.)

ruling princes,[1] to cover the walls of the Admiralty of St.
Petersburg with vast panoramic battlepieces and to be officially
appointed Historical Painter to the Czar. Yet this was the
splendid destiny of Robert Ker Porter, brother of the
authoresses Jane and Anna Maria and friend of Turner and
Girtin, who flashes like an exotic meteor across our dark
northern sky. He travelled all over the world and wrote and
illustrated a huge book on his adventures, was lavish with his
money, a magnificent horseman, and, in brief, whatever he
attempted—which was most things—he seems to have done
grandly and he seems to have done well. There is a touch of
the Renaissance about this princely, dashing figure, "distinguished alike in arts, in diplomacy, in war and in literature."[2]
Yet he remained the idol of his family. "My beloved and
protecting brother," said Jane. There is a monument to him
in Bristol Cathedral (for his brother lived in that town), but
why not in Durham? If only for his extraordinary difference,
he should be remembered amongst her sons.

Poor Mr. J. W. Ewbank, member of the Royal Scottish
Academy, was not so very different from many other artists,
successful and otherwise. After painting two great pictures,
whose contrasting subjects tickle our fancy—"The Entry of
Alexander the Great into Babylon" and "The Entry of
George IV into Edinburgh"—his "moral firmness," in the
words of a pompous Victorian, "gave way before a gradual
but rapidly progressive addiction to convivial pleasures,"[3] and
he died in the Infirmary at Sunderland in degradation and
abject poverty.[4] His daughter, who, as a pretty child of three,
was represented, by another artist, in a white dress, playing
with wallflowers and honeysuckle, was nineteen times in prison
before she had reached middle age.

Finally we must mention Sir William Eden, who was
hailed in his day as one of the leading painters in water-
colour, but has now been forgotten.

We have come to the end of our Durham painters, but,
although he was a Northumbrian, we must not omit to mention Thomas Bewick, the greatest English engraver on wood,

[1] The King of Sweden, the King of Württemberg and the Prince
Regent.
[2] *M.C.,* Vol. V.   [3] Fordyce, Vol. II, p. 458.
[4] He was born either at Newcastle or at Gateshead.

for he was a frequent visitor to our county and lived a great part of his life at Gateshead, where he died. It was at Wycliffe, on the Yorkshire bank of the Tees, that he made the first drawings of his *History of British Birds*. In his designs for bookplates he found a favourite subject in Jarrow and its old church, and he made the woodcuts of the Roman altars and of the episcopal arms which illustrate Hutchinson's *History of Durham*.

But the most distinguished artist born within the strict confines of the county, the only one to achieve a lasting reputation, whose works are today more prized than ever, was no painter, but a zealous Baptist, who was born at Stockton and there wrote *A Scriptural Illustration of the Doctrine of Regeneration*. But he later produced *The Cabinet-Maker and Upholsterer's Drawing-Book*. His name was Thomas Sheraton.

Two very learned gentlemen, both of whom have an intimate knowledge of the county, were recently asked what they considered to be (apart from ecclesiastical glories) the most outstanding and extraordinary object within its borders. One of them replied, "The Glass Vase at Castle Eden"; the other, "The Bowes Museum."

The vase, $7\frac{1}{2}$ inches high, made of green glass and elaborately decorated, is in perfect condition. It was discovered by a workman in 1775 on the estate of Mr. Burdon, its "mouth applied to a human skull, so near the surface as to leave the bottom of the vase exposed in the gutter of the hedge."[1] The estate has now been sold and the vase has been presented to the British Museum. It probably dates from the sixth century, and is of the type known as a "claw-beaker," because of the hollow glass lobes that adorn the exterior. In the case of this particular beaker these claws are decorated with an applied crimped strip of blue glass. It was doubtless of foreign manufacture and is regarded as "probably the finest and most perfect specimen [of glass found in Saxon graves] in the country."[2]

The Bowes Museum is another and a longer story. On the

[1] Surtees, Vol. I, p. 44.
[2] I am indebted for this description to Mr. K. L. S. Bruce-Mitford of the British Museum. (See also Professor G. Baldwin Brown, *The Arts in Early England*, Vol. IV, pp. 483-484.)

fringe of the little market town of Barnard Castle the traveller, preparing for the wild northern beauties of Teesdale, is astounded to perceive an enormous terraced and turreted French château. So completely out of place does this piece of Gallic magnificence appear in these rough English surroundings that he momentarily shuts his eyes, believing that he is the victim of some hallucination. But his senses have not betrayed him. This is, indeed, a translation of the Tuileries, and it was built by a Frenchman, and it is 300 feet long and 120 feet broad, and yet it is not in Paris, but in Barnard Castle, County Durham. It is the Bowes Museum, and it houses one of the finest collections of objects of art in England. And this is how it came to be built.

Mary Eleanor, only child and heiress of George Bowes, became, in 1767, the wife of John Lyon, ninth Earl of Strathmore, and was succeeded, as owner of Streatlam and Gibside, by her eldest son, John, the tenth Earl. This John married Mary Milner, the beautiful daughter of a gardener of Staindrop, but only on the day before his death, which occurred in 1820. Nine years earlier their son, John Bowes, had been born, and it was to him that his father left all his English estates, the Scottish property and earldom passing to his uncle.[1] This Mr. Bowes, a jolly, sporting country squire and a Member of Parliament, was also a patron of the arts, and as he was, besides, an extremely rich man and the owner of two magnificent houses, he was a fine parti for any English girl. But his fancy fell on a little French actress, whose stage name was Mademoiselle Delorme, and he married her. In private life she was Joséphine Benoîte. She painted pictures, had dirty finger-nails and jet-black belladonaed eyes, and was known as the Comtesse Montalbo; but when her husband brought her to England everyone called her "Madam Bowes." As Mr. and Madam Bowes had no children, they delighted in travelling and in the collection of works of art. This collection, at first housed in Paris, they determined to transfer to the neighbourhood of their English home, on account of the unsettled state of France. Thus the building arose of which Madam Bowes, whose idea it had been to found this museum for the benefit of the English public, chose one of her com-

[1] In 1885, on the death of John Bowes without issue, the Durham estates reverted to Lord Strathmore.

patriots to be the architect. She died in 1874, leaving all her
personal property to the museum, to which her husband,
eleven years later, bequeathed £125,000. With a few exceptions, the contents of this great building (as well as the
château itself) are the gift of Mr. John Bowes and "Madam,"
his wife.

The visitor to this strange exotic mansion is reminded of
the Wallace Collection, to which, indeed, in variety and size
the Bowes Museum is superior, though its contents are not so
rare. But so much has been bequeathed by those generous
donors that it has been found possible to eliminate, secrete or
bury the rubbish and still to retain a large collection at a level
of excellence which, if not quite first-rate, is not far removed
from it. This long-demanded work of Augean purification is
being undertaken at last by the present curator, Mr. Thomas
Wake. Already the changes he has wrought are marvellous.
Those who knew the museum in the old days, full, so it
seemed at a casual glance, of nothing but trash, will wonder
at its present appearance. For it is a curious fact that the
blatant and the third-rate will always attract more attention
than excellence, whether it be in pictures or in furniture or in
men; will overpower it and shoulder it out and swamp it. We
are blinded to beauty and deafened to reason by the monstrous
intrusion of ugliness and the pretentious vociferation of noise.
But now—not, alas! from the world, but from the public
rooms of the Bowes Museum—the swanks have been removed
and order and seemliness have come into their own. At least
half the nine hundred and odd pictures have been banished;
the stuffed birds, with a few exceptions placed in a new
children's room, have disappeared from sight; and the furniture has been arranged in separate apartments, according to
the century which it illustrates. One of the loveliest of the
new rooms represents a chapel. The pictures in this room—
Dutch, German, Italian and Spanish—are all of sacred subjects
and all remarkable for their beauty or interest, while a fine
fifteenth-century German altar-piece, half carved and half
painted, occupies the place of honour. The collection of china
is very large, and the nausea produced by the vulgarities of
Louis-Philippe and Napoleon III—they illustrate their period,
no doubt—is quickly counteracted by the predominating charm
and grace of the remainder: by Chelsea and Bow, by the

cornflowers of Angoulême, by Chantilly and Arras, and some lovely early Sèvres. Rich Delft, in red and yellow, gold and green, is a splendid and delightful surprise—at least to this writer and perhaps some others equally ignorant, who fondly imagined that Delft is always blue.

There is a lovely altar screen designed by Wren and carved by William Emmett, some fine French furniture and needlework, glass, Roman antiquities, a huge and noble Durham Shorthorn painted by John Glover, letters from Walter Scott, clocks and dolls, a sweet terra-cotta maiden from Versailles, and possibly the largest collection of tapestries outside London. The portraits—not very good ones—of the foundress and her husband are placed in the new "Bowes Room," where they are suitably surrounded with their own boulle and brass and majolica and lapis lazuli—the furniture with which they furnished their Paris home. She is a kindly, prim, determined little person, with a flowing sash, a large dog, a Louis-something table and a coat of arms. He sits on a boulder, as obviously English as his wife is clearly French, his heavy, good-humoured head fringed with whiskers, gaiters on his legs, a gun in his hand, a dog at his feet, and pheasants and hares strewed about him. "Ah, yes!" exclaimed Monsignor Witham when he saw this portrait in the museum. "That's my old friend Bowes, sure enough; dressed like his own gamekeeper and surrounded with more game than ever he shot in his life." These two old friends were neighbours, for Witham, a Roman Catholic whose liberality to his co-religionists had earned him his title from the Pope, lived at Lartington, just over the Yorkshire border. They both enjoyed life and were both gifted with a strong, robust individuality. One night, after a good dinner at Streatlam, Monsignor was endeavouring to make his way upstairs to bed, followed by his host and escorted by the butler with a candle. At a turn in the stairs, after vainly endeavouring to walk through the wall, he cried out in an agony of apprehension: "Bowes, Bowes! What have you done with your staircase? It's turned the wrong way round!"[1]

Of the remaining pictures in the museum the most remarkable are those which belong to the Spanish school and which include three Goyas and an El Greco. The little prison scene

[1] Told by the butler in question to a lady who is still alive.

by Goya is well known to the frequenters of the National
Gallery, to which it was lent for several years, but the superb
portrait of the artist's brother is by no means so familiar.[1]
Herrera the Elder catches the eye, and Valdes Leal, and two
fine bishops by Fernandez against a gold background, and a
well-painted but unconvincing Zurbaran of a monk flying
through the air—the translation of St. Francis, I believe.
There is a fine self-portrait of Francia Bigio, a lovely and
unusual *pietà* in pale greys and browns, a small Tiepolo, a
capital modern picture of two girls and a pig in a farmyard,[2]
a good Simon de Vos, a fascinating courtesan by Hogarth, an
unusual and attractive head of a young woman and of a child
with fair hair by I know not whom, and two good portraits by
Richelieu's painter, "le solennel Monsieur Philippe de Cham-
paigne." Mrs. Thrale by Reynolds—a lively, tiresome little
body, whom I saw with a scar on her forehead—has gone to
be mended. I spy too late, in the catalogue, yet other arresting
names—Fragonard and Watteau, Corot, Rousseau and Boudin
—all of whom I missed because I was blind or because they
were not visible at the time. But let the reader go and see for
himself, if he cares for pictures or china or tapestry or odd-
ments of virtu. Enough has surely been said to convince him
that here, within these marble halls, on the edge of this wild
moorland, are the most unexpected delights, and that he may
spend days wandering, with surprise and pleasure, amongst
the treasures of the Countess of Montalbo and Mr. John
Bowes.

[1] Its authenticity has been doubted.
[2] By Fischer, in the Children's Room.

Chapter XXIII

THE PEN AND THE SWORD

I. THE PEN

"He lives detached days;
He serveth not for praise;
For gold
He is not sold."

FRANCIS THOMPSON.

ONE great English poet was born in the county of Durham—
Elizabeth Barrett Browning. Another, Christopher Smart,
though not born within its boundaries, was the offspring of a
Durham family and far more closely connected with the
county than she was. A third, Francis Thompson, was educated
in it; a fourth, Byron, was married in it; two more, Wordsworth and Coleridge, lost their hearts in it; Scott frequently
visited it and dabbled in its ancient lore; while Gray delighted, as we have seen, in its romantic scenery and valued it
as the home of one of his best friends. Even Shelley has a
link with it; his biographer, Thomas Jefferson Hogg, was
born at Norton House, near Stockton. Thus this rude northern
Bishoprick, full of parsons and pitmen, has been brushed, at
any rate, by the delicate wing of the muses.

Coxhoe Hall, in the parish of Kelloe, where Elizabeth
Barrett was born, had been built by the John Burdon (no
relation of the family at Castle Eden) who afterwards bought
Hardwick, Sedgefield, and adorned it with those gallant and
graceful summer-houses which are now bescribbled and
tumbling to decay. After passing through several hands,
Coxhoe was let by Anthony Wilkinson to Mr. Barrett, who
had married a Newcastle girl and was waiting for a house to
be built for him in Herefordshire. Three years after Elizabeth
was born the Barretts left the North and Coxhoe remained
empty until it was bought by Mr. Wood, a mining engineer,
whose descendant has recently died. During the Nazi war the
house was occupied by Italian prisoners. There are some good
plaster ceilings and chimneypieces, some hideous coloured glass,

and in the derelict "backside" are stored some terrible county council tiles, with other horrors destined for new houses in the surrounding pit district. It is a sad place for lovers of Italy. About the little church of Kelloe the wind blows and beats, but there is a stillness within, where a plaque commemorates "the birth, in this parish, of Elizabeth Barrett Browning . . . a great poetess, a noble woman, a devoted wife." Let us hope that her soul took pity upon those exiles from her darling land.

There is a link between Mrs. Browning and Christopher Smart, for her husband singled out for highest praise Smart's solitary work of genius, the "Song to David." That wild *Benedicite* ranks high amongst the great poems of our language, but it was the only poem of any value which Smart wrote amongst a prodigious quantity of stuff, and Robert Browning has compared it very finely to a gorgeous chapel lying lost in a commonplace mansion. The master of this mansion was "no fool assuredly, no genius just as sure!"[1] You wander perseveringly and politely from room to room, finding each colder, stiffer, more correct than its predecessor; you are very slightly interested and very largely bored; you think you have the measure of this man—and then, suddenly, the doors are flung open and the chapel is exposed to your gaze, glittering with gold and jewels and fantastically carved with strange animals and exotic fruits. Here the inspiring chant of Adoration (not, it must be confessed, very easily understood, but all the more exciting for that) is raised by all created things. Here you listen enthralled to the singing and learn with wonder of "the rapid glede"[2] and "xiphias,"[3] of "Hermon's fragrant air" and the "pink and mottled vault" where the "opposing spirits tilt," and of the sparkling sea, where—

> *"By the coasting reader*[4] *spy'd,*
> *The silverlings*[5] *and crusions*[6] *glide*
> *For Adoration gilt."*

---

[1] *Parleyings with Certain People of Importance*, Robert Browning,
[2] The kite.   [3] The swordfish.
[4] The reader walking along the seashore, who sees these wondrous fish glittering to the glory of God.
[5] Kinds of fish with silver scales.
[6] Golden carp. (I owe the last three explanations to Gosse's *Gossip in a Library*. [Heinemann, 1913.])

Here you snuff the incense from that enchanted garden, where—

> *"The wealthy crops of whitening rice*
> *'Mongst thyine[1] woods and groves of spice,*
> *For Adoration grow;*
> *And, marshall'd in the fenced land,*
> *The peaches and pomegranates stand,*
> *Where wild carnations blow."*

Here you are snatched up by this Durham poet and translated, breathless, to an empyrean far removed indeed from Durham Industries and Durham Coalfields.

But Christopher Smart is probably best known for his acquaintance with Dr. Johnson and for that wise old man's remark about him. Poor Smart was mad, but said Johnson: "I didn't think he ought to be shut up. His infirmities were not noxious to society. He insisted on people praying with him; and I'd as lief pray with Kit Smart as with anyone else. Another charge was that he did not love clean linen, and I have no passion for it."[2] Smart had been confined to Bedlam for, literally, praying without ceasing, and it was there that he is supposed to have written his famous poem.

Born in Kent, where his father was steward to the Vane estates in that county, Christopher was educated at Durham School and spent his holidays at Raby, where the Duchess of Cleveland and Southampton (sister of the first Lord Darlington) took a fancy to the young man and granted him a pension of £40 a year for her life. He was of old Durham stock, probably of the same family as Peter Smart, the wild Puritan; and his grandmother, Margaret Gilpin, was a relation of the "Apostle of the North." So there was praying blood in him and excess of devotion; grandeur of thought and spirit, but no cool capacity to cope with the world. Moreover, he drank heavily. He married, but could not support his wife and children. Gray was shocked by his extravagant ways and fancies; Dr. Burney enquired tenderly after him; Johnson visited him in the madhouse; Garrick gave a benefit night for him; Fanny Burney described him as "one of the most unfortunate of men"; and he died, a prisoner-debtor, in

---

[1] From the tree "thuya." See Revelation xviii. 12.
[2] Boswell, *Life of Dr. Johnson,* edited by Arnold Glover, Vol. I, pp. 263-264. (J. M. Dent.)

the King's Bench. "One of the most unfortunate," certainly, this "little, smart, blacke-eyed man" who loved to romp with children and was forced to part from his own, but we cannot guess the compensation of his own genius or the comfort which he found in his delusions or beliefs. His way was hard and his misfortunes many and strong,

> *"But stronger still, in earth and air,*
> *And in the sea, the man of prayer,*
> *And far beneath the tide:*
> *And in the seat to faith assign'd,*
> *Where ask is have, where seek is find,*
> *Where knock is open wide."*[1]

As grand and noble as Kit Smart, even richer in imagery, deeper in thought and more sustained in genius, Francis Thompson, the last great English poet, owes not a little to our county, for he was educated at Ushaw. During the seven years which he spent there he was allowed to develop his own individuality and to imbibe that knowledge of the classics which later enhanced the native splendour of his diction and (unlike poor Christopher) brought him back sane and triumphant from the tremendous excursions of his fancy.

Byron did not owe us much more than the monotony of the waves breaking on the cliffs at Seaham, a possible glass of port at Rushyford, and a wedding which he bitterly regretted. He and Anne-Isabella Milbanke, who read Euclid and Conic Sections for fun, were married in her father's house at Seaham in the year of Waterloo. Six years later the place was bought from Sir Ralph Milbanke by Frances Anne, Marchioness of Londonderry, and in 1927 it was given to the County Council by the late Marquis for use as a hospital. Only a pretty chimneypiece in the drawing-room, where the marriage was celebrated, remains like a disconsolate ghost from that now forgotten day. It is impossible to fit in the shiny linoleum floor, the aspidistra and the waiting-room furniture with any memory of the moody poet. At Rushyford, where the unloving couple stopped to change horses on the way to their honeymoon at Halnaby, there still lingers, in spite of modern roads and A.A. sentry-boxes, some faint aroma of the past: at Croft may still be seen the huge and handsome Milbanke

[1] *Song to David.*

pew where the bored young bridegroom is said to have slept[1];
and in the broad corridors of Halnaby[2] itself, which until
the other day was filled with most beautiful eighteenth-
century furniture, we can well conceive the villain lord
pacing up and down and fingering a melodramatic dagger.
But from Seaham, in spite of the commemorating tablet
in its front hall, Byron, with all his greatness, and his little-
ness, has gone. As he loathed the place, perhaps it is just
as well. "Upon this dreary coast," he wrote to Moore, in
one of his brilliant and inimitable letters, "we have nothing
but county meetings and shipwrecks; and I have this day
dined upon fish, which probably dined upon the crews of
several colliers lost in the late gales. . . . My papa, Sir
Ralpho, hath recently made a speech at a Durham tax-
meeting; and not only at Durham, but here, several times
since after dinner. He is now, I believe, speaking it to himself
(I left him in the middle) over various decanters, which can
neither interrupt him nor fall asleep. . . . I must go to tea—
damn tea."[3]

For Wordsworth and Coleridge I must refer my readers to
the *Durham Company* of Dame Una Pope-Hennessy, where
they will find a charming account of the visits of both poets
to the Hutchinson brothers at Sockburn. Tucked away here
by the twisting river, Wordsworth rested from his travels
"among unknown men, in lands beyond the sea," and fell in
love with Mary Hutchinson, whom he afterwards married.
And here it was that Coleridge gazed at Sara in the moonlight, by the crumbling statue of the Worm-Conqueror
Conyers:

> *"She lean'd against the armed man,*
> *The statue of the armed Knight;*
> *She stood and listen'd to my lay,*
> *Amid the lingering light . . ."*[4]

And while the brother poets meditated and wooed and wrote,
the brother farmers gathered in their crops and coursed the
hares through the long, lush grass.

[1] *The Field*, November 18th, 1933. Letter from William Fawcett.
[2] In Yorkshire.
[3] *The Works of Lord Byron. Letters and Journals*, Vol. III, p. 176.
(Murray, 1899.)
[4] *Love*, by S. T. Coleridge. Written at Sockburn.

Scott we have met already, watching the pretty girls dance in the Assembly Rooms at Durham, and we shall hear of him again when we come to Robert Surtees. One of Gray's best friends, Dr. Wharton, we have seen, through the poet's eyes, at Old Park, delighting in his chickens and ducklings. Another was Richard Stonhewer, whose reverend father, of the same name, used to drive a coach and four black horses about his parish of Houghton-le-Spring.

We have left, for our last two singers, an ill-matched couple indeed, yet both of them with a touch of the true fire: Barnaby Barnes and Frederick William Faber. Barnes, the son of the Bishop of Durham, lived much of his life in our county and is buried there. He was a typical Elizabethan—swashbuckler, lover, would-be poisoner and religious enthusiast. Shakespeare knew him, and he is believed to be the prototype of Parolles in *All's Well that Ends Well*. In his preface to *A Divine Centurie of Spirituall Sonnets* there is some superb stuff with the unmistakable stamp and ring of that great age. "And if any man feele in himselfe," he wrote, "by the secret fire of immortall enthusiasme, the learned motions of strange and divine passions of spirite; let him refine and illuminate his numerous Muses with the most sacred splendour of the Holy Ghost: and then he shall finde, that as human furie maketh a man lesse than a man, and the very same with wilde, unreasonable beastes; so divine rage and sacred instinct of a man maketh more than man, and leadeth him from his base terrestiall estate, to walke above the starres with angelles immortally."[1]

Frederick William Faber was as unmistakably Victorian as Barnes was Elizabethan. Friend of Wordsworth and of Newman, he was first a clergyman in the Church of England, but was converted to the Roman Catholic faith and became, eventually, Superior of the London Oratory. He had been partly educated at the Grammar School at Bishop Auckland, where his father was secretary to Bishop Barrington. "I do not say you are wrong," said Wordsworth, when Faber announced his intention of accepting a country rectory, "but England loses a poet."[2] She gained, however, some beautiful

---

[1] "Barnabe Barnes," by Madeleine Hope Dodds, *Arch. Ael.*, Fourth Series, Vol. XXIV.
[2] *D.N.B.*

hymns, which are still sung "to welcome the pilgrims of the night."

In considering the literary and intellectual history of Durham we are struck by two aspects of it which grace our county with an individual and unexpected distinction. We are surprised by the number of brilliant women associated with the Bishoprick and by its excellence in mathematicians. Besides Mrs. Browning, there were at least seven gifted females, to whom we must at any rate pay a passing tribute of admiration; and we must also mention six remarkable men who gained their reputation in mathematics or astronomy.

Tall, dark and beautiful, Jane Porter, who was born in the Bailey at Durham, would rise every morning at four o'clock to write and to read. While still a child she had read the whole of the *Faerie Queene*, and as she grew up her stately and abstracted air earned her the nickname of "La Penserosa." Her first novel, *Thaddeus of Warsaw*, was praised by Kosciusko and ran into many editions. In 1810, some time after she had left the North, she published *The Scottish Chiefs*, a story of Wallace, more widely read than any other romance before the days of Scott, which contained passages of "terrific sublimity," was translated into German and Russian, and was banned from France by the orders of Napoleon. Her sister, Anna Maria, "L'Allegra" (for she was pretty, blonde and gay), wrote *Artless Tales* at the age of fourteen, and her chief work, *The Hungarian Brothers*, is described as full of vivacity.

In the same year (1776) as Jane, Elizabeth Smith was born at Burn Hall, a mile or two from Durham. She died, exhausted by the exercise of her extraordinarily varied talents, at the age of twenty-nine, when her namesake, Elizabeth Barrett, had just come into the world at Coxhoe. Meanwhile, during these few years, Miss Smith, according to de Quincey, had "made herself mistress of the French, the Italian, the Spanish, the Latin, the German, the Greek and the Hebrew languages. She had no inconsiderable knowledge of the Syriac, the Arabic and the Persic. She was a good geometrician and algebraist. She was a very expert musician. She drew from nature, and had an accurate knowledge of perspective."[1] She had a natural

[1] Quoted in *M.C.*, Vol. V, p. 535.

and extraordinary memory, and she rarely consulted a dictionary when engaged upon her scholarly translations. Apart from her intellectual gifts, she was a good horsewoman and a clever dressmaker; and once, when stranded in a miserable cabin in Ireland, she cooked a meal for her family without the aid of any kitchen utensil. She translated Klopstock into English, and her version of the Book of Job was described by a scholar of the period as a work "conveying more of the character and meaning of the Hebrew, with fewer departures from the idiom of the English, than any other translation whatever that we possess." In short, the extent of her knowledge appears to have been vast and only excelled by her simplicity, gentleness and humility. To judge from her portrait, she was also extremely attractive. She died of consumption.

This Smith family of Burn Hall was, not only in Elizabeth, remarkable for its high character and ability. Miss Smith's great-great-grandfather, John, Canon of Durham and Rector of Bishop Wearmouth, began an edition of the works of Bede, which was completed by his son, George, who was consecrated as non-juring "Bishop of Durham." This, described by Charles Plummer as "a truly monumental work," remained as the foundation of all later editions until it was superseded by the labours of Plummer himself.

John's brother, Joseph, was Provost of Queen's College, Oxford, which he beautified with its canopied statue of Queen Caroline; while Elizabeth's brother, Lieutenant-General Sir Charles Felix Smith, was famous for his defence of Tarifa against the French.

Dora Greenwell, sister of the archæologist and member of one of the oldest Durham families, was a deeply religious lady who, like Jane Austen, spent most of her life on a sofa and wrote works in prose and in verse which "no Christian person can read without tender satisfaction."[1] They are by no means to be despised on that account. Whittier, the American poet, praised "the singular beauty of style" of her best-known book in prose, *The Patience of Hope*, and "the strong, steady march of its argument."[2] She had met Elizabeth Browning,

[1] Poems by Dora Greenwell with a Biographical Introduction by William Darling. (Scott, 1889.)
[2] *Ibid.*

she corresponded with Christina Rossetti, and she was herself a writer of pretty, if slender, verse.

We cannot do more than briefly mention the remaining three clever women. They were Elizabeth Elstob, "the Saxon Nymph," as her contemporaries called her, who came from Foxton, near Sedgefield, and, with a knowledge of nine other languages, was the first Englishwoman to study the Anglo-Saxon tongue; Annie Ellis Raine, who, in *Sylvestra*, has written a charming account of eighteenth-century Durham from which we have frequently quoted; and, last but not least, Gertrude Bell, born at Washington, County Durham, linguist and expert in oriental affairs, traveller, archæologist and letter-writer. These seven women, with a great poetess at their head, form a cluster of feminine brilliance of which any county might be proud.

First of the Durham mathematicians, in knowledge, as in personality, comes William Emerson. He was a bear of a man, son of the village schoolmaster at Hurworth, where he lived and died, and his mathematical genius was phenomenal. But it was comprehensive of all that was then known, encyclo-pædic; not, like that of his greater contemporary at Byers Green, creative. His appearance and character have been admirably described by Hutchinson. "His person was robust, rough and masculine; his dress slovenly and mean; his manners studiously vulgar and abrupt; his way of life as singular as his person, frequently descending to the meanest labour and occupations; ale was his favourite liquor, and his diet was low, though he had a fortune sufficient to procure him all the comforts of life. Amidst these singularities he was acknowledged to be the first genius of the age in mathematics, in which he was communicative and liberal; and though he would assume an air of negligence touching his abilities, as if not conscious of them, he had infinite pride therein. He affected an appearance of infidelity in religious matters (the folly of many mathematicians), and was an example to the vulgar not a little reprehensible."[1] To which Surtees, after deploring the implied stricture on good ale, adds that Emerson was, nevertheless, "capable of very friendly and benevolent actions."[2] He refused to become a member of the Royal Society. "It is a damned hard thing," said he, "that a man

[1] Hutchinson, Vol. III, p. 158.   [2] Surtees, Vol. III, p. 257.

should burn so many farthing candles as I have done, and
then have to pay so much a year for the honour of F.R.S.
after his name. Damn them, and their F.R.S. too!"[1] He went
about with his shirt on back to front, all the buttons of his
coat undone and his legs wrapped in sacking, that he might
not scorch them as he sat over the fire. These peculiar clothes,
coupled with his eccentric behaviour and his learning, earned
him the reputation of being a wizard, and the village folk
would come and beg him to tell their fortunes, and thereby
throw him into a frenzy of rage. A woman called one day to
ask him to inform her if her husband were dead or not. He
had gone, years ago, to the West Indies, she said, and she had
not had a word from him since. Now she wanted to know if
she were free, for a man had asked her in marriage. Emerson
writhed, bubbling with suppressed rage, until the end of her
long story. Then, leaping from his stool, he yelled at her:
"Damn thee for a bitch! Thy husband's in hell, and thou
may go after him!" The woman went away, delighted and
convinced, and forthwith married her suitor.[2]

Although he lived near Darlington, Emerson's family came
from Weardale and had been successive Bailiffs of Wolsingham under the Bishop. Emerson himself still owned some
property at Eastgate. The dalesmen were very proud of him
and long remembered his skill in making dials and clocks.
"Emerson, like, ye know," they would say, "set the dial o'd
nooerth Poull; and when ye think th' matter ower, like, ye
know, t'stars is surerer nerd sun."[3] He wrote twelve volumes
on mathematics, was a fervent worshipper of Newton, and
rode regularly into Darlington on a horse as miserable as
Don Quixote's led by a small hired boy. He was visited by
mathematicians from all over England, and it is said that on
one occasion on being asked for the solution of a difficulty by
a deputation from Cambridge University, he made his brick-
layer, who was also his pupil, work out the problem for them
on the crown of his hat. In his old age, suffering tortures from
the stone, he would crawl about his room, alternately cursing
and praying, and wishing to God that his soul "could shake
off its rags of mortality without such a clitter-me-clatter."[4]

[1] *M.C.*, Vol. II, p. 31.   [2] *Ibid.*
[3] Address by Joseph W. Carr (President of the Weardale Association for the Prosecution of Felons), 1941.   [4] *M.C.*, Vol. II, p. 32.

On his tombstone was written: "As it happeneth to the fool, so it happeneth to me: and why was I then more wise?"

Emerson had a friend called Jeremiah Dixon, another brilliant and self-taught mathematician, who was born in the little mining village of Cockfield and was the son of a servant at Raby. On the recommendation of John Bird, yet another local genius, he was sent by the Royal Academy of Woolwich to observe the transit of Venus from St. Helena. The interview which preceded his appointment to this mission is said to have been conducted as follows. "Sir," said a polite member of the examining committee, "we would fain enquire whether you did study mathematics at Cambridge or at Oxford?" "At neither place." "Then at what public school did you get your rudiments?" "At no public school." "Then at what particular seat of learning did you acquire them?" "In a pit cabin on Cockfield Fell."[1] And this answer, at which a Government examiner would turn up his nose today, was evidently pleasing to the less stereotyped minds of that period, for Dixon was selected for the task. His garden wall at Cockfield is supposed to have been the first place ever illuminated by coal-gas. But his name, though not his personality, is now familiar to us, and even more to Americans, for his share in the delineation of the boundary between the possessions of Lord Baltimore and those of William Penn. This boundary line was then prolonged across the continent under the name of the "Mason-Dixon Line," and thus was brought about a little suspected connection between the coal and the sweeping winds of Cockfield Fell and the sun and the songs of "*Dixie*-land."

John Bird, of Bishop Auckland (the man who recommended Dixon to the Woolwich Academy), was a mathematical instrument maker who achieved a European reputation. Thomas Pigg, born at Bishopwearmouth, penniless and completely ignorant of arithmetic, first a farm labourer and then a trimmer, taught himself in his spare time, working out problems in coal-dust on the decks of ships, until he became a leading mathematician in the North and a contributor to scientific magazines. Finally, in point of time, a recent Vicar of Tow Law, Thomas Espin, who was, incidentally, a musician and possessed a fair knowledge of geology and botany, was, principally, a very distinguished astronomer.

[1] *M.C.*, Vol. IV, p. 245.

With his assistant, Mr. William Milburn,[1] he discovered, during his residence at Tow Law (1888-1934), no fewer than 2,575 new double stars. He was a Fellow of the Royal Astronomical Society, by whom he was awarded the Jackson Medal for his discovery of Nova Lacertæ; and he was the inventor of a spectroscope and of "Espin's star detector."

But we have reserved the greatest name to the last.

In 1785 Sir William Herschel established his claim to be considered as the real founder of modern astronomy by propounding his theory of the flatness of the stellar system. This is now accepted as essentially true. But in 1750, thirty-five years earlier, unknown to Herschel, Thomas Wright, the son of a carpenter of Byers Green, County Durham, had advanced the same proposition in his *Original Theory or New Hypothesis of the Universe*. This book, which, by means of its theory of a flat disc, explained for the first time the appearance of the Milky Way, seems to have escaped the attention not only of Herschel, but of everybody else, save of one young German scientist—Immanuel Kant. The perusal of Wright's book led Kant to compose his *Universal Natural History and Theory of the Heavens*, which contains the first hints of that theory of evolution in which he believed throughout his life, and which was later developed and popularised by Darwin and Herbert Spencer. In his book Kant specifically expresses his debt to Wright, admitting in his preface that he is unable " 'exactly to define the boundaries' between his hypothesis and that of the Englishman." With Kant's speculations on evolution, induced by this theory of the stars in space, Wright had nothing to do. In the words of Kant himself, "Mr. Wright of Durham made the happy step," but did not himself appreciate its significance. But the fact remains that this obscure Durham mathematician was the forerunner both of the greatest astronomer and of the greatest philosopher of his age. What he first suggested by reasoning as the probable nature of the stellar system was established by Herschel to be the true one, as the result of observation and measurement; while this original theory of Wright first launched the great German philosopher on his evolutionary speculations. By his association with these two mighty names,

[1] To whom, and to the present vicar of Tow Law, the Rev. J. Samuel, I am indebted for this information.

before whom, not beside whom, he may rightfully take his place, Thomas Wright may justly claim to be remembered as the greatest and the most original of all Durham's brilliant mathematicians. Yet there is no memorial to him in our county, neither in the Cathedral nor at Byers Green, where he was born and died, where the house which he built still stands[1] and the tower which he erected for the observation of his stars.[2]

With a single exception, no prose writer born within the county of Durham is familiar to the general public. But several distinguished authors are associated with it through residence or education; and some amongst the most illustrious have illumined it, in passing, with a flicker of their fame. Defoe, Smollett and Goldsmith; Scott, Dickens and Lewis Carroll—all these great men have visited the county and left some memory of them there. Defoe lived for a few months at Gateshead. Smollett, most probably, drew his portrait of the rascally Horace-quoting innkeeper in *Roderick Random* from a certain Richard Cooper, a pedagogue-cum-publican famous for his pretty daughter and his sharp business, who lived at West Auckland. Goldsmith is said to have been arrested for debt at Sunderland; Scott was frequently in the county; Lewis Carroll came to Croft at the age of eleven, when his father was made rector there; and, but for a visit to Barnard Castle, Dickens would not have written *Nicholas Nickleby* nor found the title of *Master Humphrey's Clock*. It was while staying at this little town, in order to investigate the condition of cheap northern schools, that the novelist happened one day to enter the shop of William Humphreys, clockmaker, where he saw a remarkable clock. "Did you make that?" he asked. "No, it was my lad there," replied the proud father. "Ah!" said Dickens. "So that is Master Humphreys' clock, is it?"[3] And his own phrase must have stuck in his memory.

The original of "Dotheboys Hall," as is generally known,

[1] The house is now known as "The Hall," and the tower as "Westerton Folly."

[2] The information contained in this brief summary is derived from an extremely interesting article on Thomas Wright by F. A. Paneth in *D.U.J.* for March, 1941, Vol. XXXIII, No. 2.

[3] *M.C.*, Vol. I, p. 389.

was a school at Bowes, just over the Yorkshire border, but what is not so generally known is the effect produced by Dickens's novel upon the real Nicholas Nickleby. Some time after its publication the usher of the school in question wrote to our friend Mr. John Bowes begging him to find him a job, for he was penniless. He had formerly been living, in peace and prosperity, with Mr. Shawe, the headmaster, and his wife, "when Mr. Dickens's misguided volume, sweeping like a whirlwind over the schools of the North, caused Mr. Shawe to become a victim of paralysis and brought Mrs. Shawe to an untimely grave"[1]; which shows what a nuisance reformers can be.

Henry Bradley, who under the doubly Durham sobriquet of "Cuthbert Bede" wrote that amusing tale of university life, *Mr. Verdant Green*, was educated at Durham University. He is reputed, while an undergraduate there, to have thought of and designed the first Christmas card, and he was remarkable for the pallor of his complexion. "This is 'Mr. Verdant Green'," said a friend, introducing him to Douglas Jerrold. "Really," replied that witty man. "He looks to me more like Mr. Blanco White."[2]

Hugh Walpole and Ian Hay were both at Durham School; Paley was a rector in the diocese; George Stanley Faber (a distinguished writer on evangelical doctrine) was Vicar of Longnewton and master of Sherburn Hospital; John Meade Falkner, the author of *The Nebuly Coat* and a great liturgiologist, lived for some years at Durham, where he was Honorary Librarian to the Dean and Chapter. The Catholics are strongly represented by Lingard and Waterton, Cardinal Wiseman and Lafcadio Hearn. The gentle John Lingard, who was Vice-President of the college at Crookhall and Ushaw, and was attacked for his temperate *History of England* both by Catholics and Protestants, was a wit as well as a great historian. In reply to Maltby, the very evangelical Bishop of Durham, who had strongly resented the Pope's action in sending a Papal Bull to England, Lingard wrote: "As a consistent Whig, my Lord, you ought not to oppose Free Trade in foreign cattle."

[1] *The Story of My Life*, by Augustus Hare; also *M.C.*, Vol. I, p. 294.
[2] *D.U.J.*, December 29th, 1909.

Charles Waterton, the Yorkshire naturalist, who slept on the hard floor with a block of wood for his pillow and rose every morning at three o'clock, was a pupil at Tudhoe Catholic School; and Cardinal Wiseman, the first Archbishop of Westminster and author of *Fabiola*—"the first good book that has had the success of a bad one"[1]—was educated at Ushaw.

Three natives of the county were Thomas Morton, born in Durham, from whom we first hear of "Mrs. Grundy" in his play *Speed the Plough*; Tom Taylor, born at Sunderland, one of the best-known editors of *Punch*; and Abel Chapman, the field naturalist, who was the author of *The Borders and Beyond* and other entertaining books on birds. He was born in Durham and lived where his birds lived, following them to Norway and Spain, where he appropriately bought a castle.

The charming eighteenth-century story of Robert Lamb and Philadelphia Nelson may here be introduced, with the excuse that he was not only a minor canon but probably a native of Durham, and that he wrote a *History of Chess*. She was a carrier's daughter. In 1747 Lamb became Vicar of Norham and there, in his loneliness, fell to thinking of the pretty girl with the pretty name whom he had spied on the streets of Durham. So he wrote and asked her to marry him, making an appointment with her on the pier at Berwick. She was to carry a tea-caddy so that he could recognise her! Unfortunately, he then forgot the appointment, and the poor girl paced up and down the pier, weeping, until an old naval officer asked her what was the matter. When she had told him he slapped his thigh and exclaimed: "Just like Robin Lamb! I know him well. He'll make you a capital husband. Come along!" So they were married and lived happily together until her death seventeen years later, when, to console himself, he wrote an extremely boring account of the battle of Flodden.

But now we must turn our attention to the trump card in our little pack, Robert Smith Surtees, of Hamsterley, creator of "Jorrocks."

Hamsterley Hall still stands, a pleasant house of the eighteenth and early nineteenth centuries, in lovely grounds, but hard pressed by collieries. It is supposed to be the original

[1] Archbishop of Milan. (See *D.N.B.* "Wiseman.")

of "Hillingdon Hall," for it was here that R. S. Surtees was born, where he spent the second half of his life and where he died. The estate was bought by the author's grandfather, a member of a branch of the old Dinsdale family, and is now, having been inherited through the female line, the property of Lord Gort, who has devoted much of his time—an arduous task indeed in these days—to the rescue and rehabilitation of the old and the beautiful, both in his own county and in Newcastle. Already, in his day, R. S. Surtees (who must not be confused with his senior contemporary and distant relative, the historian) foresaw the ruin of the county which he loved, prophesied the extinction of the yeoman farmer, and deplored the general exodus of landowners, which in Durham was even then taking place before the advance of the industrialist. He was a sportsman of the old school, one of those who, as has been well pointed out, associated sport with Nature, for which they had an "instinctive understanding,"[1] not with organised games and athletics; and he was the friend and admirer of the great Ralph Lambton.

Mr. Jorrocks first saw the light of day in the *New Sporting Magazine*, published in London in 1831. This was a challenge to the *Sporting Magazine*, of which "Nimrod" (C. I. Apperley) was the shining light. Surtees was the mainstay of the new rival, which owed its success, as he tells us himself, "though I say it who perhaps should not," to the sporting grocer of Great Coram Street.[2] His adventures were collected in a single volume called *Jorrocks's Jaunts and Jollities*, and in 1843 appeared *Handley Cross*.

There has been much discussion and speculation as to the originals of the characters in Surtees's novels. On only two points are all agreed: that "Pomponius Ego" was intended to represent the famous sporting writer "Nimrod," and that the original of "James Pigg" was Joe Kirk, huntsman to Jonathan Richardson, of Shotley Bridge, who hunted part of the country now covered by the Braes of Derwent. The famous incident, illustrated by Leech, when Pigg jumped into the melon frame, was inspired by the actual performance of Joe Kirk, which took place at Corbridge in Northumberland.

---

[1] Pope-Hennessey, *op. cit.,* p. 217.
[2] *Robert Smith Surtees*, by Himself and E. D. Cuming (Blackwood and Sons, 1924), p. 85.

Various places, including Croft and Shotley Bridge, have been claimed as the prototypes of "Handley Cross," but Leamington in Warwickshire is the most likely. The origins of Mr. Jorrocks himself are uncertain, but it has been said that he suggested the creation of the still more famous Mr. Pickwick. Thackeray, as well as Dickens, was a great admirer of Jorrocks, "who has long been a dear and intimate friend of mine,"[1] and Harrison Ainsworth declared that "Mr. Sponge" was "unquestionably the best sporting tale ever written and beat Nimrod all to sticks."[2]

Surtees, of course, is still read, and will be so long as there remains any love in England of what was once typically English. But it will be difficult to make a Socialist of Mr. Jorrocks and to fit him into our new cosmopolitan scene. There is a portrait of his author riding home through the twilight, spare and aristocratic, with a sad and slightly sardonic smile on his face, after a good day's hunting.

II. THE SWORD

"The tramp of squadrons, and the bursting mine,
The shock of steel, the volleying rifle-crack,
And echoes out of ancient battles dead.
So Cawnpore unto Alma thundered back,
And Delhi's cannon roared to Gujerat:

.   .   .   .   .

The voice of England's glories girdling in the earth."
FRANCIS THOMPSON.

We have already mentioned several distinguished soldiers in the course of our story—notably Sir William Lumley, the third Marquis of Londonderry and Sir Charles Felix Smith. To these we must now add the names of the late Field-Marshal Viscount Gort of Hamsterley, V.C., and of Henry Havelock. The fame of the Commander-in-Chief of the British Army in France during the earlier days of the last great war needs no refurbishing in these pages, but the figure of the great Havelock is already growing dim, melting into the haze of glory of a not so distant past, with the great Empire which he saved for us. We will, therefore, concentrate

[1] Letter to Surtees, May 30th, 1849. See E. D. Cuming, *op. cit.,* p. 245.
[2] *Op. cit.,* p. 247.

II

our attention on him. Before we do so, however, we must particularly mention one who was no great general or admiral, but a sailor lad of humble origin, whose single gallant action gave rise to a phrase which has passed into our familiar tongue; for he "nailed his colours to the mast."

Jack Crawford, the son of a keelman on the River Wear, was born at Sunderland and was present at the battle of Camperdown between the English under Duncan and the Dutch under de Winter in 1797. Several times the colours of the flagship in which he was serving had been shot down, and at last a portion of the mast which bore them was also carried away. Admiral Duncan, holding the flag in his hand, called for a volunteer to nail it to the broken mast and so save any further trouble. Crawford, climbing the rigging through a hail of shot, performed the deed, literally nailing the colours to the mast, and receiving a shot through his cheek in the process. The story is told of how the news of this great naval victory was received in Sunderland. It was a Sunday and the people were in church. Suddenly a man flung open the north door of St. John's and bellowed at the top of his voice to the kneeling congregation: "Duncan has defeated the Dutch fleet at Camperdown!" A moment's astonished pause; then the organist strikes up "Rule, Britannia!" and all the people rise to their feet and sing.

Crawford, who was given a silver medal of honour, was an improvident creature who drank away his initial glory, but he retained a fine streak of magnanimity. When in his poverty he was tempted with the splendid offer of £100 a week to appear on the stage and there repeat his performance for the amusement of the vulgar, he nobly replied: "No, I will never disgrace the real act of a sailor by behaving like a play fool."[1]

He died of cholera, and in 1890 a bronze statue to his memory was unveiled by the great-grandson of Admiral Duncan in Mowbray Park, Sunderland. Outside the Jack Crawford Inn at Monkwearmouth climbed until recently a wooden Jack, nailing a wooden flag to the mast. Inn and hero, mast and flag, were destroyed in the last war by a German bomb.

Sir Thomas Bertie, born at Stockton, was one of Nelson's

[1] *M.C.*, Vol. I, p. 8.

famous captains. He distinguished himself at the battle of Copenhagen when the great Admiral, instead of sending for him after the action, personally came aboard Bertie's ship to thank him.

Lieutenant-General Sir Henry Havelock-Allan, twice wounded in the Indian Mutiny and awarded the Victoria Cross, went out to observe the Afghan War long after his retirement from the active list, and was killed by the Pathans. He was a fiery and fearless soldier, the son of the great man, the greatest of all Durham's fighting men, to whose career and character we will now turn our attention.

Henry Havelock was the son of a Sunderland shipbuilder and of the daughter of a Stockton solicitor. He was born at Ford Hall, Bishop Wearmouth, on April 5th, 1795.

The basis of Havelock's life was religion, and the key to its conduct was his firm belief in discipline, which he imposed alike on others and on himself. Small, ascetic, stiff and prim, given to preaching to his soldiers, and cold and reserved in manner, his was by no means the character to be popular either with the troops or with his brother-officers. But he himself scorned popularity. "In public affairs," he wrote in a letter to a friend, "as in matters eternal, the path of popularity is the broad way, and that of duty the strait gate, and 'few there be that enter thereby.' Principles alone are worth living for or striving for; and of all the animals, the most ill-judging, ungrateful and opposed to their own true interests, are men, that is mankind."[1] But though this was his conviction, the deliberate judgment, after a lifetime's experience, of one who had travelled far and seen much, his was no attitude of scornful superiority. He was essentially a modest, simple man, believing not in himself, but in the overruling power of a Divine Providence, to which it was his duty to subscribe. "I entered on this campaign," he wrote after the battle of Sobraon, when he was nearly fifty-one, "fancying myself something of a soldier. I have now learnt that I know nothing. Well! I am even yet not too old to learn."[2] Such was the man, trained and toughened in Burmese, Sikh and

[1] Letter to George Broadfood. *Vide Havelock*, by Archibald Forbes. "English Men of Action" Series, p. 1. (Macmillan and Co., 1897.)
[2] Forbes, *op. cit.*, p. 69.

Afghan wars, "with the dust of Persia still in the crevices of his sword-hilt," who landed at Calcutta on June 17th, 1857, and was brought straight to Lord Canning. The Indian Mutiny had broken out during the previous month, Delhi had fallen, Cawnpore was in grave danger, Lucknow was closely besieged, the Commander-in-Chief had died. Sir Patrick Grant had been summoned from Madras to take his place, and it was he who introduced Havelock to the Viceroy. "Your Excellency," he said briefly, "I have brought you the man."

The story that follows belongs to British history: the gruelling fight all the way from Allahabad to Cawnpore, reached too late to save the women and children from massacre; the repeated efforts to relieve Lucknow by a force of 1,500 men in the face of such odds as probably no other commander has ever encountered against trained and disciplined troops; the forced marches, the pitched battles, the skirmishes, the advances, the retreats, the sun, the cholera; Havelock's anger—"Some of you fought yesterday as if the cholera had seized your minds as well as your bodies"—and his praise—"You've done that right well today, my lads"; the gradual change wrought in the feelings of the men under his command for this still stiff and severe, still upright little old man of sixty-two—dislike transformed to awe, and awe to love, and love mounting almost to adoration—"God bless the General!" "Make way for the General"; and, at last, the success, the entry of the little force into the Residency on September 25th, and the names of "Havelock" and "Lucknow" on every tongue in England. In that final advance with Outram on the besieged city only 250 of Havelock's "Ironsides" were left to take part. During the first half of the campaign, between July 12th and August 16th, a period of thirty-six days, they had engaged in two pitched battles and seven smaller fights and had been successful in every one. All these actions took place under a burning sun. The obstinate battle of Cawnpore, which was won against an enemy four times as numerous and greatly superior in guns and cavalry, followed almost immediately upon a march of twenty miles on one of the hottest days of an Indian summer. In nine days —in their vain attempt to reach Cawnpore in time—Havelock's men had marched 126 miles in this weather and fought four actions. "Better soldiers," said their historian, "have never trod this earth."[1]

The "first relief" of Lucknow by Havelock and Outram was really a reinforcement, not a relief, but it was a reinforcement which averted all danger of capture from the threatened city. The garrison was finally relieved by Colin Campbell on November 17th, and a week later Sir Henry Havelock died of dysentry. Outram, his chivalrous superior, who had waived his command and elected to serve under him, took leave of the dying man as he lay on his litter under the mango-trees. Havelock was quiet and composed. "I have for forty years so ruled my life," he said to his old comrade, "that when death came I might face it without fear."

There is no memorial to Sir Henry Havelock in Durham's great cathedral. There are memorials to him in Sunderland and in St. Cuthbert's, Darlington (near which town his grandson lives), but Durham Cathedral is, or should be, the Valhalla of Durham soldiers. The neglect can hardly be remedied now. For now it is no longer "a magnificent thing to be an Englishman." Now we have become a nation of sheep, standing in a queue, head to tail, with our rumps turned to the glories of our imperial past.

[1] Forbes, *op. cit.*, p. 104.

CHAPTER XXIV

THE FOX AND THE GAMECOCK

"Of their heart-bursting flies let the Leicestershire tell us,
Their plains, their oxfences, and that sort of stuff,
But give me a day with the Sedgefield brave fellows,
Where horses ne'er flinch or men cry, hold, enough!
Whilst the blood of old Cæsar our foxes can boast, sir,
May Lambton their only dread enemy be,
And the green waving whins of our coverts, my toast, sir,
Oh, the hounds and the blood of old Lambton for me!"
"THE LAMBTON HOUNDS," by George W. Sutton.

THE very early history of fox-hunting in this county is obscure. A Roundhead, but a long-haired Roundhead—Captain Robert Hutton, of Houghton Hall—is the first person of whom we hear in connection with this sport of Cavaliers. Mr. Apperley states boldly, and perhaps correctly, that he "hunted the Houghton-le-Spring Hounds" in 1670.[1] At any rate, he was alive at the time and was painted on horseback in front of his house "in a blue shag coat with red lining," together with several other mounted gentlemen, and hounds.[2] Probably these local squires brought their own dogs and were prepared to hunt whatever they might encounter, from a rabbit to a stag. But whether this was a regular meet of foxhounds or not, there is no doubt that George Bowes, of Streatlam, kept a pack about the year 1735, and that a few years later the gentlemen of the Sunderland Hunt were pursuing "bagmen" and other foxes. They chased one of them for twenty-six miles, practically into the sea. It is not, however, until we reach the mighty figure of the third Earl of Darlington that we find ourselves on safe ground. The first authentic records of regular fox-hunting revolve round this magnificent peer and round his scarcely less majestic junior and contemporary, Ralph Lambton.

Lord Darlington's pack at Raby was formed for him, when he came of age in 1787, by his father. He kept them for over

[1] *North Country Hunting Half a Century Ago,* by N. W. Apperley (W. Dresser and Sons, Darlington, 1924), p. 598.
[2] Surtees, Vol. I, p. 148.

fifty years, during thirty-six of which he hunted them himself, covering an enormous extent of country which was later served by no fewer than seven packs.[1] During the season of 1814-15, which gives a fair idea of the sport provided, he had ninety-five hunting days, of which one was blank, killed eighty-three foxes and ran twenty-five to ground. The meets seem to have been at all hours, mostly early; as early as a quarter to five on one occasion, very late in the season, when hounds met at Warden Law, twenty-six miles from Raby as the crow flies, in the days when there were neither trains nor motor-cars. He had eighty couples of working hounds, which "Nimrod" described as the most expensive pack of the day, put himself and his servants in hats, and his daughters (who seem to have been as hard as he was) in pink, and generally fed his "darling hounds" himself. He was the grand seigneur of sport, "the last and perhaps the greatest of those famous masters who lifted fox-hunting into a sport of kings."[2]

Lord Darlington kept a diary which reveals him as a conscientious and amusing chronicler, with a gift for vivid and forceful expression of his vivid and forceful feelings. "The fox was dying," he writes on one occasion after describing a fine run, "and only Mr. Witham, Colonel Craddock, my son William, Major Hedley, Mr. Simpson, and myself, with the hounds, when the fox turned short down wind to Middleton lodge, where the hounds were met in the lane at the gate, and turned and rode at least a mile back by several d——d skirting lane-riders, whose horses were beat, and who never rode straight nor ever will; and then told me, as an excuse for themselves, that there was a drain *somewhere*, to which I gave a mild reply, conscious of their consummate ignorance in fox-hunting."[3] On another day, after a run of two hours and a half, his wife and his three daughters were all with him at the finish, "and I will venture without fear of contradiction or presumption, and with much vanity and pride, to assert that no females have so distinguished themselves this day with foxhounds, however others may have done in the vices of

[1] Badsworth, York and Ainsty, Bedale, Zetland, South Durham and North Durham.
[2] *V.C.H.,* Vol. II, p. 388.
[3] *The Earl of Darlington's Fox-hounds*, printed by C. H. Reynell, 1816, p. 32.

public life, which disgrace their character and ruin their health, when fox-hunting promotes everything that is desirable."[1] Two years later a meet at Bishop Auckland was followed by "a good day's sport," when the fox was run very hard to the Mill Wood. But here "he was headed by a numerous set of villainous, rascally admirers of Orator Hunt, and after having committed that diabolical act, they rode and ran for another point at the worst end of Hunwick gyll, where the fox was gallantly breaking away over the open country, when the same set of damned, skirting, short-riding, nicking, scut stinking fellows, again headed the fox right down through the pack. . . ."

On February 23rd, 1815, when Lord Byron was grumbling and idling a few miles away at Seaham, the Earl of Darlington mentions our second outstanding personality, less grand in scale but more perfect than he, the Raphael, as the master of Raby was the Michael-Angelo, of Durham hunting. "Mr. Ralph Lambton was out," writes Lord Darlington, "with some gentlemen from Sedgefield, and a most immense field."[2]

Ralph Lambton, the uncle of the first Earl of Durham, hunted in his youth with the famous Mr. Meynell, of Leicestershire. He then took command of the northern part of the county, and, in 1804, when Lord Darlington handed over to him that portion of the country which is now covered by the South Durham, he set up his hunting headquarters at Sedgefield, which was destined to be inseparably connected with his fame. This little town, with its open square, where the homilies once "flew to the devil," its imposing church tower, and its general air of rustic importance, is the centre of the best hunting in the county. "Nimrod," who knew all England from a horse's back, puts this country "at the head of the provincials."[3] and Sedgefield itself was known as "the Melton of the North." There are only three towns in the world worth living in," said an early enthusiast, "and they are London, Paris and Sedgefield." Though not far from collieries and shipbuilding, iron-works and chemicals, it still remains an oasis, or almost, of rural life and sport. Here in 1804 was founded the "Tally-ho Club," and here have since

---

[1] *Op. cit.*, p. 41. [2] *Op. cit.*, p. 49.
[3] *V.C.H.*, Vol. II, p. 394.

resided four Masters of the Hunt.[1] If Sedgefield was "the centre of a setting of gems," as it was fondly called by one of its most famous votaries,[2] then the village of Bishopton, with its neighbouring covert, Foxhill, was the pearl in this carcanet. From the earliest days until the present a meet at Bishopton has seldom been followed by a blank day. In more modern times, at any rate, this meet was generally advertised for a Friday. "What happens on Good Friday?" asked the Sunday-school teacher of a Durham pupil. "The hounds meet at Bishopton,"[3] was the reply.

It was, then, to Sedgefield, to cover the surrounding country that Ralph Lambton moved his kennels in 1804, and here he hunted his hounds until 1825, when a terrible fall, from which it took him two years to recover, followed by another in 1829, prevented him from acting as his own hunts-man. But he remained the most popular Master and probably the best-loved man in the county. Sportsmen, farmers and pitmen all knew and honoured him, and he ruled supreme in his own sphere, without seeming to rule at all. He was not the sort to talk about "skirting, stinking lane-riders," but "he had the eye of an eagle for detecting a fault," said Surtees, of Hamsterley, "and the air of a Grandison in reproving one," while John Harvey, who eventually succeeded him at Sedge-field, was never tired of singing his praises. Quiet and digni-fied, he was also utterly fearless—"To go at a thing like a Sedgefield Hunt" became a proverb in the county—while one example of his "Grandison reproofs" will serve to illustrate his sense of humour. It was soon after he had recovered from his first fall, but when he was still unfit to act as huntsman, that he was one day disgusted by the performance of a group of pushing, swaggering riders, who were constantly over-riding his hounds. "Call my hounds off!" he shouted at last to his huntsman. "Call my hounds off, Jack Winter! These gentlemen will catch the fox."[4]

In March, 1838, a third fall at last put an end to the hunting career of this "perfect specimen of a highly polished

---

[1] Ralph Lambton; Richard Ord; Viscount Boyne and Major E. Ramsden. [2] John Harvey.

[3] *The Sedgefield Country in the Seventies and Eighties* (William Dresser and Sons, 1904), p. 91.

[4] *M.C.*, Vol. I, p. 33.

English gentleman." Lambton's back was broken, and he spent the remaining six tortured years of his life as a helpless cripple, but daily wheeled to the large window of his sitting-room to watch the changing seasons of the countryside he loved, and ever ready with his help and advice to those who succeeded him. "Ah!" said a sporting butcher of Newcastle when he heard the sad news, "you may get prime beef and prime mutton and Prime Ministers, but you'll never get such a prime sportsman as Ralph Lambton again."[1] He had hunted the country for nearly forty years, practically at his own expense, unfailing in dignity and humour, in patience and courage; "and the name of the man and the fame of his hounds will flourish and expand so long as the county of Durham endures."[2]

About the time of Ralph Lambton's last fall a series of resignations, accidents and disappointments threw the hunting machine out of gear for a while. In the following year the Duke of Cleveland (as Lord Darlington had now become) at last gave up his hounds. Four years later Lord Londonderry (the Cavalry General), who in the preceding year had taken on the mastership of the Sedgefield Hounds, broke his arm and was obliged to retire; and in 1844 William Russell, of Brancepeth, who had been hunting the North Durham country since 1838 and had just taken over from Lord Londonderry, decided to hunt no more. Meanwhile there had been trouble in the north-west. In 1838, after Lambton's last fall had broken up the Sedgefield Hunt, R. S. Surtees, the sporting author, formed a pack at Hamsterley to cover some of the country now abandoned. Two years later, however, he gave up his hounds and handed over the country to the Slaley, a Northumberland pack, whose rights were disputed by the Prudhoe and Derwent, formed out of an old trencher-fed pack in 1841. All this time, in the extreme south of the county, at Hurworth, the Wilkinson family of wealthy, hard-riding yeomen, having started with harriers in 1790, had been hunting the fox since 1799. One of the brothers of the older generation, Matty, was notorious for his huge size, his rough manners and his "rat-catcher" clothes. He was of the "damn-all-dandy school of sportsmen," as Surtees calls him, who thought nothing of crossing the Tees on horseback when the

---

[1] Surtees and Cuming, *op. cit.*, p. 174.   [2] *Ibid.*, p. 196.

river was in flood, though he weighed seventeen stone and could not swim.

From this confusion of masters and hounds there gradually emerged the five packs which (with one exception) still control the destinies of the county. These were the Zetland, the Hurworth, the South Durham, the North Durham and the Braes of Derwent.

In 1864 Christopher Cradock, of Hartforth (father of the admiral of the same name, who went down with his ship at the battle of Coronel), took over part of Lord Darlington's country and hunted it for twelve years, after which Lord Zetland took command and gave the name to the pack which it still bears.

In 1872 the Durham County Foxhounds, which had been formed in 1844, after Russell had given up his pack, came to a tragic end owing to an outbreak of dumb-madness and rabies. The opportunity was seized to split the county into two and to form the North and South Durham Hunts. Anthony Lax Maynard, a fine and courteous sportsman of the old school—who lived in that "grand Queen Anne mansion," Newton Hall, which is now no more—became the first master of the North Durham, and John Harvey, of whom we shall speak again, hunted the Sedgefield country with the South Durham.

In 1854 (both the Slaley and the Prudhoe and Derwent having come to an end) the Braes of Derwent were formed under the mastership of William Cowen. Today, after a long spell under Lewis Priestman, of Shotley Bridge, this hunt has returned to the care of the family which initiated it. The present Joint Master, G. A. Cowen, is the great-nephew of William. In 1923 the Braes took over the greater part of the country hunted by the North Durham, and this pack ceased to exist as a separate entity, save for book-keeping purposes. In the first season of the last war even this distinction was obliterated and there is now no longer a North Durham Hunt.

In 1888 William Forbes, formerly Master of the Kildare, took charge of the Hurworth in the extreme south, of which pack Lord Southampton was Master from 1911 to 1924, and which today is under the control of Miss Furness.

After the resignation of John Harvey the South Durham

came successively under the charge of Sir William Eden (twice), Mr. Richard Ord, of Sands Hall, and Lord Boyne. The present Joint Masters are Lord Eldon and Mr. R. H. Scrope. Here are two stories of Sir William Eden, who was, perhaps, the most singular amongst these masters.

On one very rainy morning, while being invested, in his front hall, with coat and cap and all the rest of his panoply, it occurred to him to examine the barometer lying on a table near at hand. To his amazement, it recorded "Very dry." Solemnly he tapped it, when, instead of falling, the needle rose yet higher. Thereupon, with a sudden shout of fury, Sir William seized the offending instrument and, flinging it through the open front door, exclaimed: "Go and see for yourself, you damned liar!"

About the middle of another bad day, supposing that there would be little more sport, he told his second horseman to go home. The man, however, called at Mr. Ord's house on his way back to have a gossip with friends, and it therefore happened that, on emerging from the gates, he encountered his master and part of the field, who by this time were homeward bound. Sir William was delighted to see his second horseman. It was now late in the afternoon and he was feeling hungry. "Ah, there you are! Now you can give me my sandwiches," he said. But there followed an awkward pause. Then: "I'm very sorry, Sir William. I've eaten them." "Oh! Give me my wine, then." "I've drunk it, Sir William," said the poor man. So the Master, without a word of reproach, called out at the top of his voice: "Has anybody here any food or drink he can spare?" "Yes, I have," came the answer from one of the company. "Then you might give it to this fellow of mine, will you? He's starving, poor devil!"

But we must go back to John Harvey, who, after Ralph Lambton, was the most famous of Durham hunting men. His life practically spanned the nineteenth century, and he represented the finest side of that new combination of business with sport which was to become increasingly evident throughout the course of his long career. The little man, who hunted three days a week in South Durham and devoted the remaining three to his tobacco at Newcastle, was the ancestor of the mineowners, shipbuilders and stockbrokers who, in their turn, became the devotees of the sport of kings. The regal days of

Lord Darlington and Mr. Lambton were over, but their mantle could not have fallen upon worthier shoulders. And it is fitting that there should have been an early personal link, of a remarkable and happy kind, between the aristocrat who had made the Sedgefield country famous in the hunting world and the tobacco merchant who came to rule over it nearly thirty years after his death. On New Year's Day, 1820, there was a tremendous run of Mr. Lambton's hounds, which began near Gateshead and finished at Seaham. At the finish were the Master and the hunt servants and a boy of fifteen. All the rest had been pounded. The boy looked lost, as indeed he was, for he had never been in this part of the county before and did not know his way home. But the Master rode up to him. "What is your name, boy?" he asked. "John Harvey." "And have you been with us all day?" "Yes." "Then you're a thorough-bred 'un," said Ralph Lambton. "Come along with me, and I'll put you on your road." So they rode off together and thus laid the foundations of a friendship which lasted until the older man's death.

Harvey had acted as Joint Master of the Durham County Hounds for nine years before the country was split, and it was not until he was sixty-eight years old that he assumed, in 1872, full control of the newly created South Durham. Yet this old man thought nothing of hunting three days a week from Sedgefield, though he lived at Newcastle, some twenty-six miles away. Only towards the close of his career did he allow himself to sleep at the Hardwick Arms the night before hunting. In his younger days, when he followed the Lambton Hounds, he and a small party of friends would begin the day by riding from Newcastle to Sedgefield. At Sedgefield they would mount their hunters and ride to the meet, which might be some seven or more miles further on. Then would follow the day's hunting, the ride back to Sedgefield, the light dinner on a chop and a glass of claret (nothing having been eaten since the morning's start), and, finally, the ride home to Newcastle, which had been left about 7.30 in the morning and was not reached again until ten o'clock at night. On one occasion, when hounds ran into Yorkshire, he rode altogether ninety miles in one day. He never ate or drank anything in the field, Ralph Lambton was equally abstemious, and indeed, if they had not been, they could never have performed such feats of endur-

ance. The familiar picture of the port-boozing hunting squire
may have been true of some of the rank and file, but never of
the great hunting man. These iron kings of sport, in the days
before motor-cars and even trains were available to rest and
convey the wearied limbs, set an example of clean living and
fortitude of which any specially trained soldier or athlete
might be proud. Yet Harvey by no means neglected his
business. He was always most courteous and friendly in the
field, but no one ever dreamed of taking a liberty with him.
Like his predecessor, he ruled naturally, by the sheer force of
his character, and, like him, he was a fearless rider. It was
hard, the Durham farmers remembered, to "catch the little
man,"[1] even in his old age, if ever he got a flying start. He
rode only a little over nine stone.

Such was the breed of sportsman in the late eighteenth and
early nineteenth centuries, for Lord Darlington and Ralph
Lambton and John Harvey, if they were outstanding, were
not astonishingly so. They were admired as ideals, not as
freaks, as amongst the best examples of English sportsman-
ship, of which there were a few as good and a great many
nearly as good—"of a sort,"[2] as Jack Bevans picturesquely
said, "not to be parted with." But we have parted with them.

A hunt, however, does not exclusively consist of a master
of hounds. There are the followers, both on horse and on
foot—the squires and their ladies and children, the sporting
doctors and parsons, the riding farmers, and those over whose
land the sport is held, as well as the pitmen who used to flock
by the hundred to every holiday meet, particularly on New
Year's Day, and were careful to observe the rules of the
game. Above all, there are the huntsman and the hunt
servants, those mahogany-faced, bold-hearted riders on whose
knowledge of human nature and of their own difficult art
largely depends the happiness and the success of a season. It
is all these figures, all these personalities from every walk of
life, who give to hunting its peculiar charm and distinction.
An eight-mile point, a sharp burst of twenty minutes or a
long hunting run are, in their varying degrees, exciting,
interesting or even alarming to the partakers in the splendid
sport, but they are poor reading to those who have no interest

[1] *The Sedgefield Country in the Seventies and Eighties,* p. 53, etc.
[2] *Ibid.,* p. 191.

in the chase or do not know the country. It cannot thrill the general reader to be informed that, when the North Durham met on a "dullish but fine" day in February, 1883, Mr. Maynard viewed a fox "going away for Black Banks and had the hounds put on, and they went away at a rattling pace through Black Banks, past Broadwood and Hunter Hill to Donelaford, and through Hurbeck to Bogglehole and over by Iveston and" so on. Nor is it of great moment to the modern anæmic Briton, drearily grinding up and down in his suburban train, to be reminded that on the same day the South Durham found a brace of foxes on Jordison's moors, and "after a sharp scurry at close quarters our fox turned his head northwards, leaving Dalton crag on the right, over Dove Coat farm to Elwick; then over some turnip fields towards Sheraton, thence to Cole Hill, through Roper's plantation" and so ever onward. Those runs are but old men's dreams now, the dreams of the very old by the fireside. But some of the people who took part in those runs, or in others like them, still live for us in an incomplete but sharp and vivid outline.

Lady Aline Vane-Tempest, for instance, with her beautiful hands and seat, on a little white-footed chestnut; Mrs. Ord, of Sands Hall, with her lovely blue eyes, pounding the field as she flies over a wire-rope fence on a railway; and gallant little Miss Slater, of Riding Mill, who rode a neat pony twelve hands high and painted hunting scenes "very well." So lives the huge, the kind-hearted Dicky Johnson,[1] bursting along after hounds at a surprising rate for his bulk, singing and whistling on his way; and so young George Lambton, an Eton boy of fifteen, leading the whole field on a thorough-bred mare, with his brothers hard after him.

The parsons too, they come to life once more, not in their pulpits, but preserving foxes, like old Mr. Ford, of Bishopton, or spreading a capital breakfast for all comers, like the Rev. Mr. de Pledge, of Satley Vicarage. And here come the doctors, with no thought of "nationalisation" in their robust and independent hearts—Dr. Hind, of Norton, on his chestnut mare; Dr. McCullagh, of Bishop Auckland, who loved Balzac and his clinking brown hunter; Dr. Fenwick, of Chilton Hall, with a cheery word and a glass of orange brandy for the huntsman after a hard day.

[1] R. S. Johnson of Sherburn Hall.

Horseman and pedestrian, horse and hound, the cavalcade goes on to the cracking of whips, to the faint sound of the distant horn. . . . There goes old Bachelor, Mr. Harvey's favourite hound, with his stern up; and Magnet, the thief, who stole fourteen pounds of meat from the larder at Croxdale; and poor Lively, who met such a terrible end at the bottom of an old pit shaft . . . and Ranter and Roman and Regent and Raffle . . . and Claxon, the huntsman, patient and skilful, if a little too fond of his horn, and—the best of the bunch, "the best whip ever seen," Jack Bevans, whose education had been with the keepers and who knew every fox in the country by sight.

And here are the horses: Hailstorm, the great black, and Joshua (the son of *none*), and Bailiff, the *dun*, who carried his master in the very first flight for seven seasons without a fall; and Sweetsound and Controversy, who hunted between them close upon 550 full days.

Now the footmen are passing us . . . the ubiquitous Charles Greenwell in a dark suit, a stock tie, a top-hat and an umbrella; that unknown cove in brown clothes with a red face and a pair of spats; the Monsignor and Principal of Ushaw College, who have been plying the grandson of "Nimrod" with whisky; and the pit-lads running after Bevans to ask him how many he had killed. "Thou's a lee-ar, Jack!" they told him when he replied: "A brace."[1] Ah, how friendly and happy it all sounds!

Here comes, not a horse, nor a hound, but even a special train—with Lord Londonderry and his party for the meet at Denton Cross Roads; and here is a sporting butcher on a black cob. There goes Lord Henry Vane-Tempest, a bad one to beat, who must always *handle* the fox if he gets the slightest opportunity; and there sprawls an alderman from Stockton, with himself on one side of a gate and his horse and his teeth on another. There is "Buttonhole" Cradock, the dandy dragoon, with his "haw, haw, haw!" and the butterfly bows on his knees, and there is the unknown lady who cuts a voluntary at his feet; there, the Master of the Braes,[2] quiet and courteous and particular, who only the other day was driving his coach from Edmundbyers to Shotley Bridge; and

[1] *The Sedgefield Country, op. cit.,* p. 128.
[2] Mr. Lewis Priestman.

there the Master of the South Durham[1] withering the grass with his curses as he stands by his fallen steed at Morden. Here charges a farmer on foot, furious, with a big long stick, for he cannot bear the music of the hounds; and here, by way of contrast, is another, lifted up from his deathbed to watch the passing hunt . . . the passing hunt . . . the passing hunt.

Long before Madam Softleye opened her new cockpit at Durham, in 1704, and long after cock-fighting was forbidden by law, even down to the present day, this sport has been a favourite pastime in the North. Race meetings were often the scene and the occasion of an important cock meeting as well. As many as a thousand birds are reported to have been killed during one week at Newcastle in the eighteenth century. "Depend upon it, sir," said a man who had just rented some property in Darlington, "I'll soon make a perfect paradise of this place."[2] And he turned it into a cockpit. At the Talbot, in the same town, was a famous pit, attended by Sir Harry Vane and others, where, during a four-days' meeting, "about 130 noble birds were murdered, amidst the horrid oaths and imprecations of those who were called gentlemen."[3] Whether they called themselves gentlemen or not, drove up in their phaetons and curricles, or trudged for miles through the mire, rich and poor alike delighted in the sport, at which, when distances were too great, professional "handlers" would look after their cocks for the owners and see that they got fair play. Birds would be sent by stage-coach from all over the country, by pitmen and farmers and landowners alike, to take part in the great meetings at Auckland or Stockton Races or on Newcastle Town Moor. The intervention of the law put a stop to these open proceedings, and clandestine affairs took their place. The following story was told to my informant[4] by an old "gamecocker," as such sportsmen used to be called.

It had been arranged to fight a main in a wood somewhere between Byers Green and Bishop Auckland. On the appointed

---

[1] Sir William Eden.
[2] Longstaffe, *History of Darlington,* p. 298.
[3] Heavisides, "History of Stockton." (See *M.C.,* Vol. II, p. 42.)
[4] Mr. Fred Burlinson.

day the "crows," or "lookouts," were posted, and the men, who were mostly miners, began to arrive with their birds, which they carried in special bags hidden under their coats. By ones and twos, coming from different directions, strolling casually along, they slipped into the wood. But someone had given them away. The first fight had scarcely begun when there was a crackling of the surrounding undergrowth, followed by a general scattering and scampering. The police had arrived on the scene. "Old Jack," the gamecocker who told the story, and who was young Jack in those days, escaped, but a few were caught and summoned, with two captured birds, before the Bench at Bishop Auckland, of which Mr. Shafto, of Whitworth, was then chairman. "What!" said he to the police, "do you mean to tell me that these silly little birds can fight?" "Yes, your worship." "These mangy things? Ridiculous! I don't believe it. Put them down on the floor. . . . Now, stand back, everyone, and let's see." The result was a first-rate hammer-and-tongs cock-fight—not the first, by any means, which the chairman had seen—and the case was dismissed.

Cock-fighting and racing, hunting, hawking and football were all forbidden during the Commonwealth, though not on humanitarian or even moral grounds, but because they furnished occasions for Royalist conspiracy. No doubt the ban was also welcome, for other reasons, to the sour-faced Puritan. "There is none now in power but the Rascality," said a disgusted Cavalier, "who envy that gentlemen should enjoy their recreations"; and for this he had to present himself on his knees to Mr. Speaker and beg the pardon of the House. But with the return of the King all these sports enjoyed their own again, and, not least amongst them, that of horse-racing.

Perhaps the first racecourse in the county was at Binchester, or Vinovium as it was in those days, when the Roman cavalry officers were quartered here and most probably enjoyed themselves after the manner of their kind. There was almost certainly racing at Woodham in the sixteenth century, for when James I saw a match here between the horses of William Salvin and Master Maddockes it is evident that similar matches had been taking place for some time. Bishop Cosin's wife and daughters went off "in my Lord's coache"[1] to see

_____
[1] Surtees, Vol. I, p. 164.

the racing at Auckland in 1662, and a few years later Dean Granville was complaining of the slackness of those clergy who, "for little, despicable, temporal conveniences and satisfactions, change the customary hours of God's worship and sometimes wholly lay it aside, upon no better account than that they and their people may goe to a horse-race, or some such idle sport or divertisement."[1] In the eighteenth century many landowners and farmers were breeding their own horses, and meetings were held in practically every small town in the county, until an Act of Parliament was passed, in 1740, to put a stop to so much waste of time and money and to limit racing in the Bishoprick to the two courses at Durham and Stockton. These frequent meetings were, of course, not the important arrangements they are today, but limited, generally, to a single match (or a series of them) like that which the King saw at Woodham. They seem also to have been disorderly affairs, sadly in need of a few stewards, a few policemen and a clerk of the course. "There was a great crowd," says a Scotsman, who stopped on his way home to watch the racing at Chester-le-Street (which was still taking place, in spite of the Act); and all this crowd was on horseback or in carriages or in carts, and "all of them with a keenness, eagerness, violence of motion and loudness of vociferation that appeared like madness to us." And apparently they all took part in the racing which they had come to see, or else rode private races on their own, for they were "crossing and jostling in all directions at the full gallop."[2] But, however pernicious these meetings must have been, they encouraged the breeding of fine horses and led to the formation of thoroughbred studs such as those at Croft and Longnewton and Windlestone. "A Reward of One Hundred Guineas," proclaims the sporting, cock-fighting Sir Harry Vane. . . . "Whereas the RACING STABLES belonging to me at Longnewton were broken open on the 10th instant, about twelve o'clock at night, and a mare called LADY SARAH most barbarously treated, and actually left for dead . . ."[3] This mare had been matched against another for 500 guineas on an agreed day, "play or pay." These were the usual terms of any wager of the period. No excuse was accepted. But they must have tempted every blackguard in the kingdom to make

---

[1] *Remains of Denis Granville,* Surtees Society, Vol. XLVII, p. 24.
[2] *M.C.,* Vol. III, p. 397.   [3] Fordyce, Vol. II, p. 215.

his little bit by the simple expedient of backing one horse and disabling the other. In this case they tried to strangle the poor beast.

The Durham Races, inaugurated in 1733 and always held on Easter Mondays and Tuesdays, were abolished in 1881. There is now, curiously enough, no flat racing in the county, for the Stockton course, originally in Durham, and still in the same place, has, by a diversion of the river for shipping purposes, been translated into Yorkshire. But in the grounds of Sands Hall, Sedgefield, where it was first run over a hundred years ago, there is still held a sporting steeplechase.

The big shooting days are over. Even the grouse, less affected by democracy than the lordly cock-pheasant, have grown, for some reason, sick at heart. They may recover, but the great shoots amongst the woods of Lambton and Wynyard, Raby and Windlestone are no more likely to return than the hunting of the wild boar or the Bishop's "Caza Magna." Poachers, first in the dales in the days of lead-mining, and later in the coal-mining district of the centre, have always been a nuisance, and sometimes dangerous. We have read of the terrible affray between keepers and miners in Weardale, when the former were all but killed. In 1848 the first whip to the Duke of Cleveland's Hounds was murdered by armed poachers. In the present century, between the two wars, the frequent strikes and the constant unemployment led to a spate of trespassing when, besides the genuine and forgivable poacher, badly needing "a bit rabbit" for his table, gangs of young men roamed almost with impunity about the countryside, damaging fences, young trees and plantations, molesting keepers even on the road, bent only on mischief and destruction. But it is not poaching nor trespassing which has put an end to the palmy days of the shotgun—to "Steady the beaters!" to "Come up, you cheps on the right!" to the lunch in the farmhouse and the spread of game on the grass, when the light is fast falling and the men's matches flare as they light their pipes before trudging homewards with a cheery good-night—it is not the poaching miner that has brought all these good days to an end; it is nowt but our dear young friend "PROGRESS."

Hares were numerous in the centre of the county, and at

the beginning of the present century regular coursing meetings used to be held on some estates for the benefit of the miners, who were enthusiasts of this sport and would train their own greyhounds. It was rumoured that a pitman might conceivably neglect his wife, but never his dog. Greyhounds are still popular and may be met today at exercise on the road, trotting demurely at their masters' heels, wrapped in beautiful coats; but the hare for which they are now trained is electric. The whippet, rabbit-chaser *par excellence* and once the inseparable companion of the poacher, is now seldom seen. The present age, with its paucity of food and shortage of game, does not encourage its continuance, and rabbit coursing is forbidden by law. Watching professional football matches is the great "sport" today. But men may now be observed again at the side of the road, going through a strange and solemn ritual, which betrays them as devotees of a pastime which was formerly a favourite one. These antics are the preliminaries to a pigeon race, for which much practice and preparation are necessary. During the war this racing was prohibited and many of the birds were surrendered to the Army. But the clubs are now being re-formed, and this pretty pastime may soon be enjoyed as frequently as before.

There was once an indignation meeting of miners to protest against the closing of Wheatley Hill Colliery. On the same day there was a pigeon race, and the birds were expected to arrive from Newcastle at any moment. Just as the orator was in the middle of an impassioned piece of rhetoric a voice suddenly cried out: "Haud thee hand till th' 'Slate Cock' comes in." The speech ceased immediately, and all faces were upturned to the sky in silent expectation, until, like an arrow from the bow, the expected favourite whistled over the heads of the crowd and landed on his "ducket."[1] Then the same voice said, very deliberately: "There, he's landed; thoo can gan on wi' thee speech."[2]

The practice flights from the roadside have been known to be attempted from the streets of a busy town until a crowd gathers to watch and a policeman interferes. A pitman, thus prevented from letting off his pigeon in Newcastle, put the

[1] Dove-cot.
[2] *A History of the Durham Miners' Association,* by John Wilson. (Veitch and Sons, 1908), p. 189.

bird wearily down on the pavement and said to it: "There, wa'ak home, thee little b——. And if thoo's late, tell 'em it's the fault o' Bobbie."

The old game of "pila," or foot-ball, was often the excuse and the opportunity for a free fight when the players put each other "in grave peril of their bodies." This game, or something very like it, was played (until recently, when the traffic put a stop to it) on the Great North Road at Chester-le-Street, and it may still be seen every Shrove Tuesday at Sedgefield. On the green here there is a bullring, through which the ball is passed three times by the verger or the sexton, and then the fun begins. The game is played between tradesmen and countrymen, and the object of each side is to "alley" the ball—that is, to get it into a portion of the village defended by their opponents. During the course of the contest, which lasts for hours, the ball may be taken out into the country, and if it is not "alleyed" by six o'clock it should be surrendered to the verger. But, in the words of a recent eye-witness, "as the game now resembled all-in wrestling plus Rugby football (including players being thrown into the pond near the farmers' alley), it would have taken a commando in a coat of mail to get the ball."[1] This is, surely, more fun than professional football, and it seems a pity that it is the last survivor of those games when the "butchers" played the "glovers," or the "marrieds" played the "singles," up and down the countryside, to the great benefit, from one point of view, if it were sometimes "to the grave peril" of their bodies. The origin of the game at Chester-le-Street is supposed to have been a quarrel between the apprentices of the town and a certain McHeeland, a retainer of Lumley Castle. Perhaps his Scottish ancestry was not unconnected with the result that the first football used for this game was the unfortunate McHeeland's head.

There was a type of sportsman, now no more, to whose memory I shall conclude this chapter with a tribute of admiration and regret. The old-fashioned sporting parson was sometimes, no doubt, a better priest than sportsman, like "the Rev. Mr. Sheppard, whose performances in the pulpit," wrote Lord Darlington, "are very deservedly acknowledged, but

[1] *Darlington and Stockton Times,* February 17th, 1945.

those in the field are not so conspicuous."[1] Sometimes, more regrettably, he may have been a better sportsman than priest. But when he judiciously combined the two, when, like the Rev. John Monson, he "shone in the pulpit"[2] and yet contrived to be alone with hounds over Ainderby Mires, or, like Parson Eade, of more recent memory, when he never failed in his visits to his sick parishioners, whatever the weather and however remote their sick-bed, and yet, when over eighty, could outwalk his juniors after the partridges, then he was no worse a sportsman for being a Christian and no worse a parson for being a man. No doubt there are still many clergymen who love sport—rowing men and "rugger" men and athletes —but it was not physical prowess that made these old sporting parsons, but the love and the knowledge of the countryside and of all that belonged to it—a good horse, a good crop of oats, a hedge properly laid, a field properly drained. They were the last heirs both of the priest who kept his pig and mowed his acre with his parishioners and of the country squire who associated, as a matter of course, the enjoyment of sport with the observation and the love of Nature. They were of the earth earthy, of the earth that performed wondrous miracles every year, for which they never ceased to give thanks and to lead their parishioners in glorifying God. Theirs was the robustious bearing, the loud voice, the friendly, open manner of the countryman, combined, not seldom, with the outspoken disapprobation of an honest man who scorned to cloak his feelings and with the commanding habit of a dictator. Naturally, they made enemies. "At first we didn't understand him and his haughty aristocratic ways," said one of his old parishioners of Mr. Eade,[3] Vicar of Aycliffe for over forty years. But when they came to know him, his unswerving rectitude, his unfailing kindness, they discovered that to know was to love. He was a little wild, perhaps, out shooting in his old age. It was advisable to duck if a partridge flew between you, and to keep at a respectful distance when he was climbing a fence with his loaded gun—he would never be helped, of course: "Used to helping myself, thank you"— but he was none the less welcome for the spice of danger which

[1] *The Earl of Darlington's Fox-hounds.* Diary. January 3rd, 1817.
[2] *Ibid.* Diary. 1825.
[3] The Rev. C. J. A. Eade was Vicar from 1880 to 1926.

Chapter XXV

ROBERT SURTEES, OF MAINSFORTH, ESQ., F.S.A.

"God has placed me in a Paradise. I have everything that can make a man happy."

ROBERT SURTEES.

On page 349 of the third volume of *The History and Antiquities of the County Palatine of Durham*, by Robert Surtees, of Mainsforth, Esq., F.S.A., there is a drawing which conveys a singular impression of tranquillity and charm. Yet it is simple enough. In the foreground is the portion of a field, where two old ponies are grazing under scattered trees. It is bounded by a post and rail fence in the near distance, beyond which runs a low wall. Behind the wall is a garden, where two small figures are strolling towards the house, a man and a woman; she in a large, floppy, leghorn hat. From the house—simple, square, Early Georgian, with an old tile roof and creepers climbing round the beautiful windows of that period—a stream of smoke rises into the quiet evening sky. Beyond are glimpses of more trees and a high yew hedge and the wall of an outbuilding, while, to return to our foreground and complete the picture, in the very centre of it three peacocks strut and peck and drag their tails. That is all. It was once a common English scene, such as might, before the days of mechanical invention, have been found by the dozen and the score, in any one of all our English counties. It is Mainsforth, the home of Robert Surtees, the solid house of a cultured gentleman of moderate means. But today, with its atmosphere of ordered peace and domestic security, it is the vision of an impalpable and impossible dream. Few glimpses of the past can convey to one more surely than this unpretending, innocent reproduction of an unpretending, homely scene how far we have travelled and how low we have sunk.

This, then, was the "paradise" in which God had placed the historian of our county, and these two figures, it may be, represent him indicating, with outstretched arm, some improvement to his grounds to his dearly loved wife, Annie, or his sweetly named "Cousin Ambler."

The life of Robert Surtees is interesting to us not only because he is *facile princeps* of all our Durham historians, but because we find in it the beau ideal of an English country gentleman of the eighteenth century. His death, moreover, was coincident with the death of the age which he represented so well. He was amongst "the last of the Mohicans." And we may thus fittingly complete our impressions of the county in the days before modern inventions had destroyed its individual character, with a sketch of the man who was himself a member of one of its oldest families and who devoted his whole life to the celebration of the land which he loved.

He was born at Durham on April 1st, 1779, spent his early childhood at his home at Mainsforth, near Ferry Hill, and was taught to read and write by the village schoolmaster. At the age of seven he was sent to board at the famous school founded by Bernard Gilpin at Houghton-le-Spring. Here his education was based upon the classics, but, above all, it was imbued with the spirit of an earnest religion, interpreted according to the doctrine of the Church of England. "The said schoolmaster," reads the charter of Heighington School, "shall *first and principally* endeavour to educate and bring up his scholars in the fear of God, and instruct them in the principles of the Christian religion."[1] Such was the basis upon which Gilpin's grammar school was built and on which it still rested, and in this spirit were its statutes interpreted by the clerical headmaster, to whose memory the historian paid, in after-life, his "grateful tribute of respect."[2] The influence of this school confirmed and strengthened the boy's naturally devout nature and laid the foundations of the man's self-disciplined, religious life. All through his days he strove for spiritual truth and peace and, with this object, read daily from the Bible and kept the canonical hours advocated by George Wheler in his *Protestant Monastery*. But his religion was far from smug or self-advertising. "I am very sensible," he wrote in his diary, "of the hardness of my heart and of my totally corrupt nature. . . . Libera nos, Domine Jesu, audi nos!"[3] And he detested nice argument about minor religious detail.

[1] Surtees, Vol. III, p. 317.   [2] Surtees, Vol. I, p. 161.
[3] Surtees, Vol. IV, Introduction. Memoir by George Taylor, p. 12.

"You say this and you say that," he exclaimed at last, when two clergymen had been debating for some time in his presence on some small point of doctrine, "but I say nothing, but that I stand in need of a Saviour." It is necessary, when considering the life of Robert Surtees, that we should bear in mind that in this earnest piety lay the root and explanation of it. But we will now return to the more superficial and obvious aspect of his education and career.

It was at the age of seven, then, on his introduction to Kepyer School, that Robert was made acquainted with the rudiments of Latin and, two years later, of Greek. Of both these languages he became in time a distinguished scholar, and it is impossible to read his *History of Durham* without appreciating the debt which we owe to his classical education, not only for the apposite quotations from Roman authors with which its pages are (not unduly) sprinkled, but chiefly for the elegant ease, the lucidity and often the beautiful cadence of his English style. Quotations from his great work have been given throughout this book and we must content ourselves here with one single specimen of his art. It is a description of the dene, or valley, of Castle Eden. After mentioning various gifts of land to the Church in this locality, he continues:

"It may be amusing to reflect for a moment on the state in which these grants represent a district still wild and romantic, six centuries ago. The Castle (of which the certain site cannot now be traced, but which doubtless stood near the vill, the chapel and the lake) towering above dark ancient woods; the Chapel almost hid on the edge of its little dene; and a few huts huddled together for protection round the mansion of their feudal lord. The dene and the moor useless, except for the purpose of firing, or of supplying thatch and timber for the miserable cottages of the peasantry; and the extent of moss and moor, wood, lake and waste, broken only by partial patches of cultivation, always particularised by name, 'the toft and the meadow of Nigel the steward—and the acre which Alan of Hardwick had ploughed.' If the reader would people the scene, he has only to conceive the feudal Lord in chace of the stag, with his train of half-naked serfs; or the Monks of Durham, with their black hoods and scapularies, wandering under cliffs overshadowed by giant yews which 'cast anchor in the rock,' or peeling their anthems in deep glens amidst the noise of woods and water-falls—

'*Sonantes—inter aquas nemorumque noctem.*' "[1]

Surtees was also an able Latin versifier, while of his knowledge of Greek the following story, very characteristic of that period, will amply testify. In the course of his researches he one day visited Richmond, in Yorkshire, where the Grammar School was kept by a well-known classical scholar, the Rev. James Tate. "One evening," says Mr. Tate, "I was sitting alone (it was about nine o'clock in the middle of summer); there came a gentle tap at my door. I opened the door myself, and a gentleman said, with great modesty: 'Mr. Tate, I am Mr. Surtees, of Mainsforth. James Raine begged I would call upon you.' 'The Master of Richmond School is delighted to see you,' said I; 'pray walk in.' 'No, thank you, Sir: I have ordered a bit of supper; perhaps you will walk up with me?' 'To be sure, I will.' And away we went. As we went along I quoted a line from the Odyssey. What was my astonishment to hear from Mr. Surtees, not the next, but line after line of the passage which I had touched upon. Said I to myself: 'Good Master Tate, take heed; it is not often you catch such a fellow as this at Richmond.' I never spent such an evening in my life."[2] How many schoolmasters today would enjoy such an evening? And how many squires would be able to give it to them?

After seven years at Houghton-le-Spring, Robert was sent, at the age of fourteen, to a tutor near London, who prepared boys for the university. Three years later he became a commoner at Christ Church, Oxford, where he was known as "Greek Surtees," where he delighted many friends with the originality of his mind and with the sparkle of his conversation, and where he gave decisive evidence of that sturdy independence of thought and action and that somewhat blunt habit of speech which were afterwards so characteristic of him. He called one day on the Dean to request leave of absence, and, while waiting for that exalted dignitary to finish a letter, picked up his poker and poked his fire. "Pray, Mr. Surtees," said the Dean, "do you think that any other undergraduate

[1] Surtees, Vol. I, p. 41.
[2] Taylor, *op. cit.*, p. 62.

in the college would have taken that liberty?" "Yes, Mr. Dean," was the reply, "anyone as cool as I am."[1]

This downright manner, combined with a native kindness and humility of heart, is a little reminiscent of Dr. Johnson, for, though there is no evidence in Surtees's life of any brutal bludgeoning such as enlivens Boswell's story, there is plenty to show that he was no polished courtier. In a letter to Southey, written in 1810, Walter Scott says: "If you make any stay at Durham, let me know, as I wish you to know my friend Surtees, of Mainsforth. He is an excellent antiquary; some of the rust of which study has clung to his manners: but he is good-hearted; and you would make the summer eve short between you." Much later Surtees condemned himself for this failing in a somewhat pathetic letter to the wife whom he adored. "It was all my own desire to go to Durham," he admits, now thankful to be back at Mainsforth. "But indeed it seems a settled point that bears are best in woods (at least great grey bears); and when they cry to go to Durham again, put the muzzle on. You are a good and patient wife—a lamb yoked to a bear."[2] A further example of his outspokenness, as also of his care for and interest in his dependants, is revealed in the following anecdote. "Richard," said he one day to one of his tenants, "you used to be a regular attendant at church; how comes it that I have not seen you there of late?" "Why, sir, the parson and I have quarrelled about the tithes." "You fool," was the reply, "is that any reason why you should go to hell?"[3]

In 1800 Surtees took his degree at Oxford and, moving to London, became a member of the Middle Temple. But he was never called to the Bar, for, two years later, his father died and he left London to live at Mainsforth. He was now alone in the world, for he was an only child, and his mother was already dead. So he settled down, at the age of twenty-three, in the dearly loved home which henceforth he was to leave but seldom and for brief intervals, and then always with regret. Here he straightway began to devote himself to the collection of materials for that history of his county of which he had contemplated the composition almost from his earliest years. He was, indeed, a born antiquary. Already, as a child at Kepyer, he had amused his fellow-pupils with his collection

[1] *Ibid.*, p. 9.   [2] *Ibid.*, p. 76.   [3] *Ibid.*, p. 13.

of old coins, for which he rigorously hunted and dug in his spare time, and even at this stage of his life he had carefully stored and noted any document or old paper that came his way. Now he set about his task in earnest, and, much to the boredom of his groom, spent hours driving about the country-side, noting and observing, with innumerable halts for a closer and more elaborate investigation. "Oh, sir," said the poor man to one of the antiquary's friends, "it was weary work; for master always stopped the gig: we never could get past an auld beelding."[1]

Surtees was not of robust health, and this circumstance dictated, to a certain extent, his manner of work. After the first few years of intensive labour he found that he had over-rated his strength and he was obliged thereafter to work in a more desultory fashion. "He never sat down 'doggedly' to write," said Sir Cuthbert Sharp,[2] who frequently observed him, "but would wander about on a spacious gravel-walk in front of his house; and, having well considered his subject, he would come to his library and hastily write down the result of his musings. But his ideas crowded on his mind so rapidly, and his fancy was so exuberant, that his pen could not keep pace with his creative imagination; and the consequence was that nobody but himself could read what he had written; and that not always."[3] Such a "singular mode" of writing so vast a work as his *History of Durham*, crammed with the minutest details, could only have been followed, as his biographer indicates, "by a man of extraordinary power of memory."[4] But followed it was, and the result of all these gig-drives and gravel-pacings was given, at length, to the world in four large folio volumes, of which the first was published in 1816, the second in 1820, the third in 1823, and the fourth not till six years after the death of the historian, edited by his friend James Raine, in 1840. The total number of these enormous pages is 1,635, exclusive of plates and indices, comprising, at a rough computation, some one and a half million words. It is beautifully printed, richly illustrated, often solidly bound in the thickest, choicest leather and—it is unfinished.

[1] *Ibid.,* p. 11.
[2] Author of *Memorials of the Rebellion of 1569, History of Hartle-pool,* etc.
[3] Taylor, *op. cit.,* p. 13.   [4] *Ibid.*

Enough has been said about Mr. Surtees's *History of Durham* to show that this is no bedside book to pick up with one hand and with which to read oneself happily to sleep. It is with feelings of inevitable awe and even of depression that the aspiring reader, surely rare in these degenerate days, forces himself to the gargantuan task of grappling with the heavy volumes. Apart from their contents, their weight and size alone present a ponderable problem. It is as impossible to read these books sitting comfortably in an arm-chair as it is to read them in bed. Any ordinary bookstand would collapse in fragments at the touch of them, and even a table, unless very solidly constructed, soon begins to wilt beneath the burden of them and to droop at its cabriole knees. A large pedestal writing-table provides the only solution, and a poker posture with an upright head (for, once the book is spread open, there is no room for a supporting elbow—*experto crede!*). But when these minor physical inconveniences have been overcome great is the reward and delightful the surprise of the stiff-backed reader. No doubt Surtees is weak in the philosophy of history, the broad causes underlying the revolutions in human affairs—he is an antiquary rather than a historian—but not only does he provide a wealth of extraordinarily accurate information, but, thanks to the charm and humour of his mind and to the clarity of his style, he presents it in an easy, attractive and original manner, which heightens the interest of every story, enlivens every trait of character and transforms an arid landscape of charters, conveyances or pedigrees into a friendly, smiling prospect. "The general mass of materials from many centuries collected and arranged," says his biographer, George Taylor, "exhibits something of lunar power, reflecting and prolonging the light of suns that are set; whilst the original observations and notes of Mr. Surtees are scattered round with a star-like brightness that is all their own."[1] Here is a handful of this stardust, a note by Surtees on the descent of the manor of Consett.

"Nothing was more frequent," he wrote, "than for a family, in entering the higher parts of their descent, to forget, or mistake, the exact road by which an estate had travelled, and to exhibit a sort of adumbration of the truth (founded, indeed, on the general matter of fact), without much attention to

[1] *Ibid.,* p. 65.

detail; pressing into the service any Joan or Mawdlen who seemed calculated for an heiress, slaughtering infants, who stood in the way of a clear descent, with as little remorse as Herod, and

> *Making full oft the son beget the father;*
> *Giving to maiden ladies fruitful issue."*[1]

These last two lines are, perhaps, the historian's own, for Surtees was a ballad-writer, always skilful and sometimes approaching the pathos of poetry. We have already quoted from two of the examples of this minor art of his. With another he deceived no less an authority than the great Sir Walter Scott.

Towards the end of 1806 Surtees wrote to Scott with some information about the Border which he conceived might be of value for the forthcoming edition of *The Border Minstrelsy*. This letter was the first of a long correspondence between the two writers, who naturally had much in common, and it laid the foundations of a friendship which lasted for life. Owing to the pressure of their work and Scott's numerous social engagements, they did not often meet, but when they did, both at Mainsforth and at Abbotsford, it is clear, from the increasing warmth of their own correspondence and from Scott's letter to Southey, that they delighted in each other's company and "tired the sun with talking and sent him down the sky." It has been conjectured that Scott may have written part of *The Antiquary* at Mainsforth.[2]

The main purpose of their correspondence was the communication of legends and fragments of ballads, with discussion about their origin, and as early as in the second letter which he wrote to the master, Surtees, in one of his mischievous moods, sent him a copy of a ballad on the "Feud between the Ridleys and Featherstones," which he claimed to have heard from the lips "of an old woman of Alston Moor." He accompanied the transcription with a glossary and historical notes, attempting to identify the people mentioned and to determine the date of the ballad. Scott printed it all, with suitable acknowledgments, in a note to the first canto of *Marmion*,[3] and included it later in a revised edition of his *Minstrelsy of the Scottish Border*. But the whole thing was a

[1] Surtees, Vol. II, p. 295.   [2] Pope-Hennessy, *op. cit.*
[3] Note XII.

fake. Surtees never hinted at his authorship, doubtless through fear of giving pain to Scott, but he admitted, when taxed with it, the composition of another pseudo-Border ballad, and the discovery amongst his papers of several copies of this *Death of Featherstonehaugh*, changed and corrected to the language of the period, seems to put the question beyond doubt. But whatever naughtiness may have escaped from the antiquary's pen is more than outweighed by one, to us, most happy consequence of this correspondence. "I must now tell you," writes Scott, "(for I think your correspondence has been chiefly the cause of it) that by calling my attention back to these times and topics which we have been canvassing, you are likely to occasion the world to be troubled with more Border minstrelsy. I have made some progress in a legendary poem, which is to be entitled *Marmion*."[1] . . .

Thus engaged in the delight of intercourse with kindred spirits, in drives and wanderings about the countryside, in the improvement of his property, in generous hospitality to his friends, and in many acts of untrumpeted beneficence to the needy, but, above all, in the strict exercise of his religion and in the prosecution of his great work, this cultured country gentleman lived out his happy days. For he was, in spite of his acute sensibility, essentially happy; happy in his wife, happy in his friends, happy in his labours, happy in the woods and pastures and peace of Mainsforth. "I got home without rain," he writes to his wife, "and my spirits recovered wonderfully as soon as I saw Loughbank Wood. . . . It really is a glorious change to have elbow-room, and see green fields again, and red beech, and brown oak."[2] A threat to his beloved home filled him with alarm and fury. It was proposed to run the new railway through it, and a Bill was introduced into Parliament for that purpose. But he had friends in both Houses and he fought hard, until a progressive peer waited upon him and appealed to his "public spirit," after the usual smug manner of public-spirited men. "Surtees," he said, "you are attached to Mainsforth—we deeply respect your feelings; but we hope you will not suffer that attachment to stand in the way of a scheme which has public more than private advantage for its object. Is there no other place upon which

---

[1] Taylor, *op. cit.*, p. 22.   [2] *Ibid.*, p. 76.

you could set your heart? If there be, we have perfect confidence in your honour; name your price for Mainsforth, and
you shall have it without another word." But Surtees was not
impressed by all this blarney. "My lord," he replied, with
his usual bluntness, "buy me Blenheim."[1]

The Bill was passed, of course, but with some modifications
which made it less obnoxious and left it still possible for him
to continue to live in his home. Nevertheless, his forebodings
were justified. Today the "sequestered quiet and rural elegance" in which he delighted are no more, and Mainsforth
stands, forlorn and abandoned, on the outskirts of the large
industrial village which has grown up round Ferryhill Station.

The tender heart of our antiquary was constantly suffering
from its contact with the world both of human beings and of
animals. But he did not, therefore, shrink from this contact,
but went out of his way to relieve distress. "Even a worm,
or a fly," said his wife, "was never passed, if he could render
them assistance," and she had to give up keeping sheep and
cattle for their table, for if he noticed one to be missing he
promptly sought it out and released it from the "hunger-
house."[2] How his own people trusted this goodness of his
heart is well shown by the action of Mrs. Kirkby. She was the
widow with five children of one of his tenants, on whose
death she had continued in occupation of the farm. When she,
in turn, died, it was discovered that she had left a will, wherein she bequeathed everything she possessed to her landlord,
requesting that he would pay himself what might be owing
for rent and divide the remainder amongst her children.

On more than one occasion that we know of, Surtees sought
out and helped the miserable, notably in the case of the last
descendant of the family of Conyers, of Sockburn, who,
thanks to his own generosity and his appeal in the *Gentleman's Magazine*,[3] was rescued in his old age from the
workhouse.

To throw a last light on the character of this good man
before we are obliged to leave him, we will mention the part
which he played under a very awkward circumstance which
was not of his contriving. The excellent but very resolute,
and sometimes mistaken, Bishop Barrington had omitted,

[1] *Ibid.,* p. 77.   [2] *Ibid.,* p. 69.
[3] *Gentleman's Magazine*, Vol. CXXIX, p. 1110.

without explanation to anyone, the names of two magistrates from the list which it was then the custom for the Bishop of Durham to submit to the Lord Chancellor for his nomination. The two gentlemen omitted, one of whom was a parson, had served as Justices of the Peace for some time, and it appeared, on enquiry, that their names had been deliberately removed from the list by the Bishop owing to his disapproval of some action of theirs while on the Bench. Great was the indignation. The Bishop's motives, it was pointed out, might be admirable, but he had no right thus to eliminate two officers of the King because of his own private opinion. But the good Barrington remained obdurate, whereupon several magistrates in the county declined to act in their courts, and Surtees, himself a magistrate, agreed with them. But Bishop Barrington had been most kind to him personally, taking a great interest in his work and allowing him free access to the Palatinate papers, "a favour which," as the author himself tells us, "forms only one link in a series of unsolicited kindness and attention, experienced during twenty years."[1] Most men, under these circumstances, would either have ignored the situation and continued to sit on the bench until the matter should be cleared up, or would have written to explain and regret their reasons for abstaining. Surtees did neither. He resolved to pursue the course which he thought right, but he decided that the peculiar obligations under which he lay to Bishop Barrington demanded that he should first call on him in person and tell him of his purpose, face to face. This he accordingly did, with the consequence that the Bishop accepted his decision with regret, but never allowed it to impair their friendly relationship.

On January 27th, 1834, Mr. Surtees had a cold and felt depressed. Nevertheless, he would not stay indoors, with the consequence that, a week later, though his cold seemed no worse, he complained of a pain in his side. Then the doctor was sent for and he was put to bed. "He is in danger," said the doctor, "but I am not without hope." But Robert Surtees, from the first, had none.

"Annie," he said to his wife as he left his library for the last time, "I shall never be here again: these books will be

[1] Surtees, Vol. I, Introduction, p. 9.

yours." And soon afterwards, when he was lying in bed, with the sun shining through the window, "I shall never more see the peach-blossoms," he said, "or the flowers of spring. It is hard to die in spring."

A night or two before his death he was lying, as he wished to lie, alone and in darkness when the clock struck the half-hour. He thought that it was striking one, which was the time for his medicine, and rapped upon the wall. Mrs. Surtees immediately came in. "My medicine," he said. "Surtees, it is not one yet." "Yes, it is," he replied. "You are mistaken," she answered; "it cannot be." "Nay, then," said he, with a last touch of his whimsical humour, "what is to become of the world, Annie, if you are beginning to lie?"

Of his beloved Annie he seemed alone conscious during the last hours of his life, and the last words on his lips were: "Annie, I am dead." . . . Te teneam moriens deficiente manu.

And so farewell to you, Robert Surtees, and farewell to Mainsforth—to that sweet retreat amongst the trees and peacocks, dear to me for your sake, and dear for later ties; where I, too, have dined and talked with one bearing your name and skilled, as you, in ancient lore, and hospitable and kind,[1] as you were—and watched the evening sun slant through the window painted with your famous ermine coat. Let me take my leave of you now, in the last words of the last letter written to you by your friend Sir Walter: "Adieu, my dear Surtees, et sis memor mei!"[2] And if your constant faith has been rewarded and you are now driving about in some celestial gig, to examine the respectable antiquities of Heaven, may I one day be permitted to learn about them from your lips! Adieu, my dear Surtees, and adieu to all you loved and all for which you stood—the lettered ease, the gentlemanly conduct, the quiet English home. Adieu, my dear Surtees, et sis memoir mei! For most assuredly I shall never forget thee.

[1] Brigadier-General Sir H. Conyers Surtees, K.C.M.G., D.S.O., F.S.A., born, 1858, died, 1933. Author of numerous learned pamphlets on those portions of the county not covered by the work of his great predecessor.

[2] Taylor, op. cit., p. 92.

BOOK V
OLD AGE
(1832- ?)

Chapter XXVI

THE GATHERING OF THE WATERS

"To go no further back into original causes than the Act of 1832, it is apparent that the democratic principle then established was bound, sooner or later, to become supreme over every competing influence."
ROBERT CECIL, Third Marquis of Salisbury.

THE steam-engine was to the Victorian Age, upon which we are now entering, what the internal combustion engine—hideous name for a hideous thing—has been to our age. In each case the insentient mechanical "box of tricks" created a new form of civilisation and dictated the future social, economic and political development of mankind. Between them they have largely succeeded in destroying the spiritual values of life.

The engine which made the Victorian Age was itself made by coal. It was the county of Durham, therefore, the coal country *par excellence*, which gave to the world its first exciting vision of what has now become a mechanical nightmare, of those endless iron railways, to be followed by those endless metalled roads which have today become essential to the existence of man.

Although the commercial value of coal was beginning to be recognised in the sixteenth century, the problem of its extraction from the earth was not the only one with which the promoters of the industry were, for a long time, confronted. Once the coal had been brought to the surface there remained the difficulty of transporting it from the pithead. The roads in our county were particularly bad. Even late in the eighteenth century a Mr. Hoult lost seven horses in one winter in the mire at Rushyford, while, some sixty years earlier, carriers from the North Riding, coming to fetch coal in Durham, were obliged to bring axes with them to make their ways passable. The obvious solution was to send the coal by river and then by sea. This was accordingly done. The keelmen on the Tyne and the Wear rowed the coal to the river-mouth, whence it was taken by ship to London and elsewhere. But all pits were not situated in close proximity to a navigable river, and it remained, therefore, most desirable to expedite the passage of the coal to the staiths, where it was loaded in the keels. Moreover, London and the few places that could conveniently be reached by sea were not alone in wanting coal. All over England throughout the seventeenth and eighteenth centuries the woods were falling, falling, until, at the period of time which we have now reached, fuel was becoming desperately scarce. All over England people needed coal. There were still, therefore, two major problems to be solved: one was how to get the coal quickly to the staiths on the rivers for its transport by sea, the other how to distribute it throughout the land. Both these problems were considered separately, and the solutions to both were practically contemporaneous. They were at first different solutions to different problems, but it was not long before it was appreciated that the answer to the first difficulty was the better answer also to the second. The solution, therefore, which had first been discovered for the distribution of coal throughout England was dropped in favour of that other, or a development of that other, which had been adopted to expedite delivery at the staith. In other words, the digging of new canals was abandoned in favour of building railways.

The origin of the railway dates from the time when, to ease the passage of coal from the pithead to the river, flanged wooden bars were laid down for the wheels of the horse-drawn cart. The result was so satisfactory that a heavier four-wheeled waggon was soon substituted for the two-wheeled cart, and a horse was able to pull 42 cwt., where before he could only pull 17 cwt. By 1650 these waggon-ways were numerous in the Whickham and Winlaton districts. There followed, in course of time, the iron rail and the flanged wheel, then the stationary steam-engine (on Birtley Fell in 1808), and finally Stephenson's locomotive. On September 27th, 1825, the first railway in the world was opened. It ran from near Bishop Auckland, through Darlington to Stockton, and its object was to reach the sea via the Tees, and, more immediately, to supply the pitless south-east corner of Durham, where lay the Darlington and Stockton industries, with coal. Its effect was to develop the large mining area round Bishop Auckland, Spennymoor and Crook, which had now found an outlet for its produce. From this humble thread, let down in a grubby little corner of Northern England, were spun the huge and intricate webs of English and continental railways and, inspired by this modest example, the great railroads of America were soon beginning to link, not a pithead with a river, but the Atlantic with the Pacific. The world had begun to move as it had never moved before in all its history.

The following extract from a local record of events will show what contemporaries thought about it.

"The Stockton and Darlington railway was formally opened by the proprietors for the use of the public. . . . The committee assembled at the bottom of Brusselton engine-plane, near West Auckland, and here the carriages, loaded with coals and merchandise, were drawn up the eastern ridge by the Brusselton engine,[1] a distance of 1,960 yards, in seven and a half minutes, and then lowered down the plane on the east side of the hill, 880 yards, in five minutes. At the foot of the plane the locomotive engine was ready to receive the carriages, and here the novelty of the scene and the fineness of the day had attracted an immense concourse of spectators, the fields on each side of the railway being literally covered with ladies and gentlemen on horseback, and pedestrians of all kinds. The train of carriages was then attached to a locomotive engine, built by Mr. George Stephenson, in the following order: 1, locomotive engine, with the engineer (Mr. George Stephenson) and assistants; 2, tender, with coals and water (etc.). . . . The signal being given, the engine started off with this immense train of carriages,[2] and such was its velocity that, in some parts, the speed was frequently twelve miles an hour. . . ." They arrived at Darlington, having covered a distance of eight and three-quarter miles in sixty-five minutes, and then, after "arranging the procession to accommodate a band of music," they set off for Stockton, nearly twelve miles away, and reached it in three hours and seven minutes, including stops. "By the time the cavalcade [sic] arrived at Stockton, where it was received with great joy, there were no less than 600 persons within, and hanging by the carriages, which excited a deep interest and admiration."[3]

It is not surprising that they admired. That such a Heath-

---

[1] A stationary engine.   [2] There were thirty-eight.
[3] Sykes, *Local Records,* Vol. II, p. 188.

Robinson construction as now stands on Darlington platform was able to draw this enormous load even for twenty-five yards is a marvel at which we must wonder today. The speed, it is true, was not phenomenal, and doubtless the "Highflyer" coach, which covered the whole distance from Newcastle to London in thirty-six hours, must have drawn some comfort from this four-hour journey from Auckland to Stockton. Its spanking horses could go twice as fast over more than ten times the distance. It was not for nothing that their proud heads were decorated with hollyhocks as they danced their way into London. But, alas! though they may not as yet have realised it, this day were they irrevocably doomed.

So the Industrial Revolution came to pass. Coal begat locomotive and locomotive begat more coal and more coal begat more industries. Commercial enterprise eagerly seized its opportunities, and experiment and invention hastened to its assistance. In 1812 there were twenty shipyards at Sunderland, in 1833 there were thirty-four; in 1827 Mr. Walker, of Stockton, invented the friction match; in 1831 the first coals were shipped at Seaham "amidst the firing of cannon and the cheering of about five thousand people[1]; in 1832 Mr. Cookson was urged, as "the working man's best benefactor," to continue to destroy all the vegetation round his alkali works at South Shields[2]; in 1834 cages travelling in guides and tubs on rails were first used instead of corves for drawing up coal; in 1840 the iron-works at Consett were opened, and in 1853 at Tudhoe; in 1850 mechanical coalcutters were first used, and in the same year was formed the "River Tyne *Improvement* Commission" ("I thank thee, Jew, for teaching me that word"), whose members, by straightening, widening and deepening, and by replacing "the unsightly old bridges by the present handsome structures," "have made the river the wonder and admiration of all beholders from all quarters of the globe."[3] In the whole of the eighteenth century there were approximately sixty boring and sinking operations for coal; in the first half, only, of the nineteenth century, about 260.

Thus industry begat more industry, until at length, by more industry, was begotten the motor-car, and by the motor-

[1] Sykes, Vol. II, p. 305.   [2] *V.C.H.*, Vol. II, p. 301.
[3] *M.C.*, October, 1888.

car the aeroplane, and by the aeroplane the bomb, and by the bomb the atom bomb, and by the atom bomb . . . let us hope, the end of it all at last, in one way or another. For even mechanical inventions, and mechanical thoughts, and mechanical habits of life must come one day to an end. And that is the only consolation now left to the lover of beauty. "I see that all things come to an end," said the Psalmist, "but thy commandment is exceeding broad."

The Industrial Revolution practically coincided with the French one. Between them they laid the smoke-blackened and · blood-stained foundations of our modern democracy. The seeds of Liberty, Equality and Fraternity, which, had they been planted amongst woods and meadows, might have ripened slowly with a pastoral sweetness, falling as they did upon masses freshly congregated to meet the new demands of Industry, upon poor and miserable people torn from their natural surroundings and cast, neglectfully, upon mean and miserable streets, developed all too quickly into the bitter fruit of class hatred. We do not know, for lack of evidence, how worse or better off materially was the new industrial worker in comparison with the eighteenth-century peasant. But we do know, incontestably, that there was great misery in the pit villages that sprang up like fungi all over the county, and it does not require much imagination to divine that poverty in the country home, surrounded by "the beauty of field and wood and hedge, and the immemorial customs of rural life—the village green and its games, the harvest home, the tithe feast, the May-Day rites, the field sports,"[1] was a very different proposition to poverty in a mining village, with fourteen hours of every day spent in the dangerous and abysmal darkness of the bowels of the earth. Why, then, did the people leave their trees and cornfields? It may be answered that human beings are seldom the best judges of their own best interests; that novelty always tempts; that, little though it was, there was still a little more money to be made in the pits than in the fields; that like draws like and all but the solitary-minded are prone to herd together. But there were more definite reasons than these. The population of the county was rising, while, at the same time, the village industries were

[1] Trevelyan, *Social History*, p. 475.

dying. In 1730 there were 97,000 inhabitants of the Bishop-rick; in 1801 over 149,000, or more than half as many again. And the progress of the eighteenth century revealed not only a more rapid increase in population than hitherto, owing to the gradual improvement in medical science, but also the first tendencies to organised manufacture. The Industrial Revolu-tion did not leap fully armed from Mr. Stephenson's head. It had been slowly piecing itself together for years, and he and his fellows merely puffed its hot life into it and made its wheels go round. Already there were worsted mills at Dar-lington and 500 looms there making linen. Already the Germans had banded themselves together at Shotley Bridge to forge their swords, and Sir Ambrose Crowley had formed his little community at Swalwell to make pins and anchors. Already Durham and Barnard Castle were weaving carpets, while Durham was also famous for its mustard, and Barnard Castle for its tanneries, its stockings and shoe-thread. Already an increasing number of ships was being built. Already there were glass-works and potteries at Sunderland and Shields and Gateshead; and the Beamish forges near Chester-le-Street were casting the finest cannon in England; and John Ken-drew had erected his mill at Haughton-le-Skerne and become the first spinner of flax by machinery in the world.

But we remember "the spinsters and the knitters in the sun." The village of old England was not a mere agricultural nucleus, but a self-contained, self-supporting centre, spinning and tailoring and tanning and brewing and forging, and weaving its own baskets and making its own carts. Now Mr. Kendrew and the benevolent Sir Ambrose and the busy Quakers were drawing all these village craftsmen into their large industrial net. Further enclosures of common land may have contributed a little to this exodus from the countryside, but could not have exercised, in Durham, as powerful an influence as is commonly supposed. Between 1756 and 1809 114,000 acres of land were enclosed, but most of this was moorland in the west.[1]

And so the country slowly died. But it was a lingering consumption, and flushed at first with a brightness that seemed

[1] *V.C.H.*, Vol. II, p. 359, and W. E. Tate, "A Hand List of English Enclosure Acts and Awards" (*Proceedings,* Fourth Series, Vol. X, p. 124).

to indicate health. Scientific agriculture became the order of the new day. Societies were formed for its improvement, notably one at Rushyford, of which the brothers Colling[1] and Mr. Surtees, of Mainsforth, were members. The old, casual ignorance of the northern farmer was now harassed by impatient and enthusiastic landlords. The objection to drainage on the ground that it "took the sap out of the land" was no longer considered adequate. But it was heavy work, sometimes, trying to get sense out of a Durham man who was suspiciously resolved not to supply it. "How much corn do you give your horses?" asked that other Mr. Surtees (of Hamsterley) of a local farmer. "Not a vast," was the encouraging reply. "Do they get any?" "Oh yes; whiles." "Well, how often?" "Noos and thens." "How much, then?" "Why, we dinna give them ne fixed quantity." "Perhaps a boll?" "Aye, why . . . perhaps a boll." "Or perhaps a bushel?" "Aye, perhaps a bushel; whiles one, whiles t'other."[2]

But nevertheless the work went ahead. The Colling brothers and other intelligent farmers concentrated on the breeding of cattle and sheep and horses; the home-farms of the large estates now being formed, at Wynyard and Lambton and Windlestone and elsewhere, copied the excellent example of Raby and became models for their immediate neighbourhood; and the Durham Agricultural Society, founded in 1786, was holding annual meetings by the middle of the following century. In 1832, in spite of the progress of Industry, one-third of the labouring classes was still engaged in agriculture. A hundred years later the proportion of all males with agricultural occupation to all those engaged in other work is given as one-fortieth.[3]

In 1875 began a great agricultural slump, caused by the American capture of the corn market. The prairies of the Middle West were producing at last, and their grain was being rushed to Europe by the new railways and the new steamships. The prosperity of British agriculture was destroyed. But nobody minded very much, least of all in County Durham, where the pits and the shipyards and the iron-works were smoking and clanging away; for now there was a strong

[1] Charles Colling 1751-1836, Robert Colling 1749-1820.
[2] Surtees and Cuming, p. 162.
[3] J. E. Hodgkin, op. cit., p. 17.

division of classes, and the aristocratic system of agriculture, with its landlords and its tenant farmers, was of no interest either to the pitman and mechanic or to the coal and iron and shipping magnates, who had other things to think about. The drift from the land of agricultural labourers now set in with a vengeance. In 1851 there were 10,000 of them in Durham; in 1901, in spite of the enormous increase in the population of the county,[1] the reduction of the hours of labour, better food, higher wages and better cottages, this number had been halved. Ten years later, although there had been a further general increase,[2] those employed in farming numbered under 5,000.

The country landlord, who had shown the way in the improvement of agriculture and forestry and in the beautifying of the countryside, was simultaneously fading from the picture. From 1875 dates the decline of the landed aristocracy, which was finally destroyed by the mortality and the taxation of the two great German wars. Though the Industrial Revolution itself, with all its inevitable consequences, was the fundamental reason for the death of the English gentleman, the actual fatal blow was dealt by the American Democrat and the *coup de grâce* was given by the Prussian Junker.

In the eighteenth century, as we have seen, the era of organised manufacture had already begun, but the effect of these interesting inventions and experiments was infinitesimal at first upon the life of the vast majority of people. The inspection of Sir Ambrose Crowley's works at Swalwell did not rouse "our Hutchinson" (as Surtees called him) to thoughts of commercial rivalry nor evoke from him the slightest suggestion that this enterprise was but the forerunner of a new form of civilisation. It simply sent him enthusiastically to his Virgil. The sight of the anchor-smiths at work struck him with "a pleasing astonishment" and made him exclaim:

> *"Alii ventosis follibus auras*
> *Accipiunt, redduntque; alii stridentia tingunt*
> *Aera lacu;"*[3]

and so on.

[1] By nearly 800,000.   [2] Of over 180,000.
[3] Hutchinson, Vol. II, p. 442.

But the day had now come when the hiss of molten iron and the roar of furnaces and of windy bellows would stir to eager competition a new class of men, not at all likely to quote Virgil. There was now such an opportunity to make money as only occurs once, not in a lifetime, but in generations of lives, and the business-men arose to seize it. The coal-owners, no longer limited to a few county landlords uniting in a "Grand Alliance," formed a new class of their own, which was joined by the ironmasters and the shipbuilders, and these three called in yet another new class, the technical experts, to their assistance. Thus society substituted as its primary standard of culture the smart, trained intelligence of the mechanical engineer for the simple native wisdom of the shepherd. Meanwhile, at the bottom of the scale, the ship-wrights and the iron-workers and, above all in this county, the pitmen, were congregating.

The old relationship of master and man was no longer possible. The pit apprentice could not be educated by his master nor share his roof and board nor eventually marry his master's daughter. There were too many pitmen. There was too much to do in a hurry. There was too much money to be made. And the work was altogether different. Thus a new, less personal, more antagonistic relationship was established between employer and employed. For master and man were substituted Capital and Labour—each with big letters—and, as the mounting wealth of industrialists and the accumulating sordidness of the workmen's surroundings became increasingly obvious, the rift grew wider and deeper between Rich and Poor.

Doubtless an opportunity was now presented to the natural leaders of society, the landed aristocracy, at least to lead the people in a campaign for improved conditions, if they could not bring themselves to compete with the new manufacturers on their own ground. Some of the coal-owners did, in fact, belong to old county families and many of them were enjoy-ing the direct, and all the indirect, fruits of the coal industry. But their instincts, their tastes, their inherited activities were indissolubly bound up with the countryside. They played their part in preserving that; and while, from a distance of a hundred years, it is easy to look back and criticise, it is less easy to say precisely what should have been done—beyond the exercise of a private benevolence, which was, in fact, rarely neglected. However that may be, whether the worst consequences of this industrial revolution were inevitable or not, the social results of it were that, overworked, overcrowded, underpaid and uneducated, the working men sought their own remedies for their sufferings—and found them. For education they devised the Mechanics' Institutes, of which the first, in the North, was opened at Newcastle in 1824, and which were soon spread all over the counties of Northumberland and Durham. To protect their families against the retail dealer and to train themselves in business they started the Co-operative movement. And to improve their wages and their conditions of labour and living they formed trades unions. These, with periodical "sticks" (as the old strikes were called) and an undercurrent of political agitation, were the main weapons in the armoury of the pitman and the artisan.

But there was nothing subaqueous, in 1832, about the clamour for reform. The demand for it was at least as strong amongst the manufacturers and industrialists and some of the landowners as amongst the miners. Cuthbert Rippon, Esq., and Sir William Chaytor and Messrs. Pease held dinners and meetings to support and to celebrate it; Darlington stoned Lord Tankerville, as he drove through the streets, for having voted against it; and Bishop van Mildert wrote to a friend that he dared not show his face in his own Palatinate. On the other hand, ten years later, a crowd of pitmen, all sporting the Conservative colours, refused to give the Radical John Bright a hearing. But Democracy was now on the march, and neither obstinate peers nor Conservative pitmen—whether acting from conviction or from fear of their employers—could arrest its progress. Reform followed reform and opened the way for more to follow. It was not long before the majority of the miners were members of the Liberal party. Nevertheless, there still remained much of old-fashioned North-country stubbornness, and as recently as 1907 an historical writer could then truly state that "the Durham miner is seldom a Socialist."[1] It is only within the last forty years that the social and economic dislocation caused by two great wars,

[1] Frederick Bradshaw in *V.C.H.*, Vol. II, p. 251.

combined with the artful propaganda of foreign Marxist doctrine, has destroyed the rugged and independent outlook of the North. The popular mind, already debilitated, secularised and standardised by our modern system of education, was thus prepared to renounce the teaching and principles of that individualistic religion which, in his earlier struggles, had proved to be the strength and inspiration of the Durham miner.

For it was Wesleyanism, with its offspring, Primitive Methodism, which had shed the only ray of light and joy upon the drab lives of these industrial workers, while pointing to the practical blessings of organisation and self-improvement. It was the faith inspired by these forms of religion that raised the miners' leaders above the ruck of drunkenness and immorality and set them to work with enthusiasm to seek the betterment of their fellow-men. The early history of the Durham Miners' Union is not the history of a religious movement, but of the interpretation of an earlier religious movement (whether a right one or a wrong one is beside the point) in the terms of sociology. Only as time advanced did the influence of religion gradually lose its power until the day dawned when the greatest of the miners' leaders of the past ascribed the strife and bitterness that succeeded the first world war to its final elimination. "We older men," he said, "were religious men, mostly Methodists. We feared God and kept faith with our fellow-men; but these new men who are now in the saddle care nothing about God, and make little of breaking contracts. They want victory at any cost."[1]

Here John Wilson sounds the contrast not only between the old and the new Durham leaders, but between the nineteenth and the twentieth centuries. That which essentially differentiates the Victorian Age from its predecessor is its industrialisation; that which differentiates it from ours is its individuality and its religious belief. Individuality, selfish and rampant, actuated by the spirit of gain, reckless of the beauties of Art and Nature, sowed many of the seeds of that bitter harvest which we are reaping today. But it was the individual, also, who went out to save or to govern an Empire, while the

[1] John Wilson. (See Henson, *Retrospect of an Unimportant Life*, Vol. II, p. 102.)

individual who stayed at home stayed conscious and proud of his heritage (even though his conception of its nature might be mistaken and peculiar to himself). "In Queen Victoria's reign we'es gotten a great and mighty Empire," said a Durham farmer at a Jubilee celebration; "we's gotten the wole of America, Africa, India, a canny slice out of Airsia, Australia and New Zealand. . . ." Religion was the inspiration of the best and the greatest of these Victorians. It sent forth the Havelocks with their swords and their Bibles, tempered and soothed the acrimony of industrial disputes, prompted and animated those numerous leaders in humanitarian activities who so distinguished and graced their epoch, and brought to the conduct of public and private affairs the criterion of honour and the test of duty.

Between 1831 and 1841 the population of the county increased at the prodigious rate of nearly 7,000 a year,[1] and for a long time thereafter it continued exceedingly to multiply. In 1851 it was 391,000, in 1861 over 508,000. Thirty years later it had practically doubled this number and had topped a million. It was not surprising that the Church had a hard struggle to keep up with this multiplication table, and it was fortunate for her, and for Durham, that one of her hardest-working Bishops (Baring) and two of her greatest (Lightfoot and Westcott), who between them covered the most difficult period of sixty years,[2] arrived upon the industrial scene to cope with its increasing difficulties. Though the Church of England never succeeded in recovering the chance she had missed when Wesley appeared, at least she did not lose more ground. By her new evangelical activities she kept many within her fold who might otherwise have become Dissenters, and the energies and examples of our great Victorian Bishops exercised not only a profound influence upon the spiritual, but even some upon the industrial, development of the Bishoprick. During Baring's episcopate 102 new parishes were formed; Lightfoot's régime was known as the "Golden Age"; and Westcott was dubbed "The Pitmen's Bishop." In 1882, in order further to meet the needs of a still increasing population, the new diocese of Newcastle was carved out of the old Bishoprick. In 1800 there were 82 parishes in the county, in 1920 there were 272.

[1] 1831—239,256; 1841—307,963.   [2] 1841-1901.

If we turn to the æsthetic evolution of this period, we turn to darkness and dismay. But it is a darkness which we, groping in our own Egyptian fog, stumbling over our beastly tin bungalows and our tubular furniture, have more reason to envy than to despise. The Victorians, at least, admired, and strove to emulate, the works of their predecessors. Though they destroyed much, they tried, mistakenly, to improve and restore much more. We, with far more knowledge of how things should look, and (we think) with better taste, may fiddle cleverly with an old church or house here and there, and multiply our societies for the preservation of this and that, but we will ruthlessly destroy whatever stands in the way of our utilitarian aims or tends to complicate our utilitarian problems.[1] The irremediable mischief wrought to the beauties of art and nature during the whole of the nineteenth century is as a fleabite compared to the destruction that has followed in the wake of that invention of the devil, the internal combustion engine. The sneers at Victorian taste are a little exasperating from people who have pulled down Berkeley Squares and Adelphis and evolved the ribbon road, the bungalow, the public garage, the cinema palace, the multiple store and the prefabricated house.

We owe the destruction of the beautiful in our country to three separate proceedings or events: the Protestant Reformation of the sixteenth century, the Puritan fanaticism of the seventeenth, and the Mechanical Age of yesterday and today. Of these the last is by far the most guilty. Roundhead soldiers and Scottish prisoners smashing stained-glass windows and high altars display but an impish petulance in comparison with the satanic savagery of planners and surveyors; and Dame Whittingham burning a sacred banner or Dean Horne wrecking a shrine are angels of light in contrast with those who did their utmost to degrade and humiliate Durham Cathedral by

---

[1] I may, perhaps, be reminded that, on purely æsthetic grounds, the erection of a large power station near Durham Cathedral has been (so far) prevented (see following note). But this is an extraordinary exception to the normal course of events. When we are not dealing with such prima-donnas as Durham Cathedral and St. Paul's, but with the more modest beauties of nature and of architecture, with the general charm of a village or a square or a landscape, our "necessities" in roads and car-parks, in bungalows and flats, in offices and in factories, take precedence over all other considerations.

the juxtaposition of a monster power station.[1] The Victorian "improvements," in their turn, fell far short of our own abominations, but nevertheless the advent of the industrial régime involved an immediate æsthetic decay which has only sunk deeper as the machine has grown stronger. All through the last century the terrible story goes on of removal, improvement, restoration, rebuilding and destruction. In Durham City alone much damage was done. During the reign of Bishop Barrington the Norman gateway to the Castle was modernised by Wyatt. In 1820 the tremendous North Gate at the top of Sadler Street, built by Cardinal Langley and one of the finest monuments of mediæval architecture in England, was destroyed, on the ground that it interfered with the traffic. The twelfth-century church of St. Mary-the-Less was completely "restored" in 1846. A year or two later the "Bull's Head" (or "New Place"), the old town house of the Nevilles, was pulled down to make way for the present Town Hall; and the important church of St. Nicholas, in the market-place, became of less importance when it was rebuilt from top to toe in 1858. Meanwhile, all over the county, similar glad tidings of the removal or refashioning of mean and antique structures were being announced in pompous language in the local press, while Methodist chapels of unbelievable ugliness were erected in every mining village and hundreds of necessary new churches and town halls rivalled each other in their curious interpretations of Gothic and "Early English style." The modest rambling country houses seized this opportunity to expand into mansions with pompous Palladian porticoes, with suites of rooms and marble chimneys and gilt and gingerbread.

[1] The proposed site of this power station was one mile from the Cathedral. The new building, of which the main block was planned to be 320 ft. long and 140 ft. high, was to be graced with two chimneys, each of a height of 350 ft. and three concrete cooling towers, each 90 ft. wide at the top and 260 ft. high. The new site was 100 ft. lower than that of the Cathedral, whose great central tower is only 218 ft. high and about 30 ft. square. This proposal was strongly supported (because it would bring employment to the neighbourhood) by the Trades Union, the County Council, the local branch of the Farmers' Union and the Durham City Council. It was rejected owing largely to the national feeling aroused by the efforts of the Dean and Chapter. (See article by "T.S." in *D.U.J.*, December, 1944.)

Durham Cathedral could not, and did not, escape. Already in the eighteenth century (much more than by the Scottish prisoners from Dunbar) great damage had been done to the old glass, partly by a gale which blew in the great east window, partly by local improvers. Nevertheless, the glass in the Chapel of the Nine Altars, though "mutilated" and "confused," still existed[1] until James Wyatt, called in to do his best in 1796, removed it because it darkened the church. This was, however, one of the least of his improvements. In 1796 he destroyed the Norman Chapter-house, the finest in England, in order to enlarge the Dean's garden. His simple procedure was to let down the roof with a bang, so that it smashed everything beneath it, including the old stone chair, wherein all the Bishops of Durham, from the earliest times down to Bishop Barrington, had been enthroned.[2] He has also been accused of chiselling away the exterior surface of the Cathedral, but herein, it seems, unfairly. There is a note-book in existence which belonged to a certain Mr. Ogle, who wrote in it justly and indignantly some years before Wyatt appeared on the scene. "There lives in Bow Lane," he tells us, "one George Nicholson, who . . . made Dr. Sharp and the Prebends believe he could greatly add to the beauty of the church by new chiselling it over on the outside. . . . This Nicholson is now going on with what he calls repairs in the year 1780, though I had rather see the dust of antiquity than anything which can come from him."[3] There must have been plenty of dust, at any rate. It has been computed that no fewer than 1,100 tons of stone were removed by this chiselling process.[4] Not only was the exterior of the Cathedral thereby deprived of its rich Norman-mouldings, its play of light and shade, and the quaint charm of wallflowers and stone-crop that used to lodge in its interstices, but its whole structure, its absolute existence must have been seriously threatened and its term of life curtailed. But the old Abbey has proved so tough as to stand even this, though we are left

[1] "The Stained Glass of Durham Cathedral," by W. H. D. Long-staffe, *Arch. Ael.*, Vol. VII (1876).

[2] The chair has now been repaired, as far as possible, and the Chapter House has been restored to its original dimensions.

[3] "A Note-book of the Rev. James Raine," by the Rev. C. E. Whiting, D.D., *Proceedings,* Fourth Series, Vol. X, 1947.

[4] Hodgkin, *op. cit.,* p. 101.

with only the bald, shadowless idea, only the cold, bare out-
lines of its original beauty.

But if Wyatt's chisel cannot fairly be blamed for this
disaster, he would have done far worse had he had his own
way. After he had destroyed the Chapter-house, his further
proposals included the clapping of a spire on the top of the
tower (in imitation of Salisbury, no doubt) and the driving
of a carriage road from the Castle to the great West Door,
which was once more to become the main entrance to the
Cathedral, as in its earliest days. Unfortunately, since then
Pudsey had erected his beautiful Galilee Chapel. This,
therefore, would have had to be pulled down. It must be
admitted that there is an almost magnificent self-confidence
in these sweeping suggestions, but, however magnificent, Mr.
Wyatt's plans were brought to nought by the indignation of
the public. Educated opinion was aroused at last and successfully exerted its pressure upon the Dean.

It is difficult to defend this Dean, Lord Cornwallis, though
it would be agreeable to do so if for no other reason than
because he was a peer and it is fashionable nowadays to abuse
peers. But he must bear the chief responsibility for these
outrages, though it is only fair to him to add that they were
in accordance with the spirit of the times. He could scarcely
have carried out these innovations in the teeth of the Chapter,
and we know that the Bishop also employed James Wyatt
not only at Durham Castle, but to build him a new gateway
at Auckland. Nor were the activities of this gentleman's
deforming hand limited to the northern Palatinate. They
were doubtless all, architects and ecclesiastics alike, honourable men, suffering only, like Mr. Midshipman Easy, from
an excess of zeal and too much money. There is a story, indeed, about Lord Cornwallis which shows him in a pleasanter
light than as an enlarger of his garden.

The curate of Merrington, a very poor man with a very
large family, had lost his only cow, and Surtees, of Mainsforth, with his usual kindness, was raising a subscription to
buy him another one. So he called upon the Dean of Durham
to ask him how much he would give. "Give!" said the Dean.
"Why, a cow, to be sure! Go to my steward, Mr. Surtees,
and tell him to give you as much money as will buy the best
cow you can find." "My lord," exclaimed the witty his-

torian, "I hope you will ride to Heaven on the back of that cow!"[1]

Let us also hope that he did, for most assuredly he did not get there on the shoulders of Mr. Wyatt.

[1] Surtees, Vol. IV (Memoir), p. 46.

Chapter XXVII

SKETCH OF A COUNTY

"Is there no balm in Gilead?"

JEREMIAH.

THE shape of this county is roughly that of an equilateral triangle, or a wedge, with its base to the east, where it is bounded by the North Sea. The northern line of this triangle is formed by the Rivers Tyne and Derwent, and the southern by the River Tees. Through the centre of the county twists the Wear, while the apex of the triangle is in the high lands of the west, where the four rivers spring, at no great distance from each other. From Killhope Law in the west, about 2,200 feet high, down to the seaboard in the east the countryside rolls and slopes away steadily downwards, with the consequence that, poorly protected by trees, it is much annoyed, in the spring, by the north-east wind. The difference between the climate of the north-east and the south of England lies less in the severity of the winter—the prevailing wind is then westerly—than in the persistence of this invigorating but somewhat irritating north-easter well into the summer, making it rarely possible to sit out of doors in comfort, save in some sheltered nook. But it has its compensations. On a high summer's day the little clouds sail merrily, the loveliest ripples run through the long grass, and the shadows of the rustling beech-tops dance and play with the sunshine along the woodland path. And when the day is falling the wind and the smoke between them toss and tear above a sad, mean pit village, imperial banners in the evening sky. George Moore and other æsthetes deplore sunsets, and no doubt there is a risk of vulgarity in them. But there is no need to fear that here. The smoke and the wind and the hard, crude wheels and chimneys against the vast expanse of the sky make a picture too grand and too stern for a gentlemanly French-poplar criticism. And when the night falls and the myriad little lights twinkle all over the countryside from villages suddenly grown beautiful in darkness, while the furnaces brandish their assegais and the great iron-works at Consett,

484

crowning all, tip up their regular, recurring streams of fire—
then one is almost tempted to be grateful to Industry. And
she can make beautiful sounds as well as sights. What
northerner has stood on his doorstep on New Year's Eve and
heard the weird chorus of innumerable buzzers, wailing and
moaning, faintly and more strongly, mingling with the bells
in the midnight sky, and has not brought away with him the
memory of them to southern climes and felt a blank there
where he can hear them no more? Henceforth to him the eve
of the New Year, without a buzzer and without a first foot,
has little significance. Nevertheless, all this occurs at night,
and there is another picture presented by day, on a dreary,
sunless, drizzly day. Then the pit villages do not look so
beautiful. Can nothing be said for them? They have been
much abused—and, we fear, rightly—by various authors,
social, political, topographical and poetical, while some des-
criptive writers ignore them absolutely. In *The Villages of
England* the author mentions not a single village in County
Durham, and, speaking generally of northern villages, he
says curtly: "They are altogether without the rich and varied
charm of the South."[1] In *The Landscape of England* another
writer, after praising the Cathedral, remarks that "for the
rest, the county of Durham can be dismissed quite briefly,"
and proceeds to do so in a single paragraph. "The villages
and straggling towns of the mining districts are ugly and
depressing,"[2] he says. As for the authors of *Homes and
Gardens of England*,[3] they cannot, between them, find a
single home or a single garden in the whole of our unfortunate county. These books indicate very fairly, no doubt,
the average Englishman's impression of County Durham—
some miserable mining area; part of Yorkshire, isn't it? with
a fine cathedral that can be seen from the train. But Mr.
Sharp, the author of the excellent *Shell Guide* to Northumberland and Durham, takes a very different line. He pins the
bull bravely, even roughly, almost rudely by the nose.

[1] *The Villages of England*, by A. K. Whickham (Batsford, 1932),
p. 50.
[2] *The Landscape of England*, by C. B. Ford (Batsford, 1933), pp.
6 and 7.
[3] *Homes and Gardens of England,* by H. Batsford and C. Fry.
(Batsford, 1932.)

"Whether the reader of this guide likes it or not," he barks, "I declare here and now that it is my intention not to let him pass, if I can help it, through these two counties without showing him something at least of the shameful ugliness and the social decay of some of its parts, as well as the delight and beauty of others."[1] What can we answer to all these strictures, implied and explicit?

With regard to the pit villages and the mining towns themselves, it must be admitted that we cannot say much. They are ugly; they are depressing; they are mean and sordid; and between them they combine, as Bishop Henson once told the House of Lords, "the population of cities" with "the social resources of hamlets."[2] The cottages themselves, eaveless and austere, built of hideous brick or chilling stone, are set in endless rows, one behind the other, growing dingier and more squalid as they are further removed from the main street. A heavy pall of depression hangs over the whole industrial area; the few trees in the hedgerows, between the towns and villages, have been well described as "cast in metal"[3]; the flowers in cottage gardens, wherein the pitmen once delighted, have now given place to the necessary but unattractive vegetables in a litter of unsightly allotments; the young men, their hands in their pockets, slope against the walls of the houses (less often, now, squatting on their hunkers with a whippet between their legs—there is nothing to poach!); the children play "last across" in front of the wheels of motor-cars; and the dreary blue flag of the impersonal Coal Board flies over all. Yet we must not confuse social discontent and misfortune with architectural ugliness, though the two may be closely related. At least part of the dreariness which we associate with these villages is due to the mental outlook of their inhabitants. Whatever the cause may be, the spirit in the mining area today is very different from what it was even forty years ago. No doubt the physical surroundings have played a part in influencing, if unconsciously, the minds of those who have passed their lives amongst them, but they have not played the only part. To be fair to the vil-

---

[1] *Northumberland and Durham,* by Thomas Sharp (Batsford, 1937), p. 6.
[2] *Retrospect of an Unimportant Life,* Vol. II, p. 78.
[3] *The County of Durham,* by G. E. Mitton, p. 105.

lages themselves, we must picture them, not as they are now, peopled with a disgusted population wavering between two ages in the history of mankind, but as they were when society was stable and industry was humming, the chapel was filled, and a stern purpose, whether to get more coal or to fight for better conditions from the employers, animated the spirits of the miners. "Wey," said a Victorian pitman to his marrow,[1] "wey, aa wed hev the tornpike up if it was coal."[2] No pitman would say that today.

These small towns and large villages, ugly though they be, have played a part in life all the more real for its hardness, and they have thereby acquired a certain sad and grimy dignity, far superior to the cocky vulgarity of the villas and bungalows of the South. But these, alas! are now almost as typical of the outskirts of a northern town as of London or Southampton. The new suburban blatancy of Darlington is more revolting than any pit village, and it would not be possible to say of these gimcrack abortions, as was said of Sunderland in reply to a protest against the endless sullen rows of Victorian houses: "Maybe, but it's a *solid* bit of County Durham."

Moreover, there is something to be said for "home," however disgusting it may appear to a foreigner. A detached observation may be correct and honest to any detached observer, but an observer cannot see with the eye of the native. To the northerner a slag-heap, because he has been familiar with it since his earliest childhood, may mean as much as a mountain to the heart of a Swiss peasant. It represents home. Transport a miner to the hollyhocks and thatched roofs of the South, and he will pine for his drab slate and stone and for his sunless, treeless days.

But are these "ugly and depressing villages and straggling towns" all that we can find to say about our Bishoprick? Is this the county that has been so lovingly described in the past? What has become of the "paradise" of Surtees, the "enamelled country" of Camden, the "christall rivers" of Hegge, the "orchard" and "the green and fragrant herbs" and the "sweet flowers" of Wheler? Has all, then, been destroyed by Industry, and is the "Landscape of England" justified in ignoring the landscape of Durham? Let us see.

[1] Mate. [2] *M.C.*, Vol. I, p. 111.

The mining and industrial area does not occupy the whole of the county of Durham, but, roughly speaking, the centre, the north and the east coast. The south is agricultural, though blotted in the middle by the semi-industrial town of Darlington. The west is moorlands and hills and valleys, a country of sheep and shepherds, of heather and waterfalls and wild flowers. Even if we confine ourselves to the industrial region, to the north of a line drawn from Auckland to Hartlepool, we shall find much natural beauty still escaped from the spoiler. Enough, and more than enough, has been destroyed, but there are oases here and there—the woods of Finchale, the old church in its trees at Pittington, the dene of Castle Eden, the sudden seclusion of Hamsterley—and nothing can detract from the rolling grandeur of the centre of the county and from the great skies above it. The views from lofty eminences within the area, such as Merrington, Coundon Gate and Westerton, absorb and digest with a magnificent indifference all the petty details of human activities. The Derwent Valley in the north-west, where the squirrel hopped from tree to tree, has been denuded and scarred and smudged and smutted, but the hills and ravines remain and the collieries smoke like great battleships on a tumbled sea.

There are places in this industrial region worth the seeking. Pittington Church, already mentioned, tucked away in verdure on the outskirts of a mining village, has a very fine north aisle with a curious snake-like design on the pillars, as well as a few faded remains of early twelfth-century frescoes representing incidents in the life of St. Cuthbert. These once covered the whole interior of the church and were, it is scarcely necessary to relate, mostly destroyed in the nineteenth century. Ryton Rectory, which dates from the late fifteenth century, and was altered in the early eighteenth, has a fine black oak staircase and a garden front, beautiful, sad and decaying, in the midst of the industrial devastation of the Tyne. In the sixteenth century the rector complained of the noise of the rebecks and the dancing of the people in front of his house. Would that he had cause for the same complaint today! At Horden, the largest single pit in England, is one of the best of the numerous manor-farmhouses in the county, but it has lost its fine Jacobean mantelpiece adorned with the arms of Conyers and Claxton, and its staircase. This staircase was probably the best (save for Cosin's in Durham Castle) of the many good ones in the county. Now, though intended for erection elsewhere, it lies lost—with its elaborately carved gods and goddesses, its animals and birds—in some basement or warehouse.

But it is not our purpose to make a catalogue for sightseers, only to give some evidence that, even in its mining districts, the county can present a few remains of civilisation not unworthy of the regard of the passer-by. We must, however, mention, with more detail, two remarkable buildings, very different from each other in purpose and in their present condition, but both set in the middle of pits and machinery. The first is Gibside and the second is Ushaw.

The property of Gibside, which lies, not far from Gateshead, in a magnificent country of hills and valleys, belonged originally to a family called Marley. From the Marleys it passed, through an heiress, to the Blakistons, of Coxhoe, who built the present house in 1620. From the Blakistons the property descended, again through an heiress, to Bowes of Streatlam, the descendant of that Sir George who was the hero (or the villain) of the Northern Rebellion. Finally, Mary Eleanor Bowes, yet another heiress, married the Earl of Strathmore and thus conveyed both Gibside and Streatlam to the family which thenceforth took the name of Bowes-Lyon. Streatlam has been sold, but Lord Strathmore is still the owner of Gibside.

The fine Jacobean house, with Georgian additions, stands half-way up a hill with a sheer drop into the valley to the north of it. To the south it was enclosed, at a respectful distance, by great wooded hills. Between the house and the woods were the grounds, laid out in the noble, spacious eighteenth-century manner by George Bowes. A splendid long avenue of turf was closed at one end by a charming Georgian chapel, pillared and balustraded, and at the other by a column 140 feet high, surmounted by a statue of Liberty, which still, somewhat incongruously now, commands the countryside. The house is good, the grounds are the best example of Georgian landscape gardening in the county and would be admirable anywhere, but best of all is the grandeur of the setting. "It is not easy," says Surtees, "to convey any adequate idea of the magnificent woodland scenery of Gib-

side. The best point of general view is from Bryan's Leap.
Woods, venerable in their growth and magnificent in their
extent, sweep from the height of the hills to the brink of the
Derwent, intersected by deep, irregular ravines and relieved
by plots of open pasturage."[1] Now the deserted house, bescribbled by the populace, stands in a waste of fallen trees;
now the whole property is bestunk and begrimed and shamed
by chimneys and collieries and coke-ovens and gas-works;
now it is degraded and forsaken, open to the naturally
destructive propensities of man. During the war the place was
occupied by troops, who tore up the floorboards, wrote their
names and various obscenities on the Jacobean porch, pock-
marked the back of the building with rifle bullets, and left a
litter of paper and broken glass. In the neglected undergrowth, where blackberry pickers wander by the dozen, as if
on their own land, stand the ruins of a pretty Georgian
banqueting hall or shooting lodge, also adorned by the pen
of the people. The chapel is still in use and in good condition,
but it has to be protected by barbed wire and the windows by
wire netting. The pitiful plight of this once beautiful place
and the apparent impunity with which it has been subjected
to contemptuous, ignorant and brutal treatment at the hands
of the vulgar are a disgrace to any community that pretends
to civilisation.

The College of Douay, which was founded in 1568 to
supply Catholic missionaries to England, was seized by the
French revolutionaries in 1793. The few students who still
remained within its walls were allowed to take refuge in
the very land for whose disturbance their college had been
formed, and in the spring of the following year they were
gathered together at Tudhoe, now a colliery village on the
road from Bishop Auckland to Durham, where there was a
Roman Catholic school. Amongst their number was John
Lingard, the future historian of the Anglo-Saxon Church. In
October of the same year the little band moved onwards to
Crook Hall (the earlier home of the Bakers, of Elemore),
and on July 19th, 1808, they walked over to the new house
which they had built at Ushaw moor on a high ridge over-
looking the city of Durham. Here they have remained ever
since, while their numbers have grown from eight to over

[1] Surtees, Vol. II, p. 254.

three hundred. The majority of these are educated for the priesthood. The pupils of Ushaw still retain some of the old Douay customs, for their special game of "cat," a kind of baseball or rounders, was inherited from the earlier college, and their classes—"Figs" (Figures), "Grammar," "Rhetoric"—are still called by the old Douay names. The students proudly proclaim a triple loyalty—to the Church and the Pope, to their country, and to their college. In defence of these they have laid down their lives. While, a few miles distant, Mr. Cowen, of Stella Hall, was encouraging and entertaining Garibaldi, students from Ushaw, with a few inhabitants of the neighbouring village of Esh, were fighting against him for the Pope. Some years later Pius IX, in reply to a request from the boys for a special "play-day," expressed his appreciation of the devotion of the college in the following charming message: "Servite Domino in lætitia," he wrote, "etiam in tribus pleidays."[1]

The buildings of Ushaw dominate the countryside, and it is with a shock of surprise that we encounter this vast, gaunt edifice in the scrubby world of pit villages. But the surprise is greater when we have entered the building and noted the huge dimensions of the dining-room and seen and admired the rich and elaborately impressive neo-Gothic church with its great altar by Pugin, forty feet high, its angels and pillars, its alabaster and marble, its side-chapels and mosaics. It seems strangely exotic and splendid on this barren, smoke-grimed moor, but all this richness is confined to the church and its immediate precincts, and there is no mistaking that the splendour is dedicated to God and that the atmosphere of the whole college is one of simplicity approaching to austerity, of discipline, hard work and religion. In the distance, across the moor, all that is left of the Prior's favourite Beaurepaire crumbles unnoticed into ruin.

While in the centre of this industrial region, within sight of the towers of St. Cuthbert (whose ring they cherish as their most precious procession), the children of the Old Faith are prospering once again and waxing strong, in its south-west corner the Anglican Bishop of Durham shivers in the Ser-

[1] "The Rising of the North in 1569," by George Phillips, *Ushaw College Magazine*, Vol. II.

vants' Hall of his palace for want of a bucketful of that coal of which his predecessors were the lords and owners.

The chief glory of Auckland Castle is its chapel, which has already been noticed. The house stands on the very edge of the town of Bishop Auckland in what was once described as a "dainty stately park" of eight hundred acres. Here, in 1635, a visitor to Bishop Morton saw some of those famous cattle which are now only to be found at Chillingham—"about twenty wild beasts, all white; will not endure your approach, but if they be enraged or distressed, very violent and furious." Less than seventy years later, when the cattle, destroyed by the Puritans, had been superseded by deer, the gracious deer-house was erected which Mr. Hutchinson noticed when he took a prospect from Binchester Hall. Now the park, though still retaining the remnants of beauty, can scarcely be dubbed either dainty or stately. Part of it has been thrown open to the public, and in part of it golfers from the neighbouring town, less dangerous and less beautiful, have succeeded the cattle and the deer. The hooligans who wrecked the deer-house have also broken some windows in Bishop Cosin's chapel. There are interesting, and some beautiful, rooms in the castle as well as some excellent pictures, particularly the Zurbarans, a magnificent Lawrence of Bishop van Mildert, and another very fine one of Bishop Barrington. This Bishop, one of the last who had or who could afford regal ideas, battlemented the outside walls, with no mean effect, but made rather a mess of the great drawing-room, cutting it up for the sake of a lobby and adding a Gothic pseudo-shrine over the doorway. Here, too, he installed a throne and held receptions to the neighbouring gentry. But the present Bishop of Durham does not even own this last of the numerous residences of the Palatine Princes. The Ecclesiastical Commissioners are the anonymous Princes today and the Bishop holds his castle as their tenant.

Within a short distance of Bishop Auckland is the quondam mining village of St. Helen's with some remains of old houses facing the village green. In one of these, a Jacobean house with a later addition, lived a Carr of the family who owned Cocken, in whose deserted brambled grounds we were standing a short time ago. This William Carr, M.P. for the county and renowned for his lavish hospitality, built the

large, handsome dining-room in an upper storey whose noble
eighteenth-century ceiling and mantelpiece and doors still
forlornly remain; but the floor of the room has collapsed. It
was used by the Army during the last war as a dump for
stores, and the colossal weight put upon the rafters beneath
proved too much even for the builders of that period. The
house itself, which is let to the County Council, is cut up and
occupied by smallholders, and the fine plaster-work in the
staircase hall is rapidly crumbling to pieces.

After Durham and Jarrow, by far the most interesting
church in the county, and one of the most interesting in
England, is at Escomb, another mining village, two miles
from Bishop Auckland. This tiny building, dating from the
seventh century, is the best example of an early Anglo-Saxon
church that can be found in these islands. Yet we know
nothing about its history; there are no traditions connected
with it; and it was unnoticed until late in the eighteenth
century when probably Canon Greenwell or, as is also reported, a doctor from Byers Green, was the first to discover
its extraordinary antiquity. Save for the insertion of two nineteenth-century windows, which might be worse, it is practically
unspoilt and in excellent condition. It was built of Roman
stones, which were taken from the camp at Binchester on the
other side of the Wear, and one of which, placed upside
down, bears an inscription to the "Victorious Sixth Legion."
It is strange to note, as one visits church after church, how,
quite independently of their architectural beauty, an atmosphere of religion and of peace is in some markedly present
and in others even more remarkably absent. In Edmundbyers, a little church on the top of the moors on the borders
of Northumberland, where the choir consists of one little girl
of about nine with a cloud of fair fluffy hair, a surplice and a
mortar-board perched rakishly on the side of her head, and
where the parson dashes to and fro between the organ and
the reading desk, the atmosphere is strong. Sedgefield, a much
finer church, is disappointing in this respect; Easington is a
blank; but St. Andrew's, Auckland, perched on a hill in the
middle of the dreary pit village of South Church, and St.
Mary's, Gateshead, in the very heart of the hubbub of the
Tyne, are both redolent with the piety of centuries. Durham
Cathedral, from which one expects most, does not come up to

15

expectations, and the prelude to this little Saxon church of Escomb is discouraging. One has to make one's way to it through a crowd of screaming children, who are clambering over the churchyard wall in a manner utterly regardless of the sanctity of the place. But once inside the high and narrow nave, with the door shut and nothing but the rough stones around one, with one magnificent pure Roman arch in front of the minute square chancel, one is overwhelmed by the sense of a past and of a peace stretching back into the remotest antiquity. And after one has at last regretfully departed, locked the door behind one, forced one's way back through the screaming children and surrendered the keys to the old woman who lives in the cottage opposite, she laments, with us, that now religion means nothing to youth—only the picture-house and the wireless. Certainly religion meant something to those old monks, who could thus convey it to us through the stones of their little building across twelve centuries.

We have learnt this year[1]—even after universal wars and monumental massacres, even when involved in painful social dislocation and lying in the extraordinary shadow of atomic destruction—not to despise the simple river-flood. We can therefore sympathise with the people who suffered from a series of these calamities in the eighteenth century. The worst flood was in 1771, when the rivers suddenly rose several feet, the old Tyne Bridge between Gateshead and Newcastle, with its houses upon it, was swept away, part of Gainford was flooded by the Tees, the Wear destroyed the Prebends' Bridge at Durham, and a vessel off Shields rescued a baby, alive and well, floating in its wooden cradle on the sea. Others, however, were drowned, and many beasts, and both banks of the Tyne were littered with the wreckage of boats and keels. Even the high dales were not exempt from the disaster. The "Yad Moss," a large area of spongy moorland high up between Teesdale and Weardale, unable to absorb the increment of waters, was "brust," and the flood roared down into the valleys.

But for the most part these dales were peaceful places, subject, since the days of Scottish raids, only to the occasional

[1] 1947.

outbursts of Nature, such as that which, hundreds of years ago, drowned the poor chieftain in his cave near Heathery Burn. Even Weardale, for all its lead-mines and rough lead-miners, who set the rude tone of the place in the early years of the last century, was self-contained and peculiar, a little land with its own customs and names and language. Today, with the miners nearly all gone, it is quieter than ever. Here, in these dales, is the refuge of the people of Durham, and for its exiles they remain as memories throughout their lives.

"I used to climb the summit of Intake as a boy," recalls an old Weardale man who has long been pent in cities and rushed with business, "to watch the sunrise, of Harehope Ghyll, where the waters make music amid Frosterley marble."[1] Waters and marble are typical of Weardale, and so are heather and wild thyme, and purple and yellow pansies, and the surprising apple-green of the fields and the pink of the moors, and the blue hills, and the pale blue sky, and a light heart. For Weardale is "chearing to the eye," as our old friend Hutchinson tells us. It is greener, more fertile, cosier, less grand, more *riant*, as the French charmingly put it, than the neighbouring valley of the Tees. Stanhope, in the heart of the dale, the centre of the Great Hunt of the Palatine Bishops, where later Joseph Butler was rector and wrote his famous *Analogy*, is a cheerful, friendly little town; and even the knowledge that Rogerley Hall, on its outskirts, is about to be pulled down by a timber merchant can do no more than rouse a passing feeling of indignation. It was remarkable for its oak panelling. But it is Nature who matters here, not architecture, and, unlike the rest of County Durham, unlike almost the rest of the world, she fights no losing battle in this happy valley. Indeed, the population of Weardale is decreasing, though it is still large in comparison with that which is sprinkled about the neighbouring valley of the Tees. The lead-mines in these two dales were probably not worked by the Romans, but certainly since the days of King Stephen. In the first decade of the nineteenth century there were as many as forty-eight operating in Teesdale and thirty-four in Weardale, but now they are practically exhausted. This

[1] *The Methodist Magazine* ("Letters in War Time," by Sydney Walton, 1944.)

valley was the last in the north of England to use galloways for the transport of lead ore. Each of these hardy little animals, about twelve hands high, carried two hundredweight of ore on their wooden saddles. They were unbridled but muzzled, to prevent them from grazing on grass which might be poisoned by the lead, and they moved in strings of twenty-five, their leader with a bell round his neck. "The galloways are coming!" cried the children when they heard the tinkling of this bell, and the people would come out to their cottage doors and, shielding their eyes from the sun, watch the long string of horses out of sight over the last hill. They were seen no more after about 1875.[1]

A mine is still being worked at Stanhope and another at Bolt's Burn, while recently an old one has been reopened at Wolf Cleugh. There is also an ironstone mine at Carrick, in Weardale, which employs about a hundred men. But the rural character of this happy valley is scarcely affected by these activities. It is now essentially a land of smallholders, a pattern of little stone-walled fields criss-crossing each other up and down the hills. From Westgate (the West Gate of the Bishops' Hunting Park) as far as Killhope we are in what is still known as the "Forest Quarter," and on the verge of this, at 2,000 feet above the sea, we are alone with the sky and the moors, we have reached the boundary of our county, and our feet are on "the Plains of Heaven."[2]

It is surprising—or it would be surprising, did we not know the age in which we live—to find at Stanhope today, not the Bishop's chief forester with all his hounds and underlings, not a profound philosopher lost in thought on a black pony,[3] but an "Approved School" for little boys under fourteen, run by the Home Office. Few more delectable retreats for naughtiness could have been chosen than Stanhope Castle, which is not a real castle, but built on the site of an old one by Cuthbert Rippon, a reforming M.P. for Gateshead. Now his own house has been reformed, which serves him right. The view from it down the valley is an enchanting one, the

[1] "The Last of the Carrier Galloways," by John Lee, *Proceedings,* Fourth Series, Vol. X, 1947.

[2] Not an official name, but so this high land has been called. (J. W. Carr, unpublished address on May 30th, 1941.)

[3] Bishop Butler.

rooms within are light and airy and spotlessly clean. The fitted basins, the shining taps, the rows of nail-brushes, the cheerful paint, all are so different from what we remember of our schooldays—the dark peeling walls of the candle-lit lavatory and the water cascading into the classrooms—that one cannot help wondering whether this is not "too much." It is, at any rate, interesting to compare the amenities now provided for the boys of an "approved school" with the conditions which were deemed good enough for gentlemen's sons a hundred years ago. "We used to rise at seven or eight o'clock in the morning, according to the season of the year," wrote the author of *Jorrocks* in recalling his schooldays, "and proceed to a little washing-room in which were four basins (for sixteen boys) and four roller-towels against the wall. There were no jugs and no convenience for changing the water, so the last-comer had it anything but pure. The insoluble soap was like a square of ivory, it was so hard and slippery. The ablutions, such as they were, had to be performed with one's hands—sponges, tooth-brushes, nail-brushes, anything of that sort being considered superfluous. Such a thing as a looking-glass was altogether unthought of. . . ."[1] Perhaps we altogether think too much of material conveniences in these days. Man shall not live by drains alone.

The dalesmen, living far from civilisation, harried by robbers or harrying in their turn, on the alert for a Scottish raid or counter-raid, were a hard folk in the old times, less open to the softening influences of religion than the inhabitants of the rest of the county. If these were rude and backward and ignorant in comparison with the south of England, as we have so often been told, they must still have been enlightened in comparison with the dwellers on the remote moors. Nevertheless, both Stanhope and Wolsingham (the capital of Weardale) were regularly served by parish priests from the earliest times, and the Rectory of Stanhope was one of the richest and most important livings in the Bishoprick. Here Tunstall ministered in his younger days, and Isaac Basire, and Joseph Butler, and Thurlow, who became Bishop of Durham, and Phillpotts, afterwards Bishop of Exeter. But these excellent, cultured men were scarcely of

[1] Surtees and Cuming, *op. cit.*, p. 9.

the stuff to form the ideal priest of a rough neighbourhood.
They were more interested, perhaps, in the opportunity with
which this remote living provided them for the pursuit of
learning, or even the accumulation of wealth, than in the lives
of their rude parishioners. It is, therefore, not surprising that
when Wesley appeared and preached at Wolsingham he made
an immediate impression and that it was not long before
Methodism became the religion of Weardale. In a garage at
the back of Whitfield House, in Wolsingham, are the remains
of a rough stone "pulpit" from which he preached. This
uncompromising, open-air form of worship and exhortation
was admirably suited to these frank, free and sturdy people,
indifferent to snow and rain and impervious to the appeals of
a more refined religion. The influence of Wesley and his
followers on the manners of the people was remarkable.
Henceforward "strangers were greeted with civility instead
of with insult and a volley of stones."[1] Wesleyanism was
followed in due course by Primitive Methodism, and the
Church of England fought, at first, a losing battle with both,
wasting her time in abuse of dissenters instead of mending
her own ways. For such abuse there seems to have been little
justification, save that Wesley had succeeded where his de-
tractors had failed. Some of the bishops did their best—
Bishop Barrington in particular, as we have seen, spending
much money on schools for the Weardale children—but a
few years later a dalesman still complained of the lack of
influence of the Church in his part of the world, of the absent
incumbents and the foolish curates. "The present reforming
Bishop of Durham, Dr. Maltby," he wrote, "must be ignorant
of the state of this part of his diocese. It would be a pleasant
drive for his Lordship some fine Sunday morning, when he
might see for himself these desolate and empty churches."[2]

Before we leave Weardale and its lovely names—Rogerley
Hall and Heathery Dell, Hanging Wells and Burtree Linn
—let us take a last look at it through the eyes of one of its
children. We see the stage-coach at Stanhope, within living
memory, leaving for the upper reaches of the Dale; we see
the showmen's swings and roundabouts; we see the heather
and the wild flowers and the little waterfalls, the avenue of

[1] *Weardale Men and Manners*, by Jacob Ralph Featherston (1840).
[2] *Ibid*.

lime-trees paced by Joseph Butler, the "two gracious miles" linking Stanhope with Frosterly and the five stern ones "which take the wayfarer over Bewdley into Rookhope, rewarding him with 'a land of far distances,' and the Dale in its beauty."[1]

Arthur Young, the agriculturist who praised Lord Darlington's farm, declared that it was worth a journey of four or five days from London for the joy of seeing the country between Barnard Castle and High Force. This country is still unspoilt. But let us approach it, not from so vast a distance as London, but from Darlington, wending our way along the banks of the Tees until we have reached the gates of the moorland. From Darlington to Barnard Castle are no romantic glens and waterfalls, such as we shall presently encounter, no remarkable trees, no southern thatched roofs, no palaces nor towers, no ecclesiastical edifice of extraordinary interest, nothing but an English countryside through which an English river twists its way, and a few houses worth glancing at and a village church or two not quite spoilt beyond redemption by the restorer. And yet this is an enchanting drive, for it is taken through a piece of Northern England at its very best—not reminding one of Scotland, like Teesdale, nor industrialised, like the Derwent Valley, nor wild and bleak, like parts of Northumberland, but gentle and rural, like the South, and yet retaining its own individuality. The few villages help enormously. Without Piercebridge and Gainford and Winston, with their large, wide greens, sweet colour-washed walls and the old red tiles above them, much of the singular charm of this drive would be lost. And no doubt it soon will be, for here we have entered upon the great Raby Estates, which stretch far away over Teesdale, and it is the taste and discretion of a single landowner[2] that the people of Durham have to thank for a large proportion of the beauty of their county. Alas! it is no rash speculation to presume that, at the present rapid rate of regression, the "people" will soon be the only landowners and that thenceforward the people will no longer be able to enjoy one of the prettiest drives in England. For it will have been spoilt by their officials.

Apart from the general attraction of this countryside, there

[1] *The Methodist Magazine*, Walton, *op. cit.*   [2] Lord Barnard.

are various little features of interest. There is the old George Inn at Piercebridge, with the charges for stabling still painted on the board; there is Gainford Hall, built by a Cradock and now a Jacobean farmhouse; and Gainford Church, where the parson, on three successive days, married a Pigg, christened a Lamb, and buried a Hogg. There is the famous sword of Conyers, still kept by its owners in a house on the village green,[1] and there are other houses in the neighbourhood: Selaby, once owned by Sir Robert Brakenbury, Lieutenant of the Tower when the little princes were murdered; Sledwick, which had a gorgeous ceiling when Surtees saw it, "thickly decorated with crowned roses, fleurs-de-lis and pome-granates,"[2] and which still has a priest's hiding-hole and an underground passage running round the house; Snow Hall, where died Old Drummer, the horse, at the staggering age of forty-seven, long after he had been wounded at Sheriffmuir; Stub House, where lives the great grand-daughter of "Nimrod,"[3] with its elegant eighteenth-century front, its windows removed from Streatlam, and its pretty conceit of a leaden fox let into a garden wall, with a Latin inscription beneath it recording that it was the gift of the mason; and Westholme, which is described by Surtees as "a good speci-men of the domestic architecture of the middle gentry in the age of James I,"[4] and which now, thanks to the taste of its owner,[5] rivals Headlam (also in this neighbourhood) for the first place amongst the smaller houses in the county. But it is not the houses, mostly tucked out of sight, which are re-sponsible for the charm of this southern portion of our county. It is the villages and the river and the landscape—the walk, for instance, from Gainford churchyard to Winston, or the pause on the hill, on the high road, just before Winston Church, to enjoy the calm of the evening, and the soft blue distance of Yorkshire, and the sky, like a dove's wing, tipped with pale gold.

Now we pass Streatlam and Raby, out of sight on our right, and we approach Barnard Castle. But our fancy is not engaged, as it should be, with the history of the little town. We are not conscious of Dickens, with whom it is mildly

---

[1] No longer. It is in the Dean and Chapter Library.
[2] Surtees, Vol. IV, p. 48.   [3] C. I. Apperley.
[4] Surtees, Vol. IV, p. 42.   [5] Captain F. M. C. Curtis, R.N.

associated, nor of Oliver Cromwell, who was entertained here with burnt wine and shortcake. We do not even notice this time the great museum on the outskirts, and we pass unheeding by the scattered emblems of the boar in the walls of the houses. The ruins of the castle itself serve only as a background to our thoughts. For our mind's eye is busy with the vision of a "cherry-cheeked swain, standing upright, in a close blue coat or frock with guards, a red rose in his right hand, held close to his breast, and in his left a scroll."[1] So Surtees described him when he saw him supporting an altar-tomb in the church some hundred and more years ago. On the scroll was written: "He cometh forth like a flower and is cut downe. . . ." He has been cut down. At least, his blue coat has been faded into insignificance and his red rose withered.

So we wander somewhat feebly round the town, bored with Dickens, keeping the museum for another day, pleased with the old houses in the broad main street, shocked but not surprised to hear of the damage done to one of them[2] by the soldiers of a neighbouring camp, and watching, for an idle five minutes, the frantic efforts of an enormous tank-carrier stuck in the middle of the lovely Elizabethan bridge and engaged in knocking it piecemeal into the river. Bridge and castle and rushing, bubbling river, these are the highlights in the picture of this attractive little town, "spread before the eye like a map in a fine sunset" against the background of those hills to which our steps are bound.

Some years ago Mr. Ralph Wightman, a farmer from far-away rustic Dorset, paid his first visit to Teesdale. He was surprised and he came again, and one winter he broadcast to England a homage from the South to this northern valley. "I haven't seen a waterfall anywhere in Britain to beat High Force," he said, "eighty feet high, foaming down through the rocks; and Cauldron Snout's another beauty. Everyone says that you should see Teesdale in spring, but I like it as it is now. The colour's so grand on a sunny winter's day. You know how your fells look—tawny when you're close to them,

---

[1] Surtees, Vol. IV, p. 83.
[2] Blagroves House. Once an inn where Cromwell is supposed to have stayed in 1648.

and then fading off into real deep blue in the distance. And there's a glint of ice in the river."[1] And Mr. Gowland, who has lived at Barnard Castle all his life, finished the broadcast with these words: "It's bare and wild—there's some of the wildest country still left in England up at the head of the dale. Wherever you go you hear the rushing of water—all the little becks and streams hurrying down the hillsides to join the Tees and go crashing over Cauldron Snout to High Force. There's an openness and airiness up here that's wonderfully invigorating. People from the towns come and are refreshed, and come back year after year. And to all of us who live here in Teesdale the open fells are the very breath of life."[2] Colour and space, water and air, these are the characteristics of Teesdale; the colour of the hills and the skies, of the heather and the wild flowers, of the waterfalls and the rocks, all pulled together and rendered piquant, as a savoury dish with just the right quantity of mustard, by the happy, white dotting of Lord Barnard's farms all over the far-stretched landscape; the space of the treeless, unpeopled moors and of the great shouldering hills and of the vast sky above them; the noise of the waters of Cauldron Snout and of High Force; and the open air of a high land far above the miasma of towns and untouched by the stench and toil of centuries.

You reach Cauldron Snout, at a height of 1,400 feet, after a long walk over lovely springy turf, with nothing in your eyes but great slices of sky and nothing in your ears but the cries of curlew and the occasional clutter of a grouse. It is the wilder, the more remote of the two cascades; not a single waterfall, but a series of them, one after another, like a helter-skelter rush downstairs. High Force, in more sophisticated surroundings, at the foot of a wood of fine larches, traversed with paths for the convenience of the public, is a sheer fall over the banisters, the most headlong fall in England. In spite of the somewhat Teutonised picturesqueness of its surroundings, this is no pretty water-colour waterfall—as it has been so often represented—but strong and fit for oils: the water, chrome yellow mixed with cream as it falls, and lying in a great pool of Mars red at the bottom;

[1] *Darlington and Stockton Times*, February 16th, 1946.
[2] *Ibid.*

the rocks a greyish red at the top and a dark purple half-way down. The loud yet strangely soothing roar hypnotises one into a state of agreeable imbecility, while the solid rocks fly surprisingly upwards as one transfers one's gaze to the earth after the deep attraction of falling water.

There follows a long tramp back, with the westering sun behind one, to Middleton-in-Teesdale, the little market town; and a pause on the way to chat to an old dalesman, who looks like a rugged, stately tower, but walks very slowly, very slowly indeed. He is crippled, poor man, with the "rheumatiz" and his complaints about these horrid pains are uttered with a beaming countenance and are loud as a cheerful thunderclap. It's only "saltz," he says, that do him any good.

In the churchyard at Middleton we mark the fine, tangy, robust and even lordly names of earlier dwellers on these uplands. There lies Peart (so this is where the "charming Miss Peart" has sprung from) and Tarn and Spraggon and Vipond, and John Wearmouth, of Common Top, and Nicholas Wearmouth, of Newbiggin, and Benjamin Smedley and Rebecca Lee. And as we stand musing in the gathering darkness over these forgotten dead suddenly a harassed vicar comes charging through the churchyard, pulled hither and thither by a nanny-goat and two white kids, whose chains wind and unwind themselves in a confusing and intricate game of cat's cradle about his bewildered and unwilling legs.

We must leave this land of peaceful hills and homely, friendly people, where a true civilisation still lingers and the beauty of the North lies still unspoilt. Nor will we weary our reader with a further description of scenery. He must go now and see for himself. Enough has been said to show that there would have been some justification, after all, for a word about our county in the Landscape of England, that the Bishoprick is, even now, not all coal-mines and pit villages, that there is a sovereign balm for these in Gilead itself, a physician on the banks of the Tees, and a recovery in the dales for the daughters of Durham.

Chapter XXVIII

BIRD AND BEAST AND FLOWER

"O ye Whales, and all that move in the Waters, O all ye Fowls of the Air, O all ye Beasts and Cattle, O all ye Green Things upon the Earth, bless ye the Lord."

Morning Prayer.

WHALES are not unknown to the Palatinate. In 1343 Bishop Bury, as the possessor of royal rights, laid claim to four royal fish, two whales and two sturgeons, which had been cast upon the coast. Bishop Fordham, some years later, waxed indignant over a porpoise, seized floundering on the beach by Robert Brown, of Hawthorn, and other malefactors, and commanded the sheriff to summon a jury to enquire into this act of *lèse-majesté*. A school of whales was observed in 1850 off Tynemouth and a prodigious quantity of small fish took refuge from them close to the shore, only to fall into the maw of man. Remarkable fish have been caught off the Durham coast and even in the rivers, including a brilliant king-fish, or opah (a sort of gigantic many-hued mackerel), of 77 lb., which was hauled out of the sea near Hartlepool towards the end of 1839, and a far more monstrous sturgeon, which was later landed near Stockton from the Tees, and weighed 15 stone. But these are mere freaks of Nature. The ordinary fish and the fish *par excellence* of the county of Durham, of the Rivers Tyne and Wear and Tees alike, was the salmon. So enormous were the quantities of this creature taken in the Tyne in the eighteenth century that it was sold, on occasions, for as little as 1d. a pound in Newcastle market. But the fruits of Industry have robbed us of this plethora of deliciousness. Already, about 1820, Surtees was complaining of the extreme decrease of this fish in the Tees "from the pernicious effect of the lead-mines on the higher streams and shallows,"[1] but nevertheless the salmon still made their way up to Barnard Castle, and some miles beyond, to spawn, and this mild pollution of the sources of rivers was as nothing compared to the horrors which were to come. The Tees, indeed,

[1] Surtees, Vol. III, p. 176.

504

was the last of the three rivers to succumb. In 1822 a contributor to the *Newcastle Magazine* was sorry to say "that
the proportion of Newcastle salmon in London market is very
small indeed." But he was not surprised, "for it is impossible
that such immense quantities of chemical compounds should
mingle with the waters of any river without poisoning its
inhabitants. . . . Why do not these fish-destroying establishments," he continued, "consume their refuse instead of
throwing it into the Tyne? . . . It is to the interest of every
one of us that we should not wilfully destroy one of the best
articles of food that Providence has sent us."[1] But, alas! his
words were drowned in the clang of hammers and the hiss of
escaping steam. More and more fish-destroying establishments
were to set up their headquarters on the banks of this once
beautiful river, where Bede had sat and fished and listened
to the ring-dove. In 1818 the first steam tug had appeared on
the Tyne; in 1852 the first screw collier was built at Jarrow;
and in 1861 dredging operations were begun which soon
transformed the whole river, making it much more agreeable to Industry and much more disagreeable to salmon.
They had long since ceased to appear in the Newcastle market
for 1d. and 1¼d. per pound.

Meanwhile the Wear was tarnishing its silver reputation.
Sunderland, "the marvel of the Victorian Age," was busily
engaged in straddling its mouth, and collieries were springing up on its banks, discharging their effluents into its stream.
By the end of the nineteenth century the "clear and amorous"[2]
embrace with which this river formerly clipped her beloved
city had been transformed into a slattern's hug. A few years
later the Dean of Durham[3] could safely promise to erect a
pavilion on a sports ground, on condition that he could catch
a salmon in the Wear. The Tees, however, was still holding
out. More salmon were caught in this river in 1895 than for
some time past. Ten years later the *Victoria County History*

---

[1] "A Journey from Newcastle to Edinburgh by the Mail Coach,"
Newcastle Magazine, New Series, Vol. I (February, 1822).

[2]   *"With which beloved place I am so pleased here,*
            As that I clip it close, and sweetly hug it in
            My clear and amorous arms."
                        Michael Drayton, "Polyolbion."

[3] Bishop Welldon.

could still speak of them as present in the Tees[1] (and even, though "rarely," in the Wear). Nevertheless, the end was close at hand, and Middlesbrough and Stockton have, at last, proved too strong. On May 27th, 1946, the Tees Fishery Board "passed a resolution calling the attention of the Ministry of Agriculture and Fisheries to the grave concern felt at the pollution of tidal rivers." Mr. Bainbridge said that "years ago many people made a living of netting salmon at the river mouth, but that had stopped when Middlesbrough and adjoining places just poured the sewage into the Tees. For that reason the Tees 'went to pot' as a salmon river." But Councillor W. Breckon (Middlesbrough) put the matter in a nutshell when he said that "he was inclined to think that with places like Middlesbrough with their big industries, industries came before fish."[2] He might have added that they come before man.

Today industrial pollution in the lower reaches of the Tees is not so bad as it used to be, but pollution by sewage is worse. And thus, and therefore, the salmon moves no more in the waters of Durham.

There are still trout to be found in the Tees, but even these are now threatened. The Wear, in its upper reaches, is comparatively clear, and here the brown trout may be fished, while the sea trout runs the river in the autumn. As for the smaller rivers, the Gaunless, which flows by Bishop Auckland, may serve as an example. In 1898 Canon Greenwell declared that he could remember this as "a clear stream and full of trout," but that it was "now little more than a filthy puddle in which a water-beetle could scarcely manage to exist."[3]

This famous archæologist and fisherman was the inventor of the trout fly known as "Greenwell's Glory," which was an imitation of the natural fly, the Olive Dun. The "Wilkinson" salmon fly was invented by Mr. Percival Wilkinson, of Mount Oswald, Durham.

The misled southerner (and, we must confess, the unobservant northerner likewise) does not associate Durham, its teeming population, its coal-pits and its shipyards, with a

[1] *V.C.H.*, Vol. I, p. 171.
[2] *Darlington and Stockton Times,* June 1st, 1946.
[3] *A.A.D.N.*, Vol. V (1896-1905), p. xix.

great variety of bird-life, but no fewer than 268 different species of the fowls of the air have been counted,[1] either as breeders or regular visitors or stragglers to the Bishoprick, at the present time. No doubt, were the whole of Durham stinking with Industry, as is commonly believed, this large number (which compares very favourably with the corresponding figure of 312 for the great bird-county of Northumberland) would be very considerably reduced. The reader will have guessed that the moorlands and the little hill-streams have once more come to our rescue. These western dales are not only a refuge for the people, not only a garden of wild flowers (as we shall presently see), but a land to "rejoice the ornithologist's heart."[2] Teesdale, much larger, wilder and less populated even than the upper valley of the Wear, is the cream of this country. Here, in the lower dale, driven away from many of their old haunts by the pollution of the streams, flit the kingfishers, with the dipper and the sand-piper; here the green woodpecker is seen within circum-scribed limits, and from here the nuthatch and the turtle-dove and the little owl are slowly spreading northwards. Higher up, where the meadow gives place to the moor, are the red grouse, heavier than their Scottish cousins and more abun-dant, though a succession of bad seasons has lately reduced their numbers. The shooting of grouse is popularly associated with Scotland, but the moors where run the boundaries of Durham and Yorkshire and Westmorland are the best in the British Isles. The blackcock, for some unexplained reason, is dying out, but up here, with the grouse, breed the dipper and the grey wagtail, the ring-ousel and (though very scarce) the dunlin, the golden plover and the curlew, the sprightly merlin that the pretty girls used to carry on their fists, and even a pair of peregrines, and even an occasional family of ravens in Falcon Clints. Of these the curlew has greatly increased in numbers during the last twenty years and, though generally regarded as only a moorland bird, now breeds in the lowlands also, all the way down to the sea. The common

[1] By Mr. George W. Temperley, M.B.O.U., Hon. Secretary of the Natural History Society of Northumberland and Durham. To him and to Mr. Joseph Burlinson of Heighington, County Durham, I am greatly indebted for the information contained in this section.

[2] V.C.H., Vol. I, p. 176 (by Canon H. B. Tristram).

buzzard, which Fordyce reported as practically extirpated by the gamekeeper over a hundred years ago,[1] shows signs of returning. An increasing number of young birds are arriving over the Pennines to spy out the land, nests have been built, and it is probably only a question of time before breeding begins.

It is on the sea-coast that the birds have chiefly suffered, as we might suppose, for, unlike the wild shores of Northumberland, here man has been making rapid progress with his beneficent activities, and all the rest of God's creatures find it consequently difficult to bless Him. The mouth of the Tees in particular, which, in the past, was famous for wild duck and sea-fowl, though it now presents no insuperable barrier (as to the unfortunate salmon), offers, through Middlesbrough and Stockton, such residential amenities as are more agreeable to men than to birds. Nevertheless, "our feathered friends," as we have the impudence to call them, have a measure of their own of obstinacy; so the shelduck breeds in the cavities of the sea-walls, which are made of slag from the steel-works, and the little tern and the common tern are struggling hard but mercilessly harried, and the sandwich tern has attempted to establish a colony, but in vain. The shoveller, the teal, the mallard, the tufted duck and the pochard, all these and more are known to breed here. During the years of war the barbed, banned coast was a refuge to them, they increased in numbers, and they would doubtless now establish themselves permanently if "the image of God" were to permit them to do so. But the development of Industry will spell their doom.

On Marsden Rock, an enormous, wild and rugged Arc de Triomphe, set about a hundred yards out to sea, near South Shields, where nothing of life was heard of old "but the petrel's cry and the sea-mew's shriek and the clang of the cormorant's wing,"[2] the sea-fowl had (for obvious reasons) long since ceased to breed when the fulmar petrel, extending her range from the east coast of Scotland and blissfully unaware that to choose a spot between South Shields and Sunderland was to select one of the most unpromising nurseries in England, alighted here some twenty-five years ago and confidently produced a family. Her young were destroyed, but

[1] Fordyce, Vol. I, p. 119.   [2] Fordyce, Vol. II, p. 735.

she was not disheartened. She persisted, and within a few years had established a strong colony, not only on the rock, but on the cliffs of the mainland. In 1934 she was joined by the kittiwake, who in turn underwent her period of persecution and in turn has survived. Then the war came to the rescue, a few herring gulls joined the community, and now, since the novelty of their presence has worn off and the natives are content to leave them alone, there is a possibility that, if they can side-slip the stones of enthusiastic visitors, these bold adventurers may secure a permanent footing.

In the centre of the county, in spite of Industry and the felling of woods, bird-life is not decreasing—rather the reverse—but it is changing in character. The breaking up of big estates, with the consequent loss of gamekeepers and the extension of arable land, have led to a multiplication of rooks, jackdaws, magpies, starlings and wood-pigeons. The substitution of conifers for deciduous trees has destroyed many favourite haunts of the little songbirds, for larch and fir are a poor substitution, in the bird's eye, if in no other, for oak and ash and beech. The widening of roads, the destruction of hedges, the draining of marshes (Bradbury Carrs used to be a rendezvous for wildfowl in the winter) and the uprooting of thickets have all reduced the number of nesting sites for the smaller species, but still they cling on, adapting themselves to changing circumstances, varying slightly in character. Thus the common whitethroat has greatly increased at the expense of the blackcap and the garden warbler. The linnet, thanks to the prohibition of the use of birdlime, has multiplied exceedingly. Before it was made illegal to catch and sell these birds they used to be caged like canaries, and great singing contests were held with them in the mining villages. The linnets were specially fed and then placed in covered cages facing each other. When the covers were whisked off and the birds began to sing, the one that sang longest was the victor and its proud owner pocketed his winnings. For the same reason the bullfinch is increasing, and the goldfinch and the hawfinch, once so rare, are fairly common. The redshank, previously only known along the coast, now nests freely inland in moist places and by the sides of streams. The willow tit (which seems to be replacing the marsh tit) and the lesser

16

whitethroat are both notable breeders in the southern half of the county. On the other hand, the peewit is growing scarce, for the old Durham ploughman, who used to stop his horse to lift the nest tenderly out of the way, has been replaced by the tractor juggernaut; and the corncrake, a frequent summer visitor of the past, is now but seldom heard. There is a single heronry in the county at Gainford, and it is much reduced in numbers. In the old days this bird was known to Durham folk as "Matthew Lambert's Mustardman," on account of rather an absurd story, which may, however, be worth repeating.

Old Matthew Lambert, a slightly deaf farmer of Brafferton, was expecting the arrival of a seedsman from Durham to buy his mustard. But he was a busy man with his work on the farm to do, so he directed his wife to call him when the mustardman arrived. He was busily engaged in mending a fence and wondering why he had not yet been called when, unseen by him, a heron flew over his head, uttering its harsh "Crake! crake! crake!" Matthew Lambert was relieved. "Ah!" said he, straightening his back, "there's ma wife Peggy calling me at the last."[1]

Though the native breeders and the regular movements of migrants form the chief interest of the expert, the arrival of a remarkable stranger or some freak of Nature may be likely to titillate the palate of the vague, ignorant and unobservant yet genuine lover of birds, such as is the writer, and possibly the reader, of this book. I shall therefore make no apology for introducing the following sensational bird news. On a certain day a distinguished ornithologist, Canon Tristram, was driving alone across the moors between Westmorland and Durham when suddenly a great blanket of fog descended upon him—not a rare occurrence on that moorland road—and blotted everything from his sight. So he pulled up his horse and waited hopefully for light. It came within a short time, but for a few seconds only, and then the darkness settled down as thickly as ever. But in that brief interval when the fog was lifted the man had seen, to his astonishment, motionless upon one of the low posts which mark the boundary of the road, fixing him with his great yellow eyes, only a few feet from him, an enormous golden eagle. When

[1] *Bishoprick Rhymes.*

the fog at last lifted sufficiently to enable the driver to proceed the bird had gone.[1]

The second beautiful surprise is a pure white starling,
which was seen[2] several times, both at rest and on the wing,
with a few ordinary mates, in 1909. The third is a flock of
waxwing, increasing from seven to seventy-five, which were
observed near Rowlands Gill, feeding sybaritically on guelder
rose berries, between November 1st and November 10th,
1931. The fourth is a party of three avocets (a sort of snipe)
observed in May of the same year near Stockton.[3] This year
seems to have been a particularly remarkable one, for our
fifth sensation also took place in 1931. This was no less
wonderful than the voice of the nightingale, which was heard
at Stampoly Moss, between Rowlands Gill and Winlaton, on
May 31st. The county of Durham is well without the breeding area for this bird, which is, normally speaking, never
heard north of York. It must be confessed, moreover, that
this particular creature was claimed to be one that had been
recently released from captivity in the neighbourhood.
Nevertheless, this is not the only occasion on which a nightingale has been reported, and though the experts say that, on
investigation, these other nightingales have proved to be
sedgewarblers, there was once[4] a singing in the grounds at
Windlestone which it seems difficult to ascribe to an under-
study. "We stood in the Mausoleum field," writes my informant,[5] "and definitely heard a few notes of the nightingale's song. Whether it was someone imitating the bird or not
I could not say. People came from all arts and parts to hear
it sing, bus-loads of them (horse-drawn, of course), as well
as pedestrians. In fact, one could hear people walking the
roads until the early hours of the morning." And a poem
was written on the subject for the *Auckland Times and
Herald*.

Whether the bird was genuine or not, there is something
singularly moving in this picture of tired Durham pitmen
pouring out in hundreds in their char-à-bancs, tramping the
roads for hours, all to hear the voice of a nightingale on a
May night long ago.

[1] *V.C.H.*, Vol. I, p. 177.   [2] By Mr. F. Burlinson, at Windlestone.
[3] By the late Mr. J. Bishop.   [4] 1894 or 1895.
[5] Mr. F. Burlinson.

The most famous beast ever associated with the county of Durham was the Durham Ox. This colossal shorthorn was bred by Charles Colling at Ketton, near Darlington, in 1796. John Day, who became its owner in 1801, later refused an offer for it of £2,000, a sum which must be compared to the average price for a beast in those days, which was about £17. The animal was carried round England in a special carriage and shown to farmers and the curious, many English inns were named after it, and when at last it was slaughtered its carcase was found to weigh 220 stone. With this ox Charles Colling and his brother Robert made their strain of cattle famous in England. From the animals which they bred at Ketton all modern shorthorns are descended. The two brothers lie today in the churchyard at Heighington, a village which, incidentally, when approached from the south, presents, with its groups of red-tiled cottages clustered at varying altitudes round the old church on the hill, as sweet a picture of rural England as can be found in any county. So far it has escaped the hand of the spoiler, but the Aycliffe Trading Estate and a coming "satellite town" will press upon it soon from no great distance, and nowhere in this country now may beauty long endure.

Already, some thirty years before the date of the Colling brothers, the breed of shorthorns had been begun by the crossing of a bull imported from Holland by a Sedgefield farmer with the "Teeswater" cattle, which, reared on the luscious pastures round Darlington, had long been famous for their great weight. The resulting "Durham Shorthorn" gave a high milk yield, but the quality of the meat was poor. It was from a visit paid by Charles and Robert Colling to Bakewell, of Dishley (in Leicestershire), "the great pioneer of livestock improvement," that the brothers learnt the method of selection and inbreeding by means of which they evolved their famous strain. Mason, another Durham farmer, still further improved the breed. For his cow Marcia he refused 700 guineas; his bull Charles was the most expensive in England; and his home at Chilton, near Ferry Hill, succeeded the farm at Ketton as the Mecca of the breeder and the agriculturist.

The green pastures of Darlington regaled not only cattle,

but also, and chiefly, sheep. It was by crossing these sheep, also known as "Teeswater," with the "Leicesters" from Dishley that the Border-Leicester breed was evolved in Northumberland. The breeders, two brothers called Culley, were originally Darlington farmers. The present breeds of sheep are mostly crosses between Hampshire, Oxford and Wensleydale in the lowland farms, and Swaledale on the moors. The favourite carthorse is the Clydesdale.

Sheep lead us naturally to wolves, which King Edgar did his best to extirpate in very early days. He was not entirely successful; the creatures increased again during the lawless periods of the early Middle Ages, and it was probably not until the beginning of the sixteenth century that the last wolf was turned to bay in the dales. There is a ravine in Weardale, a few miles from Stanhope, still known as Wolf-Cleugh.

The boar, or brawn (as it was generally called), was an animal of great renown in the county. It was hunted by Roman officers and Palatine Bishops, and two legends connected with particularly fierce and dangerous specimens have come down to us. The better known of these is associated with Brancepeth—"the Brawn's path," according to popular derivation. A certain Hodge, of Ferry (or, more elegantly, Roger de Ferry) undertook to rid the countryside of a formidable boar which was terrifying the little community, and he achieved his purpose by privily digging a pit in its path and then despatching it with his sword. The grateful people erected a stone cross to commemorate their delivery. This popular explanation of the meaning of Brancepeth is said to be inaccurate, but the fact remains that there is today, built into the wall of the stockyard of Cleaves Cross Farm, near Ferry Hill, a large stone which formed part of an old cross; and in the church porch at Merrington there is the lid of an ancient stone coffin, with a sword, a spear and a spade carved upon it. The other famous boar, known as "The Pollard Brawn," was killed by a member of that family, the former owners of certain acres near Bishop Auckland, which are still known as "Pollard's Land." This property was given to their ancestor by the Bishop as a reward for his prowess. The actual episcopal promise was said to be: "As much land as you can ride round while I have my dinner." So Pollard rode round the Bishop's own castle of Auckland while His Lord-

ship sat at meat within, thereby saving himself a hard ride
and securing, at the same time, a goodly acreage in exchange
for the pontifical palace. This land, which comprised Coundon
Moor, Birtley, Etherley, etc., was held in return for the
presentation of a falchion to the new bishop on his entry into
Auckland. The Pollard family died out in 1572, but successive owners of the estate duly presented the falchion until
1856, when for the last time it was offered to Bishop
Longley. In the church of St. Andrew's, Auckland, there is
the recumbent figure of a warrior with his feet resting on a
boar. The last of these animals was probably killed during
the seventeenth century.

With the exception of the New Forest, the forests of
Weardale and Teesdale were probably the largest sporting
grounds in England. Here the Bishops and the Nevilles
enjoyed a quasi-regal chase. The Bishop's "Caza Magna,"
the great hunt of the red deer, took place from Stanhope and
was followed far into the treeless hills, while the "rahunt,"
the pursuit of the roe-deer, was urged, at a different season,
in enormous woods. By the middle of the seventeenth century
there were no red deer left in Weardale, but, although there
was a terrible mortality amongst these creatures in Teesdale,
where four hundred of them perished in a snowstorm in 1673,
they lingered on in these remote uplands until the eighteenth
century. The only red deer now in the county are confined in
Raby Park, but in the Derwent Valley, in spite of all its
industrialisation, the wild roe is still occasionally started by
the Braes of Derwent Foxhounds.

For the rest, the animals are not particularly interesting.
The fox is still hunted, and the otter on the banks of the
Tees; the last polecat, whose carcase used to grace the doors
of churches, vanished about fifty years ago; the badger holds
its own, and the red squirrel has not yet been ousted by the
grey.

We come to the green things upon the earth, and first to
the most beautiful of all green things—trees; the most beautiful and therefore in this age the most hardly dealt with.
For the beauty of woods is naturally inimical to the development of Industry. The only tree now which is welcomed at
all by the impatient industrialist is the conifer, and that is

the least lovely of them all. Modern Industry, however, has not been the only enemy to the hardwoods—"the oak and the ash and the bonny ivy-tree," the wych elm, the holly and the yew in the valleys, and the birch and juniper on the high hills. These last two have been destroyed by sheep and the firing of heather. To the welfare of the rest the development of agriculture, the ruthless felling of trees for smelting purposes during the sixteenth and seventeenth centuries, the Civil War, when the fines imposed on the Royalists were largely paid with timber, the king's "hearts of oak," the heavy soil in the east of the county, the cold winds and the late frosts, have all been unhelpful, as well as the fumes and the smoke and the enormously increased population of recent times. The county has therefore never been famous for very remarkable trees, though it was heavily and beautifully wooded, particularly in the Derwent Valley and all the way between Bishop Auckland and Darlington. Probably the best individual trees were the beeches planted by the big landowners in the eighteenth century to take the place of the vanished oaks, but most of those have been felled; the large landowner, the planter and protector of trees, has been ruined, and the Raby estate is now, doubtless, the only one of importance left in the county that pursues a regular policy of silviculture. The great oak wood at Chopwell (now of 800 acres), in the days when it belonged to the Prior of Durham, was used for the building of ships of war at Newcastle. Seized by the King at the Reformation, it still remains a Crown forest. It was replanted with oak and Spanish chestnut at the beginning of the last century, but these have now been chiefly superseded by spruce, larch and other conifers. A small amount of oak, however, has been planted since 1940. We have seen what has befallen the woods at Gibside, where grew until recently probably the finest tree in the county, known as the "King Oak," with a girth of 15 feet 8½ inches, at a height of 6 feet from the butt.[1] It was felled in 1938. The total area of Durham woodlands is 28,000 acres. In Weardale in the spring and autumn the rowan-trees are still beautiful.

But if the forests are gone, the flowers in the forest are not

[1] Information kindly supplied by Mr. McQueen, agent to the Gibside estate.

"a' wede awa'." Indeed, the wild flowers of the county of
Durham are somewhat remarkable. Of the 1,500 species of
flowering plants which grow in the British Isles, no less
than 850 are found in Durham,[1] and three of them are
found nowhere else in England. These are the Bog Sandwort (*Arenaria uliginosa*) and a dog violet (*Viola rupestris*),
both of which grow in Upper Teesdale. The third is the
Loose-flowered Orchis,[2] which is found, still flourishing, in
the remains of old ballast tossed from sailing ships at Hartlepool. The place where the sandwort and the violet grow,
Widdy Bank Fell, produces, for its size, a greater number of
rare plants than any other area in Great Britain. Here are
saxifrages and violas, primulas and cinquefoils, including a
yellow saxifrage found elsewhere only in Yorkshire and
Westmorland, and here—

> *"Tread softly! For I think the gentian*
> *Is blue enamel on the smooth green grass,*
> *Painted long since by some Italian*
> *Or Dutch artificer in coloured glass."*[3]

Not far from here, at the meeting of two little streams at
the Langdon Beck Hotel, is one of the loveliest spots in the
county, whence you can follow the course upwards of the
Langdon Beck, with its waters reddened by peat and flashing
with trout as if with lightning. This rare and beautiful blue
gentian may also occasionally be found on the hills near
Stanhope, in Weardale, where, on the garden wall of the old
Rectory, grows *Erinus alpinus*, a little pink flower making a
brave show in June, which is said to have been imported from
Spain by the Roman Legionaries.

But it is not so much the rarities that delight the heart of
the casual wayfarer, but the flowers he recognises as familiar
friends: the lilies-of-the-valley and the autumn crocus in
the woods near High Force; the wonderful profusion of
pansies in Weardale, dark purple and light purple and yellow

[1] Dr. D. H. Valentine, Professor of Botany in Durham University,
is my authority. I am also indebted to him for the information about
the violet.

[2] We may have seen the last of the orchis, which is said to have
been uprooted in a (vain) attempt to make it grow elsewhere. (Information supplied by Miss Peggy Hutchinson.)

[3] *Mountain Flowers*, by Humbert Wolfe.

and cream, and the wild thyme; the lady's slippers at Castle
Eden and the yellow broom on the Derwent moors; the
daffodils at Croxdale on the banks of the Wear; the cran-
berries at the highest altitudes, the blaeberries in Langley
Dale, the crowberries at Tow Law; the globe flowers at
Norton Mill; the snowdrops at Redworth; and the little
aconites that lay in enormous pools of gold round the trunks
of the great beeches at Windlestone.

Only about a dozen of the thirty-five species of butterflies
once recorded in this county can now be found to grace the
flowers. The fumes and the towns have proved too much for
these delicate creatures, and the days are gone when Painted
Ladies danced their quadrilles with bold Red Admirals,
"sometimes in immense profusion."[1] *Erebia Blandina*, once
to be seen in Castle Eden dene, and there only, in the whole
of England, is now seen no more. A Camberwell Beauty was
carried off, many years ago, from Stockton, and another was
captured more recently at Walworth,[2] while an errant Painted
Lady was observed near Heighington in 1946.[3] The Elephant
Hawk moth is still occasionally seen.

It may be that the flowers will go the way of the butterflies, for it is unfortunately true that, while to the few the
primrose and the daffodil are sweetest peeping underneath a
hedge or tossing in a wood, to the vast majority they are a
golden booty, to be seized and dropped on the road or carried
away, roots and all. Now that there are no keepers to protect
private property and that it is almost a sin to stop a child or a
young lout from playing havoc with trees and plants, when
transport is so easy and preservation so difficult, we may
anticipate the time when not only human engines will have
stunk out the last butterfly, but human locusts will have
devoured the last flower. Only the few will mind, and only
the few will even notice. The majority, like the writer of the
following letter, have other, and in their view more important, things to consider. "With £24,000,000 already
pledged by industrial enterprise," says Mr. Max Lock in *The
Times* of December 15th, 1945, "there seems nothing to
prevent local and central government from building up a

[1] Fordyce, Vol. I, p. 120.
[2] Now in the collection of the late Mr. F. Dresser of Heighington.
[3] By Mr. J. Burlinson.

unified plan for long-term reconstruction on Tees-side, in
which the economic and scientific objectives of industry can,
all along the line, be linked with the social and human objectives of municipal planning. Thus industry and State would
be partners in a joint enterprise. To accomplish this two
things will be necessary: (1) A greater Tees-side plan em-
bracing the now separate north and south Tees-side town-
planning areas, in which the river will be treated as a link
instead of a barrier between the two banks, and the whole
problem of cross-river communication considered linking the
Hartlepools with Middlesbrough. (2) A co-ordinated pool-
ing of the scientific, social and technical skills within the
province of town and country planning which require to be
applied to make this area a model twentieth-century industrial
region." And so on.

No doubt, from the industrial point of view, this is all very
admirable, and it is high time we brought our Prayer-Book
up to date and added a few verses to the Benedicite. "O all
ye £24,000,000, bless ye the Lord; O ye objectives of
industry, bless ye the Lord; O ye social and human objectives of municipal planning, praise Him and magnify Him
for ever." But do not let us deceive ourselves, as we are so
very apt to do. The scientific, industrial development of man
and the natural beauties created by God are irreconcilable
enemies. No amount of sentimental talk about hills and trees
and wild flowers can alter that fact. No multiplication of
societies for the preservation of this, that, and the other can
evade the inevitable consequences of the progress of industrial
man. We have made our choice, and we cannot serve both
God and Mammon. Unless—an extremely improbable hypothesis—we reverse it before it is too late, unless we readjust
our values and come to regard the scientific development of
Industry, not as the immediate and ultimate and only object
of our existence, but as an entirely subordinate and unimportant adjunct to the true meaning and purpose of life, then
it can only be a question of time before gone for ever will be
the trout and the kingfishers and the Painted Ladies, fled,
with the salmon and the peewit and the twenty-three different
species of butterflies, before the face of the greater Tees-side
schemes and the human objectives of municipal planning;
gone will be the sea-birds and the oak-trees and the bright

blue gentians on the bright green grass; gone *Arenaria uliginosa* and the wild pansies and the daffodils and the aconites—as are gone now, irretrievably, never to return, the days when midsummer cushions, all stuck with roses, were made in the streets of Bishop Auckland, when there was a cherry fair at Stockton and a bank of violets near Hilton Castle, when Kelloe Bek was dark, not with foul chemicals, but with "dusky, nutant flowers,"[1] and the banks of Ferry Hill were clothed with *Anemone nemorosa*.

[1] Surtees, Vol. I, p. 67.

Chapter XXIX

SIX TOWNS

"and since men congregate
In towns, not woods—to Ispahan forthwith!"

ROBERT BROWNING.

Now we must quit our high places of refuge and face these industrial towns. They, after all, not the butterflies nor the birds, nor the castles nor the churches, are the mirrors of the face of modern man. It is in them and for them that he lives, not on nor for the hills. They reflect his activities and provide his amusements far more than the ploughed field and the wandering sheep and the random country fair. In Weardale live some 8,000 people, in Teesdale about half that number, but the five county boroughs[1] alone, excluding the municipal boroughs and the pit villages, harbour a population of over half a million, and, since it is numbers alone who rule us today, we cannot lightly set these figures aside. If we consider them in detail and in relationship to the whole and to the past, we shall apprehend by means of these simple symbols more readily than from a lengthy dissertation the prodigious and revolutionary changes wrought by the development of Industry within the last 150 years, after long centuries of gradual growth. In 1801 the population of Darlington was 4,670, of Gateshead 8,597, of South Shields 8,108, and of Sunderland (including Bishop Wearmouth and Monkwearmouth) 24,444. West Hartlepool did not exist as a separate unit until 1852. Its site was comprised within the township of Stranton, whose inhabitants in 1801 numbered 325. The total population of the county was then 149,384.

The corresponding figures in 1931 were: Darlington, 72,086; Gateshead, 122,447; South Shields, 113,455; Sunderland (including Bishop Wearmouth and Monkwearmouth), 185,824; and West Hartlepool, 68,135. Thus the population of Darlington, since the advent of the Industrial Age, has been multiplied by 15; that of Gateshead by 14;

[1] Darlington, Gateshead, South Shields, Sunderland, West Hartlepool.

that of South Shields by 14; that of Sunderland (already a
big shipping town at the beginning of the last century) by
more than 7; while that of West Hartlepool has become over
209 times greater than the old population of Stranton. If we
look at the figures for the municipal boroughs, we find that
they have a similar tale to tell. In 1801 the largest of them,
Stockton, had 4,177 inhabitants; in 1931 these had risen to
67,722. The population of this town has, therefore, been
multiplied by 16.

In Weardale and Teesdale, however, we find no such prodigious changes taking place. The township of "Forest and
Frith," in the remote moors of Teesdale, where the trout
flash and the wild flowers grow, comprised, according to the
Census of 1801, 17,270 acres; according to that of 1931,
17,698—a slight increase in extent. The population of this
township in 1801 was 460, and in 1931, of the larger area,
471. The corresponding figures for Middleton, the capital of
Teesdale, are 796 and 1,657, and for Barnard Castle, the
market town at the entrance to the valley, 2,966 and 3,884.

If we turn to Weardale we behold a similar picture. The
parish of Stanhope, by far the most extensive in the county,
was held in 1801 to comprise 54,870 acres, and in 1931
60,620 acres. In spite of an increase in extent of over 5,000
acres, the corresponding figures for the population are 5,155
and 5,338.

The total number of the inhabitants of the county in 1931
was 1,468,175, of which the boroughs and urban districts
between them accounted for well over a million. Thus within
130 years, while on the hills and dales, where Industry could
find no foothold or lost the little she had gained,[1] the number
of the inhabitants has remained practically constant, in the
whole of the county it has been multiplied by ten.

Owing to the extraordinary incursions and excursions of
war, it is difficult to draw any definite conclusion from figures
posterior to the last official Census (1931), but the latest, for
1947, seem to indicate the beginning of a decline in population. Of the five county boroughs, Darlington and West
Hartlepool have increased the numbers of their inhabitants
since 1931, West Hartlepool by over 2,600 and Darlington
by as much as 11,674. But the remaining three boroughs

[1] Lead-mining.

show a loss—South Shields almost as great a loss as Darlington's gain—so that the total decline in the population of these five major towns amounts to more than 11,800. The four municipal boroughs—Durham, Hartlepool, Jarrow and Stockton—show a net loss of over 2,800.

There is no indication that this decline in industrial population is balanced by a return to the land. The number of the inhabitants of Weardale has very slightly decreased from 8,873 in 1931 to 8,860 in 1947. The figure for 1921 was 9,544. The total population of the county has fallen, between 1931 and 1947, by 62,407.

We shall now pick the six largest plums out of our industrial cake—the five county boroughs and the municipal borough of Stockton—and have a little nibble at each, beginning with the smallest and proceeding upwards in order of size. Between them these six towns account for more than two-fifths of the county's population.

There was probably an Anglian settlement at Stockton, which moved further away from the river to Norton, for greater safety, during the Danish raids. Later the Bishop chose this pleasant site on the banks of the Tees as a residence for himself. Retainers congregated round his manor-house and some of them settled there permanently. From this little community has sprung the present town of over 60,000 inhabitants, while Norton, out of which Stockton parish was first carved in 1713, has now become a suburb of Stockton. The brick church was built at this period, and the spire added to it a hundred years later by John and Benjamin Green, the Newcastle architects. But in spite of this and the Georgian Town Hall and other eighteenth-century buildings in a main street said to be the widest in England, the general effect is not as attractive as one might expect. For there are the usual hideous plate-glass shops, the inevitable "improvements" of the nineteenth and twentieth centuries, and the typical surrounding wilderness of dreary streets. When first built, this little Georgian town must have had a singular charm, with its sailing ships laden with the corn of this fertile region, its Cherry Fair, its population of 1,800 souls, and its "pleasant society of independent gentlemen which rendered

it agreeable and happy."[1] The decline of Hartlepool had
encouraged the trade of Stockton as a seaport, although it was
situated some distance from the sea; the artificial shortening
of the course of the river almost doubled the tonnage of ships
using the harbour, and the opening of the first railway gave
the town a further fillip. But this last boon to Stockton created
also Middlesbrough, at the Yorkshire mouth of the Tees. In
1830, when the railway was extended to it, the population of
Middlesbrough was 150. Today it is 140,470. Before the
last war the annual value of imports into Stockton was
£266,000, and of exports £79,000. The corresponding figures
for Middlesbrough were five millions and seven and a half
millions. Nevertheless, the smaller town continues to go
ahead. The shipbuilding firm of Ropner and Son is one of
the best known in the North.

Matches were first invented by a Stockton chemist;
Sheraton, as we have seen, was born here; so was Brass
Crosby, Lord Mayor of London and champion of individual
freedom. About a hundred years ago a wag, instead of selling
butter, proceeded to auction his wife in Stockton market-
place, and knocked her down for half a crown.

The history of West Hartlepool is less than a hundred
years old, but that of Hartlepool itself is ancient and strangely
fascinating. The two, though administered separately, now
practically form a continuous town, and we shall consider
them here together.

Hartlepool seems to have sampled every variety of civilisation. From the double convent of St. Hieu in 640, down to
Messrs. Gray and Son and Messrs. Irvins' Shipbuilding and
Dry Dock Company in 1940, she has endured long and seen
much: the wild harts in the forest that gave her their name;
the great Bruce himself; the lordly Cliffords; the princely
Bishop and his ships; the Catholic rebels; the Scots, again
and again; and the hovering of the Spaniards and the Dutch-
men. After all this grandeur and excitement there follows a
curious quietness, a slip backwards into forgetfulness and
simplicity, to an isolated little community of fishermen who
were remarkable for their strange dress, their primitive ignorance and their courteous manners. And then, with a pounce

[1] *History of Stockton*, by John Brewster, p. 235.

and a roar, this forgotten relic of the Middle Ages, this little walled fishing port twelve hundred years old, is seized and devoured in the whirl of Victorian Industry; a huge modern fungus sprouts forth overnight from its hoary, medieval sides, and its ancient walls and buildings are smashed, engulfed, trodden under, swallowed up by an epidemic of tawdry streets and houses. But not even here comes the end of her adventures, for in 1914 the fear which had not materialised in Spaniard and Dutchman, and which had long been forgotten, suddenly leaps into horrid life, the helpless town is bombarded by German cruisers, whole streets are laid flat, and 128 people are killed and 400 injured.

Such is the strange and varied history of this deer forest by the sea, this lovely land which, not so long ago, was "diapered in summer with the burnet-rose and the purple blossoms of sea-thrift and crane's-bill."[1] It has reached its fruition in exports and imports of over two and a half million pounds per annum and the noise of riveting round the old church of St. Hilda. The only borough in the county to receive its charter from the King of England, instead of from the Bishop of Durham, has become a large commercial town in which, with the exception of the church, "there is not a single building or street which possesses the slightest architectural dignity."[2] Its docks cover an area of 182 acres, there are five miles of quays, and it is one of the most important shipbuilding centres in this shipbuilding county. The church is imposing, in spite of five separate restorations in the nineteenth century. Dominantly placed and robust in character, it stands imperially amidst the surrounding industrial waste. There is a good twentieth-century addition at the east end.

Darlington, though rudely labelled in the past "Darnton-i'-the-Dirt," cannot fairly be so stigmatised today. Compared to many other industrial towns, though it certainly is not beautiful, it is clean and open and friendly, at least in the centre, where its character of market and shopping town predominates. But even here we are allowed to forget neither the pretentious vulgarity nor the squalor of Industry. The Victorian Town Hall emphasises the first, while the recent erection of two enormous black cooling towers, looking like

[1] Surtees, Vol. III, p. 109.   [2] *V.C.H.*, Vol. III, p. 270.

receptacles for a giant game of tiddly-winks, serve very suitably to underline the second. Between them, aided by the untidy litter of the market-place, the scarlet buses and all the rest of the ragtag and bobtail of "civilisation," they have completely ruined the setting of Pudsey's beautiful church. No longer is the spire, "Darnton broach," a landmark and a guide to the wandering rustic for miles around. Thrust into third place by these later monstrosities, pining for trees and green, the old church stands as one bewildered by its sur-roundings, naked and defenceless and forlorn. The brick residential suburbs of the town are the usual characterless, stumped-tree-lined abortions of architecture which one sees all over England. Yet, within a few miles, are the old village greens and the colour-wash of Gainford and of Piercebridge, from which, one might have supposed, someone might have learnt something.

In Darlington was another of the Bishop's numerous houses. It survived as an episcopal residence for longer than Stockton, but Bishop Crewe was the last to dwell in it, and in 1703 a wandering antiquary was "concerned to see that it had been converted into a Quakers' Work-house."[1] That must have been a grim abode for the unfortunate inmates and a strange metamorphosis for a building that was first erected for Pudsey and had housed the courtly elegance of Crewe. The Board of Guardians later took over the workhouse from the Quakers, and in 1870 what was left of the old building was sold to a Mr. Luck, who demolished it and erected on its site the cottages now known as Luck's Terrace and Luck's Square. There is not much, indeed, of old Darlington left. On the site of the old Manor Mill is still a mill, but for wool, not for corn, and now worked, not by the Bishop's tenant, but by Messrs. Henry Pease and Company, Ltd. The "old houses of post and pile" which Longstaffe admired in Prebend's Row have disappeared, and, although there remains the rude carving of a bull (indicating, perhaps, some property of the Nevilles) on a corner house of Bull Wynd, near the market-place, there is little else, apart from the names of the streets—Bondgate, Skinnergate, Houndgate, Priestgate—to bear witness to the antiquity of the town. It was a borough in the days of the Boldon Book.

[1] Longstaffe, *History of Darlington,* p. 150.

17

First famous for its wool, thanks to the rich pastures around it, Darlington in the early eighteenth century became equally celebrated for its linen and produced, under benevolent and enterprising Quakers, such sweetly sounding materials as huckaback, diaper and damask—of which today, alas! we scarcely know the names. In 1810 five hundred looms in Darlington were weaving these attractive fabrics, while the woollen trade was also continued. In 1825 the building of the Darlington and Stockton railway (thanks again, very largely, to the munificence and foresight of Quakers) placed the modern town in "the *van* of civilisation,"[1] according to one of Darlington's sons—a somewhat unfortunate word to use under the circumstances. There are still important railway and iron works in the town, while on the station platform, like a mechanical toy strayed from a toyshop, stands "Locomotion No. 1," the quaint little engine made by Stephenson, which was the first to puff its way along a railroad in this world.

South Shields is older even than Hartlepool, for the Romans had a fort here to guard the end of their wall long before St. Hilda founded her monastery at the same time as St. Hieu. This town started early on its industrial career. With the exception of coal-mining, the making of salt is the earliest industry in the county, and its history is continuous from 1290, when Robert Bruce (grandfather of the King of Scotland) granted one of his tenants at Hart permission to make salt, until the present day, when it is still evaporated by the same method (but from rock salt instead of sea-water) in the same neighbourhood by Messrs. Cerebos at Greatham, near West Hartlepool. "Salt de Gretham" was famous in the fifteenth and sixteenth centuries.[2] But the centre of salt manufacture for over two hundred years was South Shields. Here, while the rest of the county was blooming unclouded, hedges were withered and no green leaf grew. "Great and extraordinary fires made of sea-cole" were rendering the place uninhabitable, for "such abondance of thicke smoake doth rise from the salt panns as all or most parte of the grasse within twenty score yards of the said panns is altogether burnt

[1] Edward Wooler. Introduction to Longstaffe, *op. cit.*, 1909 edition.
[2] *V.C.H.*, Vol. II, p. 294.

up and waisted."[1] "Why," said the parson's wife to him reproachfully, "have you brought me from Norham, frae the bonny banks o' Tweed, to Sodom and Gomorrah?" Even on Sundays the place was belching with filthy smoke, "to the great dishonour of God and the constant profanation of the Lord's day."[2] By 1791 there were two hundred of these salt pans—but fifty years later there were hardly any. Coal, which had become the open sesame to all the magical riches of the industrial world, was needed for other purposes, and South Shields was turning her attention to its export and to the building of ships. In 1839 one of the first iron vessels in the world was built here, and in 1865 North and South Shields were each made a separate port. This concentration on coal affected another old industry for which this town was famous, the making of glass. We hear of it first in 1619, and over two hundred years later more plate glass was being made in this town than anywhere else in England, but by the end of the nineteenth century it had ceased to be of first importance.

In 1789 a ship called the *Adventure* was wrecked off the coast near this harbour, and a helpless crowd watched the crew dropping from the rigging and drowning one by one, for no boat could live in the sea. Stirred by this unhappy spectacle, a committee of experts was formed to consider the building of a boat capable of riding a heavy sea. Amongst the plans submitted to them was one which embodied the principle of a curved keel instead of the usual straight one. This plan was adopted, and in the following year the first lifeboat to be constructed in England was launched at South Shields. Henry Greathead is generally recognised as the inventor, though there is a claim that a feckless genius with the happy name of Willie Wouldhave, "heedless and gay," had more than a minor share in the creation of this "new Iris, an arc of faith and hope to the gallant seamen struggling with the horrors of a lee shore."[3]

Though North and South Shields are, each of them, independent ports for Customs purposes, they are grouped with Newcastle, the third and the largest port on the Tyne, in the annual shipping returns of the Board of Trade. In 1937 the value of exports to foreign countries from these Tyne ports

---

[1] *V.C.H.*, Vol. II, p. 298.   [2] *M.C.*, Vol. I, p. 305.
[3] Surtees, Vol. I, p. 96.

amounted to over thirteen million pounds, and included just under seven million tons of coal worth five and a half million pounds of money.

Ten years have wrought so vast a change that today[1] it is no longer an insult or an absurdity to "carry coals to Newcastle."

Meanwhile Gateshead, in the heart of this industrial wilderness, continues in its pitiful ugliness. "What is Gateshead?" asked someone long ago in the House of Commons. "A dirty lane leading to Newcastle," replied Charles James Fox.[2] But Gateshead has had a history of its own. The origin of the name is doubtful. Etymologists do not differ from other experts in differing from each other, and the plausible "gate's head"—the head of the Roman "gate"[3] or "way," which is here continued by a bridge over the Tyne—is by many believed to be wrong. "Goat's Head," as Bede called it in the past—"Caput Capræ," "a headland or hill frequented by wild goats"[4]—is now regarded as the more probable explanation of the name. But Goat's Head or Gate's Head, this town has through centuries maintained its independence in spite of the jealousies, intrigues and riches of its formidable vis-à-vis—the New Castle—on the northern bank of the river. That it has not become a mere suburb of Newcastle is due both to the obstinacy of the inhabitants and to the power and protection of the Bishops, who were determined not to lose their grip on the southern shores of the Tyne. No sooner was the Bishoprick abolished by the extreme Protestant council of Edward VI than the independent charter of Gateshead was ignored and the town incorporated with its larger neighbour, but on the accession of Queen Mary and the restoration of the Bishop of Durham in the following year Gateshead reassumed its independence. A little later, however, the Newcastle merchants stole a march on their rivals by obtaining a long lease of the Gateshead coal, but the inhabitants of the town did not again become subject to their neighbours' jurisdiction. It was doubtless owing to the fact

---

[1] 1947.

[2] *Bishoprick Rhymes.* This definition has also been ascribed to Dr. Johnson. (See "The Story of Gateshead Town," by D. Lumley, *Northumberland Press, Limited,* p. 109.)

[3] Cf., "gang your own gate" = go your own way.

[4] *Oxford Dictionary of Place Names,* E. Ekwall. (Oxford, 1936.)

that Newcastle, as a Royalist town, was in disgrace with Cromwell that no second attempt was made under the Protectorate, when the Bishoprick was again abolished, to bring the Durham men to heel. The causes of this long rivalry, most serious in the past, since they were concerned not only with coal, but with such questions as the navigation of the river and the sale of the enormous quantities of fish caught in it, have been removed by the process of time and the gradual subjection of local independence to a national system of government and administration, but even today a "bonny Gyetsider" would not be pleased or flattered by being mistaken for a "Newcassel chep." The character of the two towns is essentially different, though since the last war the "austerity" (as it is politely called) common to the whole of England has practically eradicated the contrast between an alderman at a feast and a contemptuous, hard-bitten poor relation by no means begging at his gate. But here is still Durham, and there is still Northumberland; the river rolls between, and no amount of bridges linking the opposite shores can alter the fact that they are opposite. Gateshead was never a dirty lane leading to Newcastle, but since the days when Bishop Pudsey granted the town its charter it has retained its independence, if later a dirty one, and a character, if later a sad one, of its own.

But Gateshead was not always sad. It has sung its songs and rung its bells. It was a little town of windmills—eleven of them sailing together on the hills—with its people living scattered amongst oak-trees hard by a garden of safflowers.[1] As late as 1801 its population was only 8,600. Under the shade of these trees Wesley preached to the inhabitants, and from beneath them the mowers went forth to mow the Town Fields, while the fiddlers played and the pipers piped to them from the tops of the loaded wain. The name of Oakwellgate remains to remind us of those days, but not a single windmill or a single tree or a single flower is left.

In St. Mary's, the parish church, are records of the old glassmakers of Gateshead: de Thisac, with his pious motto, "Seigneur, je te prie: Garde ma vie"; and de Hennezel; persecuted Protestants who had fled from Lorraine and whose

[1] D. Lumley, *op. cit.*, p. 108, and *Proceedings*, Fourth Series, Vol. IX, p. 82. The safflower was grown for dye works.

names were "gyetsided" into "Tyzack" and "Henzel." In 1823 a sparkling seal was set upon the earlier endeavours of these old "gentilshommes verriers." For on September 12th of that year there was a grand parade of the glassmakers of Newcastle and Gateshead, who proceeded through the streets of both towns with glass stars hanging round their necks, to the notes of a sweet glass bugle and the thunder of a big glass gun.

In St. Mary's can also be seen a strange letter to *The Times* about the cholera epidemic, which again and again swept Tyneside, Hartlepool and Sunderland in the first half of the nineteenth century, when the overcrowding caused by industrial development, combined with the ignorance and carelessness of sanitation, produced such appalling conditions of living as invited and encouraged this horrible disease. The worst outbreak was in 1832, when 161 persons out of a population of 15,000 died of cholera. The letter in question, signed "Dunelmensis," suggests that, owing to "the well-founded fears of the inhabitants of Gateshead respecting the burial of cholera patients in the churches and churchyards of that town," the bodies "should be buried in the shafts of the out-worked mines." A callous and condescending postscript adds that "our well-intentioned Bishop, Dr. van Mildert, has already expressed a desire to consecrate these shafts, if that is considered of importance by the lower classes."

As the Fire of London consumed the Plague in its flames, so an appalling accident which affected both Newcastle and Gateshead, and rendered over five hundred families homeless in Gateshead alone, was probably an indirect blessing, both by the actual destruction of houses "of the most wretched description" and by the attention which it called to the conditions under which the poor were living. The cholera had been particularly severe in the quarter of Hillgate, where the accident occurred and where the Census of 1851 had shown that four houses had contained between them 52 families consisting of 215 individuals.

A little before one o'clock on the morning of October 6th, 1854, a fire was discovered in a worsted factory in Hillgate, Gateshead, fronting the River Tyne. Within a short time the building was ablaze from top to bottom, and the intense heat

of the burning wool and oil presently affected the contents of
an enormous warehouse, a hundred yards long, which stood
near the factory. This warehouse was stored with very large
quantities of iron, lead, manganese, nitrate of soda and guano,
with 5 tons of arsenic, 1½ tons of naphtha, 240 tons of salt
and as much as 3,000 tons of brimstone. It was therefore not
surprising that "streams of vivid blue flame soon poured from
its doors and afforded a most extraordinary spectacle" to the
crowds who had, by this time, gathered in the narrow streets
of Gateshead and along the quayside at Newcastle to marvel
at the wonderful sight. Soon this colossal warehouse was one
vast sheet of fire, which was seen from as far away as Yorkshire, and at a quarter-past three in the morning the whole
thing suddenly blew up. The damage done by this single
explosion was equal to that of a severe air raid in the last war.
Fifty-three people were killed on both sides of the river, a
much greater number injured, ships in the Tyne were set
alight, houses fell flat in all directions (even buildings at
Shields, seven miles away, were damaged) and two separate
fires, caused by the falling brimstone, were soon raging in
Newcastle. One of these was extinguished by six o'clock in
the morning; the other continued to roar, with intermittent
fury, for twenty-four hours and was only finally mastered by
the blowing up of houses which stood in its path.[1]

The old church of St. Mary was badly damaged by this
disaster and the chancel had to be rebuilt; but it was excel-
lently done. The church stands now in the very thick of the
hubbub of business, under the enormous modern King George
V bridge, with traffic crashing past it, but collected in its own
stillness, darkly devout, with some old Saxon stones in the
porch and a wooden cross from the battlefield of the Somme.

When we talk of Sunderland today, which is the largest
town in the county of Durham and the biggest shipbuilding
town in the world, we include under this single name not
only Sunderland itself, but the districts of Bishop Wearmouth and Monkwearmouth (the old home of Benedict
Biscop), which were formerly independent communities. Indeed, Sunderland proper, which has now given its name to
the whole county borough, was for many centuries of small

[1] Latimer, pp. 347-353.

or of no account compared to the ancient vills of Bishop Wearmouth on the south bank of the Wear, and Monk Wearmouth, on the north. Situated on a point of land which was formerly almost *sundered* from the mainland by the river and the sea, it remained subordinate to Bishop Wearmouth until 1719, when, its inhabitants then numbering six thousand souls, it was granted the privilege of a separate parish. In 1183, when we first hear of the place, the Boldon Book tells us that it was let to farm for 100 shillings; in the sixteenth century only a few poor fishermen resided here, but by 1801, though still separated from Bishop Wearmouth by fields, Sunderland, with 12,000 citizens of her own, had become twice as large as her venerable neighbour. Soon afterwards began that rapid growth which has been described as a "marvel" of the Victorian Age. Today the farm has become a gigantic town, the fishermen have multiplied into a population of 181,000, and their little cobles are represented by 2,408 ships, registering 1,853,528 tons, which cleared from the port of Sunderland in 1951.[1]

Some time before it was given an independent existence the name of Sunderland had become familiar, and it seems to have been used more or less interchangeably with that of Wearmouth or Bishop Wearmouth. It was the Civil War which first stimulated the trade of the port and brought the name into prominence. Sunderland supported the cause of Parliament, the winning cause, and thereby seized the carrying trade of Royalist Newcastle for the export of coal to London and the South. From that time she never looked back. While Hartlepool, hitherto the only seaport in the Bishoprick, was dwindling into a picturesque community of fishermen, Sunderland was reversing the process and busily exporting her coal and her salt and her glass; and Newcastle in vain petitioned the House of Commons against the making of this upstart into an independent port. The export of coal entailed the building of special flat-bottomed boats—the "keels"—to carry the produce of the mines down the river to its mouth. From the building of these to the building of

[1] These figures and all the latest shipping and shipbuilding information connected with Sunderland have been most kindly supplied to the author by Mr. A. H. J. Bown, O.B.E., F.C.I.S., M.Inst.T., General Manager and Clerk to the River Wear Commissioners.

seagoing wooden ships was but a step, which was no doubt taken some time in the eighteenth century. By 1752 the port had already grown to such importance that it had become the owner of about 190 ships, of which some at least, we may presume, were built at Sunderland, but the only definite record which we have, before the last years of the eighteenth century, dates back as far as 1346, when a certain Thomas Menvill was building ships here. It is probable that the encouragement given to shipbuilding, in this port as elsewhere, by the sea sense of Edward III and the transport requirements of the Hundred Years' War naturally ceased when England lost her overseas possessions and was plunged in civil strife, and that it was not until the stimulus of coal proved an even greater incentive than the necessities of war that the shipbuilding activities of Plantagenet days were renewed on a far grander scale. Before the end of the eighteenth century a continuous programme had been definitely established. In 1793 the firm of Laing and Sons was founded, the oldest firm still building on the Wear, and three years later the launch of the *Lord Duncan*, 144 feet long, the largest vessel built in the port up to that time, was long remembered as a famous event. Thence onwards there was a spate of building. In the early years of the nineteenth century Surtees could already write: "In Shipbuilding the Port of Sunderland stands at present the highest of any in the United Kingdom."[1] Forty years later another historian of the county proclaimed that Sunderland was "emphatically the first shipbuilding port in the world,"[2] and today it is still claimed as the largest shipbuilding town.

In 1877 forty ships were launched at Sunderland, with a net register tonnage of 39,086. In 1905 the whole of England, excluding the county of Durham, built 465,460 tons of shipping; Durham alone built 589,944. The key to this smashing triumph of Industry was provided by Sunderland, where a single firm, Messrs. William Doxford and Sons, alone produced twenty ships in that year, averaging over 4,000 tons each. This was a world record. The same firm, during the last war, produced, to the end of 1944, seventy-one merchant ships of 478,304 gross tons. The whole of England, for the same period, built over 5,700,000 gross

[1] Surtees, Vol. I (2), p. 262.   [2] Fordyce, Vol. II, p. 509.

tons, of which the output at Sunderland was over $1\frac{1}{2}$ millions, or 27 per cent. The prototype of the famous "Liberty" ships was built here by Messrs. J. L. Thompson and Sons, Ltd. During 1951 twenty-eight vessels were launched at Sunderland by eight separate firms, with a total gross tonnage of 197,920, and the town has now eight shipyards with twenty-nine building berths. In the same year over half a million tons of imports were brought to this port.

With the building of ships the shipping trade, particularly the export of coal, was naturally leaping ahead. Between 1791 and 1812, the years of the wars with Napoleon, the amount of coal exported to foreign countries varied from as much as 153,566 tons in 1793 to as little as 2,552 tons in 1809, but the total shipments, with the inclusion of English ports of destination, remained fairly constant at about 800,000 tons a year. Thus by far the greater proportion of "seacoal" was at this time shipped to the south of England. Before the beginning of the last war this figure of 800,000 had risen to nearly 5,000,000, of which approximately half, valued at £2,000,000, was exported abroad. In 1927, the peak year of the shipment of coal from Sunderland, the total shipped (including coal for English ports) was just under 5,500,000 tons. Since the war this total has been more than halved, though it now shows signs of recovery. In 1946 the corresponding figure was only 2,304,886. In 1951 the shipment amounted to 3,045,704 tons.

But Sunderland has not confined herself entirely to ships and coal. Apart from shipbuilding with its ancillary industries of marine engineering, ropemaking and so on, there are now new activities in the manufacture of clothes, in light engineering, in coachbuilding, telephone assembling and many other varieties of industry, while the town still continues the manufacture of glass and of pottery for which it was famous. In 1863 a third of the total output of English glass was being made in Sunderland. She had, and has, yet other distinctions. The Iron Bridge over the Wear, erected in 1796 and now replaced by the Wearmouth Bridge, was the largest single-arch bridge of cast iron in England and was regarded at the time as one of the wonders of the world. And in 1948 the first Aluminium Alloy Bascule Bridge ever made anywhere was

opened by the Minister of Transport. Even for the arts
a little space and time were found, and very much skill and
taste, for the creation, in the early years of the nineteenth century, of those charming jugs, with their pink lustre rims, which
were seen in so many northern cottages in the past and are now
swooped upon by the dealer and collector. And she has
another link with the Muses—a most unexpected one. In 1855
the Lyceum Theatre, Sunderland, was burnt down. On
September 29th, in the following year, the new Lyceum
Theatre was opened, and the first lines of the first piece were
spoken by a young man of eighteen who had never been on a
stage before. His name was Henry Irving.

Chapter XXX

THE END OF THE PALATINATE

"Men are we, and must grieve when even the shade
Of that which once was great has pass'd away."
WORDSWORTH.

IT was not to be expected that the proud and ancient Bishoprick could escape the consequences of the reformatory itch of the new-fangled democrats. Nor did it. William van Mildert, the successor of Shute Barrington, was the last of the Palatine Bishops of Durham. With his death, in 1836, the privileges and revenues of the Palatinate were transferred to the Crown.

"In our own time of restless and useless change," wrote Longstaffe, "the legislature decreed that this blameless prelate should be *ultimus suorum,* and the fitting splendours of his obsequies were attended by a respect and a feeling which shone brightly in the cold mists of reform."[1] It is impossible not to sympathise with this admirable sentiment. The cold, wispy mist has now thickened into an impenetrable fog, and we know not where we are nor whither we are going. Nevertheless, it must be confessed that our princely Palatinate, a most suitable setting for Bek and his kneeling knights and even for Cosin, with his angels in their scarlet petticoats, very ill became Mr. Stephenson and his steam-engine and had nothing in common with devout evangelical Bishops grappling with industrial problems. The repeal of the Test Act in 1828, the Reform Bill of 1832, the new Poor Law of 1834, and, particularly, the Municipal Corporations Act of the succeeding year, all combined to prove the impossibility of an independent ecclesiastical Palatinate in democratic times, and turned the great Prince Bishop into a "venerable absurdity."[2] The test question applied, at this period, to every human institution consecrated by time was: "What is the use of it?"[3] The question itself is far more of a venerable absurdity than the institutions which it attacked, for it dates

[1] *History of Darlington,* p. 162.
[2] Trevelyan, *England,* p. 637.   [3] *Ibid.*

back to prehistoric times, to the days before religion, art and manners had revealed to human beings the possibilities of a refined existence infinitely superior to the elementary standards of the utilitarian savage. But even to this stupid interrogation there was, so far as the Palatinate was concerned, a very definite and practical answer, as will presently be shown. The honest question, however, should have been, not "What is the use of it?" but "Is it consistent with my preconceived ideas of democracy, centralisation, industrial development and all the rest?" The answer to that question could only be: "It is not." The Palatinate was transferred to the Crown not because it was no longer of any use—on the contrary, its independent revenues were never more needed by its inhabitants than at the time when they were confiscated—but because it was ludicrous and impossible for the authority of an absolute Bishop to co-exist with the popular control of parliamentary and local government. The two conceptions of civilisation were incompatible, and one or the other was bound to give way.

Apart from the political aspect, it may be permissible to suggest that there is a virtue in grace, a power in dignity and a spiritual beauty in magnificence, and that the customs and ceremonies associated with the Palatinate of Durham were magnificent and dignified and gracious. We have come across a few in the course of our story. Let us now hear something of the last of them before we say farewell to them for ever and turn our star-filled eyes to greet the sunless, bureaucratic day.

On July 15th, 1826, Bishop van Mildert entered his new diocese over Croft Bridge. His procession was halted on the bridge to receive the customary tribute of the Conyers sword —"My Lord Bishop, I here present to you . . ."—and then continued on its way in the following order:

Sheriff's Officers on horseback bearing white wands.
Three Outriders.
The Bishop in a carriage drawn by Six Horses.
The Bishop's Wife in a carriage with Four Horses.
The Rt. Hon. and Rev. George, Viscount Barrington,[1] in
a carriage with Four Horses.
Some Fifty Carriages of the Gentry.

And so the Bishop drove to Darlington in 1826.

[1] Rector of Sedgefield (1791-1829) and nephew of the late Bishop.

In 1890 Bishop Westcott, on entering his diocese, was received at Darlington Railway Station and presented, not with a sword, but with an address.

"When the Bishops of Durham went to prayers at the Cathedral," wrote the Rev. George Ornsby,[1] "their progress thither from the Castle, as also their return, was a matter of some state and ceremony. The editor well remembers seeing Bishop van Mildert, the last Count Palatine, walking in procession from the Castle to the Cathedral. His mace-bearer went first. Then followed his secretary, in full dress, hat in hand, immediately preceding the Bishop, who was attended by a chaplain on either hand in full canonicals. The train of the Prince Bishop was borne by his gentlemen, and four footmen in purple liveries brought up the rear. All were bareheaded except the Bishop."

Let us take a last glimpse of this princely dignity through the eyes of Sir Walter Scott.

On October 2nd, 1827, the great Romantic paid a visit to Ravensworth and, on the following day, accompanied his host to Durham to meet the great soldier, the Duke of Wellington, who was making a tour of the county. The common people, said Scott, were lukewarm in their reception of the Duke because of his politics, but "he will not care a curse for what outward show he has lost." Here the writer also met Lawrence, the painter, whom he found "a little too fairspoken, otherwise very pleasant," and Lord Londonderry, the cavalryman. That night the whole company dined in the Great Hall of Durham Castle as the guests of Bishop van Mildert. "The bright moon streaming in through the old Gothic windows," wrote Scott in his diary, "contrasted strangely with the artificial lights within; spears, banners and armour were intermixed with the pictures of old bishops, and the whole had a singular mixture of baronial pomp with the grave and more chastened dignity of prelacy. The conduct of our reverend entertainer suited the character remarkably well. Amid the welcome of a Count Palatine he did not for an instant forget the gravity of the Church dignitary. All his toasts were gracefully given, and his little speeches well made, and the more affecting that the failing voice sometimes

---

[1] Editor of *Bishop Cosin's Correspondence* (Surtees Society, 1879), Vol. II, p. 349.

reminded us that our aged host laboured under the infirmities of advanced life.[1] To me personally the Bishop was very civil, and paid me his public compliments by proposing my health in the most gratifying manner. Mrs. van Mildert held a sort of drawing-room after we rose from table, at which a great many ladies attended. I ought not to forget that the singers of the choir attended at dinner, and sang the anthem, *Non nobis, Domine. . . .*"[2]

The last surviving ceremonial was connected with the periodical assize. In pre-railway days a procession was formed in Durham and rode out to greet the visiting Judges after this manner:

> Livery Men, two and two,
> Bailiffs with their rods, two and two.
> Two Trumpeters abreast, with banners pendent from their trumpets blazoned with the High Sheriff's arms.
> The Gaoler with a black wand.
> The Under-Sheriff with a white wand and a sword.
> The High-Sheriff with a white wand and a sword, his stirrups held by pages in his livery.
> The High Sheriff's relations, two and two.
> The Gentlemen of the County, two and two.
> Servants, two and two.
> The Sheriff's Coach and six horses, with a coachman and a footman on the box and two footmen on the back.
> Other Coaches.

When the Judges were met, their coach drew up alongside of the High Sheriff's. He, with the Under-Sheriff, dismounted and bowed to the Judges, and thereupon all four entered the Sheriff's coach, the county officers sitting with their backs to the horses. The procession then returned to Durham, where, on its entry, all the bells were pealed. This ceremonial has been gradually whittled down. On the advent of the railway the High Sheriff's coach met the Justices at the station, but now the trumpets and bells, the pages and liveries and coats of arms all belong to the past, and the Judges drive up in closed motor-cars. During the Assizes Bishop van Mildert used to entertain over two hundred

---

[1] He was 62, but evidently old for his age.
[2] Lockhart's *Life of Scott*, Vol. VII, pp. 72 *ff*. (Cadell, 1837), *cf*. *M.C.*, Vol. IV, pp. 39 *ff*.

guests at Durham Castle, where rooms are still reserved for the Judges' use.

Bishop van Mildert was an orthodox and learned prelate of firm opinions, gentle manners, great dignity and princely generosity. Besides his splendid banquets at Durham Castle, he used to entertain nearly three hundred guests on his four public days at Bishop Auckland, and his charity was so unbounded that, in spite of his large income, he died, comparatively speaking, a poor man. He voted against the Reform Bill and deplored the tendencies of his day. In his Primary Charge he spoke strongly and reproachfully of the growing disposition to "wage war with established opinions, chiefly because they are established," and he maintained that the modern mind was too much occupied with these controversies.[1] But, recognising that it is idle to fight against a flowing tide and that the Palatinate would be abolished after his death and its income confiscated, he made a virtue of necessity and persuaded the Dean and Chapter to found the University of Durham, to which he surrendered his Castle and £2,000 a year out of his income. His funeral, as if to celebrate the passing of the Palatinate, was conducted with a special pomp and solemnity, and he was buried in the Cathedral.

It is a strange and ironical fact that the immediate result of the progress of Democracy and its Industrial Twin, on whose altars the Palatinate had its throat cut for the sake of its golden fleece, was an increase, instead of a decrease, of the episcopal income. The intention of the Government was that the "princely revenues" of the Bishop of Durham should, for the most part, be taken from him and be devoted by Ecclesiastical Commissioners to the general welfare of the Church throughout England. But in point of fact Bishop Maltby, the democrat, was a far richer man than his predecessor, Bishop van Mildert, the prince. This state of affairs was brought about through lack of foresight on the part of the Commissioners. For some years before the death of van Mildert the revenues of the Bishoprick had averaged £19,200 per annum. It was decided that henceforward the episcopal income should be limited to £8,000. The new Bishop of Durham, Maltby, was therefore offered the alternative of either accepting a fixed

[1] *V.C.H.*, Vol. II, p. 71.

income of £8,000, leaving the Commissioners to collect the remaining revenues, whatever they might amount to, or to pay the Commissioners £11,200 a year and himself to take the residue, whatever it might be. Maltby very generously (and very wisely) raised the income payable to the Commissioners to £13,200 and announced that he would be satisfied with the remainder. But the great industrial boom had come. The coal in the Bishoprick was soon being worked on a hitherto unprecedented scale, with the consequence that its revenue soared and that the remainder due to the Bishop, instead of hovering in the neighbourhood of £6,000 as had been anticipated, rose to £30,000 and more. Thus Bishop Maltby's own share of the total became greater by at least half than the whole of that of his princely predecessor. But this mistake was corrected after the Bishop's retirement. The fixed episcopal income of £8,000 was then substituted for this ecclesiastical gamble. In spite of the tremendous decrease in the purchasing power of the pound this income has now been halved. £4,000 a year represents today all that is left of his Bishoprick to the present Bishop of Durham. The Ecclesiastical Commissioners have, in their turn, been deprived of their coal royalties for secular purposes, and thus the proudest and wealthiest See in England has been beaten to its knees.

In spite of the trend and purpose of the times the Palatinate was not surrendered without a struggle. Numerous petitions from all parts of the county were received against its abolition, and Lord Londonderry became the champion and the mouthpiece of the petitioners in the House of Lords. The objections to the proposed Bill were on two grounds. The first was that it withdrew a large revenue, derived exclusively from the Bishoprick, to expend it on general purposes throughout the country. Thus the local inhabitants were to be deprived of the direct benefits they had hitherto received from this income at a time when, owing to the phenomenal expansion of industry, the workmen and their families were multiplying exceedingly and the people of the Palatinate were consequently standing more in need than hitherto of religion, instruction and charitable support. "My Lord," wrote the Vicar of Stockton to Londonderry, "at the request of my parishioners I take the liberty of placing the inclosed petition in your Lordship's hands,"

18

which he supports by stating that "in the return of the number of churches endowed, no mention is made of the sums of money given by his Lordship annually to the incumbents of poor populous livings"—Barnard Castle, Hartlepool, Etherley and others; nor of the Bishop's charities to Stockton, Shildon, etc., "independent of money given to assist in building churches"; nor of the schools founded by Bishop Barrington, which were so badly needed and which completely changed the character of Weardale. "My intimate acquaintance," concludes the vicar, "and general connexion with every part of this diocese for upwards of thirty years enable me to say that the want of moral and religious instruction is greater in this part of the country, especially in the populous towns and mining districts, than is stated in the petition." The Vicar of Pittington, who had previously forwarded a petition to Lord Melbourne signed by a thousand of his parishioners, also wrote to Lord Londonderry. He complains of the inaccuracies and the repeated corrections of the Commissioners' three reports, and states that their recommendations amount to "a virtual subversion of the general principles on which property is held." He further points out that his own parish, extending "over the most valuable coal-field" in England, had risen from a population of 500 in 1827 to 6,000 in 1836, and that "it would be an act of extreme injustice if the wants of such a population were not amply provided for, both as regards religious and moral instruction," before any portion of the wealth which they brought to the surface was expended elsewhere. A third letter, from South Shields, states that Bishop van Mildert out of his episcopal income augmented livings, endowed churches and erected schools, and that his local charities, amounting on an average to between six and seven thousand a year, were raised to as much as £13,000 in the last year of his life.

All these points Lord Londonderry emphasised before the House and did his utmost "to open their Lordships' eyes to the cruel, the unparalleled situation in which the county would be placed if this Bill succeeded." The Commissioners, he declared, were pursuing a course of parsimonious economy, "but he believed if they had a cheap hierarchy they would soon have a cheap monarchy."

The Government was, in fact, proposing to confiscate the revenues of the Bishoprick on a scale for which Queen Elizabeth would have blushed, precisely at the time when they were most needed. But the fact was that the Church, however strong and true its utterance, could no longer claim to speak on behalf of all the people. There was a large element of Dissent in the county which practically coincided with the large element of Democracy. On religious grounds the Nonconformists were most unwilling that the revenues of the Bishoprick should be reserved for the sole use of their theological opponents, and for political reasons the Democrats rebelled against the continuance of authoritarian power to an ecclesiastical Tory hierarchy. Even if it were not proposed to confiscate the riches of the See for purely secular purposes, at least it was in their view a step in the right direction to bring down that brazen image, the Palatine Count and Bishop of Durham, to the level of an ordinary democratic man. The opponents of the Bill were, moreover, embarrassed in their opposition by the parliamentary tactics of its supporters. These affirmed that there was now no question of the revenues of the Bishoprick, beyond putting them at the disposal of Parliament, and that their ultimate fate would be decided later. It was now, they told Lord Londonderry, only the question of the Palatine Courts which was under consideration. Thus by evasion and postponement of their obvious intentions they successfully contrived to take the edge off Lord Londonderry's attack.

It was against the abolition of these separate Palatine Courts —the County Court, the Court of Chancery and the Court of Common Pleas—that the second serious objection to the Bill was stoutly maintained. It was argued that the abolition of the Courts would simply result in greatly increased expense to the inhabitants of the County without any compensating advantage: "that no case of abuse in the practice of the Courts of Pleas and Chancery can be established and that no proper inquiry has been instituted, all information obtained having been procured from one or two irresponsible individuals." Even Mr. Joseph Pease, Member of the Southern Division of the County, and "decidedly in favour of the principle of this Bill," demurred to carrying this "general principle of centralisation too far."

The result of it all was that, on June 21st, 1836, only four months precisely after the death of Bishop van Mildert, the independent Palatine privileges and revenues ceased to exist.

Only as a sop to their opponents the Government allowed the separate Courts of Pleas and of Chancery to remain. The Court of Common Pleas was abolished, simultaneously with all the others in England, in 1873, and today the "Court of Chancery of the County Palatine of Durham and Sadberge" is "the sole surviving symbol of the great powers formerly exercised by the Prince Bishops of Durham."[1]

There is indeed another, but it seems to be a mistaken one. In Burke and Debrett the arms of the Bishop of Durham are still shown with a coronet over the mitre and a crossed sword and crozier (instead of crossed croziers as for other bishops). But as the King of England, not the Bishop of Durham, is now Count Palatine, this sword (to represent temporal power) and this coronet (which, moreover, is drawn as a duke's instead of an earl's or baron's) are incorrect.

The Bishop of Durham is, alone of all the bishops, still hailed as Bishop "by Divine Providence" instead of "by Divine Permission." With London and Winchester he takes his place amongst the first three bishops of the realm, regardless of the personal seniority which determines the precedence of the remainder. At the coronation of the King he stands at His Majesty's right hand.

[1] *V.C.H.*, Vol. II, p. 173.

CHAPTER XXXI

SCHOOL AND UNIVERSITY

"Fundamenta ejus super montibus sanctis."
PSALM lxxxvii. Motto of Durham University.

WHEN the secular clergy were turned out of Durham to make room for the Benedictine monks they formed elsewhere their own communities round a central church, and the earliest English parishes were probably served by these or similar "collegiate churches," as they are called. It was not long before the bishops began to look with favour upon these little groups of priests and to seek in their numbers, who were well educated and learned in the law, for clerks, advisers and administrators to help them to counteract the increasing influence of the monks. So Pudsey built their own church for the secular clergy of Darlington, and Bek added Lanchester and Chester-le-Street to those already established—St. Andrew's Auckland, Darlington, Norton, Heighington and (probably) Easington. All these he turned into regular collegiate churches, with a dean and prebendaries. Staindrop, which came later into being, was of a slightly different order. St. Andrew's, with a dean and twelve canons, was the largest of these communities. Walter Langton, the chief minister of Edward I, was at one time a member of it.

To each of the collegiate churches a public grammar school was attached, and when they perished in the Reformation the schools perished with them.

But new schools soon came into being under Protestant direction. Some, such as those at Darlington and Auckland, covered the same districts as were served by the old colleges, while new ones were established elsewhere.[1] As the years advanced these schools were multiplied by a steady flow of endowments and benefactions, while a few private schools, generally run by clergymen, were added to their number in the eighteenth and early nineteenth centuries. To this last category belonged, amongst others, a well-known school at Witton-le-Wear where Joseph Stevenson began his educa-

---

[1] Heighington School was founded in 1601 by Mistress Jenison.

tion; the school, just over the Northumberland border, attended by R. S. Surtees; the Yorkshire specimen at Bowes which was denounced by Dickens; and a Catholic school at Tudhoe remarkable for much beating (as doubtless they would all be today), where the cat once kittened in the headmaster's wig.

The Churches of the different denominations took an increasing interest in the instruction of their respective flocks, but apart from the institutions they directed there was no public supervision of education until the Charity Commissioners took over the general control of endowed schools in 1869. In the following year primary education was first undertaken by the Government, and in 1902 the County Councils were made responsible both for primary and secondary education. Since that happy day no Government nor County Council has been able to hold its eager hand, with the consequence that now nearly all education has become utilitarian, secular and stereotyped, all individuality of character and intellect, with all lively and picturesque parochial idiosyncrasies, is being rapidly effaced, and the daily newspaper has become the only form of literature for the vast majority of the English people.

Gilpin's school at Houghton-le-Spring, which had educated the great scholar Hugh Broughton, George Carleton (Bishop of Chichester), Robert Surtees, Christopher Hunter (a distinguished antiquary) and other worthies of the past, was brought to an end in 1924. For many years before its dissolution it had fallen from its high place, with other institutions of a similar character, owing to the increasing influence throughout the nineteenth century of the so-called "public school." The centralisation of the education of the wealthy from all parts of England in such places as Eton, Winchester and Rugby, was one more, but perhaps not the least serious, of the effects produced by the invention of the steam engine. The children of the squire who, of old, were as familiar with the local inhabitants and local customs, with the animals and the trees, as the butcher's and the farmer's sons, who knew as well as they did the bird's nest in the hollow poplar by the mill and the pond where the kingfisher flew, were now separated at their most impressionable age from the natural influence of their own environment, and instead of wandering the Durham woods and the hedgerows of home, catapulting a wandering pheasant with Cuddie Anderson or plundering a neighbouring orchard with Tom Dunn, grew up as strangers from their own people and wasted their time playing organised games with young gentlemen from Tooting and Tewkesbury. Thus the old grammar school with its parson schoolmaster, its single usher and its score or so of little boys came to an end or changed its character. So Gilpin's school died, and Mistress Jenison's at Heighington ceased to instruct its pupils "in the accidence and Lily's grammar"[1] and the principles of the Christian religion, and became an ordinary "undenominational" elementary school. At the other extremity of education their local University was soon abandoned by the gentlemen of Durham for the sake of Oxford or Cambridge.

One or two of the old schools still survive. Amongst them are the "Free Grammar School of Queen Elizabeth" at Darlington, the only school in the county whose original endowment was royal and not episcopal nor private, and the "Free Grammar School of King James I" at Bishop Auckland. In spite of its title this school has not a royal foundation, but owes its origin to Mistress Ann Swifte, who endowed it, and its name to her petition to the king to grant it the light of his countenance. Lord Armstrong was educated here, the ingenious inventor of the automatic gun, and here, too, the author of hymns, F. W. Faber; nor will the undistinguished writer of this volume soon forget the debt which he owes to its late headmaster, the distinguished cricketer, Robert Bousfield.

The little school at Rushyford, which was no grammar school and may be taken as a specimen of the "elementary" school before the days of Government supervision, aimed at a standard of education which would certainly not be regarded as elementary today. Amongst past relics in the possession of my friend Mr. Fred Burlinson[2] is an exercise book used by his grandfather's uncle while in attendance at this school. Its subject is trigonometry. A hundred years ago, when the opportunities for learning were fewer and more prized, pupils used

[1] *V.C.H.*, Vol. I, p. 399.
[2] To whom I am indebted for many interesting reminiscences.

to come from long distances to this little school mounted on their galloways and ponies and cuddies.

The large school at Barnard Castle, formerly called the "North-Eastern County School," though established within comparatively recent times, has its roots in the early Middle Ages. It owes its eventual existence to the founder of the famous Oxford College, John Balliol, and can claim an even earlier origin than that venerable foundation. But whereas Balliol College awoke immediately to life and activity the idea of the Barnard Castle school lay dormant for centuries. About the year 1229, according to Hutchinson,[1] Balliol founded the Hospital of St. John in Barnard Castle for the permanent relief of three poor women. The income derived from the property with which this hospital was endowed is still received by the Charity Commissioners, and part of this income is still expended, as stipulated by the original donor over seven hundred years ago, on the support of three almswomen. But the amount now received is in excess of what is required for this charitable relief. In 1829 it was pointed out that the successive masters of the hospital had for some time been granting leases for the various portions of the property and pocketing as their rightful due the large "fines" (or, as we should now call them, the "premiums") which were paid by the lessors in consideration of an infinitesimal rent. The last of these leases expired in 1863, and the inhabitants of Barnard Castle then decided that the office of master, as an expensive sinecure, should be abolished and that, after the beadswomen had been paid, the balance of the income should be set aside for a future school. A further £1,000 were later to be raised on mortgage for the same purpose. Finally this fund was combined with that derived from another charity, and in 1883 the school was opened at its temporary premises at Middleton-St.-George, near Darlington. Three years later it was transferred to Barnard Castle, where it fulfilled its purpose for many years as an institution which provided the advantages of the larger "public schools" for the sons of professional men, tradesmen and farmers of the Northern Counties. Latin and religion formed the basis of education, which, however, was mainly modern in character and concentrated on agriculture and engineering. The school still continues to flourish, but now

[1] Hutchinson, Vol. III, p. 237.

as a "Direct Grant Grammar School" (and no longer as the "Northern Counties") it has been brought under the ægis of the ubiquitous Minister of Education.

Of all the schools in the county the oldest and the most famous is Durham School. The date of its foundation is doubtful, but it is possibly one of the oldest schools in England, for it may have been in existence before the Norman Conquest. The Benedictine Monastery of St. Cuthbert, besides the special instruction which it gave within its walls to the novices, had established, as we have seen, a school for certain poor "children of the almonry" just outside the Abbey gates. But the monks were not alone in encouraging learning in the city. The Bishop likewise had founded a school long before the monks had established theirs, perhaps even before the See had been removed from Lindisfarne. There is, at any rate, some evidence that the Bishop's grammar school "was already in existence in the city soon after the See was removed to Durham in 995."[1] Little is known, however, of this school's history until, in the year before the battle of Agincourt, Cardinal Langley reorganised it, amalgamated with it the Novices' School and erected new buildings for it on the east side of Palace Green. Two masters were appointed to this school, of which the senior was to teach Latin grammar and the junior to give instruction in song, and they were "diligently to teach and instruct all willing to learn and study under them, the poor indeed freely (*gratis*) for the love of God, if they or their parents have humbly asked for this,"[2] but taking a reasonable fee from those who could afford to pay it. One of these early masters was John Claymond, protégé of Bishop Fox and friend of Tunstall and Thomas More. He later became the first President of Corpus Christi College, Oxford.

So the school continued until the Reformation, when it was refounded by Henry VIII and placed under the control of the Dean and Chapter. At the same time the Almonry School was incorporated with it. Thus the three separate schools which had existed side by side through the early Middle Ages were amalgamated, by two separate stages, into one. Apart from these alterations the school continued much as before. It was

[1] *Durham School Register*. Third Edition. Edited by T. H. Burbridge (Cambridge University Press, 1940), p. xix.
[2] *V.C.H.*, Vol. II, p. 372.

still divided into "grammar" and "song," of which the latter half, consisting of ten boys, acted as a preparatory school for the former. There were eighteen Grammar boys, "of apt parts," on this foundation, and they correspond with the "King's Scholars" of the present school. They were "to be brought up at the expense of the church until they have gained a fair knowledge of Latin grammar and have learnt to speak and write Latin, for which a period of four years, or, if the Dean see fit, five at the most and not more shall be allowed." During this period the Latin authors to be mastered by the boys included Cicero, Livy, Ovid, Horace, Virgil and Lucan. They had likewise to learn how to write Latin verse, to speak Latin always when in the vicinity of the school, to write a weekly Latin essay and to deliver a weekly Latin oration of their own composition before the master and the class. Nor was Greek neglected. Homer, Hesiod and Demosthenes were the principal authors to be studied in this language. Whole holidays (except for Sundays) and half-holidays during term were unknown, but, "for recreation's sake," the boys were allowed to read such jolly books as the epistles of Roger Ascham or Paulus Manectius (whoever he may be). The school hours were from 7 to 11 in the morning and from 12.45 to 5 o'clock in the afternoon. Even during the regular holidays, which were not unduly long—a fortnight at Christmas, ten days at Easter and ten days in the summer—the boys had to go back to the school twice every day "to repeat such things as the Schoole maister shall think profitable." But nothing apparently quenched their spirits, for on breaking-up day there were scenes, we are told, of "intolerable disorder," so that it was most strictly forbidden to "use in or nere the schoole noe weapons, as dagger, sword, or staffe, cudgell or such like."

So the Abbey School continued undisturbed in its industrious way until the outbreak of the Bishops' War. Then the Scots destroyed the school buildings and the masters had to teach where best they could—how the boys must have enjoyed that time!—until the Dean and Chapter erected new premises on the opposite side of Palace Green. Here the school remained until, having grown too big for its beautiful surroundings, it was moved to its present site. The old building is now used as a lecture room for Durham University.

Many distinguished men throughout the ages have been educated at Durham School—from John Balliol, King of Scotland, who "had been for a long time at School at Durham,"[1] down to the late J. W. Fawcett, who was the son of a Brancepeth farmer. At the age of fourteen he walked from Durham to Newcastle for extra lessons in Hebrew and Latin. At the age of twenty-five he could speak thirty-three foreign languages. Christopher Smart, the mad poet, was at school here; so was the most sane author of "Jorrocks." Here, too, were Bishop Creighton, the great historian, with his "red hair and cold blue-grey eyes";[2] and here the first Viscount Hardinge. Lord Hardinge was present with Sir John Moore at Corunna and fought with Wellington in the Peninsula. He was three times wounded, lost his hand at the battle of Ligny, and became successively Secretary of State for War, Governor-General of India, Commander-in-Chief of the British Army and Field-Marshal. He was the son of a Rector of Stanhope; so, though not quite by birth,[3] this gallant soldier may be claimed by early residence and by education as a Durham man. One of the school's headmasters, Edward Elder, who ruled from 1839 to 1853, was then appointed to Charterhouse. "He lies buried in Durham Cathedral graveyard but, as Thackeray's Dr. Senior in *The Newcomes*, he lives on today."[4]

Durham School is remarkable for its prowess in rowing and in Rugby football. Ever since 1854 a crew from the school has been entered annually to compete for the Grand Challenge Cup for Fours in the regatta held on the Wear, and, apart from the distinctions won in the southern universities by old Durham boys, these form the backbone of the best crews in the North.

When Durham Regatta was at its height as many as eight crews used to compete for the great race, and the preliminaries must have been delightful to attend. First came a band down the river, playing "Meet me by moonlight" and other sentimental ditties of the period; then Mr. Wharton of Dry-

[1] His own words, given as a reason for declining to assist Ralph Neville in his quarrels with the Prior, |*Durham School Register,* p. xx.
[2] "Mandell Creighton," by Edmund Gosse, *Portraits and Sketches.* (Heinemann, 1912), p. 195.
[3] He was born at Wrotham, Kent, six years before his father moved to Stanhope.
[4] *Durham School Register,* p. xxv.

burn, master of the ceremonies, standing in a white top hat in the bow of an eight-oared out-rigger; then the competing crews, who raised their oars opposite the Count's house, while all on river and shore sang "God save the King." Next, to the waving of the white hat, came three loud cheers, followed by "Rule, Britannia," and then the race.

In Rugby football the school has trained nineteen Oxford and Cambridge "Blues" and twenty internationals. No fewer than five old boys (including the referee) appeared on the field at Twickenham in 1929 when England was playing the Rest. This is a remarkable record for a comparatively small school, whose numbers today amount to 220.

Towards the maintenance of this school the Chapter contributes a sum of £3,000 a year.

When Henry VIII seized the possessions of the monks of St. Cuthbert there was some question of founding a college at Durham and devoting a portion of the former monastic revenues to its support. It came, however, to nothing more than the eighteen Grammar boys and the ten Song boys whose establishment or, rather, whose continuance we have just noticed. The old Durham Hall at Oxford was re-cast as Trinity College and ceased to maintain its connection with the North. Thus the Palatinate jogged along with no special form of senior education attached to it until Oliver Cromwell strove to shed light in the dark place by the realisation of the old Tudor idea of a college for students in Durham. The definite steps which he took would doubtless have met with success but for his death and the subsequent collapse of the Protectorate. Thereafter the scheme lay dormant again for many years until, after the death of Barrington, it became clear to his wise and practical successor that the old order of society was doomed and that a storm was about to burst, particularly on bishops and cathedral clergy, only comparable in its fury to the tempest of the Reformation. He therefore determined to anticipate, so far as he was able, the confiscation of the ecclesiastical revenues of Durham and to ensure that some portion of them at least should be retained for the exclusive benefit of the Bishoprick and of the Christian faith. The Dean (Jenkinson) and the Chapter shared his alarm and discussed with van Mildert the best means of forestalling and softening the effects of the coming shock, and thus the idea of a college for Durham was revived for the second time. In 1831, when the atmosphere all over England was electric with "reform," the Chapter unanimously resolved that "an academic institution should be established, to be called Durham College,"[1] and that one-fifth of the total capitular revenues should be devoted to it, in addition to an annual amount to be decided by vote but not to exceed £2,000. Bishop van Mildert, however, convinced that "nothing short of a university with the power of granting degrees would answer the expectations of the public,"[2] carried the Chapter with him, and on July 4th, 1832, the Bill for the establishment of a university at Durham received the Royal Assent.

But this measure was not passed without opposition, not from the "reactionaries," as might have been expected, but from the "progressives." The influence of Dissent was now powerful throughout the county, and it was the religious nature of this foundation that stuck in the gullets of the Nonconformists. The new university was to be "in connexion with the Cathedral Church of Durham, and under the direction and control of the Dean and Chapter of Durham, as Governors thereof";[3] the Bishop was to be Visitor; and no one could be granted a degree who did not recognise the supremacy of the King and subscribe to the Book of Common Prayer and the Thirty-Nine Articles. This excluded from the benefits of a university education all those who were not members of the Church of England, and "Radical Jack" Durham made himself the mouthpiece of their indignation in Parliament. But in vain. Nonconformists would be allowed to attend lectures, but the main object of the foundation of the university—the continuance of the influence of the Church under a new form adopted to meet changing circumstances—would have been defeated, had the Dean and Chapter given way. They had no intention of doing so. A hundred years ago there was a profound conviction of the vital importance of religion in public affairs, and particularly in education. The adherents of the

[1] C. E. Whiting, *op. cit.*, p. 36.   [2] *Ibid.*, p. 39.
[3] *Durham University*, by J. T. Fowler (Robinson and Co., 1904), p. 27.

Church of England—above all, its chief priests, its guardians, teachers and expounders—were less inclined to compromise than to fight for their faith. The Government, therefore, simply informed Parliament that if the clause to admit Nonconformists were approved by the majority there would then be no university at all; for they could not (in those days) compel people to do what they did not like with their own money.

But the history of the development of Durham University is largely a reflection of the development of national democracy, which has now popularised and practically secularised even this citadel of exclusive ecclesiasticism. The institution displays progressively (or retrogressively) less and less of a religious character and becomes less and less subject to private control. It was, however, never the intention of the founders that the University should become a training ground for Anglican clergy. As early as 1837 the curriculum included a school for civil engineering, which is believed to be the first established in the country. But it is indisputable that it was a *sine qua non* of the foundation that the principles and practice of the Church of England should be punctiliously observed by the members of the University and that these principles were essential to its constitution. The authorities of the Church doubtless hoped to substitute for the old episcopal breakwater against the violence of reformatory floods a more up-to-date system of ecclesiastical engineering. But Time has disappointed them. In this disappointment they were not, of course, alone in England to suffer, or even to suffer most severely. The religious background of this University is still apparent, more noticeable perhaps than that of any other. But the University itself is no longer of an essentially religious nature, and thus the main purpose and intention of its clerical founders has been defeated.

This defeat has been inflicted by successive stages, which were accelerated by the financial difficulties in which the Dean and Chapter soon found themselves involved.

In 1834 Bishop van Mildert, who had already offered his castle and set aside a portion of the episcopal revenues to the new University, raised his annual subscription to £2,000 and gave a further donation of £1,000. But the endowment still fell far short of what was required, and on the death of van

Mildert the Ecclesiastical Commissioners appeared on the scenes. These graciously agreed to recognise "the engagements entered into by the late Bishop and the Dean and Chapter,"[1] but proposed to reduce the prebendal stalls from twelve to four, to give each of the four remaining canons a fixed salary, and to confiscate what was left of the revenue for the general welfare of the Church throughout the land, leaving the new institution to fish for itself. Bishop Maltby protested strongly to the Prime Minister, with the consequence that the lands belonging to the Deanery and to the eleventh stall and, later, those of the first and second stalls, were all made over to the new University. But the local magnates, now waxing rich on coal and from whom much had been expected, helped but little; the revenues of the Deanery and of the three stalls proved quite insufficient; the great feudal castle weighed upon modern academic shoulders like an elephant; and by 1857 the state of affairs had become so perilous that there were serious thoughts of closing down altogether. This drastic step was avoided, but the first warden was removed; the wardenship was thenceforward attached to the deanery and a set of ordinances was issued for the reform of the University.[1] These included the shortening of the preparatory period for a degree[2] and the abolition of compulsory attendance in chapel for Nonconformists.

Meanwhile, in 1834, a School of Medicine, in no way connected with any religious foundation, had been established in Newcastle, and after diverse vicissitudes had become "the Newcastle-upon-Tyne College for Medicine in connexion with the University of Durham." In 1870 this College became an integral part of the University, and in the following year was founded, also in Newcastle, the "University of Durham College of Physical Science," eventually to be known as "Armstrong College." In 1937 this college and the College of Medicine were joined together in one great block of buildings and received the title of "King's College." In 1946, of the 3,094 students of Durham University, no fewer than 2,423 were members of King's College in Newcastle, where not only medicine and science but all normal University subjects are now taught, with the exception of theology and Oriental languages.

[1] C. E. Whiting, op. cit., p. 74. [2] This mistake was later corrected.

In 1896 the first four women students were matriculated, and a women's hostel, opened on Palace Green in 1899, later developed into St. Mary's College, for which Princess Elizabeth in 1947 laid the foundation stone of a new building. There are, besides, two licensed halls of residence for women —St. Hild's and Neville's Cross.

In 1907 the chief officer of the University ceased to be the Dean of Durham (who from 1862 had been Warden *ex officio*) and the reins of power were transferred to the hands of a Chancellor and Senate. In the following year all compulsory attendance in Church was abolished, even at Sunday Services in the Cathedral; and in 1910 the Dean and Chapter ceased to have any control over the University. Today all degrees and all official positions are open to men and women alike and no religious test is required either from students or teachers. Thus the religious nature of the original foundation has been obliterated.

The gradual effect of the slackening of ecclesiastical bonds and of an increasing modernity of outlook has been reflected in the advance in the number of undergraduates. From 41 in 1862 this had risen to over 200 within thirty years, and by 1932 to 1,600. Today this last figure has been trebled.

Professor Whiting, to whose book, *The University of Durham*, I owe most of these facts, writes[1] (in 1932) that "the old ties between Chapter and University have been modified and not severed." Apart from the peculiarly theological character of one or two of the colleges, such as St. Chad's and St. John's, there remains, no doubt, a strong, sentimental attachment between the University as a whole and its original founders. Moreover, the Bishop of Durham is still the Visitor, and so theoretically the First Officer of the University, as when it was first instituted; the Dean is a member of the governing body, there are still two Canon Professors, and every college has a daily service in its chapel for those who wish to attend. Not least, perhaps, the bells of the Cathedral constantly ringing in the ears of the student, its shadow ever cast upon the path of the passer by, must produce even an involuntary effect upon the academic life. Nevertheless, if an outsider may be permitted to judge on the strength of the

[1] C. E. Whiting, *op. cit.*, p. 61.

facts submitted, it seems that "modification" is too mild a term to describe the changes in the relationship between Chapter and University. The ties certainly have not been severed, but they have been weakened to the verge of severance.

We should expect to find some remarkable characters amongst the professors of a university founded a hundred years ago by an ecclesiastical hierarchy. Today all over England the spice and flavour have been taken out of life and the insipid dish of uniformity is served to scholar as to clown. Even archdeacons must have food coupons and lecturers in Hebrew wear utility clothes. Today it needs a man of gigantic proportions to keep his head distinct, in sunshine, above us shadowy ghosts that lag in a murky world. But then it was comparatively easy to live and walk erect, unstarved. Men naturally played and looked their own parts and no other's. They were free to square their shoulders and to wag their beards, to show what manner of men they were and to rejoice without fear in the showing. So a host of Professors and Canons and Tutors, of clear-cut figures, of dominant personalities crowd about us from this nineteenth-century university, and our only difficulty is one of selection.

Archdeacon Thorp, the first Warden, was indefatigable in his zeal, the sacrifice of his money and the determination with which he pursued his own way. He had a kind heart, a lisping voice and several pretty daughters—"Now, behave, Jennie," he used to say to the youngest, "you know you were a mistake"—but as he would not give his tutors a free hand, all the best men, save only Canon Jenkyns, left him; and when at last the poor autocrat fell and soon afterwards died, the darling of his heart, "*my* university," had fallen into "almost absolute decay."[1] This Canon Jenkyns, who had stuck through thick and thin to his old Warden, was famous throughout England as a teacher of theology. To him and his renown it was chiefly due that the University was kept alive during these difficult years. Profound in learning, impeccable in conduct,

[1] *Memorials of Dean Lake*, edited by Katherine Lake (Arnold, 1907), p. 115.

"cold as ice, clear as ice, hard as ice,"[1] he was the last survivor of the "Golden Canons," a Tory in politics and a High Churchman of the old school. Canon Fowler has borne witness to his "sweet smile" at the ceremony of the Loving Cup; and when he resigned in 1864, after a bad accident, the last link was severed with the old gracious ways and elaborate courtesy of the eighteenth century.

Dean Waddington, who succeeded as Warden on the retirement and death of Thorp, was a man of stately presence and soldierly carriage, who addressed the Bishop at his installation "as if he were addressing a regiment of cavalry."[2] He enjoyed the side-shows of life, visited the boxing-booths at Durham races and even, perhaps, put on the gloves himself; and he loved dancing at a County Ball. "I hope I may go to another," he said to his young partner, "before I enter Paradise." But when he did enter Paradise he seems to have left rather a mess behind him. "I have had infinitely more real trouble," wrote his successor, Dean Lake, "in getting the Cathedral into order (after Waddington's laxity) than even the University has cost me."[3] And this cost him a good deal. For it was largely thanks to Lake's rough energy and his go-ahead views that the University was rescued from its moribund condition. As for the Cathedral, he hacked the plaster from its great pillars, rebuilt the Chapter House and revived the services. For Queen Victoria's Jubilee in 1887 he packed the huge building with children, and on another occasion, in the morning, sixty bishops processed up the nave, the Bishop of Western New York preached the sermon, while the Bishop of Durham,[4] surrounded with his chaplains, reigned aloft on his high throne; in the afternoon two thousand choristers filled the old Abbey with their song. But this tall, dignified, white-haired man with the black skull cap did not achieve all his reforms and infuse fresh life into the Cathedral and University without inevitable opposition and trouble. "What! Is my old

[1] So described by Dr. Townsend, a brother Canon. "Senilia," by J. T. Fowler. (*D.U.J.*, December, 1918.)

[2] "Reminiscences of Cosin's Hall," by Dr. Scudamore Powell. (*D.U.J.*, December, 1918.)

[3] Letter to Archbishop Tait. November 29th, 1879. Lake, *op. cit.*, p. 241.

[4] Lightfoot.

friend Lake dead?" asked Archbishop Tait in mock surprise when he heard that all was peaceful at Durham.

It would be pleasant to linger over many more of these noble characters, but we must respectfully hurry the dignified steps of Dean Kitchin, the uncompromising pro-Boer, who kept his mind serene by his "happy gift of forgetting things";[1] Canon Greenwell, the fisherman-archæologist whose book on *British Barrows* was "a perfect treasure of information for the man of science";[2] Canon Tristram, a great authority on birds; Dr. Kynaston, Professor of Greek, whose sermons were patterns of beautiful English; Professor Sanday, the chivalrous, in whom "the helpless and unfortunate always found a champion";[3] and his friend Dr. Plummer, pale-faced, bearded and deep-voiced, who died at the piano while playing to his wife her favourite tune. These last two, under Dean Lake, did more than any others to raise the University from the low estate into which it had fallen.

The knowledge of Professor Chevalier, one of the earlier dons, was encyclopædic, but, "wrapped in astronomy and abstruse calculations," he was unable to impart it in an elementary form. He was not only a profound mathematician but a good Hebrew scholar, and he spent his spare time skating with all the zest of youth or watching rooks through a telescope from the window of his house.[4] Joseph Stevenson, at one time Librarian to the Dean and Chapter, was a famous historian. One of the editors of the Rolls Series, he was pensioned by Gladstone for his services and eventually became a Jesuit at Farm Street, where he died. The Reverend H. J. R. Marston was a classical scholar, Reader in English to the University, spoke German, had preached in French, was a brilliant musician and—blind, since the age of twelve.

Perhaps the most attractive figure of all these Canons and Professors is that of T. S. Evans, the lover of words, the beautiful Greek and Latin versifier, he who liked the unpopular Bishop Phillpotts immensely because "he really has an excellent appreciation of the aorist." He was so absentminded that on one occasion he took off his boots during ser-

---

[1] *D.U.J.*, June 11th, 1904. His own expression.
[2] *Saturday Review*, Vol. XIV, p. 147.
[3] W. Hooper in *D.U.J.*, December, 1920.
[4] Powell, *op. cit.*, and Fowler, "Senilia" (*D.U.J.*, December, 1918).

vice in the Cathedral and placed them on the book-ledge in
front of him. At another time, it being his turn to preach, he
left his stall for the purpose, but, instead of going into the
pulpit, strolled absent-mindedly down the nave and so home.
His hair was black as a raven's plumes, his figure tall, his
manners grave and elaborately polite; "beautiful to see," said
Professor Sanday, for they "sprang from genuine kindliness
of heart."[1] Unlike most scholars and artists he never resented
criticism of his verses, which were described by the greatest
authority of the time as combining "the utmost accuracy with
the utmost grace in a degree never surpassed and rarely
equalled."[2] Evans died composing a Latin verse on the dark
colour of his medicine; and after his death, the very memory
of him, wrote one of his friends, "makes me feel young
again."[3]

A. S. Farrar, Professor of Divinity, stalked through life
with his chest thrown out and flourishing an umbrella. He was
very particular about dress. "Dear and Reverend Sir," he
wrote with stately courtesy to a young minor canon to con-
gratulate him on his black coat and trousers, his old-fashioned
collar and his chimney-pot hat. But when the same young man
appeared in the Cathedral in grey flannels Dr. Farrar, who
was beside him and about to conduct the service, remarked:
"I cannot think, Mr. Dolphin, why you have taken to dressing
like a cad. Let us pray."[4]

Another formidable personality was that of Archdeacon
Watkins, Professor of Hebrew, the "Black Archdeacon," as he
was called, for his dark complexion, his flashing eyes, his huge
head and his great black beard. He has been described as "cast
for a Cardinal," a Richelieu of tremendous power rather than
a scholar; a man who, kind and even tender at heart and most
happy in his home, found his field of work too narrow for him
and was consequently "extreme to mark what is done amiss."
He was never late, he never drank wine or spirits, he never had
a doctor or breakfast and he loathed smoking. "Who's that,"

---

[1] *D.U.J.,* October 26th, 1889.
[2] Robinson Ellis, of Balliol and Trinity College, Oxford. (*D.U.J.,*
May 25th, 1889.)
[3] Archdeacon Sandford of Exeter. (*D.U.J.,* November 23rd, 1889.)
[4] A. R. Dolphin. Reprinted from *Spectator.* (*D.U.J.,* December,
1923.)

he would exclaim as a whiff of tobacco came through his open window, "burning incense to the devil?" His hearing was extraordinarily acute. On one occasion when preaching in the Cathedral he quoted from an early Father of the Church. "He never said anything of the sort," murmured the Professor of Divinity to his neighbour. "For the benefit of the *ignorant*," continued the Archdeacon, turning towards the interrupter, "I will give chapter and verse," and thereupon proceeded to do so.

Perhaps the best known of all the dons was the gold-spectacled J. T. Fowler, author of a history of his University. "Durham?" asked someone. "Oh yes, that's where Fowler is." In his character, it has been said, there was "something of the sublime." He was a fully qualified doctor of medicine, a lecturer in Hebrew and an antiquarian who edited many volumes for the Surtees Society. He had no love of sport, but used to ride a tricycle, which he took with him on many excursions to the Continent. For a short time, indeed, he used a bicycle, but he was always, in his own words, "liable to be nervous about mounting and dismounting" it. Nevertheless, in spite of a petition signed by the ladies of the Close, he persisted for a few years in obstinately and dangerously riding it. Then he went back to his three-wheeled machine.

And last we come to Canon Cruickshank, "a scholar, a gentleman and a Christian," who succeeded Kynaston as Professor of Greek and was an authority on Massinger; and to Bishop Welldon, Dean of Durham, enormous and friendly, who once, after an accident when he was attending service in a long chair, was mistaken in the shadows for one of the monuments of his Cathedral.

We must let them go now, these learned, wise and witty men, who have made enduring the fame of this great University and who loved it as their child. For their love was repaid and they were happy there. They lived in an age when learning was honoured, character was respected, and there was a smiling appreciation of those little idiosyncrasies, those traits of a rare or robust personality that set men apart from the herd. So to them, indeed, the Lord had shown, in the words often quoted by Canon Fowler, "marvellous great kindness in a strong city."[1]

[1] *D.U.J.*, March, 1920.

Durham Castle was built about 1072, on an earlier site, as a stronghold for Walcher, the first Norman Bishop of Durham. Thenceforward it remained the official episcopal residence until 1837, when it became, what it now is, the headquarters of University College. Of Walcher's original buildings, the mound (on which stands the Victorian keep) and the beautiful Norman Chapel are the only distinctive features left. But the magnificence of Walcher's successors has added new glories which can scarcely be rivalled elsewhere and have made of this castle "the finest example in England of the secular architecture of the period."[1] The undergraduates of University College may enter their home through Pudsey's unequalled doorway; dine in Bek's great hall, "larger than that of New College and more beautiful than that of Christ Church";[2] receive their food from Fox's kitchen, only surpassed by that of Cardinal Wolsey, also at Christ Church; go to prayers in Tunstall's Tudor Chapel; walk to bed up Cosin's famous black staircase, certainly the noblest in the county and one of the best in England; and fall asleep at last in rooms carved out of the "Norman Gallery" or Hall which Pudsey had built for the use of the Constables of his castle. Such was the setting which, twenty years ago, was threatened with absolute destruction.

In the early years of this century increasing anxiety had been felt about the fabric of the castle. The struggle which the University had had to keep its head above water had precluded any possibility of serious expenditure on the building which housed it. This severe limitation of funds was still imposed upon the authorities. Though they were alive to their responsibilities and took careful notice, through their own architect, of shiftings and sidlings and bows and bends, and did their best to prevent and delay them by such small precautions and repairs as they were in a position to undertake, it was becoming increasingly obvious that something drastic and thorough would soon have to be attempted if the castle, or at least the most important part of it, were to be saved from tumbling into the river. The west and the north were the sides

[1] Report of Dr. Oscar Faber on the condition of Durham Castle (1927). See *Durham Castle,* by Brigadier-General H. Conyers, Surtees (1928), p. 20.

[2] *V.C.H.,* Vol. I, p. 387.

which were threatened, and these included all that was best—Bek's hall, Pudsey's gallery and doorway, and Cosin's great staircase. They included, moreover, the hall where the undergraduates dined, some of the rooms where they slept and the rooms assigned to the Judges of Assize. The danger was urgent, not only to the building itself, but to life and limb. By 1927 the position had grown so desperate that the University, on the strength of two separate reports by independent experts, warned the High Sheriff that the Judges' rooms were no longer safe, and in the following year a similar warning was given with respect to the Great Hall. "It is, I think, impossible to exaggerate," said Doctor Faber, one of the experts, "the urgency or the necessity of underpinning and strengthening the battlement wall on the west front, and no guarantee could be given by a competent engineer that the whole of this part may not collapse at any moment."[1] And Mr. Fletcher, the other expert, added: "The south wall (of the Norman Gallery) should at once be secured by temporary shoring. . . . It is a matter of urgency."[2] The whole trouble was due to the fact that, unlike the Cathedral, which was built directly on the solid rock and has not, therefore, budged an inch, the castle was founded on beds of loose shale and earth. In order to put the matter right it was necessary to underpin a tottering, enormous building down, through fifty feet of earth, to the solid rock. Even to touch it was dangerous, and the whole operation had to be conducted on the edge of a precipice. The cost of this permanent repair, essential to prevent the "total or partial collapse" of the castle, was estimated at £150,000.

Already, in 1925, the Bishop of Durham (Hensley Henson) had broadcast an appeal for help. "I cannot doubt," said he, "that patriotic Englishmen, justly proud of this majestic building and acknowledging the obligation to maintain one of the noblest of England's historical monuments, will willingly and quickly contribute the money needed for its due preservation."[3] But patriotic Englishmen were slow and faint in performance. About three years later the Bishop had to write: "The financial result is almost nothing, and I am completely baffled by the invincible indifference of the public."[4] In the

---

[1] Report of Dr. Faber. General Surtees, *op. cit.*, pp. 21, 22.
[2] *Ibid.,* p. 24.   [3] *Durham Castle*. An address, p. 14.
[4] Henson, *op. cit.*, Vol. II, p. 206.

CHAPTER XXXII

COAL

"The history of mediæval Durham is the history of the Bishopric; the history of modern Durham is the history of its coal industry."

H. R. TREVOR-ROPER.

No single substance, no animal, nor vegetable, nor other mineral has exercised so profound an influence upon the development of man as coal. Not only materially, as the source of locomotion and the life-blood of industry, but even intellectually, as the begetter and as the translator into practical effect of modern theories of political government and social improvement, it has wielded a power hitherto more revolutionary and absolute than that of any other discovery, invention or device of man. It has already profoundly affected, and may eventually completely transform, the spiritual values of his life. Without coal the greed of Dives would have been constrained within pastoral limits; Karl Marx would have found no dark soil for his dragon's teeth; the furies of Hitler would have been limited to the range of a sword's thrust and an arrow's flight; and no stiff, mechanical Frankenstein would today be clutching its creator by the throat. Coal has much to answer for. It is not for nothing that its colour is black and that it is found, far from light and beauty and growth, in the horrid bowels of the earth; the associate of greed and suspicion and anger and sorrow; inseparable from toil and danger, and minatory of death. Coal has much to answer for. Yet without it, it is probable that we would never have been born; without it, it seems certain that we could not now continue to live. Some two hundred years ago men seriously began to build upon it the fantastical, convoluted structure of a new age. Today we are awake to the discovery that this deep foundation is also a fundamental problem in our present lives and for our future development. It is the problem of how to separate the evil and the mischief, both social and individual, which are apparently inherent in the extraction of coal, from its apparent necessity; of how to reconcile intellectual and spiritual progress, without which man must inevitably perish, with that industrial continuity which is now infused into the blood and bones of our physical existence. It may well be that the new atomic discoveries will provide the solution of this problem and will turn us into angels, in one way or another, but meanwhile it is imminent and threatening, pervasive through the lives of each and every one of us, greatly aggravating the strain of the present and rendering the future of all civilisation dark and forbidding, doubtful and insecure. It is against this gigantic background that we must look at the story of the Durham coal-field. It is not a cheerful background, but it will enable us to see the details with some sense of proportion.

The story of the development of coal, in Durham as elsewhere, is not a single story but two stories. Though each in the process of telling reacts upon and changes the course of the other, each has a distinct and separate theme. There is the story of the gradual process of extraction, of commercial gain and loss and speculation, of mechanical improvements, of setbacks and disasters, of practical difficulties encountered and overcome; and there is the story of the men engaged in that adventure and of the progress of relationship between employers and workmen. There is the mining story and there is the social story, and, so far as we are able, we will here treat them separately, while endeavouring constantly to bear in mind their close interdependence. We will take the mining story first.

The discovery of the combustible nature of coal, whenever this may have taken place, had no immediate revolutionary consequence, nor did its first working produce any frantic effect, or indeed any appreciable effect at all, upon the structure of society. The way to industrial revolution was arduous, long and, at first, very slow. The Romans who excavated coal, and the Saxons who gathered it on the shores of the German Ocean, did not, we may believe, suppose for an instant that in so doing they were acting as the forerunners of the breakers and makers of worlds nor that such innocent and casual employment might one day be subject to the anxious scrutiny of a Minister of Fuel and Power. Nevertheless, the black link is there. From the opening chapter in those far distant days down to the latest bureaucratic injunction on the consumption of electricity the story of coal goes rambling on, though at first more hinted at than told and much subject to blanks and hiatuses. After the conquest of this island by the Normans it is probable that the severity of the Forest Laws prevented more than surreptitious scratching of some waste piece of ground, for once these begin to be relaxed we find our first definite pronouncements on mining. The uncertainty about this early history is partly due to the fact that the Latin word "carbo" has the significance both of "coal" and of "charcoal," and it is not, therefore, easy to determine, when the Boldon Book, for instance, talks about "carbones," to which of these two substances it is referring. But it seems certain that open-cast working had begun at least in the twelfth century, for early in the following it was well under way. In 1228 a street in a London suburb was known as Sea Coals Lane; in 1239 Henry III granted his royal authority to Newcastle merchants to dig for coal; and in 1256 the approaches to this town were already noted as dangerous because of unfenced excavations. Throughout the following two centuries the development slowly continued, for the most part, as was natural, on the convenient banks of the Tyne; but in 1350 a mine was opened in Coundon (at a cost of 5s. 6d.), and about the same time coal was being dug at Lumley, Cocken and Rainton on the Wear, as well as Cockfield (in 1375) and other places in the county. At the beginning of the fourteenth century the monks of Jarrow converted their wood-burning hearths into an iron fire-grate provided with "1 porr (poker) and 1 pare of tangys," and twice during the reign of Edward III the king intervened to protect the coal traders of Gateshead from the more go-ahead rapacity of the burghers of Newcastle. In 1354 Thomas of Ferry leased the coal in his land to the Prior of Durham in return for half a cart-load every week—perhaps the first mention of those much abused coal royalties which were abolished nearly six hundred years later.

But the commercial and financial importance of coal was little appreciated until after the Reformation, until we reach the period of transition between the old world and the new and pass from the imperium of the Church to the domination of the counting-house. Commercial capitalism was the brave new key which was to unlock the wonders of this brave new world, and "the forces of capitalism in northern England,"

says Mr. Trevor-Roper, "consisted in one word, in coal."[1]
Those greedy Newcastle merchants, who were constantly giving the good Gatesiders so much trouble, had been foremost
amongst the few to realise at least the potential wealth of
those mineral deposits upon which the pompous Prince Bishop
and his backward subjects were so ridiculously squatting. They
gazed across the river, their river as they conceived it to be,
with impatience and envy at the great coal-fields on the other
bank situated just within the orbit of the Palatinate. Not only
during the reign of Edward III, but in that of his grandson and
frequently thereafter, we find them leaping into Tom Tiddler's
ground and constantly being rapped on the knuckles. In 1416
Cardinal Langley obtained judgment against the mayor and
burgesses of Newcastle and was confirmed in his possession of
the south side of the Tyne, and more than a hundred years
later the Durham Chancellor of Cardinal Wolsey was still
complaining on the same theme. "Please it your grace," he
writes, "to be advertised that ther be thre cole pytts at a township of yours called Whikam where be allredy gotyn a gret
substance of colis. . . . It is no reason that the marchaunts of
New Castell shuld enforce your grace to sell your colis only
unto theym at their own prices. . . ."[2] But the merchants of
Newcastle had plenty of reason for their continued interference, and they did not rest until their activities were crowned
with success. They believed that they had achieved it when
the condottiere Duke of Northumberland, John Dudley,
abolished the Palatinate and promised, in return for their support, to hand over to them the coveted mines. But Dudley fell
and the Church returned to power, so that it was not until the
days of Queen Elizabeth, when, by making use of an obscure
Southern money-grubber called Thomas Sutton and of his
influence with another Dudley, the Earl of Leicester, these
cunning business men at last obtained their hearts' desire. On
the death of Bishop Pilkington, Leicester secured for Sutton
a lease of the Gateshead and Whickham coal-mines, which
Sutton exchanged later for a still longer lease of ninety-nine
years. Stella, Ravensworth and other collieries were soon afterwards engrossed in this lease. In the year after he had effected

---

[1] "The Bishopric of Durham and the Capitalist Reformation," by
H. R. Trevor-Roper, *D.U.J.*, New Series, Vol. VII, No. 2.
[2] Hutchinson, Vol. I, p. 404.

this exchange, having in vain tried to make himself a freeman of the town, Sutton was out and the Newcastle merchants were in. They had bought the whole lease from him for £12,000.

As the result of this "Grand Lease," as it was called, the Bishoprick was largely excluded, until the end of the seventeenth century, from the increasing revenues derived from coal. This was the period which "saw an increase in the coal trade, hardly less astonishing, in the circumstances of that earlier time, than the second great increase in the early nineteenth century."[1] But the mines were in those days concentrated round the Tyne, and Newcastle obtained the almost exclusive benefits from this first boom. In 1609 under 12,000 tons were exported from the Wear and over 239,000 from the Tyne, while in 1635 the income received from Whickham and Gateshead exceeded by a hundred times that of the Bishop's coal-pits. So the burgesses of Newcastle waxed fat and proud, believing themselves to be citizens not only of the richest town in the North but soon of the richest in England. They laughed and snapped their fingers at London herself. "Our staiths their mortgaged streets will soon divide," they sang; "Blaydon own Cornhill, Stella share Cheapside."[2] But already, when this song was published, the Civil War and the growing importance of Parliamentary Sunderland, with the consequent development of the pits on the Wear, had begun to check at last the absolute predominance of the Newcastle merchants. Presently, on the expiry of the Grand Lease, the Bishops of Durham once more enjoyed their own and entered, with increasing revenues, upon the golden age that preceded the Industrial Revolution.

Now the momentum was gathering weight and speed. Early in the eighteenth century two inventions of prime importance gave a tremendous impetus to the coal trade. About 1718 the first steam-engine to drain a coal-mine was erected on Washington Moor by Thomas Newcomen, and in 1735 coke was first used for the smelting of iron. Thus early was heralded "the most potent and characteristic phase of the whole Industrial Revolution"[3]—the connection of iron with coal. These

---

[1] Trevelyan, *Social History*, p. 284.
[2] *History of the Parish of Ryton*, William Bowen (1896).
[3] Trevelyan, *Social History*, p. 393.

inventions were followed throughout the century by others. Already in 1676 Sir Francis North, a visiting judge, had described the new method of bringing the coal to the staiths, which was succeeding their transport in panniers or their lumbering progress in a loaded wain. "The manner of the carriages is by laying rails of timber from the coalliery down to the river," he wrote, "and bulky carts are made with four rollers fitting those rails, whereby the carriage is so easy that one horse will draw down four or five chaldrons of coal."[1] He did not know that he was witnessing the first step towards our modern railways. A hundred years later a little progress had been made. Two iron wheels had been substituted for two of the wooden ones,[2] and a contemporary account tells us that a great difficulty and danger was the speed reached by the waggons when coasting down a decline. In coming to a "run," we are told, the horse is generally "unloosed," lest the waggon should kill him, but, in spite of this, owing to derailments or to the careless blocking of the route, "many hundred poor people and horses have lost their lives."[3] At the end of the century iron rails (with four iron wheels) were substituted for the wooden ones. In 1813 " an ingenious and highly interesting experiment was performed in the presence of a vast concourse of spectators on the railway leading from the collieries of Kenton and Coxlodge, near Newcastle, by the application of a steam-engine, under the direction of Mr. John Blenkinsop, the patentee, for the purpose of drawing the coal waggons."[4] The experiment was successful; Stephenson was also working on the same lines, and in 1825 his first train, bearing coals (as well as passengers) from Auckland to Stockton, fairly ushered in the Industrial Revolution.

All these inventions and the consequent deepening of coal-mines, with the opening of new ones, resulted in an increasing number of accidents. The first recorded explosion of fire-damp took place at Gateshead in 1621, but for many years thereafter few precautions were taken, and it was not until the end of the eighteenth century that those responsible began to examine the question seriously. The miners, for their part,

---

[1] "Life of Lord Guildford." (See Hutchinson, Vol. III, p. 498.)

[2] "The two front wheels are made of metal, the two back wheels of wood." (Local newspaper, 1777.)

[3] Local newspaper, 1777.   [4] Sykes, Vol. II, p. 74.

thought that a devil lurked in the pit, and any hint that he might be bent on mischief on a given day—such as the sight of a woman in a white apron or of a crow on the pulley frame of the shaft—was more gravely taken than any reasonable precaution. More lives were doubtless saved through super-stition[1] in the old days than through scientific means.

> "As me and my marrow was ganging to wark,
> We met with the de'il it was in the dark;
> I up with my pick, it being in the neit,
> I kocked off his horns, likewise his club feet."[2]

But many of these brave men, who thus defied the devil and his fiery breath, paid for their courage with their lives. Fire-damp, being lighter than air, tends to accumulate near the roof. Prior to the invention of the Davy lamp the method of testing for the presence of this gas was for the "fire man" to go ahead bearing a long pole with a naked light at the end of it and, lying at full length upon the ground, to thrust his stick upward and hope for the best. It was not surprising that the "de'il" often got him, nor that throughout the seventeenth and eighteenth centuries there were frequent explosions when men, women and children were blown to pieces and sometimes whole families destroyed. No inquests were held upon these deaths,[3] and it was not until after the terrible explosion at Felling, near Gateshead, in 1812, when ninety-one men and boys were killed, that societies were formed for "Preventing Fatal Accidents in Coal-mines," and, before long, the Davy lamp was evolved. A contemporary account of this single disaster will serve for all and will illustrate the courage which was required of the rescuers.

"About half-past eleven on the morning of May 25th, 1812, the neighbouring villages were alarmed by a tremend-ous explosion. . . . A slight shock, as from an earthquake, was felt for half a mile around the workings; and the noise of the explosion, though dull, was heard to three or four miles

[1] And it has lingered far into modern times. Even that up-to-date and valuable functionary, the District Nurse, has had to bow down to it within living memory, remaining indoors until the men had gone down the pit, in case they should meet her on their way to work and so be compelled to return home.

[2] From an old pitman's song. *Durham*, by William Whellan and Co. (London, 1856), p. 96.

[3] Before 1815, Trevelyan, *England*, p. 607.

distance, somewhat resembling an unsteady fire of infantry. Immense quantities of dust and small coal rose with these blasts into the air in the form of an inverted cone; the heaviest part of the matter fell near the pit, but the dust, borne away by a strong west wind, fell in a continued shower from the pit to the distance of a mile and a half. In the village of Heworth it caused a darkness like early twilight, and covered the roads so thickly that footsteps were strongly imprinted in it; pieces of burning coal, driven off the solid stratum of the mine, were also blown up one of the shafts. By twelve o'clock thirty-two persons, all who survived, were brought up by the gin rope, which was wrought by human strength in the absence of horses; the dead bodies of two boys were also recovered; and of the thirty-two who came up alive, three died within a few hours. . . . At a quarter after twelve Mr. Straker, Mr. Anderson and seven others descended the John pit in hopes of meeting with some of the workmen alive. As the fire-damp would instantly have ignited at candles, they lighted their way by the *Steel Mill* (a small machine which gives light by turning a plain thin cylinder of steel against a flint).[1] Knowing that a number of the workmen would be at the crane when the explosion happened, they attempted to reach it by the plane board;[2] but their progress was intercepted at the second pillar by choak-damp;[3] the noxious fluid filled the board between the roof and the thill,[4] and the sparks from the flint fell into it like dark drops of blood. In retracing their steps to the shaft they were stopped at the sixth pillar by a thick smoke, which stood like a wall the whole height of the board; the flint mills were useless, and to the total despair of success in their enterprise was added the certainty that the mine was on fire and the probability of a second explosion at every moment burying them in its ashes.

---

[1] This was, still, a dangerous method of illumination, but safer than candles and more satisfactory than phosphorescent fish, which were used, in earlier times, to give a ghostly glimmer to those who worked in darkness.

[2] A main haulage underground road running east and west. The modern spelling is "bord." Roads running north and south are called "walls."

[3] Firedamp (carburetted hydrogen) explodes; choke-damp (carbonic acid gas) poisons.

[4] The floor of the seam.

At two, Messrs. Straker and Anderson had just descended the John pit with three of the workmen; two were in the shaft, and two were left below, when a second explosion (though infinitely slighter than the first) did actually occur. . . . Haswell and Anderson, who were below, heard its distant growling, and, like the Arabian, who falls prostrate to let the fiery Simoom pass over him, fell on their faces, and by keeping firm grasp of a strong prop which supported the roof near the shaft, experienced no other inconvenience from the blast than its lifting their legs and poising their bodies in various directions, as the waves toss and heave a buoy at sea. . . ." It was not until July 8th that the fire was got under and that the bodies were brought out of the pit. "As soon as a cart-load of them was seen the howlings of the women, who had hitherto remained within their houses, but now began to assemble about their doors, came on the breeze in slow fitful gusts, presaging a scene of extreme distress and confusion at the pit. Happily the representations made to them as to the state of the *one* body already found . . . induced them either to return home or remain silent in the neighbourhood of the pit. Every family had (with a feeling very general in these classes) made provision for some entertainment of their friends on the day the bodies of their relatives should be discovered, and it was generally given out that they intended to take the corpses to their own houses. The weight, however, of Dr. Ramsay's opinion, and other friendly remonstrances, prevailed with them to waive the usual practice and to consent that the bodies should be interred as soon as discovered. . . . The effects of the blast were most various: round the *crane* twenty-one bodies lay in ghastly confusion, some shattered to pieces, others lying as if overpowered by sleep and others scorched as if by the fiery wind of the desert; others lay prostrate with their hands extended, as if attempting to escape the blast."[1]

It was believed that, with the invention of the safety lamp, the pitman could thenceforward "traverse the most dangerous recesses of the subterraneous realm with impunity."[2] But such was not the case. Though the risks of disaster were very greatly reduced by this invention the danger still remains.

[1] "An Account of the Explosion in Brandling Main Colliery at Felling," by Mr. Hodgson, the local parson. Quoted in Surtees, Vol. II, pp. 87-88. [2] Surtees, Vol. II, p. 89.

The slightest spark, such as that caused by a pick striking against some hard substance, or a flash from a fault in an electric cable, may be sufficient to cause an explosion if the presence of gas has been undetected. As recently as 1909 one hundred and sixty-eight men and boys were killed by a pit explosion at West Stanley, whose cause was never clearly ascertained.[1]

Nevertheless, the value of the safety lamp can scarcely be exaggerated; for not only is its light so protected that there is no possibility of explosion from its contact with fire-damp, but the manner of its burning, if carefully observed, will reveal the presence of even a minimum quantity of this gas. Thus, though the occasional explosions which still occur are the most sensational, they are far from being the most frequent examples of pit accidents. Of the deaths and serious injuries in the collieries of the United Kingdom in 1938 only 6 per cent. were caused by explosion of fire-damp. By far the greater number (49 per cent.) were due to falls of roof and 28 per cent. to haulage accidents.

The development of the coal trade in the North during the eighteenth century was dominated by a team of monopolists who called themselves the "Grand Allies." These comprised the Russells of Brancepeth, the Brandlings of Gosforth, the Liddells of Ravensworth, Lords Strathmore and Wharncliffe, and Matthew Bell of Woolsington. William Russell bought Wallsend, which produced the finest coal in the world, and between them all they owned the best pits in the North. Their object, which they successfully enforced for over seventy years, was, by limiting the output and the sale of coal, to keep up its price on the London market. By these means they made fortunes for themselves and we owe, amongst other things, the hash that was made of Brancepeth Castle to this "limitation of the vends," as it was called. But the monopoly was brought to an end by the spread of the railway system and the increasing number of pits which were sunk as a consequence of this revolution in transport. For, although the

---

[1] There were two explosions. "The main explosion may have been initiated by an explosion of gas but was undoubtedly propagated by coal dust. What the means of ignition were we cannot say." Report by R. A. S. Redmayne and Donald Bain.

eighteenth century was indeed a time of industrial progress, we must not lose sight of the fact that, until the advent of the railway, the county was still far from being industrialised. The great majority of the workers still worked on the land. Throughout the whole of the eighteenth century only about sixty new mining operations were undertaken, as compared to some five hundred in the nineteenth.

Then, indeed, in the new Coal and Iron Age the face of the county was changed and the lives of the people of the Bishoprick were transformed. In 1810 there were 10,000 pitmen working on the Tyne and the Wear; in 1913 there were 223,000. Soon after the beginning of the nineteenth century, coal was discovered in the east of the county under the limestone, and in 1821 the first colliery in this area was opened at Hetton, which, with others, combined to increase the trade of Sunderland and led to the building by Lord Londonderry of Seaham Harbour. Meanwhile, mechanisation was going ahead. Ponies were brought down the pits for haulage and were regularly replacing hand labour before the turn of the half-century, but underground steam haulage was already in use at Hetton Downs Colliery in 1826, eventually to be succeeded in its turn by the present electrically driven conveyors. In 1863 Thomas Harrison of Tudhoe invented the first compressed air coal cutter; by the end of the century these were being worked by electricity; and only 19 per cent. of the total coal excavated in County Durham is now hewn by hand.

In 1787 two million tons of coal were shipped from all the ports on the Tyne and Wear. A hundred years later the coal produced in the County of Durham alone amounted to over thirty million tons. By 1913, the peak year of production, this figure had risen to over $41\frac{1}{2}$ millions. In 1946 the county produced $24\frac{1}{2}$ millions.

Certain Durham coal is the best for household use and is also remarkable for its excellent quality for coking purposes. Indeed, the manufacture of coke absorbs about a quarter of the total output of the collieries. Moreover, by far the greater proportion of the coal used by the London and South Coast Gas Companies comes from Durham. There are believed to be still left in the ground within the county area, excluding any portion beneath the sea, over three thousand million tons of coal capable of being worked under present-day conditions. So that it does not appear that the Coal Age will soon come to an end through exhaustion—at least, not through exhaustion of the fuel. In an endeavour to increase the output today, recourse is once more being had to open-cast working to supplement the production of the pits. Thus the wheel has come full circle, and we return at the end of our story to something very like that system of untidy grubbing for coal which was followed in the earliest days.

We shall not begin to understand the temperament of the coal-miner until we can grasp something of the conditions under which he works and lives. These conditions have been essentially the same since the time when the first pit was sunk and the first group of colliery houses was built in its vicinity. Coal still must be dug out from the depths of the earth, can still not be hauled down from the top of a tree, and this essential nature of the blackened and degraded vegetable must control and dictate the tenor of the lives of all those associated with its extraction. But although the miner's life and work have, therefore, remained essentially the same, so many details of both have been progressively changed, that we may fairly draw a contrast between the picture of conditions as they are now and as they were in the earlier days of the last century. For this purpose we will take a look at a modern pit (not with the eyes of a mining engineer but through those of an ignorant visitor) and we will then contrast it and its working conditions with those of a hundred and a hundred and fifty years ago. From these different sketches we may be able to conceive a setting for the modern miner and for the problems which are connected with him and with which society is today confronted. For it is surely necessary, in order to comprehend a picture, not only to look at the immediate foreground but also behind it. Only those who ignore the past and despise the influence of heredity will believe that the difficulties with which we are now faced are solely difficulties of our own making. Between us and their solution there is a whole crowd of unhappy, black-faced ghosts that start and mutter.

For our first picture let us take an account of a recent descent of a coal-mine by a layman who was ignorant as any Southerner of the conditions that predominate over the ex-

traction of coal. His visit took place on a holiday, when, perhaps, the abnormal silence and the absence of human activity
within the recesses of the mine may have contributed to the
depressing and even alarming effect.

"The pit is only 500 feet deep (a deep mine is 1,800 feet)
and we went down in the 'cage,' which is a rectangular, oblong
box, with rails in it and room for two tubs on each of two
decks. The sides are of steel, the ends open, except for lattice
gates which come down to within a couple of feet of the
ground after you are in: and the floor has puddles of water
on it. (I was previously decked up in overall trousers and
jacket, a thick and heavy pair of boots, a handkerchief round
my neck—a very nice bandana—and I was given a stick and
an electric lamp; while a small black 'tin' hat[1] was put on my
head.) The descent was not alarming, and on stepping out of
the cage I was relieved to find quite a high and broad passage,
about 12 feet each way, which was whitewashed and dimly
lit by electricity. It sloped slightly upwards and two sets of
rails ran along it for the full tubs going to the cages. The
empty tubs go round a different way and are hauled up by
electric power. The loaded ones run down the slope towards
the shaft, and at intervals there are devices designed to
catch and hold them in case they are going too fast. We
walked up this passage for a considerable distance, stepping
aside once to see the pumps. These also are electrically run
and were beautifully kept. (Most mines have these pumps
to remove the water which is usually found underground
and sometimes in great quantities.) At intervals along
the passage were 'man-holes' or recesses into which to step to
avoid the Juggernaut Tub.

"We then turned at right angles into a somewhat narrower
and distinctly lower passage, the height here being about 6 feet
with slight variations up and down. This passage was supported by curved steel girders, spanning the roof in the shape
of an arch. I was glad of my helmet, for I caught my head a
hard crack on one of these girders, and thenceforward walked
as one slightly bowed in grief. But it was encouraging to
observe that the air, which in the first broad passage had surprised me with its friendly rush, was still perfectly agreeable.
It smelt rather like a hot-house.

[1] It is, in fact, made of strong fibre.

"In this branch road there were two sets of rails, one for the full and one for the empty tubs. It was quite dark here, so that the hand-lamp was indispensable, and as the floor was not as even as in a palace, one was inclined to stumble over it in one's heavy boots and over the rails and into an occasional small puddle of water. By this time I was beginning to sweat; partly from exertion, partly perhaps because it was fairly warm though by no means hot, chiefly from fear of what might lie before me. Eventually we came under a fixed electric light and saw a still smaller passage, again branching off at right angles. This miserable-looking track[1] was half filled by a rubber belt[2] about 2 feet broad, which ended at one of the rails in the road down which we had walked. To this moving belt the coal was transferred near the coal-face from a similar belt running parallel to the seam. At our end the coal is tipped off into a tub, and here a man stands to supervise the loading and send off the tubs, each with 12 hundredweight of coal, on their career to the shaft.

"As I had feared, we proceeded, my back awkwardly inclined, down this narrower and lower passage, and soon came to a heavy canvas curtain which reminded me of a gas-chamber. 'This is not a very satisfactory method of conducting the air,' said my guide cheerfully as he passed through; an extraordinary observation, it seemed to me, for if I wanted to 'conduct' air I would not attempt to do so through a curtain! However, I said nothing, for fear was now definitely overcoming curiosity and a scientific explanation would inevitably delay my exit from this horrible place. I was content to be certain that these very clever people know what they are about and frequently obtain remarkable results by methods which savour, to the elementary mind, of the follies of *Alice in Wonderland*.

"Presently we passed through another curtain, and by this time I was very near panic, with the feeling that I would never see the light of day again. Only shame and my conductor's matter-of-fact explanations kept me from calling out to him to stop and carry me back to die under the open sky. 'I bet you thought it would be much worse than this, didn't you? No crawling about on your stomach, you see! This is one of the easiest pits you can be in and I am taking you only to the

---

[1] Technically, a "road."
[2] An electrically driven "conveyor."

easiest portions of that.' This certainly reassured me a little, but probably his ideas of what was 'easy' and mine differed considerably. It was, however, certainly not 'difficult'; it was only terrifying; terrifying, at least to me, through the appalling sense of being buried alive. Yet even here the passage was as much as 4 feet high, and although we had to climb round a tub once and another time wade through water ankle deep, it was not these impediments that worried me, but only pure and unadulterated funk of the enclosed space. By this time the sweat was cascading off me in all directions, but it was not long before we reached the end of the passage and came at last to the coal-face, where the men (had it not been a holiday) would have been working. Here there was a scooped out hollow, sloping from 3 feet high downwards, into which my conductor crawled—oh, horror of horrors!—and where I followed him, like a whipped, obedient dog, and lay down, completely exhausted.

"There are three main methods of getting coal: (1) By coal-cutter. After being undercut by this machine the coal is blasted down with explosive. (2) By pneumatic picks worked by compressed air, on the same principle as the pneumatic drill that breaks up a London street. (3) By hand-pick. The miner who puts the coal on the conveyor, after it has been blasted as in (1), is called a 'filler.' The miner who operates the picks, as in (2) and (3), is known as a 'hewer.' The method followed in this pit was that described in (1).

"The 'Brockwell' seam, with which we were now face to face, is 2 feet 8 inches thick, and this is the height in which the men must work. But the 'Victoria' seam, 60 feet below this, is only *15 inches thick,* and men have to crawl in and work in that 'height.' I should be screaming mad within five minutes, but apparently they do not mind.

"My conductor told me of an actual incident, such as might have occurred in any pit, and which will give a fair idea of one of the dangers of a coal-mine. A pitman had done 'rather a stupid thing'—taken some unnecessary risk—as a consequence of which he had become buried by a fall of stone. On his arrival at the scene the manager of the pit realised that the man would soon die of exhaustion unless he were released as speedily as possible, and that the only way to do this was to cut through a wooden pit prop at the risk of bringing another fall down on the top of the rescuer. He ordered a man to do this. 'All very fine,' said the man. 'This may be the only way to rescue the fellow, but what about me? I shall then be buried, and you'll have two to get out.' 'You'll be all right,' said the manager. 'Don't think so much about your own life! What does that matter? Think of the other fellow and then you won't worry about it.' Eventually he persuaded the man to do it by lying down beside him all the while holding his light. The victim was released and the roof did not fall.

"This story made me feel very ashamed of myself, for I knew that nothing would have induced me to do the same—to lie there quietly, thinking that it might well be in one's tomb, encouraging another man, who at least had the advantage of having something to do.

"So we went back, back—oh, wonderful thought!—clambering over the tub, splashing through the water, stumbling over the uneven ground, until we reached the electric light and the second passage (with the double truck-lines). Here two officials were awaiting us, and presently my conductor went off with them to inspect some other portion of this inferno. 'You won't mind waiting here for a few minutes?' How thankful I was that he did not suggest that I should come too! For nothing would have induced me to move in any direction further away from home. So I sat on a little seat by a recess, rather like a shrine, in which was an empty tin for sandwiches and an oil-burning safety lamp. Although electric lamps are the order of the day now, a light on the principle of the Davy lamp is still used for the detection of gas. The flame is turned as low as possible, and if then a light blue 'cap' appears above it, that is an indication that there is gas about. Its proportion to the air can be determined by the height of the 'cap.'

"I sat on my little seat for some time. The silence was awful. I seemed to be all alone in the pit. How right the psalmist was to regard mountains as the abode of God and the 'nethermost pit' as synonymous with hell. No sky, I thought, no green grass, no trees, no birds, no movement, no light, no air, no space—nothing but blackness, constriction and silence. Supposing my conductor were never to come back? Supposing I were left alone down here? Could I find my way out by myself? I could if I kept my head—a big 'if.' I thought of that awful story by Conan Doyle of the man who deliberately led his secret enemy astray in the catacombs and left him there to perish alone in the dark. . . . Presently I heard steps and voices, and a small light glimmered in the inky distance. My party was returning. . . . Incidentally, every man (including myself) on descending the pit is given a small metal label stamped with a number, called a token or tally. These are surrendered when you emerge into daylight once more. At the end of every shift these numbers are checked, and if there is one missing it is known that the bearer of it must be somewhere in the pit. Thus no one, who might be working by himself and perhaps be suddenly seized with illness, could long be overlooked—quite apart from the frequent visits of inspection that are made.

"So now we made our way back, and with every step my heart grew lighter and I found it difficult not to break into a run. But I was not really happy until we had emerged from the cross passage into the broad main thoroughfare, and indeed I had some reason for alarm, for my guide suddenly pointed to the right and said: 'There is a road there leading to a steep drift to an upper seam. We have put in some nice concrete steps—about 125 of them—for ease in travelling; but I don't suppose you want to go there, do you?' 'No, *thank you*,' I replied with perhaps unnecessary emphasis, but the mere thought of climbing up this nightmare staircase nearly started a fresh panic in my craven breast. 'Yes,' said the manager cheerfully, 'it is much more convenient for the men, if they want to get from this seam to the upper one, to go this way than to walk all the way to the shaft and all the way back again on the higher level.' ('No doubt,' thought I, 'and if they wish to do that, let them do so by all means. But for my part I would rather climb a mountain than walk up ten of your "nice concrete steps."')

"When we emerged at last into the main thoroughfare I said to myself: 'This is much better, but I have a long way yet to go, and I shall not be really happy until I get to the lift or whatever they call the thing.' And when at last we reached the bottom of the shaft I told myself that I would be really happy when I came out into the open air. And so it proved. I could have danced and sung aloud with joy when at length we stepped out of the cage into the dreary-looking shed which covered it, and I marvelled that my companions grumbled because it was raining. I have seen few sights more welcome than this delicious rain, and I could have run about in it for hours and soaked myself with joy. For it came down from the skies above me and there was nothing at last between me and the manifestations of a natural world.

"What agonies had I then endured? None, except mental agonies, and these I realised well were due to the constant attempts of my imagination to run amok—attempts which I was just able to keep in check more through a sense of shame than by any effort of will. My will down there was like paper pulp. I said to myself that I would not have missed, and that I would not repeat, the experience for a thousand pounds. But, all the same, I would not so very much mind if I knew that I would only go through *exactly the same* procedure again. This time it would not have the same terrors for me, for there would be no fear of the unknown. I could even understand that, in course of time, one could get quite used to a pit and regard it almost as one's second home; that familiarity would breed contempt. But when every allowance has been made for the terror of the unknown and for the workings of a too ridiculously imaginative mind, still it remains a fact that the occupation of a miner, besides having in it an inevitable element of danger, is utterly unnatural. My guide hit the nail, I think, on the head when he said that God had put the coal deep down in the earth, presumably because He thought it was a good place for it, well out of everybody's way, and that we, with all our machinery and cunning devices, were flying in the teeth of Nature in order to extract it. So I believe. This is not work comparable to the ploughing of a field or the felling of a tree or the building of a house. This is uncanny work. And however little, or not at all, the miners themselves may be consciously affected by this aspect of it, it must produce, in time, a deteriorating effect on the mind and on the character. Other occupations may be harder and even exposed to greater danger—such as the life of a sailor—but none, surely, can be more unnatural. As the mind of a sailor, however small and limited, or of a forester, however unpoetical, must be enlarged by the vastness of great skies and mighty waters or smoothed by the green dignity and quietness of woods, so must the mind of the miner, however naturally sweet and reasonable, suffer from this perpetual contact with a close and pitiless blackness. If to this daily occupation in the bowels of the earth you add a daily return from them to a dreary pit village, made up of stone or brick houses with slate roofs, often (though not always) without a garden to be seen to relieve their dreariness, common and meaningless in shape and revolting in material, with even more ugly chapels and churches occasionally breaking the monotony of the line of grey roofs under a grey sky— what wonder is it if a man living and working under these conditions becomes warped in his mind and feels that his hand is against every man and every man's hand against him? The marvel to me is, not that the miner is collectively so difficult, but that he is individually so easy and friendly. The young men of today do not want to go down the pit. When I consider that I have only seen the best parts of one of the easiest and most up-to-date pits in the county, that I spent only two hours in it and did no work in it whatever, and that I came out in a state of mental, moral and physical prostration—while making every allowance for my own weakness and appreciating that it would probably not even be understood and certainly not shared by the born and bred miner—I should still say today to any man who announced his firm intention of never going down a pit again, 'I am not in a position to blame you.'"

The payment of pitmen is extremely complicated. They are divided into two classes: "datal workers," who are paid by the day or shift; and piece workers, who are paid by results. This second class comprises hewers, fillers, coal-cutter men, stonemen, putters and several others. These are the crack troops of the miner's army. The datal workers, who are responsible for haulage, the cleaning of roads, the renewing of timber and the numerous odd jobs that must be done in a pit, are paid a regular, fixed wage; but the wages of the piece worker vary according to the amount of work and the kind of work he does, as well as the conditions under which it is done. Some coal, for instance, may be easy to extract, while in other places it may be difficult. The actual amount paid is, therefore, fixed by agreement between the Government (until recently, the owners) and the men's representatives, while, in order to give each man a fair chance, lots are drawn every three months whereby his particular working place in the pit is decided. These lots are known as "cavils." But, apart from this system of payment, there is now a minimum, unconditional wage of £5 a week for every hewer, which was fixed in January, 1944, by what is known as the "Porter Award." According to this arrangement the mere presence of a hewer in the pit, whatever he does or does not do, is sufficient to ensure him £1 per shift—that is, £5 per week.

The time of a miner's shift in Durham is reckoned at $7\frac{1}{2}$ hours, in addition to the time of one winding, which is usually about 20 to 25 minutes. The proportion of this time spent at the coal-face must vary, of course, according to the distance to be travelled underground, but, roughly speaking, after making allowance for covering this distance and for a meal, one may say that the actual time spent in work is about 6 hours.

In addition to his wage, a miner today gets a free house or 5s. a week rent and either 12 or 15 tons of coal a year, according to the size of his family and the number of workers in the house.

Let us now compare this account of modern mining conditions with a contemporary description of a hundred years ago.

"First, then, how to descend. We see a vertical hole, or pit, pitchy dark, and surmounted by wheels to facilitate the raising of coal from the bottom of the shaft. Into one of the 'tubs,' or 'buckets,' used for this purpose we must now contrive to get, a matter which requires no small amount of nerve to effect. If the bottom of the bucket should give way, or the rope break, or—but it is fearful to speculate on such ifs when you are swinging over a depth of several hundred feet. Now we are descending. It is said by those who ascend in balloons that no feeling of motion is perceptible, but that the earth seems to be flying away from them while they are perfectly still and motionless. Much the same idea may be said, in reverse, in descending a coal shaft (*sic*). You have no idea of the descent, but the little round hole of light seems to be flying faster and faster over your head upwards, as if it were going to the skies, and at length, in a couple of minutes, perhaps, the orifice of the shaft has apparently turned itself

into a day star, which shines far, far above you in the firma-
ment.

"Arrived at the bottom of the pit, what do we see?
Nothing, or nothing but 'darkness made visible.' Every
vestige of daylight is effectually shut out, and it requires
some time to accustom one's eyes to the light of the candles,
which appear as mere sparks or points of light in the midst
of intense darkness. By degrees, however, our eyes become
accustomed to the strange scene, and men are discerned moving about in galleries, or long passages, working in positions
which would break the back of any ordinary workman, while
boys and horses are seen to be engaged in bringing the coal
to the mouth of the pit. Some of these horses go through the
whole of their career without seeing the light of day—they
are born in the pit, reared in the pit, and die in the pit. . . .

"The actual coal digger is called the *hewer*. Whether the
seam be so narrow that he can hardly creep into it on his
hands and knees, or whether it be lofty enough for him to
stand upright in, he is the responsible workman who loosens
the coal from its bed; arrangements below ground are made
to suit him; he is indeed the key of the pit, the centre of the
mining system. Next to the hewers come the *putters*, who
are divided into *trams, headsmen, foals* and *half-marrows*.
These are all youths or children, and their employment
consists in dragging or pushing the coals from the workings
to the passages where horses are capable of being employed
in the work. The distance that a corve, or basket of coal, is
dragged in this manner averages about a hundred and fifty
yards. When a boy 'puts' or drags a load by himself he is
designated a *tram*, when two boys of unequal age and
strength assist each other, the elder is called a *headsman*
and the younger a *foal*, and when two boys of equal age and
strength help each other, both are styled *half-marrows*.
When the corves are 'put' to a particular place, where a crane
is fixed, the *crane-man* manages the crane by which the corves
are transferred from the tramway to the rolleys and keeps an
account of the number so transferred. The *corf* is a wicker-
work basket containing from four to seven hundredweights,
the *rolley* is a waggon for transporting the corves from the
crane to the shaft, and the *rolleyway* is a road or path sufficiently high for a horse to walk along it with the rolley,

and is kept in repair by the *rolleyway-man*. The *driver* takes charge of the horse which draws the rolley, and the *on-setter* is stationed at the bottom of the shaft to hook and unhook the corves and tubs which have descended or are about to ascend the shaft. . . .

"The seams of coal, and the apertures where such seams have been, often give out carburetted hydrogen and other gases, which, when mixed with common air, become very explosive. Hence it is important to drive these gases out of the mine as quickly as possible, and this can only be effected by causing a current of air to pass constantly through the workings. A complete system, as now adopted at the best collieries, comprises the *downcast-shaft* for the descent of fresh air, the *upcast-shaft* for the ascent of the vitiated air, well-planned galleries, doors and valves throughout the whole of the mine, and a furnace at the bottom of the upcast-shaft to heat the air and cause it to ascend more rapidly. . . . In former times the dangerous contaminated passages were lighted only by sparks struck from a small instrument called a 'steel-mill,' but the beautiful safety lamp, or 'Davy' as the miners familiarly call it, has superseded this. . . . If the lamp be properly tended it is one of the most precious boons that science gave to industry; if it be neglected, as it often is by the miners, those explosions take place which so frequently give rise to such fearful results. . . .

"Hard as a pitman's life seems to be, yet it is agreed by those who knew the northern collieries half a century ago that it was then much more laborious. The following is a description given of it by a Newcastle merchant, who had himself experienced the severity of boyish labour some forty or fifty years since. His description of that period was sad indeed, and it was very detailed. Then, according to his account, the boy would go into the pit to work at two o'clock on the Monday morning, and arrive at his home between eight and ten at night entirely exhausted. He would again repair to work the next morning at the same hour, half asleep and sometimes half naked. This continued through the week, and he would not see much daylight from Sunday till the next Saturday afternoon. Although this state of things might not be permanent as regarded the long hours, yet the labour was always extreme, and two boys were often bound to 'put' together without the adequate strength; this led to quarrels between unequally matched boys, and though these were often brothers, fights and foul language was frequent among them. One great cause of improvement was the employment of metal or iron plates for the trains to run upon, and another was the blasting of coal with powder. Before this the boys had often to drag their coal over a fir plank or even the bare floor, but now the whole way is laid with metal plates, even up to the face of the workings, and by this improvement one boy can perform the previous work of two.

"It might naturally be expected that the very unnatural position in which the children employed in the pits are placed, and their exclusion from daylight and the open air, would materially influence their physical health, not only at the time, but would so affect their constitutions as to render them liable to particular forms of disease in after life. Nevertheless, experience will not warrant the inference that any very pernicious effects result from the circumstances in such numerous instances as to justify anything like a general conclusion. . . . That the health of the boys is for the most part good, their favourable recovery from severe wounds and other accidents sufficiently proves, and though their persons are thin and their complexions pale, their general appearance is muscular and athletic.

"The 'outward man' distinguishes the pitman from every other operative. His stature is diminutive, his figure disproportionate and misshapen; his legs being much bowed and his chest protruding, while his arms are long and oddly suspended. His countenance is not less striking than his figure, his cheeks being generally hollow, his brow overhanging, his cheekbones high and his forehead low and retreating. 'I have seen,' says Mr. Morrison, 'agricultural labourers, blacksmiths, carpenters and even those among the wan and distressed stockingweavers of Nottinghamshire to whom the term "jolly" might not be inaptly applied, but I never saw a jolly-looking pitman.' The same gentleman partly traces this to the fact that the whole of the pitmen have been pitboys at an early age, during which the form is injured by the cramped positions occupied by the boys in the mine; but he also adduces other reasons: 'Pitmen have always lived in communities, they have associated only among themselves, even their amusements are hereditary and peculiar. They almost invariably intermarry, and it is not uncommon, in their marriages, to commingle the blood of the same family. They have thus transmitted natural and accidental defects through a long series of generations, and may now be regarded in the light of a distinct race of beings.'

"Everybody seems to award credit to the wives of the pitmen as being indefatigable in their exertions to keep everything right and tidy at home, so far as the arrangements of the houses and the employment of the people will permit. The household duties of a pitman's wife are very numerous. The male portion of her family may be divided into 'putters' and 'hewers,' the former going to the mines when the latter leaves, and the hours of labour and rest are consequently not the same, thus there is entailed the necessity of preparing numerous meals and at irregular and various hours of the day.[1] . . . Mr. Morrison, the gentleman above quoted, gives the following picture of the manner of living among the pitmen: 'The children of colliers are comfortably and decently clothed. Cleanliness, both in their persons and houses, is a predominant feature in the domestic economy of the better females of this community. The children, although necessarily left much to themselves and playing much in the dirt, are never sent to bed without ample ablution. Pitmen, of all the labouring classes I am acquainted with, enjoy most the pleasure of good living. Their larders abound in potatoes, bacon, fresh meat, sugar, tea, and coffee, of which good things the children partake as abundantly as the parents—even the sucking infant, to its prejudice, is loaded with as much of the greasy and well-seasoned viands of the table as it will swallow. In this respect the women are foolishly indulgent, and I know of no class of persons among whom infantile diseases so much prevail. Durham and Northumberland are not dairy counties, consequently the large population, excepting the *hinds* in the northern part of Northumberland, are very inadequately supplied with milk. Did this wholesome and nutritious beverage more abound, probably the infant population would be more judiciously fed.'

"If we follow the pitmen to Newcastle, their great metropolis, we find them still a characteristic race. Their velveteen dresses, with large and shining metal buttons, distinguish

[1] This domestic difficulty still remains.

them from the rest of the population. Mr. Holland states that the pitmen used formerly, perhaps more so than at present, to delight in gaudy colours. Their holiday waistcoats, called by them *posey* jackets, were frequently of very curious patterns, displaying flowers of various hues, and their stockings were blue, purple or even pink, or mixed colours. Many of them used to have their hair very long, which on weekdays was either tied in a queue or rolled up in curls, but when dressed in their best attire it was commonly spread over their shoulders. Some of them wore two or three narrow ribbons round their hats, placed at equal distances, in which it was customary to insert one or more bunches of primroses or other flowers. Such were the pitmen of past days, and many of their holiday peculiarities still remain."[1]

This last is scarcely true today. The pitman, like the rest of us, has suffered the mortification of uniformity. Now, save for an occasional pigeon-flying contest (and perhaps a surreptitious cock-fight), his "holiday peculiarities" consist of listening to the wireless and watching football matches. His posey jackets and even his purple stockings (though these lasted well into the present century) have been sacrificed on the altar of "utility." But he still retains his love for flowers.

"The idea," wrote F. S. Oliver, "gives birth to the organisation, and the organisation then kills the idea." We may apply this maxim to the story which now remains for us to tell. The idea, in this case, is Freedom and the organisation is the Trades Union.

We have had a glimpse of the conditions under which the miners, including the children, were obliged to work at the beginning of the last century, and we must not suppose that they were better off before this period. It was not because their conditions of labour were worsened, but because their numbers were greatly multiplied, that our attention is particularly drawn to the misery of the coal workers during the first half of the nineteenth century. Physical hardships may be endured in a small rural community which become intolerable when people are accumulated in masses amid surroundings which

[1] Whellan, *op. cit.,* pp. 93-99.

become progressively uglier. The plaintive miaow, moreover, of a neglected kitten is not so well calculated to attract attention as the roaring of a wounded tiger. But in the eighteenth century, also, children were employed in the pits, and even women worked underground, dragging sledges laden with baskets of coal along the ink-black "roads" or climbing up ladders with the corves on their backs. In 1842 this was forbidden by law, as was also the employment below ground of children under ten, but in Durham women had ceased to work in the pits some sixty years earlier. In 1861 no boy under twelve was allowed to go down the mine unless he could read and write, but in 1865 the Durham delegate to the Northumberland and Durham Joint Union could still say, of the older boys, that their average hours were fourteen a day and that "they never saw the light of the blessed sun from Sabbath to Sabbath."[1] Schools were being established for these boys, but to these a fair answer was "Thank you for nothing." To provide schools for children who still worked thirteen hours a day was, as another delegate maintained, six years later, "like preparing food for persons who had no appetite."[2] As for their housing conditions, we are told that as late as 1855 the best class of pitmen's houses "possesses only two rooms on the ground floor, with a kind of loft above," and that the worst consisted of a single room.[3]

Such was the state of affairs against which the miners had to fight for themselves. The owners, at least until the latter half of the nineteenth century, seem to have been too busily engaged in getting money to bother about them, and although there were doubtless individual acts of private charity no charitable organisation existed to combat these evils. It is only today, when the sufferings of the working classes are of insignificance compared to what they were, that we wax indignant about them and loudly proclaim our allegiance to their cause at the expense of everybody else. The bulky, ponderous mind of the general of mankind, ever failing to understand the significance of events at the time of their occurrence, will suddenly awake to a truth when it is ceasing to be true and will fly from one extremity of error to the other in a frantic

---

[1] *A History of the Durham Miners' Association, 1870-1904*, by John Wilson (Veitch and Sons, 1908), p. 7.
[2] John Wilson, *op. cit.*, p. 32.   [3] Whellan, *op. cit.*, p. 98.

endeavour to catch it up. Now it amounts almost to a crime to challenge the right of the masses to rule the world and direct the course of civilisation, and every political party, from the Conservative to the Communist, subscribes with enthusiasm to the same interpretation of "Democracy." Then, when help was really needed, when the miners, wretched, politically powerless and overworked, were fighting with their backs to the wall against a phalanx of powerful, selfish speculators, scarce a finger was lifted to assist them.

But Mr. Wesley had shown a light in the darkness of the pit, and his successors, the Primitive Methodists, taught the people how to lift up their hearts and their heads and to band themselves together for defence. Their methods were, indeed, more "primitive," more crude and violent than those of the Wesleyans, but they served their ends. There was a vivid splendour about them which scorned to shrink from ridicule and captured the imagination of rough men. The Reverend Joseph Spoor, for instance, one of their most famous preachers, would act and dance his sermons before a congregation which came to hear for merriment and remained for wonder and awe. Whether he strode up and down the aisle, as the sower casting his seed, or dashed out of the chapel to seize a loitering plough-man and drag him in with the triumphant cry, "This, my son, was dead, and is alive again; he was lost and is found"; whether he made a bundle of his coat and waistcoat and bowed down under it as under the weight of sin, or stood on the top of the pulpit and shouted through a paper trumpet, like the Angel of the Revelation, "Time shall be no more! I say, Time shall be no more!" his tremendous, his almost appalling sincerity swept his audience off their feet.[1]

Thus, instigated by the sufferings around them and inspired by their religion, a few men set to work to sacrifice themselves for the majority.

Tommy Hepburn was one of these. After the repeal of the Combination Acts in 1825 he formed the "Pitmen's Union of the Tyne and Wear," which fought against the Yearly Bond (the system by which men were tied to their work for a year) and against payment of wages in the form of tokens for the "Tommy Shop" (a general store at the pithead from which the pitmen were practically compelled to buy their provisions).

[1] *M.C.*, Vol. V.

The strike failed, the union broke down, and Tommy Hepburn was left to starve. He was given work, at last, on condition that he would thenceforth take no part in trades unionism, and he faithfully kept his promise until his death forty years later. Another union was formed, and again, in 1844, struck for the abolition of the Yearly Bond. Thereafter, although the men had to return to work on the employers' terms, the bond was dropped until 1864 and a fortnightly contract gradually took its place. The next nineteen years disclose a story of unions formed and dissolved again, through lack of funds and lack of agreement, and of the first steps towards Government control of safety in the mines. Inspectors were appointed in 1850, and as the result of the great disaster at Hartley, in Northumberland, when over 200 lives were lost,[1] it was ordained that every mine was to be provided with two shafts. In 1863 another Northumberland and Durham Union was formed, from which, owing to constant disagreement and the lack of interest displayed by the Durham miners, Northumberland broke away under their great leader Thomas Burt. Left to themselves, the Durham men at last formed their own union, and in 1872, the owners having followed suit, the first meeting took place in an atmosphere of friendliness and temporary prosperity between the Durham Coal Owners' and the Durham Miners' Associations. The Yearly Bond, which had been re-introduced, was then finally abolished, advances of wages were agreed upon, and a joint committee was appointed to meet regularly every fortnight to discuss and, if possible, to settle all differences, and if not, to submit them to arbitration. Thus, thanks to several years of hard work by the miners' leaders—W. Crawford, A. Cairns and J. Richardson—and to the goodwill of the owners, this extraordinary advance was made on the previous unhappy lack of arrangement, and the year 1872 is marked as the first turning point in the relationship betwen masters and men. "The idea had given birth to the organisation." Thenceforward, thanks largely to the arrival upon the scenes shortly afterwards of the great figure of the Durham Miners' Association, John Wilson, the record of this relationship, in spite of temporary disputes and setbacks, was a record of steady progress. It was not until after the war of 1914 and the Russian Revolution that a dissolving element

[1] January 12th, 1862.

was introduced into the gradually hardening cement of industrial friendship and quickly disintegrated it. The political exponents of Socialism found in the large industrial trades unions the ready-made means for the propagation and enforcement of their uncompromising doctrine. Not a further improvement in the relationship between masters and men, but the imposition upon all classes of a definite theory of national government was the new programme of the leaders of trades unionism.[1] Adherence to that creed soon became, to all intents and purposes, the sine qua non of trades union membership. Thus freedom, though more loudly proclaimed than ever, became nothing but a loud and empty name. And thus "the organisation killed the idea."

Nevertheless, such a fundamental change in the industrial outlook cannot alone be accounted for by the social upheaval and economic dislocation caused by war. The ready acceptance of and fidelity to a "foreigner" like A. J. Cook, after forty years under the guidance and instruction of such a man as John Wilson, cannot only be ascribed to the sudden effects of a new Socialist propaganda. The seed had been germinating for years. Though the leadership of Crawford and Cairns, of Richardson and Wilson, had been accepted, it had not been accepted even from the earliest days of the Association without a struggle. It was through the strength of their own individual characters more than thanks to the popularity of their methods that the great Durham leaders had established their ascendancy. Again and again, throughout the enthralling story told by John Wilson, we read of the difficulties encountered through the opposition and hostility of the men they were trying to save, of how the leaders were often insulted and sometimes maltreated and how strikes were embarked upon in defiance of their warnings, advice and expostulations. When, during the course of a dispute in 1879, by a series of mutual concessions the difference between the owners' and the miners' committees was growing appreciably less the men themselves

[1] "During the last few weeks we have gone through . . . a period which found for the first time a united and determined working-class effort to challenge the existing order of Parliamentary Government. . . . That our course of action was bold none can deny, that it definitely challenged the Constitution there can be no doubt."—J. H. Thomas, President, to Trades Union Congress. *Times*, September 7th, 1920.

were holding mass meetings of furious protest at which "orators, vehement if not polished, sprang up from every quarter, whose stock-in-trade consisted of foul epithets which they hurled at the Committee and Federation Board."[1] And a strike was proclaimed. Similarly, the great Durham strike of 1892, with all the misery which it entailed, might have been averted had the men given their own representatives that free hand to settle the dispute for which the leaders twice appealed in vain. Suspicion, baseless in this case but bred of past suffering and fostered by ignorance, was already inherent in the miner's mind, induced him always to lend a willing ear to the abuse and sweeping misrepresentations of agitators, and still presents a major obstacle to good cheer and good will in the coal-field. It is not surprising. The miner's history is a history of unceasing warfare. He has had to fight in the past for the elementary decencies of existence, and the very nature of his work is dark and destructive. Man's purpose in life is to create, but the miner's business is to destroy. Man's habitat is the green field in the open air, but the miner's is the blackness of the pit. His subconscious instincts have thus become those of a born antagonist, those of a man who, when called upon to serve the cause of his country, has proved himself to be one of the best fighters in the world—the record of the Durham Light Infantry is amongst the finest in the British Army—but who, when misled and misdirected, has involved himself and others in sorrow and suffering and has even been in danger of undermining the very existence of our land.

Such were the difficult natures, apart from the difficult problems, with which John Wilson and his colleagues had to contend, and all through his story one can hear the clash of opposing forces, not only between employers and employed, but far more between those who held that the way to peace and prosperity for the miners lay in the search for mutual understanding with the owners and in the practice of mutual forbearance, and those who believed, or pretended to believe, that it could only be achieved on a basis of hatred and through the disruption of society. And all through the long years of Wilson's leadership that great man was lifting up his voice counselling wisdom, patience, honesty, moderation. "When the employers," he and his fellow leaders wrote in a circular

[1] John Wilson, *op. cit.*, p. 145.

in 1876, "arrogated to themselves the right to judge both for them and for us, we were not slow in applying the words 'tyranny,' 'despotism' and even 'villainy' to their actions. Don't let us then be guilty of an imprudence, both by a repudiation of our own principles and going into battle when everything is against us."[1] And again, "The true test of institutions, as of men, is their action in a variety of conditions. *No arrangement can make trade prosperous. They are dreamers who think so, and are liable to a rude awakening.*"[2] And again, "The more certainty we can infuse into our industrial relationship with our employers the better it will be for the workmen; and there is nothing more calculated to foster this desirable condition than the principle of conciliation."[3] At the end of his long career he looks back and compares the feeling in his early days with that which predominated when he surrendered office.[4] "At that time Capital and Labour were looked upon as being natural enemies, and all their relations were on that principle. We see now how foolish was that idea. . . . Where hate was endangering the general weal by its unreasoning action we now have regular business relations." And he takes leave at last with these final words of wisdom to the young miners: "My young brothers, two things we must avoid: impetuosity in associated work and stagnation in the individual life."[5]

He was applauded, no doubt, but we now know that his wise words fell on barren ground. "Impetuosity in associated work" is now the order of the day, not only in the mining field but throughout the land, while "stagnation in the individual life" becomes increasingly more marked. The folly of the enmity of Capital and Labour and the power of the spirit of conciliation, the wickedness of the gospel of hate, the idle dream that any arrangement can make trade prosperous— these principles repeatedly enunciated and emphasised as sober truth by the man who devoted his life to the cause of the Durham miners have now themselves been rejected as idle dreams. The public utterances of responsible Ministers of the Crown today are completely at variance, in temper, in general policy and in detail, with the doctrine and practice of this

[1] John Wilson, *op. cit.,* p. 116.   [2] *Ibid.,* p. 269 (my italics).
[3] *Ibid.,* p. 295.   [4] In 1907.
[5] John Wilson, *op. cit.,* pp. 41, 347, 354.

comparatively irresponsible trade union leader fifty years ago. A spirit alien from that of the old Durham leaders has triumphed. A conception of society totally different from that in which they worked and for whose betterment they strove has been accepted by the country, and Socialism and National-isation have replaced the principle of conciliation between masters and men. They have yet to prove their worth.

We cannot leave the Durham miners without a reference to their gala day. This was first held in Wharton's Park, Dur-ham, on August 12th, 1871. In the following year it was held on the old racecourse, and here it has been held ever since on the last Saturday in July. The pitmen troop into the city from all over the county, bands and banners process through the streets, a special service is held in the Cathedral, where the sermon is preached by the Bishop or the Dean, and speeches are made on social and political subjects. We are reminded of the old processions of the guilds on Corpus Christi. At first this influx of rude, rough men was viewed with considerable alarm by the citizens of Durham, who barricaded their shop windows and hid behind their doors. But they soon learned that their fears were groundless. Even at political meetings, though the temper on occasions has been bad, the average miner (as distinguished from the political agitator), while blunt and boisterous and sometimes disconcerting, is good-humoured and even friendly with those who sincerely disagree with him. On these gala occasions, though politics form a part of the order of the day and he may be momentarily whipped up by a flight of oratory, he is out to enjoy himself. On one occasion a housewife in a hurry decided that she had time to slip across the road between the tail of one miners' lodge and the head of another. But half-way across her large paper bag burst and a stream of golden oranges cascaded all over the street. Up went the hand of the lodge's leader, the procession stopped, and the pitmen broke their ranks and helped the harassed woman to pick up her fruit.

Chapter XXXIII

GREAT VICTORIANS

"We are assured that this is an age of progress. Parties commend their claims to us on the ground that they are progressive. It is assumed we are agreed on the meaning of the terms, and yet a very little reflection will show that this is not the case. There are serious differences of opinion as to the sphere, scope, and standard of progress. Change, even when popular, is not necessarily progress, nor movement, however rapid. Before we can determine whether a movement is really progress we must determine the end it is desired to reach. Progress is an advance towards an ideal. If we wish to estimate human progress we must fix the human ideal."

BROOKE FOSS WESTCOTT, BISHOP OF DURHAM.

As the nineteenth century advances the difference in classes becomes accentuated, not only between rich and poor but between those engaged in different occupations. The village had ceased to be the atom of society wherein squire and parson, tradesman, farmer and labourer all revolved about each other like microcosmic suns and between them composed the apparently indivisible unit of civilisation. Now that unit had been divided, the atom had been split, and its particles were gyrating independently of each other in megalomaniacal dances. The squire had built his palace and was acquiring a host of servants and pheasants and a conglomeration of acres; the parson (thanks largely to Mr. Wesley, though the result was far from his intention) had exploded into several parsons—all of whom were glaring and glowering at each other; the tradesman (carrying a bit of the squire away with him), instead of rattling a loom in the shadows of a village barn, had departed to fresh fields whose verdure he withered and deflowered with his smoke, whose waters he polluted with his chemicals, and whose sweet circumambient air he poisoned with his money. The farmer had caught the infection of Industry and become scientific and grand, parading cattle through England blown up to bursting point like animal balloons and forming societies for the promotion of agriculture; and the labourer was steadily streaming away from the home of his fathers to the new centres created by the tradesman, where he multiplied himself out of all proportion and

597

waged his own war with his own poverty and the other's wealth. So the village, the hub of the old English wheel, became of less and less importance to the progress of our society under its new mechanical form. Today it is little more than a collection of houses on a road, distinguished by yellow signs for the benefit of the motorist, and graced perhaps by an old church, generally shut, aloof in the background under a group of elms. It has ceased to exist as an entity, its schools are being closed and centralised, its churches are more than half empty, its distinctive activities and amenities are going or gone, its larger houses are decaying for lack of labour and domestic assistance. It will soon be impossible for any but the actual toilers on the land to live in that English countryside whose fibres are deep-rooted in all our English hearts, whose history had been for centuries the history of England; which has cradled our children and buried our fathers, inspired our poets and moulded our old warriors and statesmen.

Thus the stage was set for democracy. Thus, through all the years of the century, its theory grew apace, and particularly in the County of Durham, where a ruthless industrialisation, with its consequent prodigious increase in population, encouraged and even enforced its growth. We will attempt in this chapter to give some impression of this hurly-burly in which our county was now to be involved. It was accentuated and thrown into relief by the old customs and habits of thought, which were dying indeed, but dying hard; and it was bravely tackled by a succession of remarkable Bishops who strove —and not immediately in vain—to exert their influence upon the course of events. The first of these was Edward Maltby.

And he was not the most successful. It was partly owing to the tardiness of the Church in adapting itself to rapidly changing conditions, during the twenty years of Bishop Maltby's episcopate, that his successors were so hard pressed in their efforts to deal with the ever-increasing problems. But he can scarcely be blamed for this. It is easy to look back and to see that a revolution of life was already in full swing. It was very difficult at the time to estimate either its radical nature or its prodigious velocity. Nor could a single Bishop bereft of his Palatinate, however individually rich, be expected to tackle it

alone. It would have needed a phalanx of wealthy, self-sacri-
ficing, far-seeing and determined men to divert the roaring
engine to the runway where it would bring the most benefit,
or involve the least affliction, to mankind. Such a phalanx was
not forthcoming. "The wealthy and the great are entirely
wrapt up in themselves and their own interests," wrote Havelock on his return to England in 1850,[1] and though we must
make some allowance for his puritanical cast of temper, this
stricture was no doubt in the main true. Those interests, which
included agriculture, were not unconcerned with national
interests, but, whether defensible or not, they diverted the
attention of those best qualified by tradition and influence to
deal with it, from the cancerous sore in their midst. The Durham magnates had not the excuse of ignorance which may be
advanced on behalf of their brethren in the South. They lived
in the heart of the hubbub and even profited from it. It was
within a mile or two of their homes that their own coal was
being dragged out of the pit by children while they were
gallantly breaking their necks in the hunting field. In 1844,
the same year in which Ralph Lambton died, occurred "the
most momentous of all the Durham strikes"[2] which settled the
question of the Yearly Bond. Nevertheless, it is not true that
the miners were entirely ignored even in the first half of the
century by those who enjoyed the fruits of their labours. A
colliery disaster elicited sympathetic response for the victims[3]
and there were subterranean balls and other rejoicings, particularly for the pitmen, on such gala occasions as the first
winning of coal. Frances Anne, Marchioness of Londonderry,
entertained on more than one occasion "upwards of 3,000 pitmen and workpeople, employed on her ladyship's collieries"
to a feast on "eight bullocks, fifteen sheep, a ton of plum
pudding, a ton and a half of bread, one hundred bushels of
potatoes, and fifty barrels of ale."[4] By her declaration, at
another festival "that if her workmen were willing to combine
for the purpose of supporting their aged and infirm brethren,

[1] *Havelock,* by Archibald Forbes, p. 76.
[2] *The Story of the Durham Miners,* by Sidney Webb, p. 43.
[3] The coal-owners on the Wear and the Tyne and "a long list of
individual contributors" subscribed nearly £3,000 to the sufferers from
the Felling disaster. (Surtees, Vol. II, p. 89.)
[4] Latimer, p. 376.

she would readily be at the expense of erecting a suitable building,"[1] she appears to have been the first to have suggested an Aged Miners' Home, which did not materialise until over forty years later.

As the century advanced the sense of social duty and responsibility was quickened and those charities, both private and public, were multiplied, for which the wealthy Victorians of the later period have received too little recognition and gratitude from posterity. Cottage Hospitals, Nursing Associations and Ambulances, Church Schools and Home Missions, Working Men's Clubs and Young Helpers' Leagues, Chambers of Agriculture and Dairy Classes, Bird Shows and Pigeon Societies—every conceivable form of benevolent local activity was initiated, encouraged or supported, in addition to such national organisations as Dr. Barnardo's Homes and the N.S.P.C.C. Food and clothing were distributed privately on a lavish scale, the sick and suffering were relieved from many a private purse, charades and theatrical entertainments were constantly being organised for some charitable purpose or other, and great bazaars, in warm town halls decorated with palm trees and gay with red baize and Union Jacks, were opened here, there and everywhere by distinguished peers and statesmen in frock coats or chatelaines in feather boas, enormous hats and trailing dresses. Here, at stalls served by bevies of young ladies, were to be seen "bewildering assortments of the nic-nacs which go to make a home beautiful," or "star-like chrysanthemums, delicate ferns, and flowers of varied form and hue," or "good things from Witton that may safely be bitten," or "Mrs. Goose presiding over a brilliant array of toys."[2]

It is questionable, of course, whether all this was much to the good. Wise men, even at that time, were inclined to doubt it and to sigh for the days when the rich—but the less rich—were happy with their trees and kine and the poor were left unmolested in a pastoral silence. "There is no peace, no repose now," wrote Canon Greenwell in 1900; "but there is hullabaloo, this society and that society, this must be done and that must be done, until it has become to an old fellow like me by no means a pleasant world. . . . I wish I could live again in those days when I saw Jory White, Tim Wheatley and Bill

[1] *Ibid.*, p. 401.   [2] *North Star*, November 2nd, 1892.

Sharpe looking over the bridge for hours at the fish working his tail."[1]

Moreover, if it is indisputable that a large proportion of distress was relieved and a large measure of goodwill promoted by all this hurly-burly of beneficence, it is equally true that the root of social discord was not thereby uprooted, nor even disturbed and examined. The fundamental problem of the relationship between employer and employed—that relationship upon which the whole future of England was to depend—was not touched upon except by those immediately concerned.[2]

Though a great Bishop of Durham, in the full vigour of manhood and armed with all the authority and power of the past, might have done much, the first of the Bishops under the new democratic order could do but little. He was, moreover, an old man of sixty-six when he came to the See, and a fumbler at that, according to Queen Victoria.[3] His immediate province was, in any case, to supply the spiritual needs of the galloping population, and this, generously, out of his own pocket, albeit for the needs of the time in too small a measure, he proceeded to do. He formed the "Maltby Fund" for the building of new vicarages and rectories, to which he contributed, by arrangement with the Ecclesiastical Commissioners, the additional £2,000 a year which he had voluntarily surrendered to them and a further annual sum averaging nearly half as much again. He was a low churchman, and therefore benevolent to the numerous Dissenters, and he helped and encouraged the new University during his life and bequeathed to it his valuable library. But perhaps Queen Victoria was right when she called the poor old man "maladroit," for it may have been his rage against the Roman Catholics, or a simple senile error of judgment, which induced him to publish an "unpremeditated and unguarded effusion"[4] from the Prime Minister which seems not to have been intended for publica-

---

[1] *A.A.D.N.*, Vol. V. (1896-1905), pp. li-lii.

[2] Bishop Westcott, by his action in 1892, seems to have provided the solitary exception to this rule.

[3] "The Bishop of Durham stood on the side near me, but he was, as Lord Melbourne told me, remarkably *maladroit*, and never could tell me what was to take place."—*The Queen's Journal,* on her Coronation. (June 28th, 1838.)

[4] Fordyce, Vol. I, p. 96.

tion. This did both himself and Lord John Russell, who had fairly let himself go, not a little amount of harm.

The occasion was the saucy introduction by the Pope of a Roman Catholic hierarchy into England, which was announced in terms well calculated to annoy by our old Ushaw friend, the great Cardinal Wiseman. Henceforth there were to be Roman Catholic Bishops, no longer "in partibus infidelium" (which was, surely, a compliment), but of Southampton and Hexham and so forth, and Wiseman himself was to be Archbishop of Westminster, from which exalted throne "we govern, and shall continue to govern, the counties of Middlesex, Hertford and Essex."[1] Immediately there was a howl of Protestant fury. Bishop Maltby, not at all amused by Lingard's little joke about foreign cattle, wrote indignantly to the Prime Minister and received, in reply, the famous "Durham Letter."

"My dear Lord," wrote Lord John Russell, "I agree with you in considering 'the late aggression of the Pope upon our Protestantism' as 'insolent and insidious.' . . . There is an assumption of power in all the documents which have come from Rome—a pretension to supremacy over the realm of England . . . which is inconsistent with the Queen's supremacy, with the rights of our bishops and clergy, and with the spiritual independence of the nation, as asserted even in Roman Catholic times. . . ." But "there is a danger which alarms me much more than any aggression of a foreign sovereign. Clergymen of our own church, who have subscribed the Thirty-Nine Articles, and acknowledged in explicit terms the queen's supremacy, have been the most forward in leading their flocks 'step by step to the very verge of the precipice.'[2] The honour paid to saints, the claim of infallibility for the church, the superstitious use of the sign of the cross, the muttering of the liturgy. . . . What is the danger to be apprehended from a foreign prince of no great power compared to the danger within the gates from the unworthy sons of the Church of England herself? . . . But I rely with confidence on the people of England, and I will not bate a jot of heart or hope

---

[1] *A History of Modern England,* by Herbert Paul, Vol. I, p. 197. (Macmillan, 1904.)

[2] The Oxford Movement had begun in 1833. Newman was converted to the Roman Catholic Church in 1845. This letter was written in 1850.

so long as the glorious principles and the immortal martyrs of the Reformation shall be held in reverence by the great mass of a nation which looks with contempt on the mummeries of superstition, and with scorn at the laborious endeavours which are now making to confine the intellect and enslave the soul."[1]

That last sentence is a fine one. Perhaps the Prime Minister did, after all, intend the letter for publication. At any rate, it was received at first with enthusiasm, but when passions began to cool, the accusation of disloyalty to the Crown (for it practically amounted to that) levelled not only against English Roman Catholics but against the unfortunate Puseyites, who had nothing whatever to do with the Pope and his edicts, made wise men look askance at the Durham Letter and strongly criticise the Bishop for its publication. It seems to us now but a storm in a teacup, though even today there are scenes against "mummery" in our churches, and in those days the Protestant religion was not only trumpeted but generally practised. The George Liddells (of the Ravensworth family), who lived in Old Elvet, had a very hard day on Sundays, which included a double dose of Church and prayers and long sermons at home. On weekdays, after morning prayers, every member of the family had to read to himself all the psalms and both the lessons for the day before he went about his business. No doubt this was exceptional even for that time, but there was scarce a household, from the richest to the poorest, which was not familiar with a large proportion of the contents of the Bible and the Prayer-Book. These, with *Good Words*, or some such excellent magazine, to which well-known writers contributed essays and sober serial stories, and a large illustrated edition of Bunyan, were as familiar objects in the homes of that period as are the wireless and the newspaper today.

It is as the champion of this uncompromising Puritan strain in English Protestantism that Bishop Maltby stands forth, no frilled gentlemanly prelate, but a kindly, rather worried, rather stern old man, a great Greek scholar, "grave and very impressive in the pulpit."[2] Six years after the publication of the Durham Letter he resigned his See, at the great age of eighty-six, and soon afterwards died in London. Before he left, the transfer of all the episcopal lands to the Ecclesiastical

[1] Fordyce, Vol. I, pp. 94-95. [2] *D.N.B.*

Commissioners had been finally effected.[1] The only exception was the house and grounds of Auckland Castle, which remained in the possession of the See until 1945, when they too were handed over to the same public body. There is now nothing left of the great Patrimony of St. Cuthbert.

Already the proposal was being seriously considered that the diocese should be divided into two, and Maltby's successor, Charles Thomas Longley, was appointed to the See on the understanding that such might be its fate. Longley, however, a strong Protestant, "handsome and winning," and a steady, reasonable supporter of Lord Palmerston, was not long in the North. After a preliminary transfer to York, he became Archbishop of Canterbury. He was succeeded at Durham by Henry Montague Villiers, a young man of only forty-seven, from whom great things were expected. He had made a name for himself in a large London parish, where his tact and energy, his particular appeal to the poor and his kind heart seemed to indicate him as one born to grapple with the difficulties of an industrial diocese. He was, moreover, an extremely low churchman and, therefore, likely to win the favour of that great body of Dissenters of which the mining population was chiefly composed—even, perhaps, to restore them to the fold. His comparative youth seemed to promise a long reign, during which his great qualities might have re-established the influence of the Church in the North which had been lost in Wesley's time. But it was not to be. In the year following his elevation to the See he died at Auckland Castle. He was succeeded by Charles Thomas Baring, a member of the great banking family.

It is interesting to note, by the way, that all the seven Bishops of Durham, from Maltby to Moule, whose consecutive reigns cover the whole period of industrial development and whose aggregate of wisdom, learning and piety was higher than that reached by any corresponding number since the foundation of the See, were of strongly Protestant inclination. No doubt the existence of a large dissenting element in the county was partly responsible for the fact that no High Church prelate was appointed. It is also curious (though doubtlesss of small significance) that of those seven learned Bishops six were educated in only two university colleges, and these two

[1] April 4th, 1856.

the most famous in the land. Three of the Bishops (Longley, Villiers and Baring) were at Christ Church, Oxford, and three (Lightfoot, Westcott and Moule) at Trinity College, Cambridge.

Baring has been somewhat overshadowed by his mighty successors and has, perhaps, not received the full meed of praise which is his due. Though a Double First at Oxford, he had not the international reputation for scholarship of Lightfoot and of Westcott, and from the date of his appointment to Durham he abandoned all outside interests and devoted himself entirely to his diocese. There he found more than enough scope for his labours, and he toiled away without ceasing, grimly evangelical, earnestly simple, practically forgotten by the rest of the world. But his clergy, particularly those who ventured to differ from him in doctrine, were well aware of his presence. The Dean of Durham,[1] the twin stars of whose life were Arnold and Newman, and who set to work on his appointment to beautify the neglected cathedral and to bring order to the slovenly services, was publicly condemned by his bishop for "unwise, lavish and wasteful expenditure."[2] Mr. Dykes, the hymnologist, who had resigned his precentorship to become vicar of the large parish of St. Oswald's, was refused the help of curates because he declined to give an undertaking that they should not take "the eastward position" at Holy Communion. Baring was, in short, no tolerant, humble Christian like his successors. There was gall in his composition. Though, no doubt, his extremely low church views were valuable to a diocese containing so large a population of Nonconformists, on the other hand his uncompromising spirit kept many good men away from seeking service under his authority. Some of those who were already in the diocese found a slight consolation in punning on his name. "I confess," a young clergyman is said to have confided to his friend, "that I find our good Bishop somewhat *overbearing*." "Do you?" was the curt reply. "I have long since found him *past bearing*." But Bishop Moule has more seriously appraised "the unpretending greatness of his work and character and his large and wise pecuniary liberality."[3]

[1] William Lake.   [2] *The Guardian.* (October 25th, 1876.)
[3] *The Evangelical School in the Church of England* (James Nisbet and Co., 1901), p. 55.

Although a number of our prelates have been remarkable for their munificence, Baring is probably unique in having put back into the See more wealth than he took out of it. The fact that he was a rich man and could afford to do this rather enhances than detracts from the merit of his performance. For the rich, ipso facto, know the value of money. He devoted it to the now much needed spiritual extension of the diocese, creating 102 new parishes, building 119 churches—would that he had had the taste as well as the liberality of Cosin!—and increasing the number of clergy by 186. Such was the prodigious performance of this dour old man, more severe to himself even than to others, who "with a stern modesty"[1] refused to have his portrait painted for inclusion in the episcopal gallery at Auckland Castle and when he retired declined a pension. A few months after he had left the county he died, at the age of seventy-two, worn out by his labours. He had admitted that even for his unflagging energy the diocese had proved too great—it had risen by 350,000 since his enthronement—and he recommended its immediate division.[2] More respected for his virtue than popular in his personality, lacking in that charm with which Villiers might have done so much, he had, nevertheless, through sheer force of work and character, saved the position of the Church in Durham. It had definitely taken a strong place in the race of interests which was now absorbing the attention of the old Bishoprick.

During the nineteen years of Baring's episcopate the hum of industry had risen to a roar. Already the county was producing as much coal as today[3] and pit after pit was still being opened. Shipbuilding was going ahead, blast furnaces were blazing at Tudhoe and a revolution had come about in the relationship of masters and men. The Co-operative Movement was spreading, the Durham Miners' Association had been formed, and the pitmen were gaining in strength and confidence. There is a story that one of them forced his way into his owner's office to complain that he had not been fairly paid for

---

[1] Bishop Creighton in *D.N.B.*

[2] Bishop Henson, however, regarded this division as a mistake. (Henson, *op. cit.*, Vol. II, p. 91.)

[3] 23,278,556 tons in 1873, according to the Report on the Durham Coalfield by the Ministry of Fuel and Power. In 1883 the tonnage had risen to 29,878,435. The corresponding figure in 1946 was 24,668,066.

the tubs he had filled. A stranger happened to be present at the time. "How much did he earn last fortnight?" asked the owner of his clerk. "Two pounds for eight days," replied the clerk. "That is far more than my men make," said the stranger. "And whe's yor men?" asked the pitman angrily. "Weavers," was the reply. "Weavors!" exclaimed the other contemptuously, "weavors! Wey, aa cud eat two or three weavors ivvory day aa gan hyem frae the pit!"[1]

Meanwhile, perhaps at the moment in which the audience was shedding tears over *Lost in London*, a melodrama at the Theatre Royal, Newcastle, in the course of which the heroine descends a coal-shaft, the Duchess of Cleveland was contemplating the beauty of the deer in Raby Park; and in the same year[2] in which took place the first momentous official meeting between the coal owners and the men, Mr. John Harvey was appointed to the mastership of the South and Mr. Anthony Lax Maynard to that of the North Durham Hounds. The old world was not dead yet.

The man who succeeded Bishop Baring stands like a boulder in midstream of a turbulent torrent. Fifty-four years separate his accession from the opening of the first railway and sixty-two years separate us today from the date of his death. It is difficult to say whether his world would have seemed stranger to us or to Bishop Shute Barrington: to us for its lack of motor-cars, wireless and aeroplanes, for its plenty and security, its formal manners and its aristocratic society; or to that earlier Bishop for its trains and factories and chimneys, its enormous population, its lack of manners and its bustling democracy. A little more than a century of time, an insignificant fraction even of the recorded history of man, but the difference—and how slight that is!—between Henry III and Edward III, divides us from the first fruits of mechanical invention. But from the peaceful riparian lawns of the eighteenth century to the dark and unfathomable ocean whereon we now find ourselves adrift, pilotless and afraid, the change of scenery and environment is vast indeed. Looking back, up the stretch of the river down which we have been hurried with ever-increasing velocity, we can just discern a rocklike figure looming large, even at this distance, in the midst of the stream.

[1] *M.C.,* Vol. I, p. 141.   [2] 1872.

It is that of Joseph Barber Lightfoot, "the cherub with the face of an ox which Ezekiel saw"[1]—so a Free Church Minister described him—"the man whose voice seemed to come out of a coal-pit"[2]—so a miner appraised him—the greatest of all the Bishops who have ever succeeded to St. Cuthbert's throne.

He has been compared more than once to Bishop Butler for the extraordinary combination in both of deep thought and profound learning with practical sagacity and statesmanship. And it was no accident, but a similarity in temper, that induced Lightfoot to regard the eighteenth-century philosopher as the greatest of the Bishops of Durham and to select him as the subject of the sermon he preached on his enthronement. Lightfoot had been a pupil of Prince Lee, the famous Headmaster of King Edward's School, Birmingham, and later[3] of Westcott (who was destined to succeed him as Bishop), and he was Senior Classical Scholar of Trinity College, Cambridge. He could read easily French, German, Italian, Spanish, Latin and Greek, and had at least a working knowledge of Hebrew, Syriac, Arabic and Ethiopic, and a little of Armenian. But he was essentially a historian, and the great work of his life was on the Apostolic Fathers, of which the Epistles of Ignatius and Polycarp were declared by a German professor to be "the most learned and careful Patristic monograph which has appeared in the nineteenth century."[4] He was, in brief, one of the greatest scholars, if not himself the greatest, of his age. And it is not, therefore, surprising to find him also such a master of the English language as to rank him foremost even amongst those notable exponents of the beauties of our tongue who have graced the throne of Durham both before and since his day. The following passage from the sermon already mentioned is worthy of Donne. After referring to Butler's perpetual consciousness of the Eternal Presence, he adds: "And what more seasonable prayer can you offer for him who addresses you now, at this the most momentous crisis of his life, than that he—the latest successor of Butler—may enter upon the duties of his high and responsible office in the same

---

[1] *Lightfoot of Durham*, by George R. Eden, D.D., and F. C. Macdonald (O.U.P., 1932), p. 35.

[2] *Ibid.*, p. 77.   [3] At Cambridge.

[4] "Bishop Lightfoot." Reprinted from the *Quarterly Review* (Macmillan, 1894), p. 36.

spirit; that the realisation of this great idea, the realisation of this great fact, may be the constant effort of his life; that glimpses of the invisible Righteousness, of the invisible Grace, of the invisible Glory, may be vouchsafed to him; and that the Eternal Presence, thus haunting him night and day, may rebuke, may deter, may guide, may strengthen, may comfort, may illumine, may consecrate and subdue the feeble and way-ward impulses of his own heart to God's holy will and pur-pose!"[1]

Such language we may expect from so mighty a scholar and such aspirations from so pious a priest. But who could have divined that this bulky, shy, humble, Newfoundland dog of a man, whose thoughts were so deep and recondite and whose ambitions so sublime, would prove himself to be a great administrator of a modern industrial diocese, would inspire the devotion of youth and leave a loving remembrance of his liberality, his self-sacrifice and devotion to the daily concernments of his See, exceeding even his reputation as a scholar? It was a stroke of genius which appointed this Cam-bridge Don to the spiritual oversight of shipwrights, iron-workers and pitmen, but it was a stroke for which the Muses wept.

For Lightfoot, though he did not abandon his scholastic labours, working at them whenever the opportunity offered— in his carriage, on railway journeys, during his holidays— always put the cares of his episcopate first. And these were tremendous. Though the diocese was divided in 1882, when the new Bishopric of Newcastle was formed, and though his predecessor had done much to meet the needs of the time, the population was still growing, industry was still spreading, and much still remained to be done. Still more parishes had to be formed, still more mission districts established, still more churches built, and this at a time of great agricultural and in-dustrial depression, when the boom in coal which owed its origin to the Franco-Prussian War had been succeeded by a series of slumps. Six times within three years the new sliding scale, by which arrangement wages were to depend on the market price of coal, had had to be adjusted anew to the steadily increasing detriment of the workers. And now, in

[1] *Leaders in the Northern Church*, by J. B. Lightfoot, D.D. (Mac-millan, 1890), pp. 164-165.

1879, a seventh request for reduction had led to a strike, against the wishes of the miners' representatives. This was scarcely a moment in which to raise money for the Church. Yet money had to be got; the sheep must be fed; and Lightfoot, unlike Baring, was not, apart from the episcopal income, a rich man. He called a meeting of the notables of the county, put the case before them, set them the example of generosity by announcing his own personal contribution towards the new churches and mission rooms required, and before the meeting broke up had already secured promises amounting to £30,000. Such were the methods by which this thinker dealt with his practical problems. They were the methods of personal contact and the use of his own personal authority, which was great and impressive. At a meeting of the Newcastle Church Congress, when feelings ran high in a controversy about ritual and the language was strong, the Bishop slowly stood up and raised his hand. The argument ceased abruptly and he sat down again without having uttered a word.

His influence, indeed, was extraordinary, not only upon his clergy but upon all who knew him. "And if I were asked," said Dean Lake, "what it was which inspired so wide an affection and formed so unique a character, I should answer that it was not merely his vast learning and his untiring labours, but joined to these, and more than these, it was that meekness of wisdom and unselfish humility by which in him, more than in any other person I have ever known, we could understand the full meaning of our Lord's promise, so real and yet so hard to realise, that 'the meek shall inherit the earth.'"[1]

Lightfoot was unmarried and therefore, his appetite for work unglutted by his diocesan and literary labours and by the larger Church issues of which he never lost sight, he decided to found a peculiar family of his own. He took in a number of young men as boarders in his own palace at Auckland and had them trained for Holy Orders by his own chaplains under his immediate supervision. Besides his usual work, each candidate was obliged to visit one of the numerous surrounding pit parishes three times a week and to work in the mission rooms and institutes. These were his sons, as he called them, the "Sons of the House," or the "Auckland Brotherhood," to give

[1] *Memorials of Dean Lake*, edited by Katherine Lake (Arnold, 1901), p. 137.

them the name by which they were more generally known, or
"Lightfoot's Lambs," as irreverent laymen used to dub them.
Eighty of these young men passed through his hands during
the ten years of his episcopate, some of whom were afterwards
distinguished in the annals of the Church. Every year the
Bishop's successors would welcome these former students to
an "Old Boy" reunion in the Castle, when the ties which they
had formed in their youth were strengthened afresh and when
the memory of their personal devotion to the father who had
trained them was revivified by contact with the old familiar
place. The last reunion took place during the episcopate of
Bishop Henson.

But Bishop Lightfoot offered no sweet inducements to his
sons, no modern system of education with frequent intervals
for rest and recreation, no jolly, popular form of religion, but
"toil; to spend and be spent; in some form or other, a cross."[1]

And so he spent himself, killed himself with the excess of
his labours. On the day of his death he was still writing, like
Bede, and he left the world, worn out, at the early age of
sixty-one. But it did not matter to him. His last illness did not
disturb him. Though he was well aware that the cause of it
might have been avoided, he did not regret his indifference to
his own health. "For what after all," said he, "is the individual
life in the history of the Church? Men may come and men may
go, individual lives float down like straws on the surface of the
waters till they are lost in the ocean of eternity; but the broad,
mighty rolling stream of the Church itself—the cleansing,
purifying, fertilising tide of the River of God, flows on for ever
and ever."[2]

It is impossible to mention Lightfoot without at once speaking of Westcott. They are the Castor and Pollux, the heavenly
twins of our Bishoprick, who shed a double but continuing
lustre, from 1879 till 1901, through the dark industrial
northern night. They were pupil and master, and it is touching and in their case seems even appropriate that the pupil
should have preceded the master and the master have become,
in a sense, the pupil of the pupil. "I can only hope," wrote
Westcott, when he accepted the See, "that I may be enabled,

[1] Eden and Macdonald, *op. cit.*, p. 33.
[2] Eden and Macdonald, *op. cit.*, p. 75.

if I enter on the work, to fulfil it according to the full measure of my power in the spirit of the late Bishop."[1] They were both educated at the same school. They were friends from youth. They were alumni of the same university and brethren of the same college. They were both mighty scholars. They were partners in the same scholastic enterprise[2] and loving rivals, each pushing forward the other, for the scholastic honours which were heaped upon them. They were destined to become successive Bishops of the same diocese and to lie side by side, at last, in the same chapel. Yet the one was no pale reflection of the other. They were both great men and their personalities were distinct and different.

Brooke Foss Westcott was an old man of sixty-five when he succeeded to the See. The offer had been made to him only after considerable hesitation and the refusal of other nominees to accept the honour. The persistence of the Queen at length overcame the reluctance of the Prime Minister, for Lord Salisbury was averse to the appointment. "As a learned man," he wrote to Sir Henry Ponsonby, "he would be thrown away, as Lightfoot was thrown away. His time would be occupied in the petty details of diocesan administration; and his un-equalled erudition would become useless to the world for the want of leisure to produce it."[3] A more cogent reason, per-haps, was that Lord Salisbury doubted the suitability of this aged and esoteric scholar to the practical business of an indus-trial diocese. In these reasonable doubts he was not alone. "How can that mystic seer ever take the place of the great organiser?" asked a Northern clergyman on hearing of the appointment.[4] At an early date, when Westcott was a Canon of Westminster, the great preacher Dr. Liddon had wittily written: "The fog is very heavy in London today. It is rumoured that Canon Westcott left his bedroom window open last night in Westminster."[5] But three consecutive refusals of the See by others, the persistence of the Queen, the urgent

[1] *Life and Letters of Brooke Foss Westcott,* by Arthur Westcott (Macmillan, 1903), Vol. II, p. 93.

[2] Commentary on the New Testament.

[3] *Life of Robert Marquis of Salisbury,* by Lady Gwendolen Cecil (Hodder and Stoughton, 1932), Vol. IV, p. 210.

[4] *Handley Carr Glyn Moule,* by J. B. Harford and F. C. Mac-donald (Hodder and Stoughton), p. 210.

[5] Cecil, *op. cit.,* Vol. IV, p. 212.

advice of the Archbishop of Canterbury, and the anticipation of the diocese itself at length left the Prime Minister with no alternative. Westcott, however, was not the man to jump at such an offer. He was acutely conscious of his imperfections. "To some I am a cloud," he had written some time before, "and I do not see how to help it." And he was old. Could he dare to accept? In his humility he felt "utterly overwhelmed."[1] For five days he wrestled in prayer and then sent off his acceptance. He would rely on a Strength other than his. "Οὐκέτι ἐγώ," he wrote in his diary. "No longer I."

The new Bishop of Durham was, in truth, a mystic. He spoke sadly of the latest inventions and discoveries. "Perhaps we may hope to realise some day," he said, "that the five senses are not the measure of the universe, nor even of our universe."[2] And again, "Does it seem to you that many appear to regard the phenomena of the outer world as the very type of reality, and the knowledge which we gain of these as the type of knowledge? To me, I confess, they are no more than shadows, witnessing to that which casts them."[3] When in his earlier days he had prayed alone at night in the great Cathedral of Peterborough he did not feel unaccompanied, and in later years the empty chapel at Auckland Castle had seemed to him to be "full." The account of his first sight of him by Canon Scott Holland and a glance at the portrait of the Bishop reproduced in this volume from his *Life* leave us no doubt that we are here in the presence of a man who drew his power from mysterious sources. Scott Holland in his youth, accompanied by a young friend, first saw Canon Westcott giving a lecture on St. John in a side chapel in Peterborough Cathedral. "We could hardly believe our eyes. This tiny form, with the thin small voice, delivering itself with passionate intensity of the deepest teaching on the mystery of the Incarnation to two timid ladies of the Close, under the haughty contempt of the solitary verger. . . ." It almost made these students of Divinity laugh. But a little later, when they were established as his pupils, "We had never before seen such an identification of study with prayer. . . . He taught us as one who ministered at an altar; and the details of the Sacred Text were to him as the Ritual of some Sacramental Action. . . . Sometimes

[1] Arthur Westcott, *op. cit.*, Vol. II, p. 92.
[2] *Ibid.*, Vol. II, p. 82. [3] *Ibid.*, Vol. II, p. 87.

he would crush us to the dust by his humility. . . ."[1] The portrait referred to confirms this eager, this almost fierce intensity of spiritual life. The face is rugged and masterful and humour plays about the lips, but the look directly challenges and demands and searches, will accept no compromise with the truth. Yet even as his eye pierces, even as you guiltily shrink from his gaze, you realise that he is looking, not at you, but through you, to some glory which he has discerned— beyond. So it was that the personal appeal and influence of Lightfoot, the devotion of the diocese to its Bishop was replaced by an atmosphere less nobly human and more spiritually awful. The counsellor and guide, the familiar friend, the father even, in its most intimate sense, was gone. A being not quite on the plane of mortals had succeeded him. "Men will remember (in Westcott) not the mesmeric control of a great man, but the presence of and above them of a faith and an insight into eternal ideas, which did not aim at achieving situations but at opening the eyes of men."[2]

That last sentence gives the clue to his success as a diocesan. It explains why his spiritual powers were no hindrance to but the inspiration of his practical work. He was not lost in the clouds, as people had supposed of him, as they had supposed of Butler before him, but he drew down manna from them, manna for human life. He was bent on opening the eyes of men. It was to this end that he had trained his great intellect as a youth, rising at five every morning and working until midnight or later. It was to this end that he now used this intellect for the service of his See. It might have been expected, particularly by those who hazily confuse the doctrine of Socialism with sympathy for the sufferings of the poor, that this saintly Bishop who was so devoted to the welfare of the miners, would have welcomed the rule of the masses to which we are subjected today. On the contrary, he anticipated it with dread. "These Ordination times always bring hope," he wrote from Bishop Auckland soon after he had settled the miners' strike; "but it is impossible not to feel here that things are moving with alarming rapidity and that power is going to those who have not learnt to use it." According to Thomas Burt, the miners' leader, he boldly proclaimed to a meeting of

---

[1] *Ibid.*, Vol. I, pp. 310 *ff.*
[2] Bishop Boutflower. (See Westcott, *op. cit.*, Vol. II, p. 363.)

pitmen that he was "in favour of inequality of social condition. 'He believed it was well that some men should have a high place and large means;' but then, he hastened to add, such men were in the position of trustees and administrators who were bound to use their means 'simply and solely for God and the nation, without any distinction of class.' "[1]

It might have been supposed, moreover, that this mystic, spiritual pastor, who made it the true business of his episcopate to "maintain and set forward, as far as should lie in me, quietness, love and peace among all men,"[2] would have shrunk from war under any condition and welcomed with open arms our modern policies of appeasement and surrender. But in his sermon on the Boer War he declared that "it was impossible for us to submit to arbitration the fulfilment of our imperial obligations." And again he said, "The duty of fulfilling a trust is not a matter for arbitration, and, if need be, must be preferred to the maintenance of peace."[3]

It might have been expected that he, with his great tenderness of heart and love of children, would have acclaimed with delight the eager enthusiasm with which we prepare the silken path of dalliance for the modern child. But he suggested as a subject for an essay "The Danger of making Children's Lives too Pleasant." "It is good for a man (and for a woman) to bear the yoke in his youth."[4] And he would hardly have approved the exchange of parental responsibility for the tutelary benevolence of the State. He believed that the family, not "the community" or "the State," was the essential unit of civilisation. "When the family is held in due honour," he wrote, "as you most rightly say, the better times for which we look will be near at hand."[5]

In short, there is no evidence, in his sermons or speeches, his writings or actions, of any sentimentality or foggy saintliness, of that unpractical unworldliness which had been fearfully anticipated. Those who dreaded it had overlooked, or did not appreciate, the power of his intellect and the strength of his character, and they had misunderstood the nature of his mysticism. For him the Unseen Presence was not passive but active, did not serve as a refuge from the world but as its only inspiration, as the only force to drive it. Thus the concrete

[1] Westcott, Vol. II, p. 388. [2] Ibid., p. 393.
[3] Ibid., p. 287. [4] Ibid., p. 160. [5] Ibid., p. 218.

problems of life were not resolved in a dangerous dew of dreamy benevolence but were tackled individually with an eager intensity; thus he did not drift with the times, murmuring generalities about universal love, but turned the fierce light of his intellect upon every problem, accepting no solution, no general trend of conduct or belief merely because it was popular. For all his saintliness, more probably because of it, he had few delusions. He had no easy faith that all was for the best. He believed that there was wickedness in the world. "Are there demons among men," he once wrote in his textbook, "clothed in humanity?"[1] And again: "Is no tendency to be resisted? It is the old, old story. Our rulers say to us, What should you like and we will do it."[2] And again, in a heart-cry to his wife: "To me the wretchedness and apparent failure of the world is terrible."[3] Lack of character, he believed, was largely responsible for it. "Mould your character, make it firm, even self-willed. . . . Character *alone* will move the world and influence your generation, but genius *alone* is like the bread cast upon the waters which will return to you after many days."[4] These are not the words of an idle visionary.

It was this strong, practical streak in him, this honesty of thought and purpose, that enabled him to be of real service to the miners and earned him the sobriquet of the "Pitmen's Bishop." When, in 1892, after carefully and anxiously watching the progress of the great strike, he decided that the time had come for him to offer his mediation, both sides accepted, for both knew that they had no humbug to deal with. Both expected, as they received, no harmless, charitable aspirations, but practical guidance and advice. This was the position.

The principle of agreement between masters and men based upon the "sliding scale" having, unfortunately, been operated during a bad period of depression, had been condemned by the miners and had come to an end in 1889. Better times had followed, but these were again succeeded by a fall in the market, and in 1891 the owners had presented the men with three alternatives. First, an immediate reduction of 10 per cent. in wages; or, secondly, agreement to arbitration on the matter; or, thirdly, a counter-offer from the miners which the owners would consider. The Federation Board, representing the pit-

---

[1] *Ibid.*, p. 24.   [2] *Ibid.*, p. 44.
[3] *Ibid.*, p. 59.   [4] *Ibid.*, p. 33.

men, asked the members of the union to give them full power
to settle on the lines of the third alternative proposed by the
owners. But by a large majority the members of the Miners'
Union rejected all three alternatives. In February of the following year the owners amended their proposals, offering now
an immediate $7\frac{1}{2}$ per cent. reduction with discussion as to the
future, or an immediate reduction of 5 per cent. with a further
5 per cent. on May 1st. Again the Board urged their members
to let them deal with the matter, and again the members refused. So the strike began on March 12th, 1892. After eight
weeks, on being tentatively approached, the owners let it be
known that, owing to the losses they had meanwhile suffered,
they would not reopen the pits unless a reduction of $13\frac{1}{2}$ per
cent. were agreed to. On May 7th the miners at last agreed to
leave the matter in the hands of their representatives, who
promptly offered a $7\frac{1}{2}$ per cent. reduction, or the terms which
the owners had proposed in February. But it was now too late.
The owners would accept nothing less than $13\frac{1}{2}$ per cent. And
meanwhile misery was mounting. Over 80,000 miners were
out of work, shipbuilding was being paralysed, the railway
had almost come to a standstill, the tradesmen were losing
heavily—and the Bishop was watching with anxious eyes,
eager to help, but fearful of making matters worse, for the
men had issued a warning (perhaps intended for his address)
that they "wanted no outside interference." But he had begun
probing, tentatively, since the very beginning of the strike,
and on May 2nd he wrote an open letter which was published
in *The Times*. In this he suggested the appointment of a
special Board to which an absolute decision should be entrusted; the Board to consist of three owners, three miners
and "three business men unconnected with this special industry." Towards the end of the month he followed up this
letter with another addressed directly to both sides. In this he
suggested an immediate reduction of 10 per cent. and the
reference of any further reduction to a Wages Board which
should be established "with full powers to deal with this and
with all future differences" on the question of wages. The
Bishop further invited owners and men to meet at Auckland
Castle on a given day to discuss this proposal. The meeting
accordingly took place under the Bishop's chairmanship, when
he urged them to consider "not merely the settlement of the

present difficulty, but, what was far more important, the establishment of real fellowship between Capital and Labour."[1] After a long joint discussion the two sides consulted in separate rooms, and the Bishop passed from one to the other, endeavouring, at first in vain, to find a point of agreement. The miners had raised their offer to 10 per cent. but the owners remained firm for $13\frac{1}{2}$ per cent. Meanwhile the crowds were gathering in the streets of Bishop Auckland and thronging the market-place before the Palace gates and even the drive inside the park (which had been thrown open to the public), pressing against the inner gates which screened the gardens and the immediate approach to the Castle. In spite of their anxiety and distress, their orderly behaviour was remarkable. They were careful to keep off the grass and they refrained from smoking within the park precincts. At length the Bishop appealed to the owners to abate their claim, not on the grounds that it was unreasonable or unjust, "but simply, he would use a very strong word, imploring them," in view of the state of destitution in which the men now found themselves, "to be generous to the utmost."[2] On this consideration the owners gave way at last, and the secretary of the Miners' Union appeared at the window of the conference room and dramatically signalled the basis of agreement to the expectant crowd by holding up his ten fingers.

So the century drew to its close. Mining affairs were taking on more and more of a national aspect, becoming less and less concerned with immediate local conditions. The officials of the Durham miners found themselves involved in disputes not only with the owners on the one hand and their members on the other, but with the increasingly powerful Miners' Federation of Great Britain, which would tolerate no independence of action. Never again would a Bishop be able to intervene in a local dispute, for there would be no more local disputes. All industry was becoming centralised and national. The Consett Ironworks had grown enormous, turning out vast quantities of steel shipping plates, with the whole world for their market. Several small foundries in Darlington had welded themselves together into the Darlington Forge and were making castings for the great Atlantic liners. Two great piers, the Roker and

---

[1] *Ibid.*, p. 124.   [2] *Ibid.*, pp. 124-125.

the New South Pier, were being built at Sunderland, and by
the opening of the St. Bede works the old, peaceful home of
the saintly scholar at Jarrow had been turned into "the
dreariest district in the whole of England, in the very centre of
industrial activity."[1] Rock salt was being excavated in prodigious quantities[2] on either side of the Tees, the exodus from
the land was proceeding apace, and the internal combustion
engine had been invented. Everything was changing, everything was growing bigger, everything was moving faster.

The great landowners kept up the pace at their end. The
hunting fields were larger than ever. Mr. Hamilton-Russell[3]
had taken over the South Durham from Sir William Eden;
Captain Christopher Cradock, R.N.—soon to find death and
fame at Coronel—was galloping fearlessly at the Zetland
fences; and the grandson of the great Havelock was jumping
walls of such a height that the top of his hat was invisible from
the other side.[4] Enormous house-parties assembled and dis-
persed, for Stockton and Catterick races, for pheasants and
partridges. Four guns at Windlestone seized the partridge
record for the county with 138 brace, and a wit wrote in the
Duchess's Visitors' Book at Raby that he had come "to see
their Graces and to shoot their Grouses." To the old country
life were now added all the fruits and resources of industry
and science, and everything here, as in commerce, was on a
grand scale. Hospitality and generosity were profuse. Expense
was boundless. Ritual and order were elaborate. The be-
ribboned cart-horses and the curly woolly sheep of the Home
Farm, even the pigs that were prodded with a meditative
walking-stick on Sundays, all were the sons and daughters of
a Champion This or a Champion That; and heavy prize oxen,
on their way to market or an agricultural show, broke down
the carts in which they were travelling. Orchids and gardenias
intoxicated the hot-houses and malmaisons were fixed in the
buttonholes of departing guests. A thousand brace of grouse
and half a thousand of pheasants were the orders of the day;
and brilliant shots, crumpling tall birds in the head before a

---

[1] *V.C.H.*, Vol. II, p. 293.
[2] 231,000 tons in 1892.   [3] Afterwards Viscount Boyne.
[4] Sir Henry Havelock-Allan, Bt. Though a Durham man, it was
actually in Ireland that he performed this feat. (See "Memories of a
Huntsman," by Bert Thatcher, *Field,* December 9th, 1933.)

gallery of critical, softly swearing pitmen, had taken the place of the solitary pot-hunting, muzzle-loading sportsmen. The dead game was despatched hither and thither, as presents, throughout the countryside, and a careful account was kept of its distribution. No messenger came to a country house without being regaled with beer and cheese for his departure; servants solemnly processed in order of rank to their meals; and major-domos in white ties, with butlers and visiting valets, toasted "Lord and Lady" in their glasses of port. Crested carriages, their horses glistening in the firelight, were driven into the very hall of Raby Castle.

There was a simpler, gentler side to this rich and splendid life, this last, fine burst of grand manners in grand houses, while all around democracy was stoking up its steam. Not all the country people had gone. Even a few, with the blood of their fathers strong in their veins, sickened of the smoke and stench and returned to find rest and refreshment where feudalism at its best was now enjoying its St. Martin's Summer. Through the kindness of an old friend, whose recollections date back to that period, I am enabled here to give a glimpse of life on a large estate in the County of Durham towards the end of the nineteenth century.

"Life had been a struggle with my father and mother in the town. Times were hard and men were having to work what was called 'short time'—not a full week—and there seemed no prosperity for anyone. It was in these circumstances that father was sent by the firm he worked for to do some work at the Hall, and when it was nearing the finish the squire asked him how he would like to work there permanently. . . . Within a week of the removal to the cottage the squire brought his lady to see the improvements there—all the old paper removed from the walls and an extra window fixed in the kitchen, and more especially to see the cream coloured walls. I was still working in the town, and when I came home on the Wednesday half-holiday how delighted my dear mother was to tell me all about the visit and what they had said and how pleased they were with the look of the lightsome walls in the June sunshine. The roses were just ready to bloom on the front of each of the six cottages, and I think we all believed we had come to fairyland. . . . Cottage No. 1 was the home of two Scottish gamekeepers, who were their own house-keepers and cooks. One of the men used to play the fiddle in the winter evenings, going over many of the old Scottish songs that we knew, and he could play well—or we thought so. Cottage No. 3 was occupied by a farm worker who had a large family of boys and girls, very lively and happy. Their father had worked on the Home Farm, as his father before him. An uncle of these children lived in the next cottage, and had worked all his life on the same farm. He was married and had two children. We used to be rather sorry for him. His wife was very house-proud and had her house always in beautiful order. One of her plans was that William, on coming home from work, must put off his boots and change into his slippers. We never heard that he objected. Cottage 5 was the home of two nice neighbours who had no children. The husband was a notable gardener. He always had the earliest of the vegetables that grew under his hand and there was some rivalry, but as far as I remember it was friendly too. The clerk in the Estate Office lodged with these people for years.

"One of the grooms and his wife and family lived in the sixth cottage. There were four boys and one girl. They were very well behaved children and we were great friends with this family. The husband took a good deal of drink, which was the cause of their being poor, but they kept their garden in good order and they had fowls and kept rabbits. So they took no harm—so long as they remained. But when the man received his notice for drunkenness and they had to leave it was a sad story.

"On Sunday afternoons a church service was held for the people in the schoolroom. The squire's lady was at the organ and the vicar or his son took the service, which was well attended. . . . A visit to the town was a great event and did not happen every day, seeing it meant an eight mile walk—there and back again. What a bustle there was and how we enjoyed helping mother to collect all her things and get a list ready of what was wanted and how we laughed and teased her, and she laughed too. She had to be met coming home again by one or two of us, to carry parcels and hear the news from the town.

"When I begin to think of the many ways in which kindness and help were shown, I feel I hardly know where to begin.

23

. . . A free cottage, a supply of wood to cut into logs, our coal led from the colliery to the cottage door. So much milk a day free—I don't remember the quantity. A good garden, as well as a long row of potatoes on the farm for each of the workmen, grown alongside those grown for the Hall—and what potatoes! Sound and shapely and *one* of them roasted was a meal, so floury and good to eat, very unlike the potatoes we see today and before the war. Many helps in cases of sickness, and for every member of a workman's family who died all the undertaker's fees were paid. But as I recall things in those days, the people were healthy and strong—they were in great measure free from care—as I know was the case in our family.

"A reading room and a billiard room were provided for the men, and the squire's lady, at one time in the early days, had weekly afternoon meetings for the womenfolk, at which tea was provided, and she read aloud to them or they had games. For the young women or girls who were not away working, the squire's lady had a meeting for them to be taught embroidery. At all times she visited the cottages and often brought her children with her, so that we were never strangers to each other. At the wonderful entertainments from time to time given at the Hall the estate people were given the privilege to attend and enjoy them. Also, for long, a ball was held yearly and there were invitations for those for the home people. For Christmas, a farm cart, scrubbed clean, came round with a big joint of prime beef for each family—a gift. At the shooting-parties there were gifts to the cottagers of two rabbits or hares, and what fine creatures they were, clean and plump, and the fur was beautiful to see. . . . Happy days. Blessed memories."

"Faith in persons," as Bishop Westcott once wrote, "is stronger than faith in systems."[1]

But his day, too, was now drawing to its close. On July 20th, 1901, in very hot weather, he preached the last sermon of his life, and, very suitably, to the pitmen on their gala day in the Cathedral. As the Bishop, supported by the Dean and the Archdeacon of Durham, entered at the south-west door, a miners' band entered from the north-west. "This band was playing with much feeling 'Abide with me: fast falls the

---

[1] Westcott, Vol. II, p. 354.

eventide,' and many of the large congregation assembled in the Cathedral were visibly affected by its moving strains." Little hints that he had recently let fall had shown that the Bishop, through that sixth sense which was so powerfully developed in him, was inwardly aware of his approaching departure, and now, though cheerful and not ill, though he spoke in "a voice which for fulness and vigour I have never heard him use before,"[1] he made a definite allusion to his imminent death. The allusion was, naturally, not understood and caused bewilderment at the time and much speculation. "At the present time Durham offers to the world," he said, "the highest type of industrial concord which has yet been fashioned. Much, no doubt, remains to be done; but the true paths of progress are familiar to our workers and our leaders, and are well trodden. While, then, so far I look back, not without thankfulness, and look forward with confident hope, I cannot but desire more keenly that our moral and spiritual improvement should advance no less surely than our material improvement. And therefore, since it is not likely that I shall ever address you here again, I have sought to tell you what I have found in a long and laborious life to be the most prevailing power to sustain right endeavour, however imperfectly I have yielded myself to it—even the love of Christ; to tell you what I know to be the secret of a noble life, even glad obedience to His will. I have given you a watchword which is fitted to be the inspiration, the test, and the support of untiring service to God and man; *the love of Christ constraineth us.*

"Take it, then, my friends, this is my last counsel, to home and mine and club; try by its Divine standard the thoroughness of your labour and the purity of your recreation, and the Durham which we love, the Durham of which we are proud —to repeat the words I used before—will soon answer to the heavenly pattern."[2]

Exactly a week later Bishop Westcott was dead.

DATES OF THE BISHOPS OF DURHAM
MENTIONED IN THIS CHAPTER

Edward Maltby	1836-1856
Charles Thomas Longley	1856-1860
Henry Montague Villiers	1860-1861
Charles Thomas Baring	1861-1879
Joseph Barber Lightfoot	1879-1889
Brooke Foss Westcott	1890-1901

[1] *Ibid.,* Vol. II, p. 393.   [2] *Ibid.,* Vol. II, pp. 393-394.

Chapter XXXIV

THE DELUGE

"The ultimate subjugation of the individual to the community is fatal to the highest interests of the community. For it dulls the individual conscience, and the collective conscience, after all, is but the summing up of millions of individual consciences."

H. C. G. MOULE, BISHOP OF DURHAM.

"We have entered on an epoch of tragedy, and anything calamitous is congruous with this evil time."

H. H. HENSON, BISHOP OF DURHAM.

THE man who, on the death of Westcott, became the eighty-fifth Bishop of Durham, Handley Carr Glyn Moule (whose name must be pronounced as "Mole") seems at first sight to be overacting his part. We are almost shocked by the closed eyes, the very sweet smile, the hands a-washing in invisible soap, the surely too episcopalian "dear, dear, dear"s and the "yes, yes, yes"es. But it is not long before we realise that all these apparent "tricks of the trade" are, in fact, perfectly sincere and unconscious; they are the manifestations of an extreme but genuine humility. The conclusion of his first letter, as Bishop-elect, to the clergy and people of his diocese "I am, Dear Brethren, with full purpose of heart, altogether yr. servant in the love of God"—was not only a beautifully worded phrase but the candid expression of an inward conviction. He was their servant; and he proved it by living as their servant.

And therefore it might be supposed that he was ill fitted to rule. Such was, no doubt, to a great extent the case. Bishop Moule, although a pupil of Lightfoot and a "Double First," unlike his great master, was no organiser nor administrator. Unlike his own successor, who delighted to find in the House of Lords a "candour and intelligence"[1] surpassing that of almost any other audience, he had no interest in statecraft. "Thank God there isn't much of the House of Lords in my life," he wrote; "I don't love the atmosphere more for this first taste of it."[2]

[1] Henson, *Retrospect of an Unimportant Life,* Vol. II, p. 83.
[2] *Handley Carr Glyn Moule, Bishop of Durham,* by J. B. Harford and F. C. Macdonald, p. 243. (Hodder and Stoughton, n.d.)

But he was, nevertheless, far from being a negative "saint."
If he failed to be a great diocesan, if he was no leader of men,
if he was out of his element in ecclesiastical business and could
only sigh deeply to express his agreement or groan heavily in
disapproval, he could not renounce his great intellectual
honesty. His father, it is supposed, was the original of Hardy's
old parson, "the earnestest man in all Wessex," and he himself, the earnestest man in all Durham, proved that he could
speak out on matters which nearly touched his faith and his
heart. Moreover, he possessed the power of stamping his utterances and actions with the indelible impress of a distinctive
personality. No one but he would or could have *run two miles*
in pouring rain at the age of seventy (after the breakdown of
his motor-car) in order to keep an appointment with a village
congregation. And he had a sense of humour. No one,
again, but he, on being told by a clergyman that he desired a
change as he had worked so many years in that particular
parish, would have replied, warmly clasping him by the arm,
"So many years, my dear brother! How you must be wedded
to the place!" Nor is there anything facile or indeterminate
in the following plea for courage and independence of thought
which was only one of the many precepts which he enforced
by his personal example. "So I would say to every man here,
whatever his special social or political views may be, 'So reverence yourself that you shall never consent to be merely a cog
in the vast wheel. Refuse to rank with those who have no independent moral judgment of their own, and who dare not
stand, each for himself, as those who, when the occasion calls,
can face the world for a principle and say "Yes" to God even
if millions on the other side say "No" to Him.'" For all his
sweetness and humility he was no Mr. Facing-Both-Ways.
For all his dislike of the practical business of politics, he saw
clearly and spoke strongly against the fatal tendency of the
times to drift with the popular tide.

When, on the succession of Bishop Westcott by Bishop
Moule (we must remember here how to pronounce his name),
a Canon of the Cathedral was asked for his opinion of the
change, he wittily replied: "Oh, well, you know, it takes a
good many moles to make a waistcoat." This was a just criticism and perhaps a deeper than the speaker intended. For all
that was essential, all that was fundamental in the composition

of the greater man was present in the less—"even," as Bishop Westcott said, "the love of Christ." It was this that carried Bishop Moule, if not faultlessly, at least faithfully and unfalteringly, through the performance of a task for which he was not temperamentally suited. He may have wept where he should have admonished and grieved where he should have condemned; he may have left his successor with acute diocesan problems owing to his passion for foreign missions, his lowering of the intellectual standard of the clergy and his general over-tenderness in episcopal handling; he may have been a weak bishop but he was not a weak man. His irreverent laymen laughed and called him "Holy Moly." They did not know that behind that unfailing ultra-gentleness and rare courtesy of manner lay a naturally virile, nervous and irritable disposition. They did not know that they had dubbed him with a sobriquet which he, in fact, and thoroughly and literally deserved.

The first thirteen years of his episcopate were the last thirteen of a triumphant industrialism and of an epicurean aristocracy. There were significant signs indicative of the ultimate fate of both—twenty-nine "Labour" Members of the House of Commons in 1906, the final ingurgitation of the Durham miners by the National Miners' Federation in 1908, the affiliation of this great Union with the Labour Party in 1910, the drafting of the first Nationalisation Bill in 1912,[1] above all the very significant Parliament Bill of the preceding year— but in spite of all these and the troubles in Ireland and the vociferations of Mr. Lloyd George, the London seasons were gayer than ever, the country houses were full of laughter and flowers, and the wheels of industry went on turning and turning with a phenomenal rapidity. In 1913 the peak was reached in the production of coal. In the winter of this year the Durham fields were dotted with galloping scarlet coats, the Durham coverts were a-rattle with the sticks of beaters, and the port went the round of warm, untroubled guests in the candlelight and the firelight. In the summer of the same year a different company of guests, eight hundred aged miners, had been entertained by the Bishop at Auckland Castle.

In 1914 the deluge began.

[1] By the Miners' Federation of Great Britain for the handing over of the mines to the community.

In 1915 every considerable house in the county had been turned into a hospital and the heirs of some of them had already fallen in the field. They were never again to teem by day and to blaze by night on the old, well-ordered, brilliant scale.

The Durham Light Infantry surpassed even its own distinguished record. Thirty-seven battalions of this regiment were raised for the fight and the Butte de Warlencourt[1] became for ever associated with the glory of the "faithful Durhams." The Bishop was not slow to encourage them. This gentlest and humblest of men flamed with indignation at the conduct of the Germans. He was never in doubt as to the justice of our cause, while the acuteness of his intellect and the honesty of his nature could not tolerate the confusion, so commonly accepted today, of personal humility with national humiliation. Thus those who advocated a passive submission in the name of Christianity were unequivocally denounced, and the great county regiment was sent upon its way "with the Bishop of Durham's Greeting and Godspeed."[2]

But the toll of the war was fearful and the consequences, not only of social upheaval and economic dislocation but of the loss of the finest and the bravest individuals in the country, were quickly perceived. In 1918, although the headquarters of the Durham Miners' Association still looked upon trade unionism as an activity independent of politics, "a new spirit," as Mr. Sidney Webb remarked, had become apparent in the mining districts, ten lodges ran their own candidates in the local elections on "a definitely Labour party programme" and returned a majority to power on the County Council.[3] In the following year a strike was voted for the nationalisation of the mines, for a 30 per cent. advance in wages and a 25 per cent. reduction of hours. The figures for Durham showed 76,000 in favour and 16,000 against. This strike was called off by the nomination of the Sankey Commission. But now the country was reaping the aftermath of war. It was in a turmoil and the pace was hot. In August, 1920, the miners demanded a reduction in the price of coal to the consumer together with increased wages, and in the same month the new Bishop of

[1] November 5th and 6th, 1916.
[2] Harford and Macdonald, p. 276.
[3] *The Story of the Durham Miners*, by Sidney Webb, p. 92.

Durham noted that "England has ceased to be a constitutional monarchy, and is making its first advance towards the 'dictatorship of the proletariat.'"[1] In October of the same year every pit had stopped in the country.

Meanwhile the old Bishop had died, with his mind filled with care for his diocese. "My whole heart is in it," he had said when begged to think no more of it. "It is my life." He was succeeded by Herbert Hensley Henson, who retired on the eve of the last war and died in 1947.

It has been noticed on an earlier occasion that at every period of violent change in their history the people of the Palatinate have been under the care of a Bishop remarkable as one of the noblest products of that form of society which was passing away. Thus, at the time of the Reformation, the saintly Catholic Tunstall was in charge of the Bishoprick; in the days of triumphant Puritanism, the no less saintly churchman Morton; and when Reform was sweeping all before its path in the early years of the last century, the courteous, wise and princely "reactionary" van Mildert was at the helm. In every case the personal qualities of these bishops, which, we cannot doubt, would have secured for them a lasting influence in more settled times, were to a great extent nullified by the revolutionary conditions prevailing in England during their tenure of the See. They were none of them revolutionaries. They were all out of sympathy—though none of them totally out of sympathy—with the age in which they lived. They all provided the finest examples of those habits of thought and those principles of belief which were condemned by the progressives of their respective periods. We must now regretfully add a fourth example of this conflict of personality with circumstances.

It will be admitted at last, even by the most casual, that our social system is undergoing today a revolutionary change at least as thorough as any which it has experienced in the course of our history. Every reasonable person will, further, agree that such a change, though finally expedited by the last war, has been proceeding apace for many years and that it received a special impetus from the great international conflict of 1914. Now, if we were obliged to mention a single outstanding feature of those Victorian times whose last faint

[1] Henson, *op. cit.,* Vol. II, p. 24.

agonies we are still enduring, we would probably choose its individualism. Particular religion, personal wealth, private property and, above all, individual thought, character, responsibility and influence, these are typical of that age and chiefly distinguish it from ours. And it was precisely at the time when these were receiving their death-blow, in the throes of the mortal struggle between the old world and the new, between the Man and the System; when the governor was yielding to the governing committee, the squire to the County Council, and John Wilson to the Miners' Federation of Great Britain that there was appointed to the See of Durham—an individual. He was an individual, moreover, who possessed not only the intellectual strength and honesty to think for himself but the moral courage publicly and repeatedly to express his thoughts. The pursuit of Truth—and more than its pursuit, its proclamation, its sometimes aggressive proclamation—was the main purpose of his existence. To this he rigidly adhered throughout his life, regardless of the consequences to himself, with an almost contemptuous courage. Such a singular combination of reckless intrepidity and acute discernment, expressed in a vivid and pungent phraseology, was not likely to secure a warm welcome from ecclesiastics and politicians chiefly remarkable for their nervous anxiety to do the popular thing. Bishop Henson made the mistake of hitting the nail on the head too smartly and too frequently for the comfort of the vaporously benevolent and the mildly anarchical. He shocked and alarmed his contemporaries, and he derived, no doubt, a certain satisfaction from doing so. "I voted against this resolution in a minority of one," he wrote of some meeting of enthusiastic churchmen. "It appeared to me to have small importance. Its phrases were grandiose, but their precise meaning was obscure."[1] Yet he was no mere episcopal *enfant terrible*. His passionate love for his country made him grieve for the state in which he found her and shudder at the terrible future which he predicted for her. Only an earnest faith, none the less real because it was not trumpeted, and a religious humility, all the more remarkable for the naturally proud nature with which it had to contend, saved him from the worst pangs of personal disappointment and patriotic despair. No doubt, also, his remarkable gift of

[1] Henson, *op. cit.*, Vol. I, p. 207.

expression proved a real solace to his overcharged emotions and a genuine relief to his indignant intelligence. For he was the master of a splendid and compelling diction which enabled him to unburden his feelings with a poignancy with which it was impossible not to sympathise and to advance his arguments with a logical cogency, relieved with flashes of dry humour, which is as delightful to read as it is difficult to resist. Only incommunicable truths, the thoughts that fret in vain for expression, prove intolerable to their possessor. Bishop Henson's clarity of thought and command of language invested him with a power to present his truths in a manner which must have satisfied even his critical mind. He was never smothered by the nebulous burr of his fancies; and he had at least the satisfaction of knowing not only that he had written his best but that no man could have written better. If people would not listen to arguments couched in such lucid and magnificent English they would listen to nothing. The autobiography[1] which he wrote after his resignation is remarkable not only for its ruthless exposure of the general weakness of the times, but even more so for its perhaps unconscious record of the sufferings and frustrations of a single great intellect and a single noble spirit in that prolonged attempt to wrestle with fatality. It will take its place—at least, the first two volumes— amongst the greatest and the most human memoirs in our language.

Such was the man who arrived in Durham to take up his episcopal duties while a miners' strike was still unsettled. As will now be expected, he took the very first opportunity which was offered him—a speech at the banquet given in his honour on the day of his enthronement—to dive at once beneath the smooth, ceremonial waters of welcome and to hazard his popularity at the outset of his career by speaking out his mind on strikes in general. But "I do not care one straw about popularity," he had written in his youth and often illustrated in his maturity, "for I know that it is generally purchased by a sacrifice of the truth."[2] On this occasion, "I do not venture to express any opinion on subjects highly technical," he said, "with respect to which more special knowledge than I possess is required in the man who would pass a judgment, but I do not scruple to say this, and I desire my words shall

[1] *Retrospect of an Unimportant Life.*   [2] *Ibid.*, Vol. I, p. 27.

carry to every corner of my Diocese, that strikes and lock-outs are methods of violence which ought to become obsolete.

"These methods have come down to us from a time when the workmen were uneducated and unenfranchised and the strike was perhaps the only available weapon they possessed for winning those political powers which are the proper birthright of free citizens. But that battle has been won, and the strike is now—I speak as a close student of our economic public life for a good many years—a dangerous rival to constitutional action. Its political analogue is war as that of the lock-out is a blockade, and both are open to the same moral objections."[1]

So he entered bravely upon an episcopate which, if it was to bring him no sensational success, to advance him no further upon the road of ecclesiastical preferment and to win for him no popular applause, earned for him at least a general respect, the love of those who were close enough to discern the man behind the potentate, and the admiration of all who can appreciate a prophetic intelligence, recognise an unswerving integrity and value an extraordinary courage.

Concerning his successor, Alwyn Terrell Petre Williams, the present and eighty-seventh Bishop of Durham, we can but repeat the words which Surtees wrote during the lifetime of Shute Barrington: "Addressed to living merit, the voice of legitimate praise can scarcely be distinguished from that of flattery."[2]

But now that we have reached the end of our episcopal parade, let us take this opportunity to withdraw awhile from the raging social torrent on whose waters we must presently be rushed to our conclusion, in order to cast one lingering look behind at the long line of Bishops of Durham and at the house which was essentially their home. The procession stretches back so far into the misty past that we are tempted to regard it as endless and to see no reason why it should ever stop. The sandals and the staff, the sword and the jewel, the miniver and the velvet cap, the bob-wig and the lawn sleeves, the gaiters and the shovel hat—these have succeeded each other over a thousand years; and is there any reason why, suitably adapted to the costume of the period, these episcopalian

[1] *Induction, etc., of the Rt. Rev. H. H. Henson.* (Durham, 1921.)
[2] Surtees, Vol. I, p. cxxiv.

insignia should not continue for another thousand? Alas, we must recognise that a Bishop is a great dignitary of the Church, a notable in an antique hierarchy, and that neither dignitaries nor notables nor hierarchies can long be permitted to survive in an age self-dedicated to the Common Man. A Bishop is an uncommon man, and as such, with all uncommonly good things, he must come to an end. Not even a utility vestment will serve to disguise or save him. Let us then make a last obeisance before the Durham throne ere the overwhelming judgment of this world condemn such a reverent gesture as lèse-populace.

The manor house at Auckland was an episcopalian possession in the tenth century, if not earlier. Since that time practically all the greatest Bishops have been closely associated with it. This was the favourite of their many residences. Here the splendid Pudsey built his banqueting hall and gorged himself, where later the ascetic Bek sat, spare and proud, attended humbly by his hundred knights. Here "our most dear secretary," Richard de Bury, entertained his pupil Edward III, a splendid young man of twenty-four, clothed in rich velvet spangled with flowers of gold. Bishop Hatfield first called this manor house a castle, though it was Bek who had enlarged and castellated it. It was from here the English army marched to Neville's Cross. Ruthall grumbled to Wolsey about the number of people he had to entertain here—at least three hundred a day, which "is the way to keepe a man poore." This Bishop and Tunstall built the long dining-room and the room beneath it. Charles I and Archbishop Laud were entertained in this house by the gentle old Morton; Cosin transformed the banqueting hall into the chapel; Crewe built the deer-house; Butler paced and meditated along a terrace which now bears his name; and it was at Auckland that Scott talked and told old tales to Bishop Barrington over their nuts and port. Here, in the same hall which had witnessed such splendid scenes of mediæval entertainment, now before the chapel altar, flanking the indomitable bibliophile Cosin, lie those great scholars Lightfoot and Westcott. And here, in the dim light of a fast falling splendour, we can still almost catch the incisive tone of voice and see the aggressive lift of eyebrows of Bishop Henson as he denounces the "Christian" drift towards "Communistic sentiment," the prevalence of "clerical toadies," and the contemptibility of "prophylactic verbiage."

Lightfoot and Westcott chose different rooms for their studies, Lightfoot's being downstairs and Westcott's immediately above. Since their day the Bishops have alternated these two rooms for their personal use with curious and becoming regularity. Moule, who succeeded Westcott, chose Lightfoot's study, Bishop Henson returned upstairs to Westcott's, and Bishop Williams has descended again to Lightfoot's. But we must go back into the counting-house of our everyday affairs. We must go back into the workshop. For this place has little now in common with the vulgar world. It is full of mighty ghosts. . . . Pudsey, Bek, de Bury, Hatfield, Tunstall, Morton, Cosin, Crewe, Butler, Barrington, Lightfoot, Westcott and Henson. We have met them all. We have wondered at them all. We have gained from them all. We have taken once more the refreshment of their names.

But need we, nevertheless, go on with this business? We have reached almost the present day. Does not discretion, as well as inclination, urge us to take leave here, not only of our Bishops, but of them all? To usher them out, to bow them out, to thank them for their custom and to wish them all goodnight? Must we, indeed, now tell of the long, sad years of unemployment and of yet another war? Must we enter into further schemes and plans and hopes and fears and arguments? Speak of the huge ordnance factories, perhaps, which sprung to sprawling, strenuous life at Aycliffe and at Spennymoor; or of the trading estates now seeking to infuse new blood into the old pit villages; or of the Imperial Chemical Industries, pioneers of progress, whose enormous factory at Billingham has, in the uplifting words of the Board of Trade, "turned a barren area of a thousand acres into a mighty centre of the chemical industry"?[1] . . . Not so. For closing time has come. The time has come to put the shutters up. The long and busy day is done.

Yet, although we have had about enough of them, we must part from our kind customers with regret. They loom and

---

[1] *Industrial Opportunities in the Development Areas* (H.M. Stationery Office, 1946), p. 20.

cluster in the twilight and press their way out through our narrow workshop door. Bishops and monks, professors and prebendaries, barons and miners; and the charming Miss Peart; and pretty little Elizabeth Smith with her head full of Hebrew. . . .

They are gone. And as we wave them farewell from the entrance our eyes are lifted up to the great Cathedral, the old Norman Abbey, the Sion of all these children of Durham, standing high above the narrow street. Down here all is dusk and wavering uncertainty, but there is an enduring strength and beauty, there the last rays of the setting sun turn the great windows into shields of gold. Surely it will remain for ever. Hath He not founded it upon a rock?

An aeroplane passes above it.

Which of the two is the truer symbol of the times in which we live?

APPENDIX A

BISHOPS OF LINDISFARNE, CHESTER-LE-STREET AND DURHAM

BISHOPS OF LINDISFARNE

	Accession	Death, Translation or Resignation
Aidan	635	651
Finan	651	661
Colman	661	664
Tuda	664	664
Vacancy	664	678
Eata	681 (from Hexham)	685
Cuthbert (St.)	685	687
Eadbeorht	688	698
Eadfrith	698	721
Aethelweald	721	740
Cynewulf	740	780
Hygebeald	781	802
Egbert	802	821
Heathwred	821	830
Ecgred	830	845
Eanbeorht	845	854
Eardwulf (Eardulf)	854	See transferred to Chester-le-Street 883

BISHOPS OF CHESTER-LE-STREET

	Accession	Death, Translation or Resignation
Eardwulf (same as above)	883	899
Cuthheard	900	915
Tilred	915	928
Wigred	928	944
Uhtred	944	—
Seaxhelm	944	—

Ealdred	944	968
Aelfsige	968	990
Ealdhun (Aldhun)	990	See transferred to Durham
		995

Bishops of Durham

	Accession	Death, Translation or Resignation
Ealdhun (same as above)	995	1018
Vacancy	1018	1020
Eadmund	1020	1042
Eadred	1042	1042
Aethelric	1042	1056
Aethelwine	1056	1071
Walcher	1071	1080
William of Saint-Calais	1081	1096
Ralph Flambard	1099	1128
Geoffrey Rufus	1133	1140
William of Saint Barbara	1143	1152
Hugh du Puiset (Pudsey)	1153	1195
Philip of Poitou	1197	1208
Richard Marsh	1217	1226
Richard Poore	1228	1237
Nicholas Farnham	1241	1249
Walter Kirkham	1249	1260
Robert Stichill	1261	1274
Robert de Insula	1274	1283
Antony Bek	1284	1311
Richard Kellaw	1311	1316
Lewis de Beaumont	1318	1333
Richard Bury	1333	1345
Thomas Hatfield	1345	1381
John Fordham	1382	1388
Walter Skirlaw	1388	1405
Thomas Langley	1406	1437
Robert Neville	1438	1457
Laurence Booth	1457	1476
William Dudley	1476	1483
John Sherwood	1484	1494

Richard Fox	1494	1501
William Senhouse (or Sever)	1502	1505
Christopher Bainbridge	1507	1508
Thomas Ruthall	1509	1523
Thomas Wolsey	1523	1529
Cuthbert Tunstall	1530	1552 (deposed)
Cuthbert Tunstall	1559 (restored)	1559
James Pilkington	1561	1576
Richard Barnes	1577	1587
Matthew Hutton	1589	1595
Tobias Matthew	1595	1606
William James	1606	1617
Richard Neile	1617	1628
George Monteigne	1628	1628
John Howson	1628	1632
Thomas Morton	1632	1659
John Cosin	1660	1672
Nathaniel Crewe	1674	1721
William Talbot	1721	1730
Edward Chandler	1730	1750
Joseph Butler	1750	1752
Richard Trevor	1752	1771
John Egerton	1771	1787
Thomas Thurlow	1787	1791
Shute Barrington	1791	1826
William Van Mildert	1826	1836
Edward Maltby	1836	1856
Charles Thomas Longley	1856	1860
Henry Montague Villiers	1860	1861
Charles Baring	1861	1879
Joseph Barber Lightfoot	1879	1889
Brooke Foss Westcott	1890	1901
Handley Carr Glyn Moule	1901	1920
Herbert Hensley Henson	1920	1939
Alwyn Terrell Petre Williams	1939	—

The above dates are taken from Powicke's *Chronology*.

APPENDIX B

PRIORS AND DEANS OF DURHAM

PRIORS OF DURHAM[1]

1083-1087	Aldwin
1087-1109	Turgot
1109-1137	Algar
1137-1149	Roger
1149-1154	Laurence
1154-1158	Absolom
1158-1162	Thomas
1162-1188	Germanus
1188-1209?	Bertram
1209?-1214?	William of Durham
1214?-1234	Ralph Kerneth
1234-1244	Thomas of Melsanby
1244-1258	Bertram of Middleton
1258-1272	Hugh of Darlington (resigned)
1273-1285	Richard Claxton
1286-1290	Hugh of Darlington (again)
1290-1308	Richard Hoton
	(Henry of Luceby intruded *de facto* Prior 1300; never *de jure*)
1308-1313	William of Tanfield
1313-1321	Geoffrey Burdon
1321-1341	William of Couton
1341-1374	John Fossor
1374-1391	Robert Berington of Wallworth
1391-1416	John of Hemingbrough
1416-1446	John of Wessington
1446-1456	William Ebchester
1456-1464	John Burnaby
1464-1478	Richard Bell
1478-1484	Robert Ebchester
1484-1494	John Auckland
1494-1519	Thomas Castell
1520-1540	Hugh Whitehead

[1] I am indebted to the Rev. Canon S. L. Greenslade for the above list of Priors.

Deans of Durham

1541-1548	Hugh Whitehead
1551-1553	Robert Horne (deprived)
1553-1557	Thomas Watson
1557-1559	Thomas Robertson
1559-1560	Robert Horne (restored)
1560-1563	Ralph Skinner
1563-1579	William Whittingham
1579-1581	Thomas Wilson
1583-1595	Tobias Matthew
1596-1606	William James
1606-1620	Sir Adam Newton
1620-1638	Richard Hunt
1639-1645	Walter Balcanqual
1645-1659	William Fuller
1660-1661	John Barwick
1662-1684	John Sudbury
1684-1691	Denis Granville
1691-1699	Thomas Comber
1699-1728	John Montague
1728-1746	Henry Bland
1746-1774	Spencer Cowper
1774-1777	Thomas Dampier
1777-1788	William Digby
1788-1794	John Hinchliffe
1794-1824	Lord Cornwallis
1824-1827	Charles Henry Hall
1827-1840	John Banks Jenkinson
1840-1869	George Waddington
1869-1894	William Charles Lake
1894-1913	George William Kitchin
1913-1918	Herbert Hensley Henson
1918-1933	J. E. C. Welldon
1933-1951	Cyril Argentine Alington
1951-	John Herbert Severn Wild

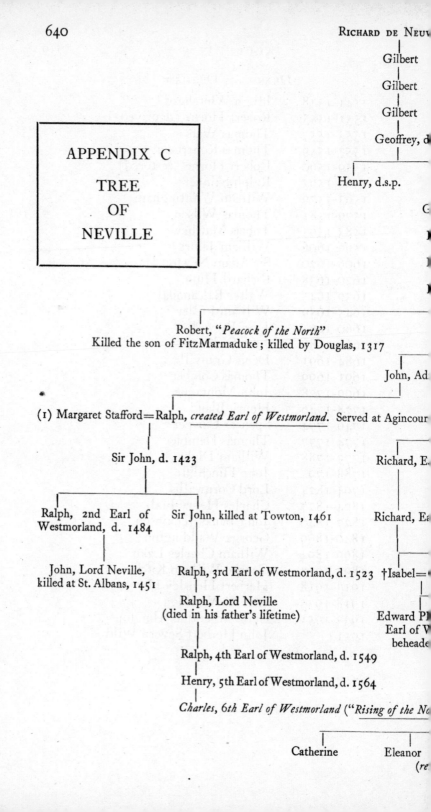

Gilbert

Gilbert

Gilbert

Geoffrey, d

Henry, d.s.p.

Robert, "*Peacock of the North*"
Killed the son of FitzMarmaduke ; killed by Douglas, 1317

John, Ad

(1) Margaret Stafford = Ralph, *created Earl of Westmorland.* Served at Agincour

Sir John, d. 1423   Richard, E.

Ralph, 2nd Earl of   Sir John, killed at Towton, 1461   Richard, Ea
Westmorland, d. 1484

John, Lord Neville,   Ralph, 3rd Earl of Westmorland, d. 1523   †Isabel=
killed at St. Albans, 1451

Ralph, Lord Neville
(died in his father's lifetime)   Edward Pl
                                                        Earl of V
                                                        beheade

Ralph, 4th Earl of Westmorland, d. 1549

Henry, 5th Earl of Westmorland, d. 1564

Charles, 6th Earl of Westmorland ("*Rising of the No*

Catherine   Eleanor
                                                        (*re*

a, heiress of Bertram de Bulmer, lord of Brancepeth and Sheriff Hutton

FitzMaldred, lord of Raby

ook the name of Neville

a ("Wel quha sal ys hornes blaw")

i of wounds=*Mary, heiress of Ralph FitzRanulf, lord of Middleham*

, lord of Raby, Brancepeth, Middleham and Sheriff Hutton
  (This Ralph made the scene about the stag, p. 103)

alph, *Victor of Neville's Cross*, d. 1367

nd, Seneschal of Bordeaux,   Eufamia=de Clifford
by Castle, d. 1389   (Clifford Tower, Raby, named after her)

er bird, p. 117) d. 1426=(2) Joan Plantagenet (Jane's Tower, Raby, named
                after her)

v, beheaded at Wakefield, 1461 Cecily,   Richard,
          "The Rose of Raby"=Duke of York

k, *The Kingmaker*, d. 1471 King Edward IV George, King Richard III
                 Duke of =Anne Neville*
                 Clarence
                 =Isabel Neville†

of Clarence *Anne=Richard III

  Margaret,
Countess of Salisbury,
 beheaded 1541

), d. 1601=Jane Howard ("*Twinkes*")

aret Anne   Sons died young
p Hutton, p. 206)

APPENDIX D—A LIST OF DURHAM CHURCHES

Date of Original Building (Year or Century).	Dedication.	Place.	Comments.
Early 13th	St. Andrew	Auckland	Collegiate. N. wall of chancel with original windows destroyed 1881
Late 12th	St. Helen	Auckland	"A very good example of a Durham parish church"
c. 1200	St. Andrew	Aycliffe	A pre-Conquest core. Restored 1880
1130	St. Mary the Virgin¹ (or St. Margaret)	Barnard Castle	Altered 15th C. Restored "out of all recognition" 1868-70
c. 1050	St. Cuthbert	Billingham	Death watch beetle. Much restored and extended c. 1938
Early 13th	St. Michael	Bishop Middleham	Fine church. Memorial to Robert Surtees
12th	St. Michael	Bishopwearmouth	Enlarged 1806. Rebuilt 1932. E.E. tower and chancel remain. (Was (1) wooden, (2) earlier stone church, on same site)
13th	St. Peter	Bishopton	Completely demolished. New church built 1846
1220	St. Nicholas	Boldon	Many interesting features left. (An earlier church here)
Early 13th	St. Brandon	Brancepeth	Lovely 17th C. woodwork. Fine church. "Peacock" Neville's tomb
14th	Friarside Chapel (Dedication unknown)	Burnopfield	Ruin. Chapel of a small hospital
12th	St. James the Apostle	Castle Eden	Built by Bruce. Chapel served by Durham Abbey. Rebuilt 1764
1262	St. Mary and St. Cuthbert	Chester-le-Street	(Earlier churches: wooden, 883; stone, 1045.) "Not violently" restored 1862. Collegiate. Spire 156 ft.
c. 1200	St. Mary	Cockfield	Great alterations 1911
Early 13th	St. Edwin	Coniscliffe	Lovely position. "Decorated" spire. Repairs (1844) "as bad as bad can be"
Norman	St. Bartholomew	Croxdale	New parish church, same name, 1846. Original became Salvin chapel
12th	St. Andrew	Daltron-le-Dale	Major restoration 1907. Norman door. Effigy of Bowes, Knight
1192	St. Cuthbert	Darlington	Fine woodwork. 183 ft. to top of spire. Collegiate
1190	St. Mary	Denton	Burnt by Scots in 1321
c. 1200	St. John the Baptist	Dinsdale	Restored 1875 (home of Surtees family)

¹ Dedication uncertain.

Date of Original Building (Year or Century).	Dedication.	Place.	Comments.
1112	St. Giles	Durham	Church for Kepier Hospital. North wall original
12th	St. Margaret	Durham	Interesting. Former chapelry of St. Oswald's. Chantry to St. Thomas-à-Becket
Early 13th	St. Mary (-le-Bow)	N. Bailey, Durham	Rebuilt 1685. Traditional site of first wooden church for St. Cuthbert's bones
12th	St. Mary (-the-Less)	S. Bailey, Durham	Built by the Nevilles. Rebuilt à la Norman 1846
1450	St. Mary Magdalene	Durham	Ruin. Church for Hospital of same name. There was earlier church here
Norman	St. Nicholas	Durham	Completely rebuilt 1858
12th	St. Oswald	Durham	The parish church of Durham. Much restored in 19th C.
12th	St. Mary the Virgin	Easington	Rebuilt in 13th C. Much restored in 19th
c. 1100	St. Ebba	Ebchester	Site of earlier monastery destroyed by Danes (?). Stands on Roman fort
c. 1150	St. Edmund	Edmundbyers	Good gargoyles. Restored 1858. Some old bits left
12th	St. Mary the Virgin	Egglescliffe	Norman doorway. Restoration woodwork
12th	St. John	Elton	Rebuilt 1841. Original chancel arch remains
c. 1200	St. Peter	Elwick	Restored 1813. Was "a little, picturesque, grey structure"
7th	St. John (?)	Escomb	"The most complete and unspoilt example of the earliest type of Anglo-Saxon church to be found in this country". (B. Colgrave)
13th	St. Michael and All Angels	Esh	Chapelry to Lanchester. Mostly rebuilt, 1770. Restored, 1850
c. 1220	St. Mary	Gainford	Built by Gilbert de Lacy. Some original portions left
13th	Holy Trinity	Gateshead	Part of old St. Edmund's Hospital turned into a church in 1864
11th	St. Mary	Gateshead	Tower, 1740. Chancel rebuilt after explosion, 1854
Early 12th	All Saints	Great Stainton	Entirely rebuilt 1876. Elizabethan cup
12th	St. John the Baptist	Greatham	Rebuilt 1792. Altered 1855 (Hospital chapel was destroyed 1785)
12th	St. Thomas-à-Becket	Grindon	Norman chancel. A wreck "rapidly deteriorating from neglect and wilful vandalism"

Date of Original Building (Year or Century).	Dedication.	Place.	Comments.
12th	St. James	Hamsterley	Norman doorway. Lancet windows. Several restorations
c. 1000	St. Mary Magdalene	Hart	E., W. and N. walls remain. Fine 15th-C. font
1190	St. Hilda	Hartlepool	Fine church well restored, 18th, 19th, 20th Cs. Norman doorway, Bruce chapel. (St. Hilda's monastery was destroyed by Danes)
c. 1150	St. Michael the Archangel	Heighington	Norman tower intact. N. wall destroyed 1875. Pre-Reformation pulpit
7th (?)	St. Mary	Heworth	Chapelry of Jarrow. Rebuilt 11th C., 17th C. and 1822, 14th-C. pattern
13th	St. Michael	Houghton-le-Spring	Designed by Elias, builder of Salisbury Cathedral. Fine "Decorated" E. window
12th	All Saints	Hurworth	Rebuilt 1831 and 1871
681	St. Paul	Jarrow	Tower, part Norman, part Saxon. 12th-C. nave destroyed 1782
Norman	St. Helen	Kelloe	Perp. windows. Chancel (Dec. and E. English) as long as nave
12th	All Saints (or St. Mary)[1]	Lanchester	One of best in county. Fine chancel arch. Collegiate 1283
13th	St. Mary	Longnewton	Rebuilt 1806 and 1856. Very little of old left
Early 13th	St. Mary Magdalene	Medomsley	Restored 1878. Beautiful lancet windows. Chapelry of Chester-le-Street
11th	St. John the Evangelist	Merrington	Was finest Norman example in county. Rebuilt with old stones, 1850
c. 1170	St. Mary the Virgin	Middleton-in-Teesdale	"Wantonly demolished" and rebuilt (1886) on another site
13th	St. George	Middleton St. George	1790, nearly all rebuilt; 1888, tower added
Early 12th	St. Mary	Monkhesleden	Norman doorway. Roof and windows altered c. 1796
674	St. Peter	Monkwearmouth	West wall and porch original
12th	Unknown	Muggleswick	Rebuilt 1728. Restored 1869, 1886. (Part of Prior of Durham's house remains)
c. 1050	St. Mary the Virgin	Norton	Pre-Conquest design. Aisles 1190 and 1876. Chancel 13th C. Effigy of a Knight. Collegiate church

[1] Dedication uncertain. See *Proceedings*, 3rd Series, II, 397, note.

Date of Original Building (Year or Century).	Dedication.	Place.	Comments.
c. 1180	St. Lawrence	Pittington	Transitional. "Unique in county and perhaps in England." Frescoes
12th	St. Cuthbert	Redmarshall	Norman doorway, nave, tower. 13th-C. chancel
Early 13th	Holy Cross	Ryton	"Suffered from ignorant restoration." Curious E. English spire
12th	St. Mary	Seaham	Probably pre-Conquest foundations. Restored 1914. Late Norman tower
1245	St. Edmund the Bishop	Sedgefield	Perpendicular tower (1430). Fine Restoration screen
c. 1300	All Saints	Sockburn	Destroyed save for Conyers chapel. (Probably was 7th-C. church here)
648	St. Hilda	South Shields	Nothing left of 7th C. Rebuilt 12th C. and 1810. Contains model of Wouldhave's Lifeboat
1170-90	St. Mary the Virgin (formerly St. Gregory)	Staindrop	Fine sedilia. Altered 13th C. Stained deal substituted for oak roof with Neville arms which was in perfect condition
1200	St. Thomas	Stanhope	Restored 19th C., reroofed 20th; fragments of old glass
1710	St. Thomas	Stockton	Three-decker pulpit. Death-watch beetle affecting Regency pews
12th	All Saints	Stranton (West Hartlepool)	Much restored in 19th C.
1719	Holy Trinity	Sunderland	Brick
11th	St. Margaret of Antioch	Tanfield	Rebuilt 1748, 1853, 1864. Old piscina left. Chapel to Chester-le-Street
12th	St. Mary Magdalene	Trimdon	Was chapel of ease to Kelloe. Restored
13th	St. Mary the Virgin	Washington	Rebuilt 1832
c. 1088	St. Mary	Whickham	Chancel arch and S. door, Norman; nave, late Norman; S. aisle, Decorated. Original font. Restored 1862
Early 13th	St. Andrew	Whitburn	1867. "The great restoration." Fish window
12th	Unknown	Whitworth	Rebuilt 1803. Restored 1848. Chapel of ease to Merrington
?	St. Mary	Whorlton	Rebuilt 1853
Early 13th	St. Andrew	Winston	"Very badly and unsympathetically" restored, c. 1846

Date of Original Building (Year or Century).	Dedication.	Place.	Comments.
12th	St. Michael	Witton Gilbert	14th-C. East window. Much restored 1859. Fragments of old glass
Norman	St. Philip and St. James	Witton-le-Wear	Chapel to St. Andrew's, Auckland. Much restored. A "monstrous window" (1850)
11th	St. Mary and St. Stephen	Wolsingham	Rebuilt 17th C. (called "St. Matthew"). Rebuilt 1848 and renamed as in 11th C. Some Norman work left
12th (?)	(old) St. Mary Magdalene (new) St. Peter	Wolviston	Rebuilt and rededicated 1716. Demolished and rebuilt 1876

I am particularly indebted to the incumbents of the parishes for much of the above information.

INDEX TO VOLUMES I AND II

A

"Barony, The," I. 127
Barrington, George, Viscount, II. 537
  Shute, Bishop of Durham, II. 293, 375, 381-383, 482, 492, 498, 607, 632, 633
Barwick, John, I. 228, 229, 238
Basire, Isaac, I. 168, 229-231, 268; II. 497
  Mrs., I. 230-231
Bathurst, Dr., II. 290
Baxter, Mrs., of Edmundbyers, II. 308
  Richard, I. 267
Beamish, I. 128
  Forge, II. 472
Bear Park. See Beaurepaire
Beauchamp, Guy, Earl of Warwick, I. 86
Beaufort, Jane, I. 91
Beaumont, Lewis de, Bishop of Durham, I. 88, 103
Beaurepaire, I. 104, 106, 142, 242; II. 491
Becket, St. Thomas à, I. 32, 76, 94
Bedale Hunt, II. 435
Bede, The Venerable, I. 27, 28, 29, 43-57, 74, 156
  Shrine of, I. 96
"Bede, Cuthbert," II. 426
Bede, St., Works, II. 619
Bedlingtonshire, I. 65
Bek, Antony, Bishop of Durham, I. 66, 80-87, 118, 119, 142, 144, 145, 156, 194, 241; II. 545, 562, 563, 632, 633
Bell, Gertrude, II. 421
  Matthew, of Woolsington, II. 574
Bellasis, family, II. 331
  John of, I. 111, 250
  Mary, II. 399
  William, Sir, I. 233; II. 295
Bellasis (game), II. 365, 366
Bellasis (place), II. 331, 348, 350
Bello Monte. See Beaumont, Lewis de
Ben, II. 374
Benfieldside, I. 246
Benson, Edward, Archbishop of Canterbury, II. 613
Bernicia, I. 24, 26
Bertie, Sir Thomas, II. 430-431
Bevans, Jack, II. 442, 444
Beverley Church, I. 75
Bewdley, II. 499
Bewick, Thomas, II. 407-408
  William, II. 406
Biddick, North, II. 384, 387
Billingham, I. 146, II. 350
Binchester (Vinovia), I. 12, 15-18, 20, 24, 248; II. 446
  Hall, I. 248, 249

Bird, John, II. 423
Birkett, Joseph, Vicar of Stranton, II. 305
Birmingham, King Edward's School, II. 608
Birtley, II. 514
  Fell, II. 468
Biscop, Benedict, I. 44-46, 156; II. 531
Bishop Auckland (see also Auckland), I. 21, 123, 187, 233, 241; II. 366, 423, 436, 468, 514, 519, 540, 618
  Grammar School, II. 418, 547
Bishop Middleham, I. 241, 245
Bishops of Durham. See Appendix A and under individual names
"Bishops' War," I. 224
Bishoprick, Barons of the, I. 66, 67, 113, 114, 120-129
Bishopton, I. 124, 125, 193; II. 358, 437
Bishopwearmouth (see also Monkwearmouth and Wearmouth), I. 147; II. 331, 423, 520, 531, 532
Black Death, I. 90, 130, 146, 202
Black Dyke, I. 13
  Rood of Scotland, I. 97, 117
Blagroves House, II. 501
Blakiston, family, I. 232; II. 330, 349, 489
  Frances, II. 349
Blakiston, Mr., I. 265
Bland, Henry, Dean of Durham, II. 315
Blaydon Races, II. 395, 396
Blue Bell Farm, II. 356
Blue-coat School, II. 328
Boer War, II. 615
Bog Sandwort. See Arenaria
Bolam, I. 228
Boldon Book, I. 74; II. 525, 532
Bolihope Common, I. 19
Bolt's Burn, II. 496
Bonny Bobby Shafto, II. 362, 399, 400
Bonny Moor Hen, II. 401
Boroughbridge, I. 190
Boruwlaski, Count Joseph, II. 320-322
Bost, Father, I. 208, 209
Bosworth, I. 153
Boulder Clay, I. 7
Bousfield, Robert, II. 547
Bouyer, Archdeacon, II. 320
Bowes, family, II. 334, 489
  Adam, Sir, I. 184
  George, II. 409, 434, 489
  Sir, I. 181-197
  John, II. 409-412, 426